AND A WOODSTOCK IN A BIRCH TREE

© 1958, 1965 United Feature Syndicate, Inc.

by Charles M. Schulz

Holt, Rinehart and Winston/New York

PEANUTS comic strips by Charles M. Schulz
Copyright © 1978, 1979 by United Feature Syndicate, Inc.

Published by Holt, Rinehart and Winston,
383 Madison Avenue, New York, New York 10017.

Published simultaneously in Canada by Holt, Rinehart
and Winston of Canada, Limited.

First published in book form in 1979.

Library of Congress Catalog Card Number: 79-1926

ISBN: 0-03-053291-4

First Edition

Printed in the United States of America

10 9 8 7 6 5 4 3 2 1

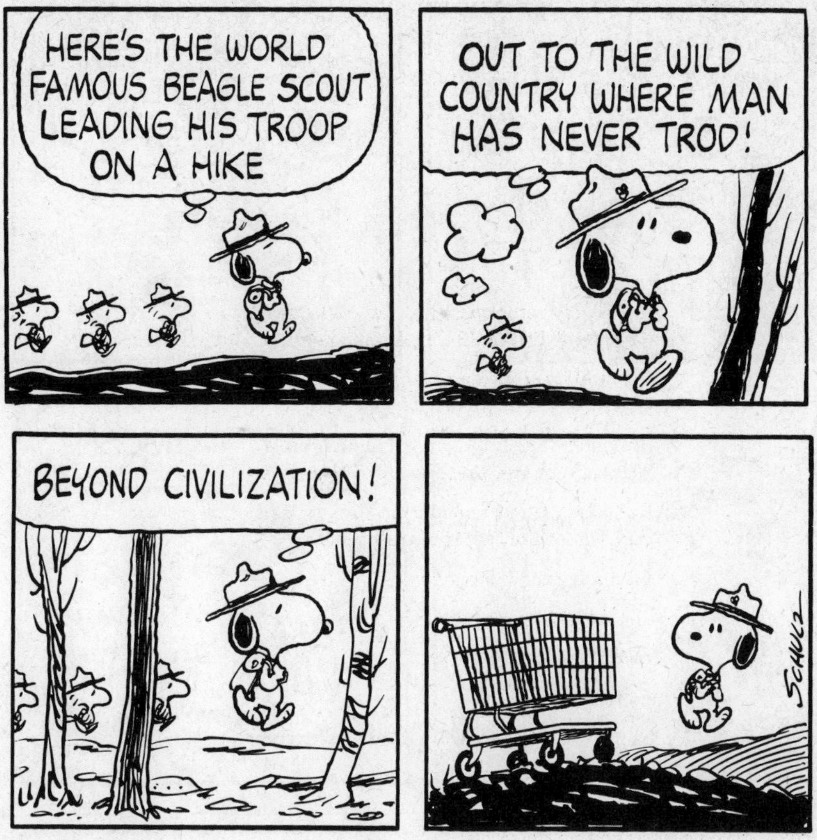
HERE'S THE WORLD FAMOUS BEAGLE SCOUT LEADING HIS TROOP ON A HIKE
OUT TO THE WILD COUNTRY WHERE MAN HAS NEVER TROD!
BEYOND CIVILIZATION!
SCHULZ

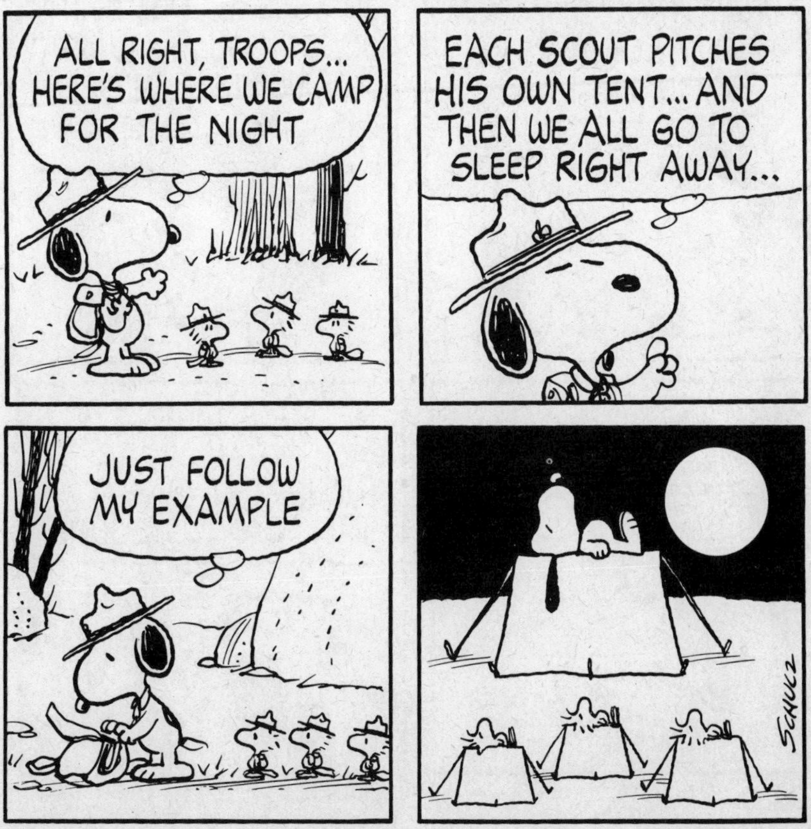
ALL RIGHT, TROOPS... HERE'S WHERE WE CAMP FOR THE NIGHT
EACH SCOUT PITCHES HIS OWN TENT... AND THEN WE ALL GO TO SLEEP RIGHT AWAY...
JUST FOLLOW MY EXAMPLE
SCHULZ

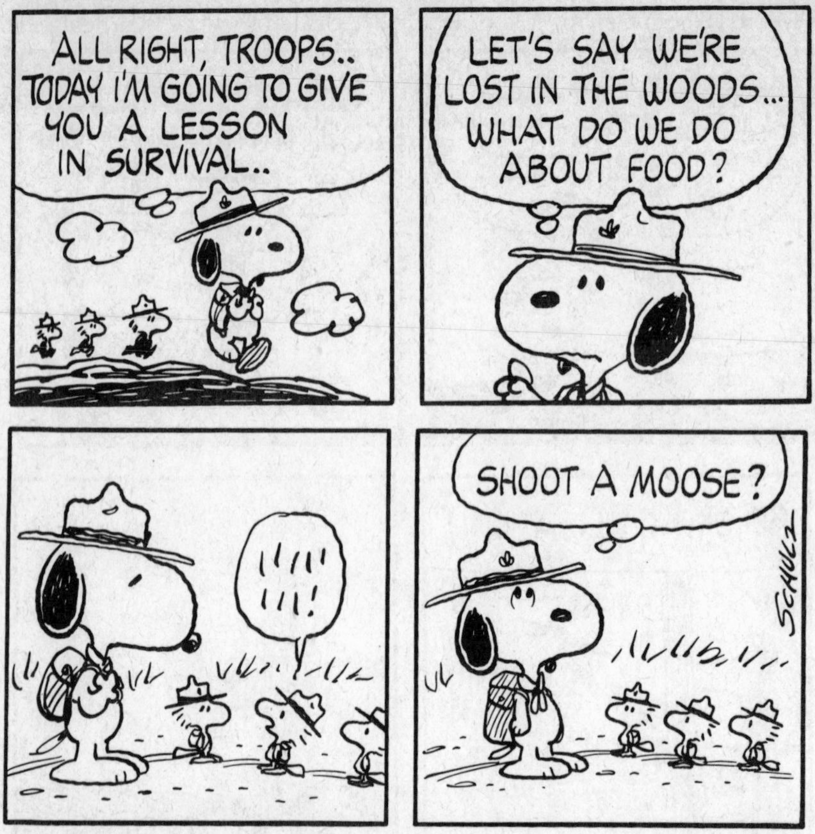
ALL RIGHT, TROOPS.. TODAY I'M GOING TO GIVE YOU A LESSON IN SURVIVAL..
LET'S SAY WE'RE LOST IN THE WOODS... WHAT DO WE DO ABOUT FOOD?
SHOOT A MOOSE?
SCHULZ

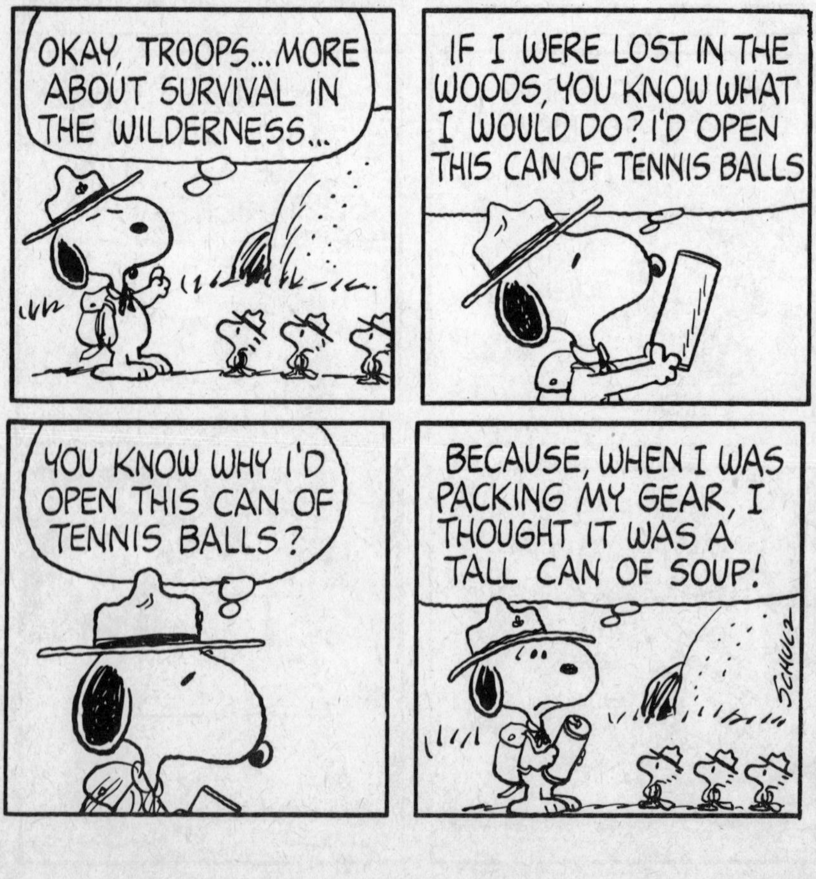
OKAY, TROOPS... MORE ABOUT SURVIVAL IN THE WILDERNESS...
IF I WERE LOST IN THE WOODS, YOU KNOW WHAT I WOULD DO? I'D OPEN THIS CAN OF TENNIS BALLS
YOU KNOW WHY I'D OPEN THIS CAN OF TENNIS BALLS?
BECAUSE, WHEN I WAS PACKING MY GEAR, I THOUGHT IT WAS A TALL CAN OF SOUP!
SCHULZ

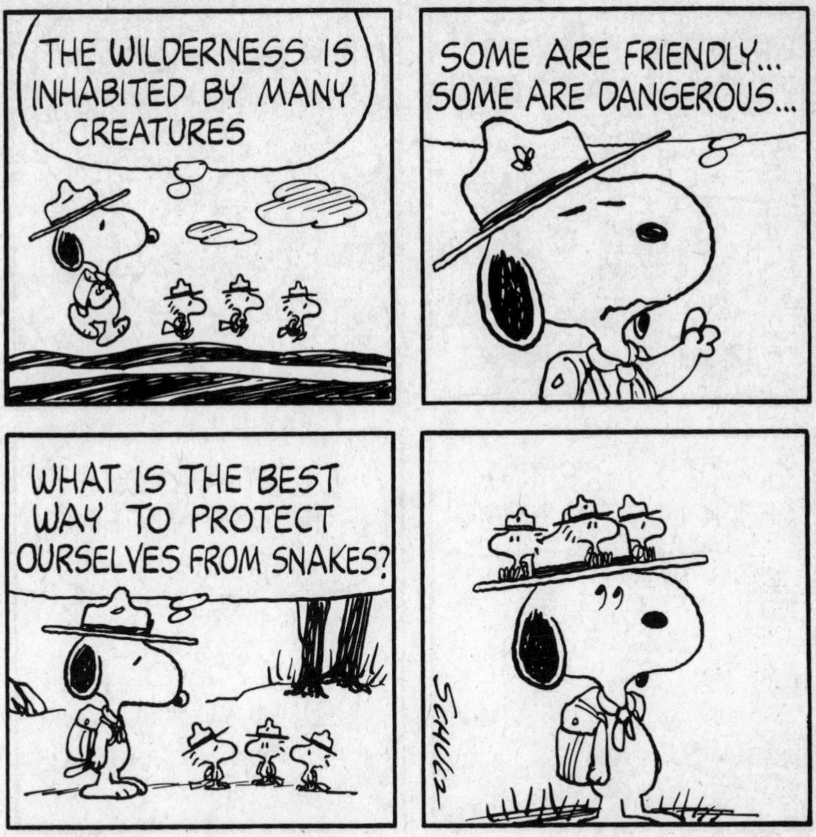
THE WILDERNESS IS INHABITED BY MANY CREATURES
SOME ARE FRIENDLY... SOME ARE DANGEROUS...
WHAT IS THE BEST WAY TO PROTECT OURSELVES FROM SNAKES?
SCHULZ

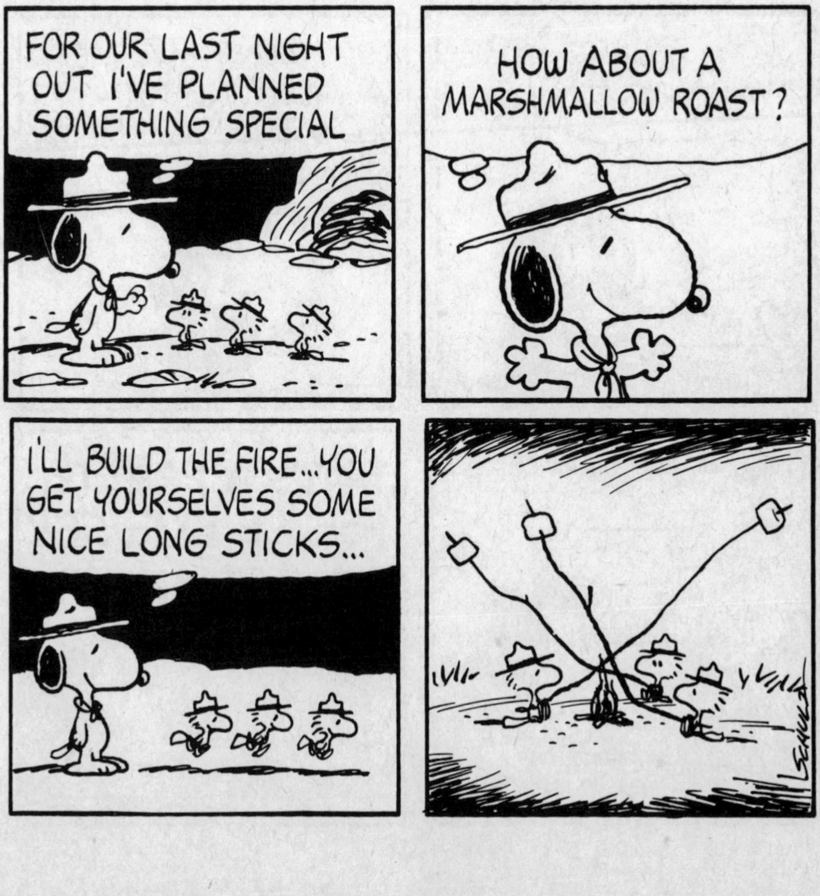
FOR OUR LAST NIGHT OUT I'VE PLANNED SOMETHING SPECIAL
HOW ABOUT A MARSHMALLOW ROAST?
I'LL BUILD THE FIRE...YOU GET YOURSELVES SOME NICE LONG STICKS...
SCHULZ

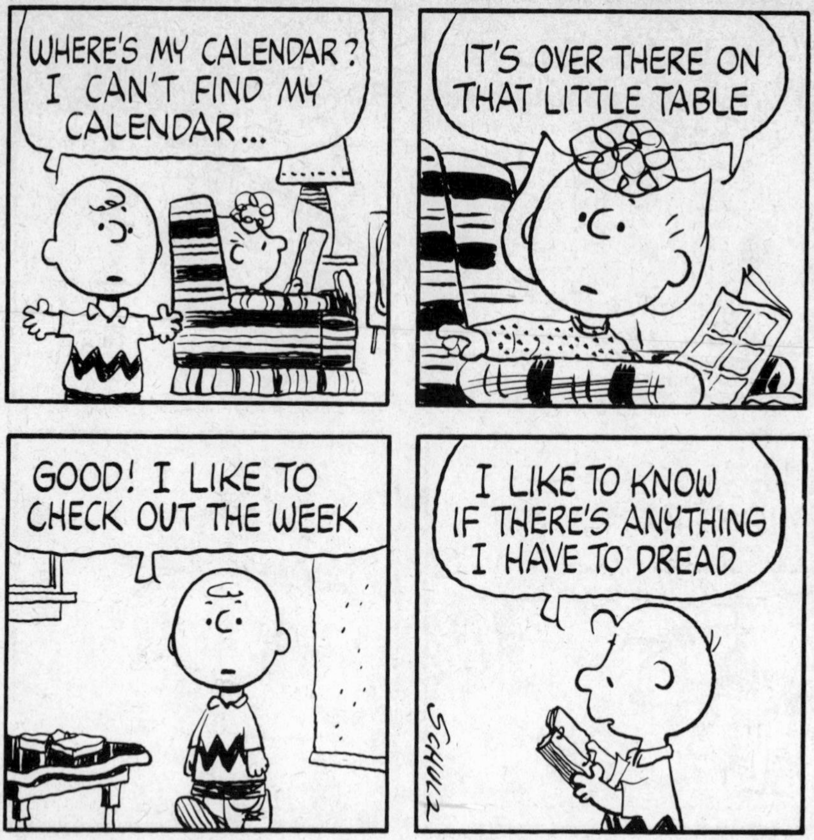
WHERE'S MY CALENDAR? I CAN'T FIND MY CALENDAR...
IT'S OVER THERE ON THAT LITTLE TABLE
GOOD! I LIKE TO CHECK OUT THE WEEK
I LIKE TO KNOW IF THERE'S ANYTHING I HAVE TO DREAD
SCHULZ

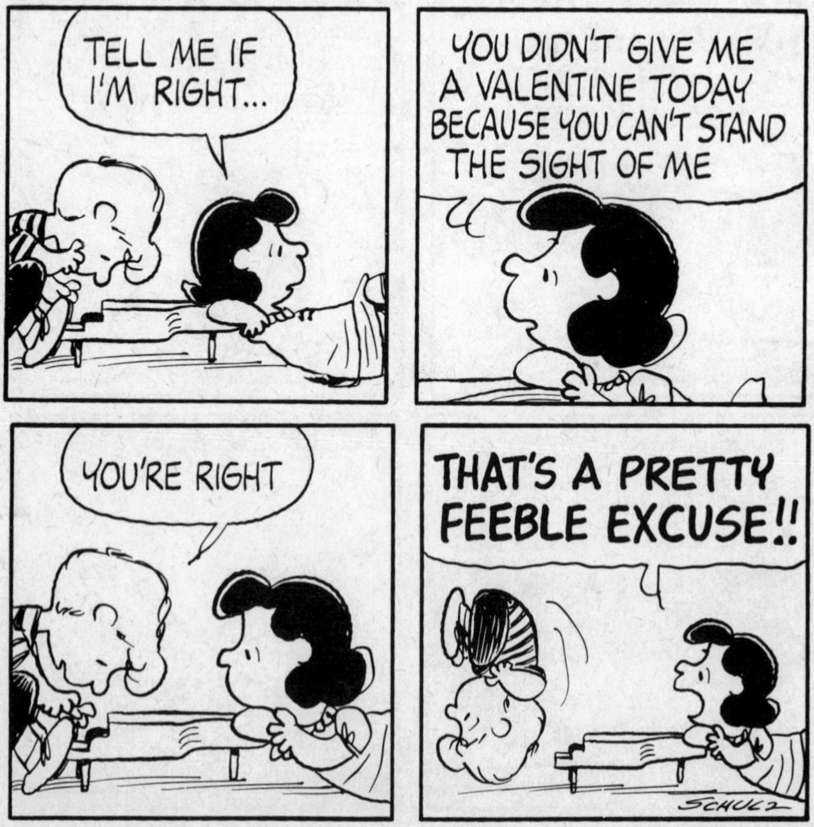
TELL ME IF I'M RIGHT...
YOU DIDN'T GIVE ME A VALENTINE TODAY BECAUSE YOU CAN'T STAND THE SIGHT OF ME
YOU'RE RIGHT
THAT'S A PRETTY FEEBLE EXCUSE!!
SCHULZ

GOOD GRIEF, I'M DROWNING!
WHERE ARE ALL MY FRIENDS?!
SCHULZ

THIS IS A FLEURON..YOU THOUGHT IT WAS AN ASTERISK, DIDN'T YOU?
A FLEURON DOES NOT APPRECIATE BEING TAKEN FOR AN ASTERISK!
PROBABLY SOMETHING THAT GOES WAY BACK, AND BOTH SIDES OF THE FAMILY HAVE FORGOTTEN
WHAT DID YOU SAY?
NOTHING
SCHULZ

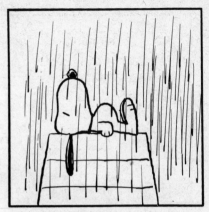

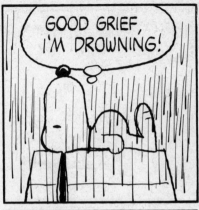

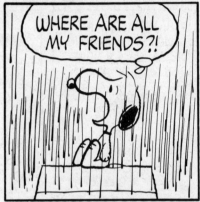

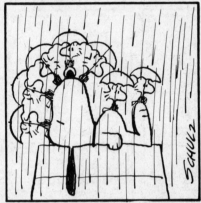

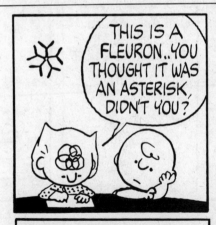

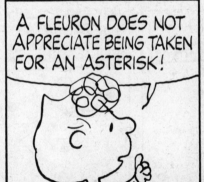

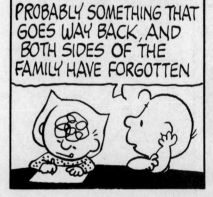

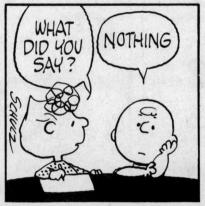

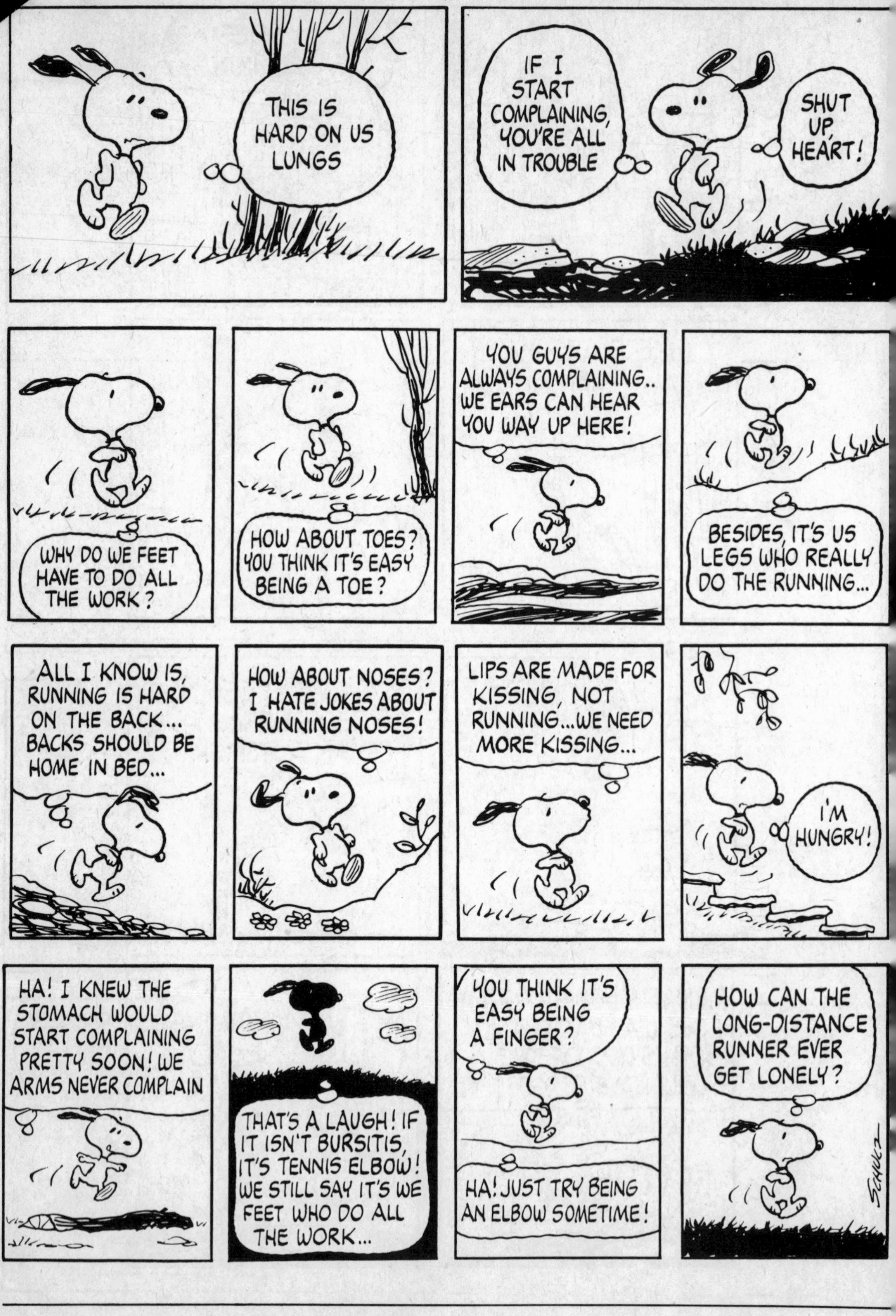
THIS IS HARD ON US LUNGS
IF I START COMPLAINING, YOU'RE ALL IN TROUBLE
SHUT UP, HEART!
WHY DO WE FEET HAVE TO DO ALL THE WORK?
HOW ABOUT TOES? YOU THINK IT'S EASY BEING A TOE?
YOU GUYS ARE ALWAYS COMPLAINING.. WE EARS CAN HEAR YOU WAY UP HERE!
BESIDES, IT'S US LEGS WHO REALLY DO THE RUNNING...
ALL I KNOW IS, RUNNING IS HARD ON THE BACK... BACKS SHOULD BE HOME IN BED...
HOW ABOUT NOSES? I HATE JOKES ABOUT RUNNING NOSES!
LIPS ARE MADE FOR KISSING, NOT RUNNING...WE NEED MORE KISSING...
I'M HUNGRY!
HA! I KNEW THE STOMACH WOULD START COMPLAINING PRETTY SOON! WE ARMS NEVER COMPLAIN
THAT'S A LAUGH! IF IT ISN'T BURSITIS, IT'S TENNIS ELBOW! WE STILL SAY IT'S WE FEET WHO DO ALL THE WORK...
YOU THINK IT'S EASY BEING A FINGER?
HA! JUST TRY BEING AN ELBOW SOMETIME!
HOW CAN THE LONG-DISTANCE RUNNER EVER GET LONELY?
SCHULZ

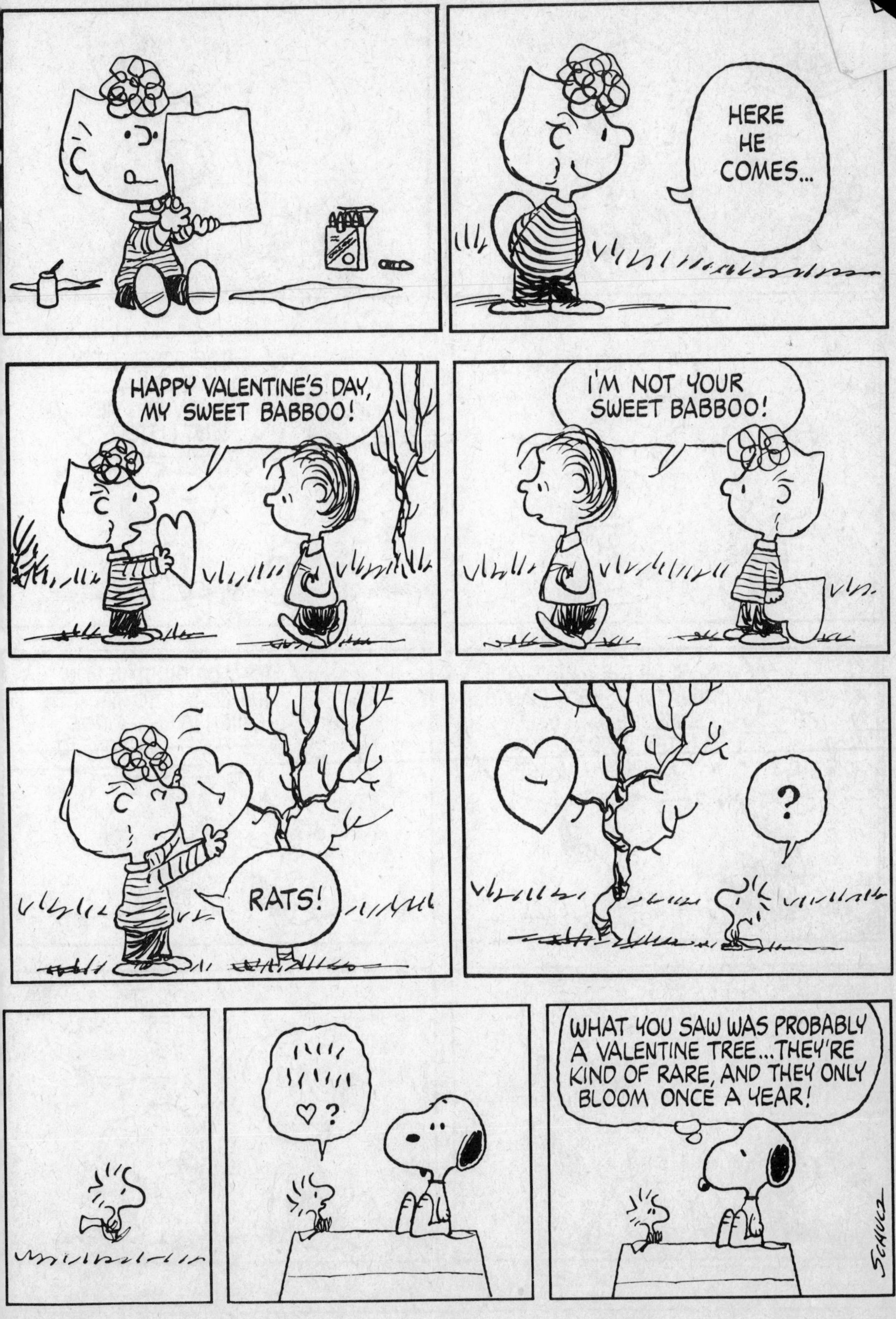
HERE HE COMES...
HAPPY VALENTINE'S DAY, MY SWEET BABBOO!
I'M NOT YOUR SWEET BABBOO!
RATS!
?
♡ ?
WHAT YOU SAW WAS PROBABLY A VALENTINE TREE...THEY'RE KIND OF RARE, AND THEY ONLY BLOOM ONCE A YEAR!
SCHULZ

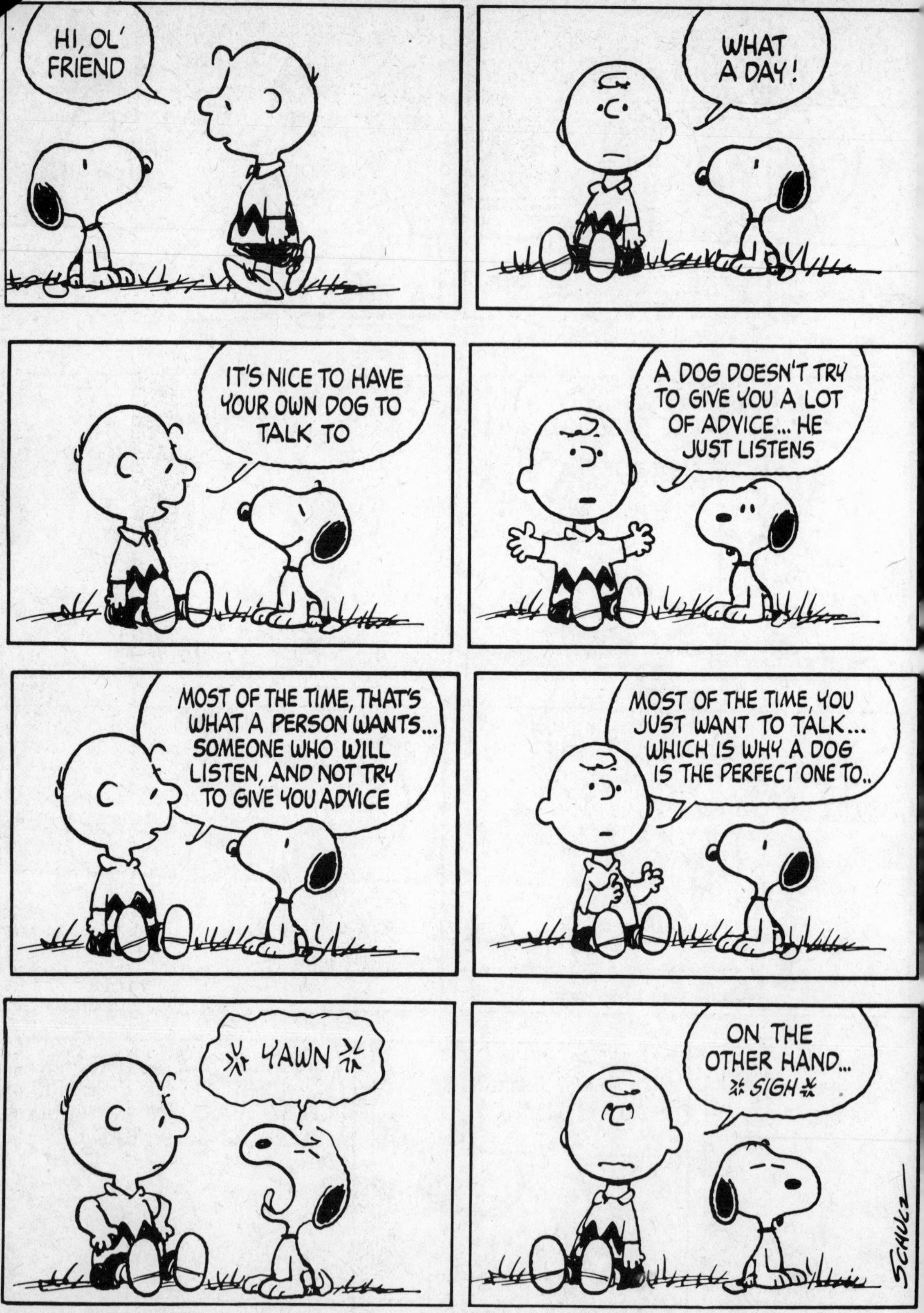
HI, OL' FRIEND
WHAT A DAY!
IT'S NICE TO HAVE YOUR OWN DOG TO TALK TO
A DOG DOESN'T TRY TO GIVE YOU A LOT OF ADVICE... HE JUST LISTENS
MOST OF THE TIME, THAT'S WHAT A PERSON WANTS... SOMEONE WHO WILL LISTEN, AND NOT TRY TO GIVE YOU ADVICE
MOST OF THE TIME, YOU JUST WANT TO TALK... WHICH IS WHY A DOG IS THE PERFECT ONE TO..
YAWN
ON THE OTHER HAND... SIGH
SCHULZ

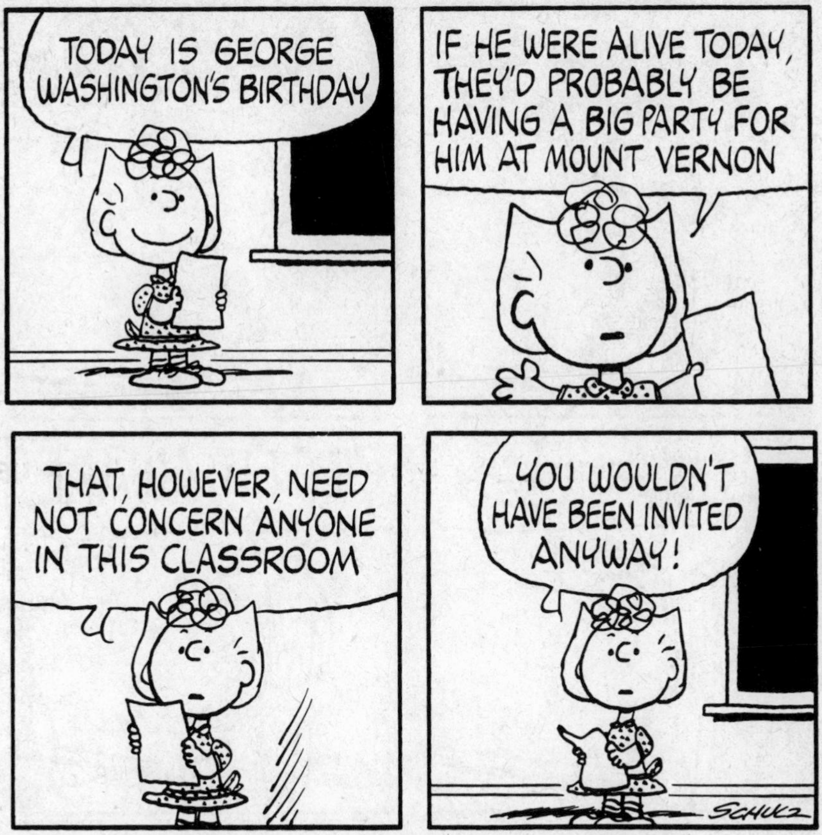
TODAY IS GEORGE WASHINGTON'S BIRTHDAY
IF HE WERE ALIVE TODAY, THEY'D PROBABLY BE HAVING A BIG PARTY FOR HIM AT MOUNT VERNON
THAT, HOWEVER, NEED NOT CONCERN ANYONE IN THIS CLASSROOM
YOU WOULDN'T HAVE BEEN INVITED ANYWAY!
SCHULZ

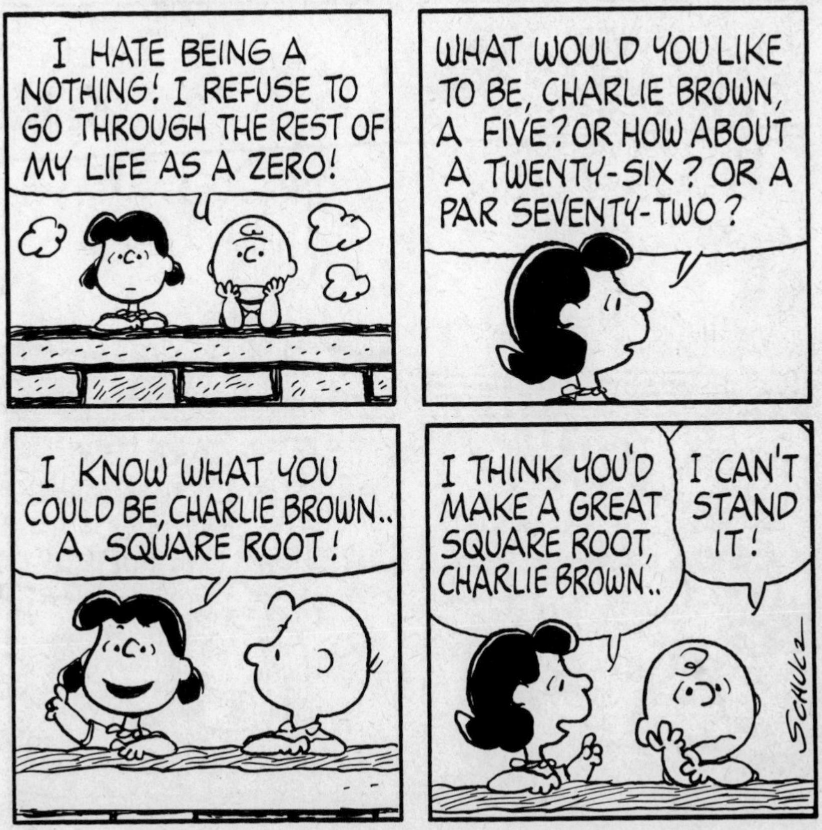
I HATE BEING A NOTHING! I REFUSE TO GO THROUGH THE REST OF MY LIFE AS A ZERO!
WHAT WOULD YOU LIKE TO BE, CHARLIE BROWN, A FIVE? OR HOW ABOUT A TWENTY-SIX? OR A PAR SEVENTY-TWO?
I KNOW WHAT YOU COULD BE, CHARLIE BROWN.. A SQUARE ROOT!
I THINK YOU'D MAKE A GREAT SQUARE ROOT, CHARLIE BROWN..
I CAN'T STAND IT!
SCHULZ

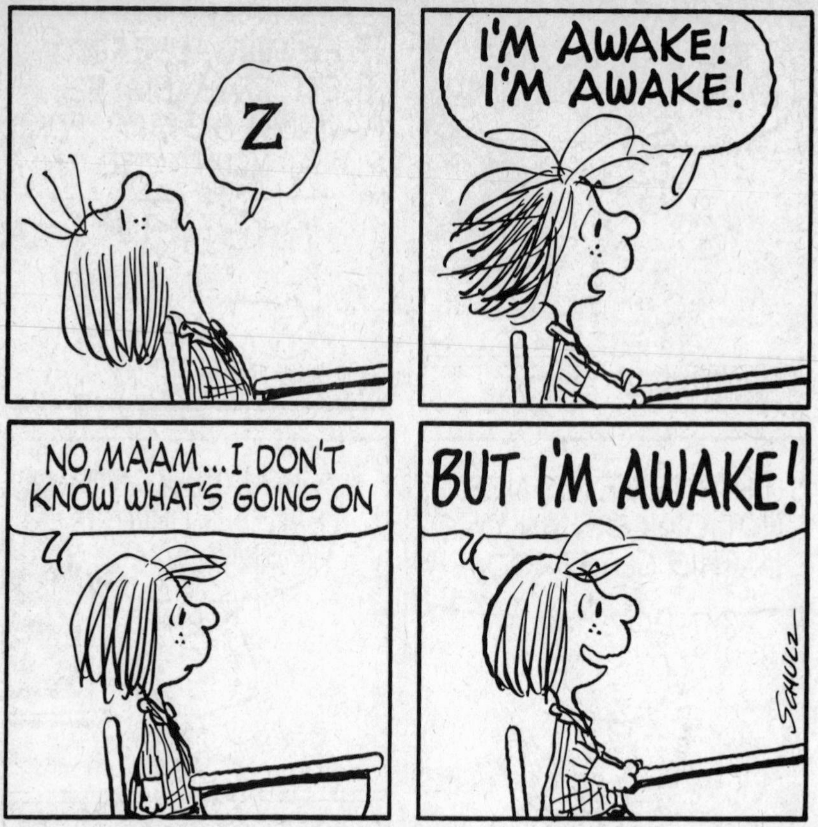
Z
I'M AWAKE! I'M AWAKE!
NO, MA'AM... I DON'T KNOW WHAT'S GOING ON
BUT I'M AWAKE!
SCHULZ

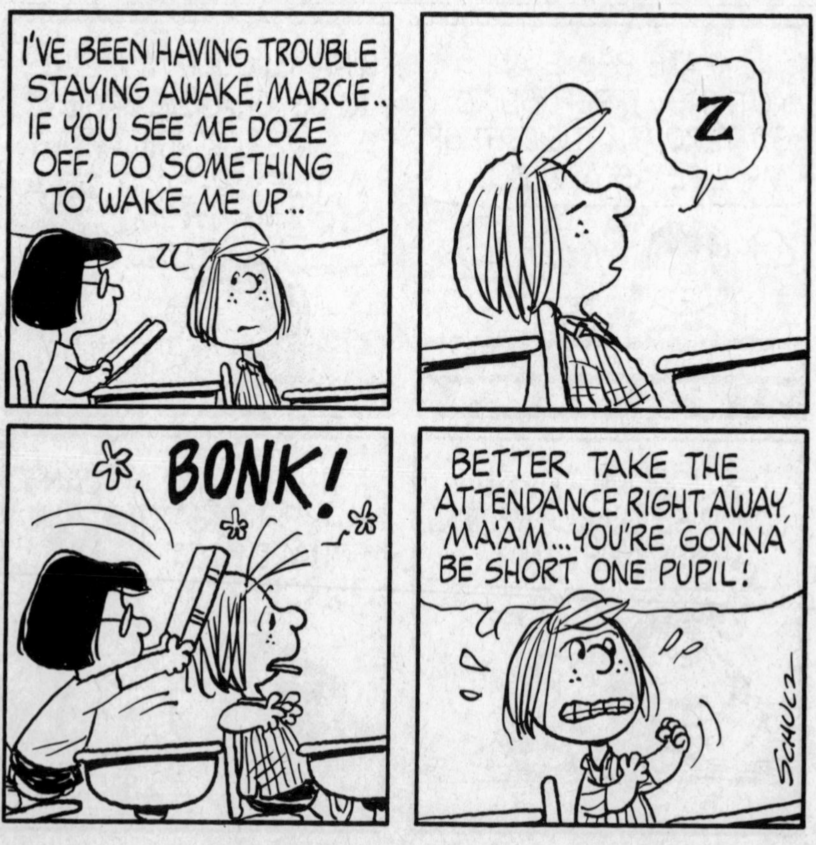
I'VE BEEN HAVING TROUBLE STAYING AWAKE, MARCIE.. IF YOU SEE ME DOZE OFF, DO SOMETHING TO WAKE ME UP...
Z
BONK!
BETTER TAKE THE ATTENDANCE RIGHT AWAY, MA'AM... YOU'RE GONNA BE SHORT ONE PUPIL!
SCHULZ

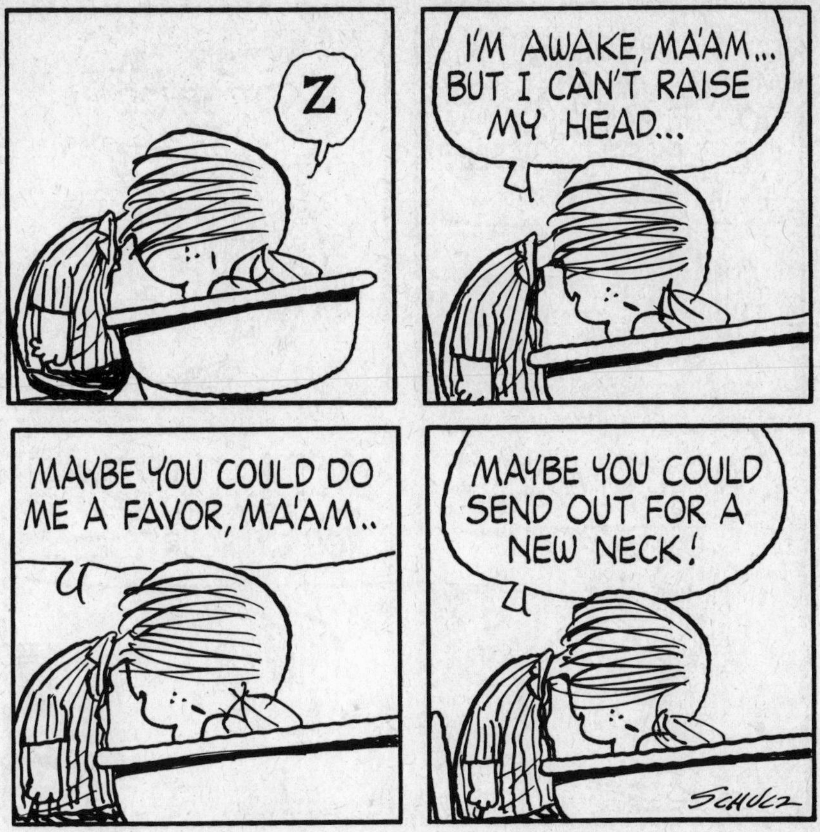
Z
I'M AWAKE, MA'AM... BUT I CAN'T RAISE MY HEAD...
MAYBE YOU COULD DO ME A FAVOR, MA'AM..
MAYBE YOU COULD SEND OUT FOR A NEW NECK!
SCHULZ

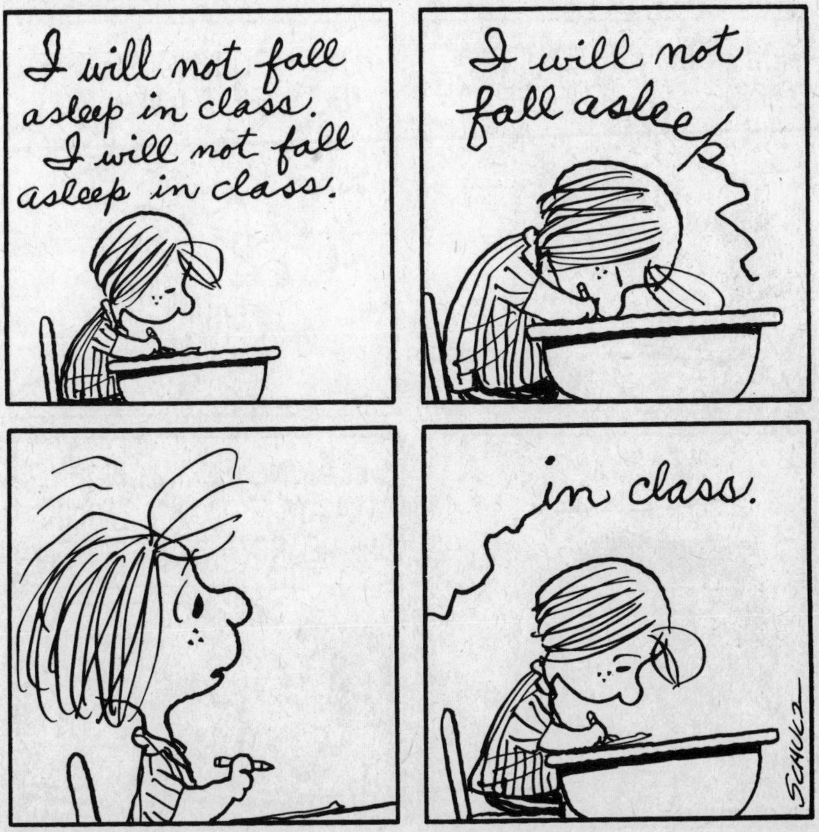
I will not fall asleep in class. I will not fall asleep in class.
I will not fall aslee
in class.
SCHULZ

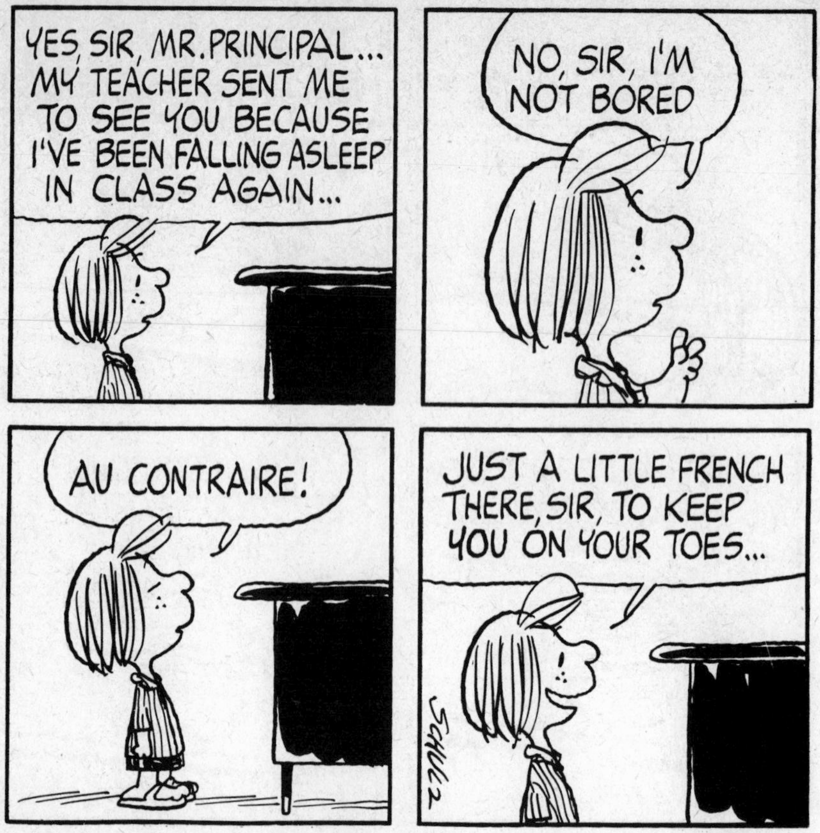
YES, SIR, MR. PRINCIPAL... MY TEACHER SENT ME TO SEE YOU BECAUSE I'VE BEEN FALLING ASLEEP IN CLASS AGAIN...
NO, SIR, I'M NOT BORED
AU CONTRAIRE!
JUST A LITTLE FRENCH THERE, SIR, TO KEEP YOU ON YOUR TOES...

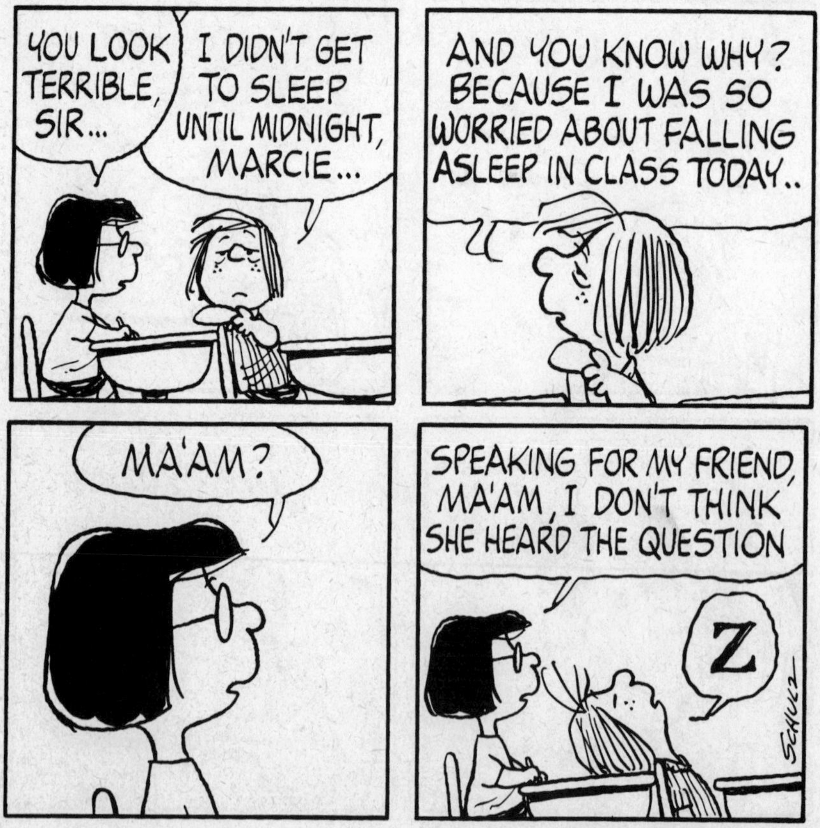
YOU LOOK TERRIBLE, SIR...
I DIDN'T GET TO SLEEP UNTIL MIDNIGHT, MARCIE...
AND YOU KNOW WHY? BECAUSE I WAS SO WORRIED ABOUT FALLING ASLEEP IN CLASS TODAY..
MA'AM?
SPEAKING FOR MY FRIEND, MA'AM, I DON'T THINK SHE HEARD THE QUESTION
Z

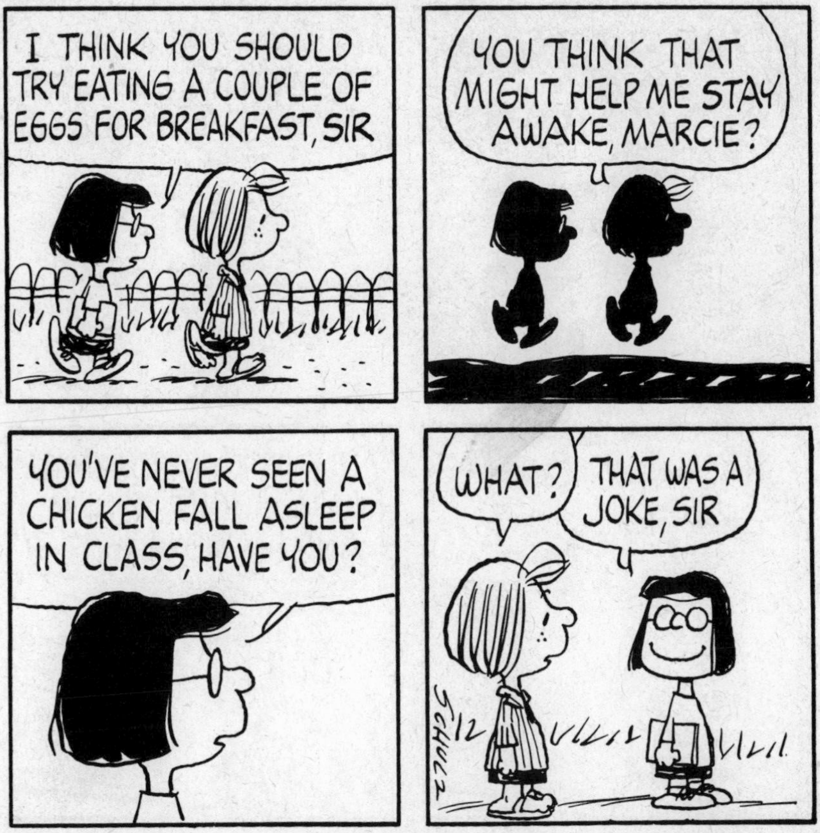
I THINK YOU SHOULD TRY EATING A COUPLE OF EGGS FOR BREAKFAST, SIR
YOU THINK THAT MIGHT HELP ME STAY AWAKE, MARCIE?
YOU'VE NEVER SEEN A CHICKEN FALL ASLEEP IN CLASS, HAVE YOU?
WHAT?
THAT WAS A JOKE, SIR
SCHULZ

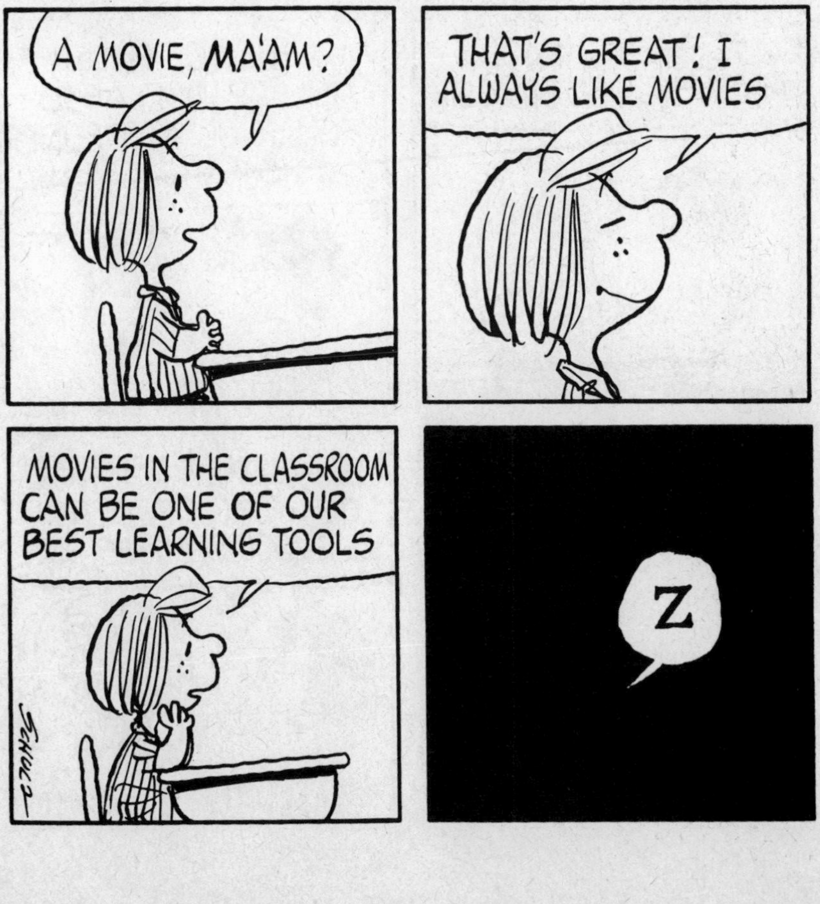
A MOVIE, MA'AM?
THAT'S GREAT! I ALWAYS LIKE MOVIES
MOVIES IN THE CLASSROOM CAN BE ONE OF OUR BEST LEARNING TOOLS
SCHULZ
Z

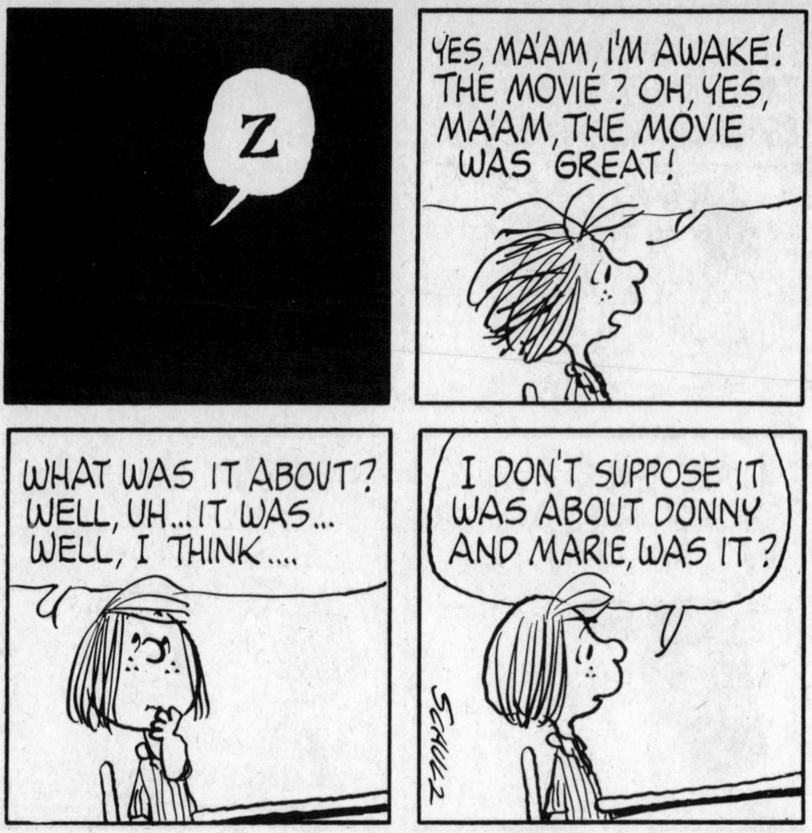
Z
YES, MA'AM, I'M AWAKE! THE MOVIE? OH, YES, MA'AM, THE MOVIE WAS GREAT!
WHAT WAS IT ABOUT? WELL, UH...IT WAS... WELL, I THINK....
I DON'T SUPPOSE IT WAS ABOUT DONNY AND MARIE, WAS IT?
SCHULZ

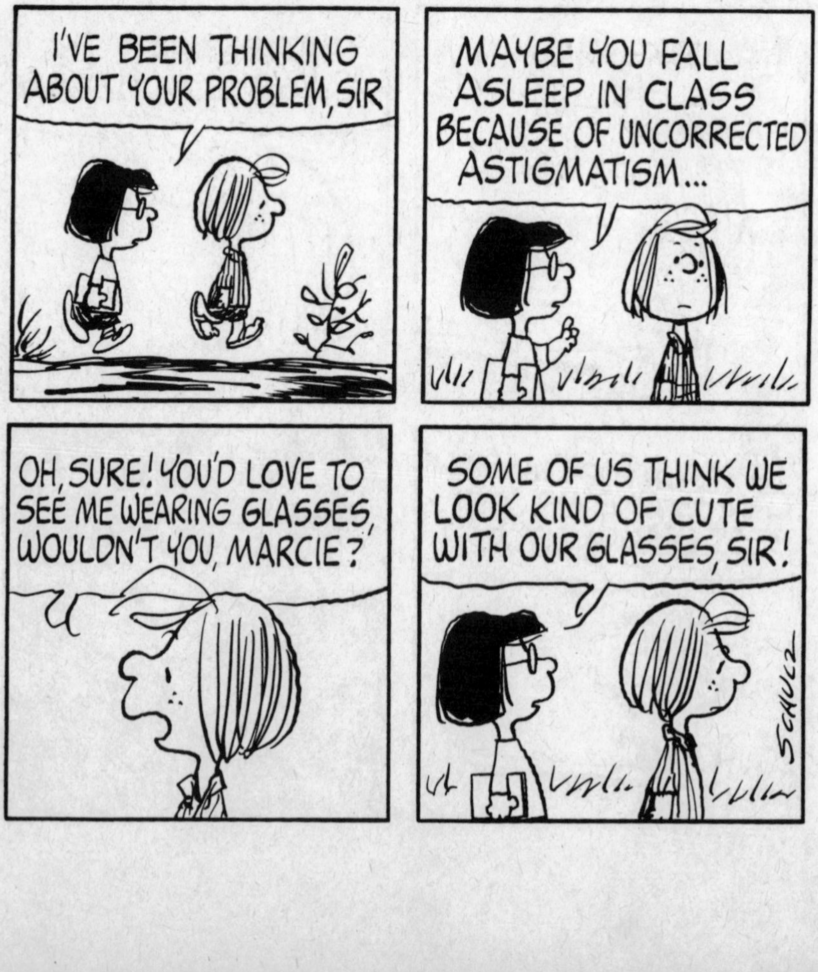
I'VE BEEN THINKING ABOUT YOUR PROBLEM, SIR
MAYBE YOU FALL ASLEEP IN CLASS BECAUSE OF UNCORRECTED ASTIGMATISM...
OH, SURE! YOU'D LOVE TO SEE ME WEARING GLASSES, WOULDN'T YOU, MARCIE?
SOME OF US THINK WE LOOK KIND OF CUTE WITH OUR GLASSES, SIR!
SCHULZ

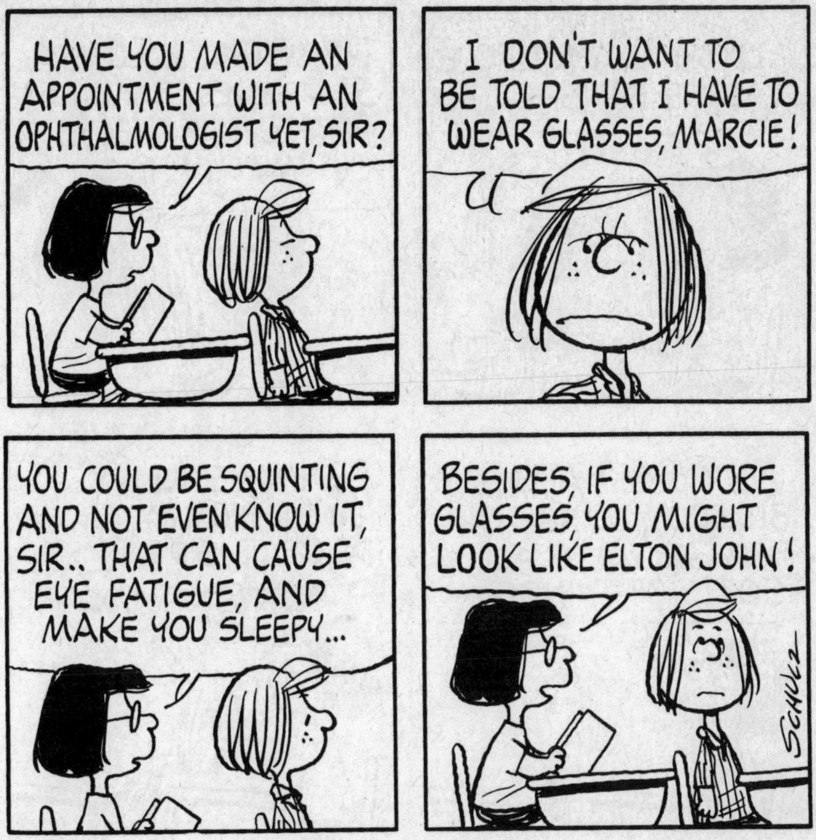
HAVE YOU MADE AN APPOINTMENT WITH AN OPHTHALMOLOGIST YET, SIR?
I DON'T WANT TO BE TOLD THAT I HAVE TO WEAR GLASSES, MARCIE!
YOU COULD BE SQUINTING AND NOT EVEN KNOW IT, SIR.. THAT CAN CAUSE EYE FATIGUE, AND MAKE YOU SLEEPY...
BESIDES, IF YOU WORE GLASSES, YOU MIGHT LOOK LIKE ELTON JOHN!
SCHULZ

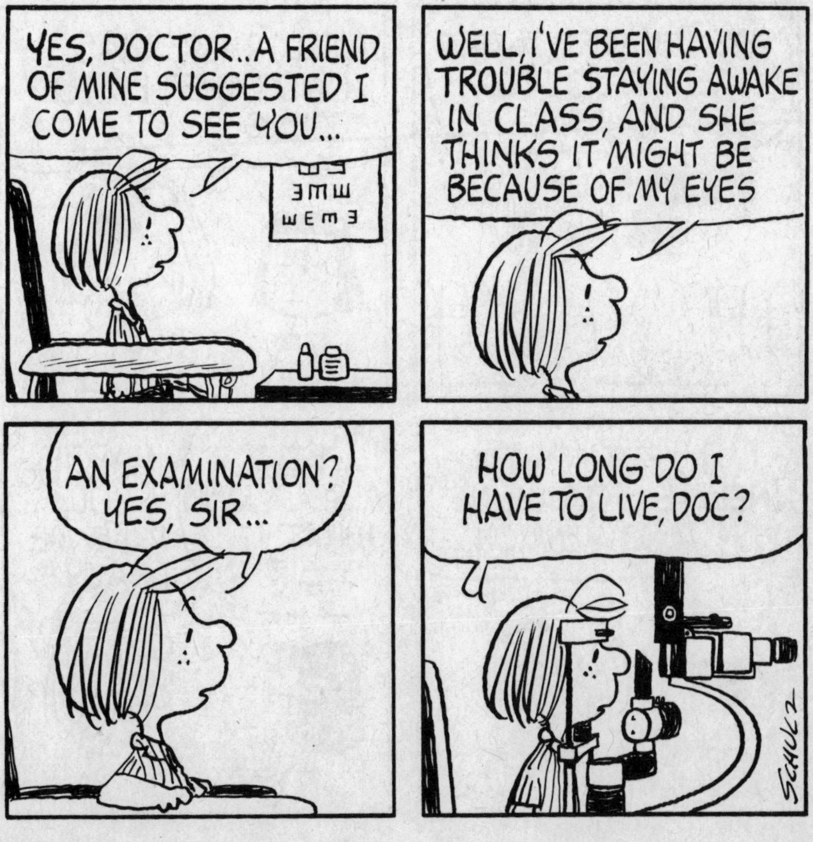
YES, DOCTOR..A FRIEND OF MINE SUGGESTED I COME TO SEE YOU...
WELL, I'VE BEEN HAVING TROUBLE STAYING AWAKE IN CLASS, AND SHE THINKS IT MIGHT BE BECAUSE OF MY EYES
AN EXAMINATION? YES, SIR...
HOW LONG DO I HAVE TO LIVE, DOC?
SCHULZ

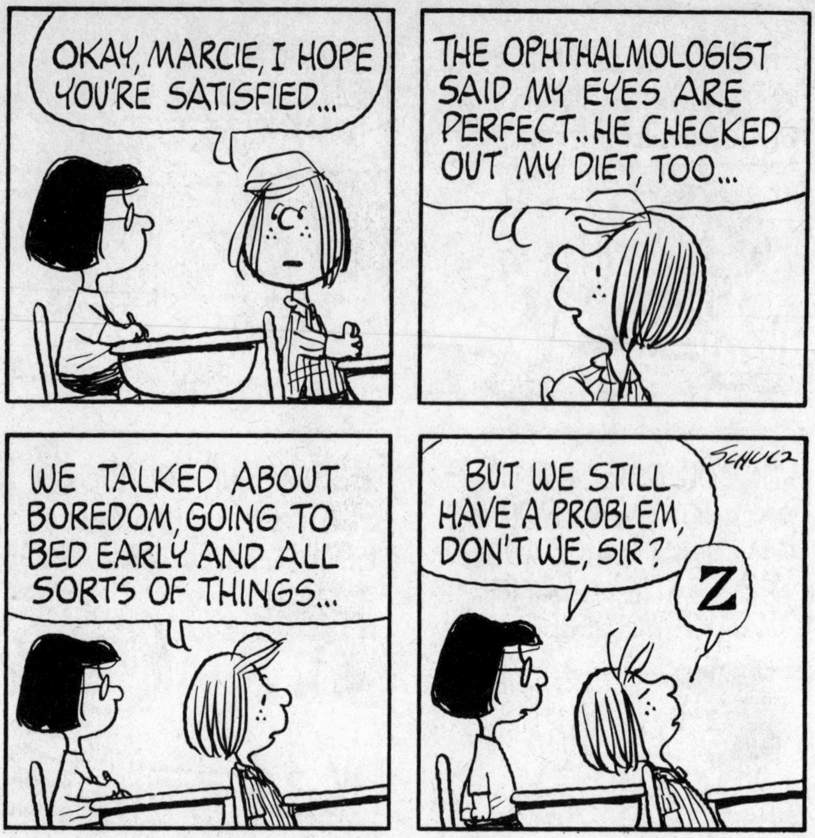
OKAY, MARCIE, I HOPE YOU'RE SATISFIED...
THE OPHTHALMOLOGIST SAID MY EYES ARE PERFECT.. HE CHECKED OUT MY DIET, TOO...
WE TALKED ABOUT BOREDOM, GOING TO BED EARLY AND ALL SORTS OF THINGS...
SCHULZ
BUT WE STILL HAVE A PROBLEM, DON'T WE, SIR?
Z

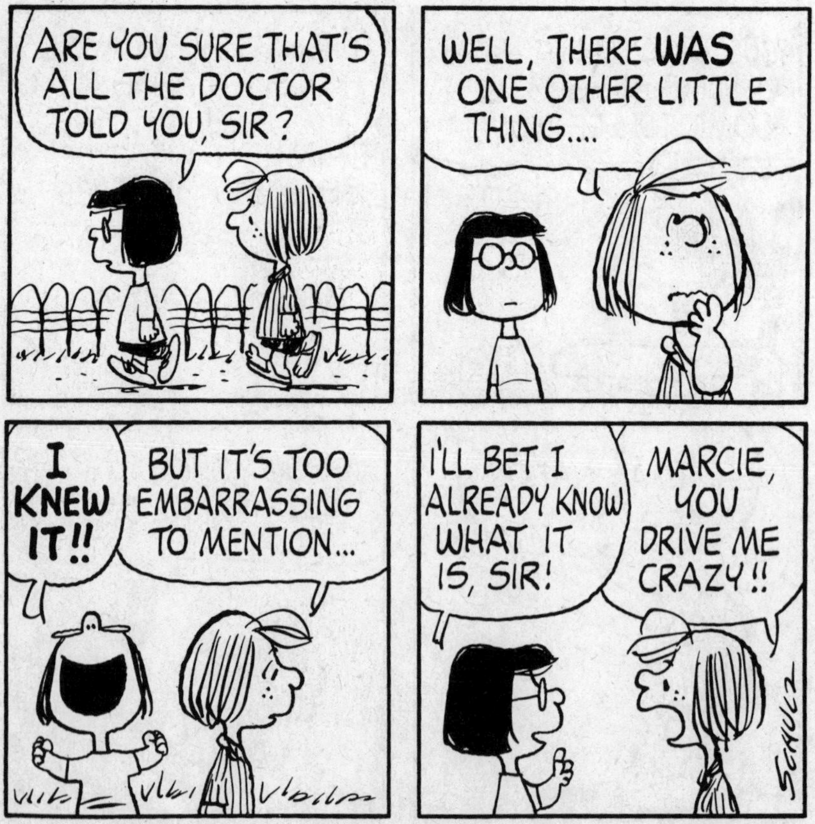
ARE YOU SURE THAT'S ALL THE DOCTOR TOLD YOU, SIR?
WELL, THERE **WAS** ONE OTHER LITTLE THING....
BUT IT'S TOO EMBARRASSING TO MENTION...
I KNEW IT!!
I'LL BET I ALREADY KNOW WHAT IT IS, SIR!
MARCIE, YOU DRIVE ME CRAZY!!
SCHULZ

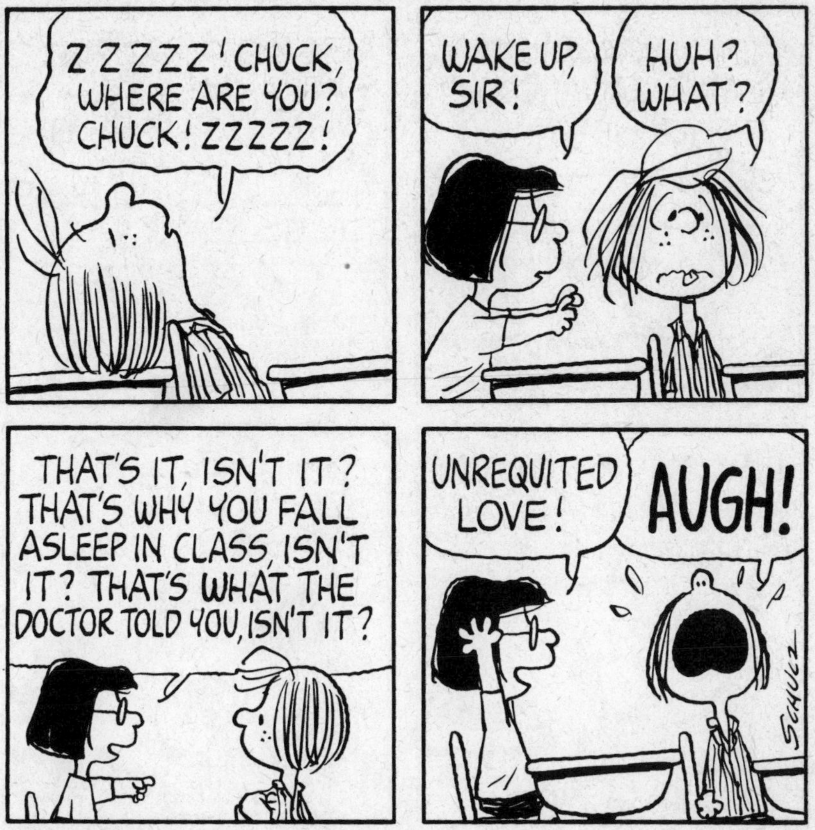
ZZZZZ! CHUCK, WHERE ARE YOU? CHUCK! ZZZZZ!
WAKE UP, SIR!
HUH? WHAT?
THAT'S IT, ISN'T IT? THAT'S WHY YOU FALL ASLEEP IN CLASS, ISN'T IT? THAT'S WHAT THE DOCTOR TOLD YOU, ISN'T IT?
UNREQUITED LOVE!
AUGH!
SCHULZ

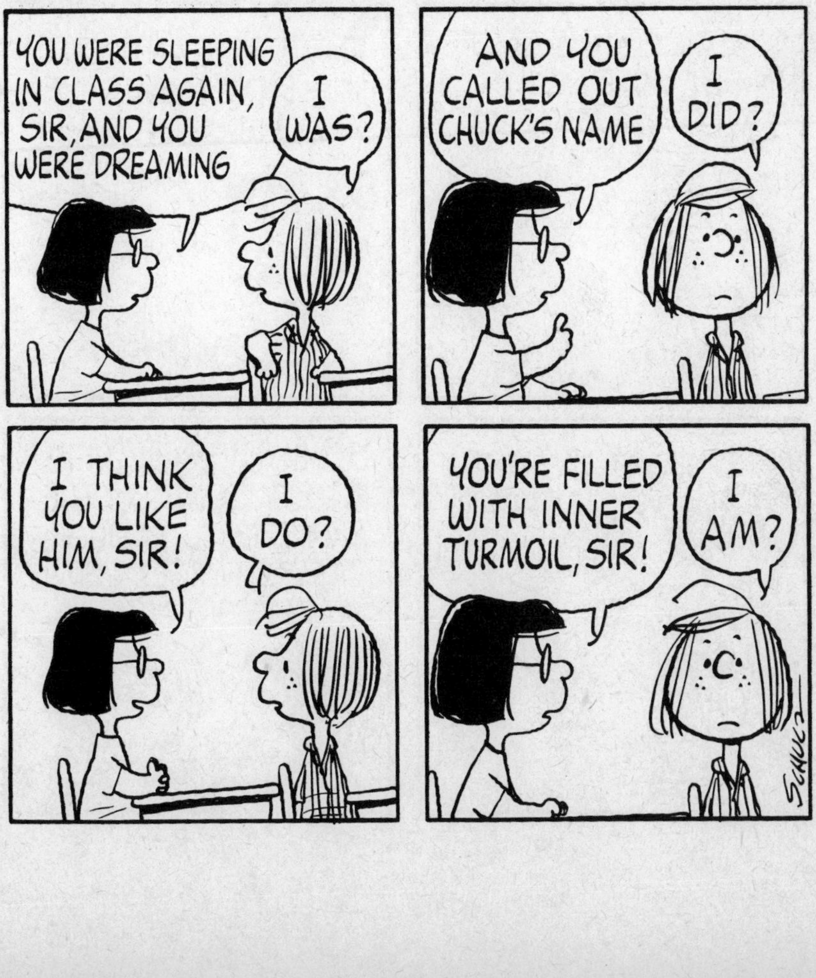
YOU WERE SLEEPING IN CLASS AGAIN, SIR, AND YOU WERE DREAMING
I WAS?
AND YOU CALLED OUT CHUCK'S NAME
I DID?
I THINK YOU LIKE HIM, SIR!
I DO?
YOU'RE FILLED WITH INNER TURMOIL, SIR!
I AM?
SCHULZ

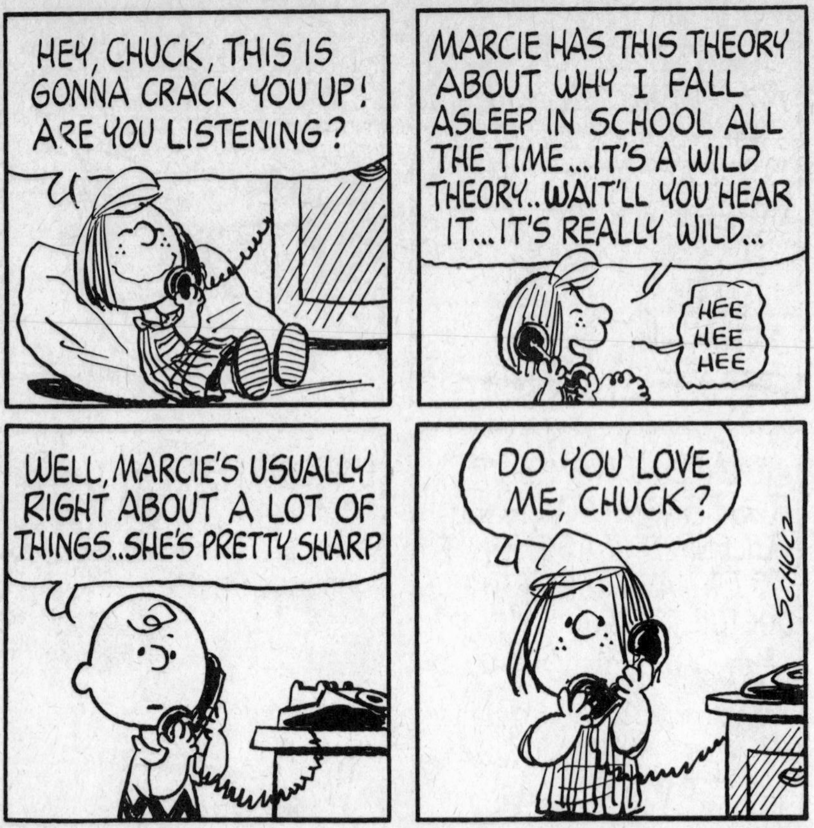
HEY, CHUCK, THIS IS GONNA CRACK YOU UP! ARE YOU LISTENING?
MARCIE HAS THIS THEORY ABOUT WHY I FALL ASLEEP IN SCHOOL ALL THE TIME...IT'S A WILD THEORY..WAIT'LL YOU HEAR IT...IT'S REALLY WILD...
HEE HEE HEE
WELL, MARCIE'S USUALLY RIGHT ABOUT A LOT OF THINGS..SHE'S PRETTY SHARP
DO YOU LOVE ME, CHUCK?
SCHULZ

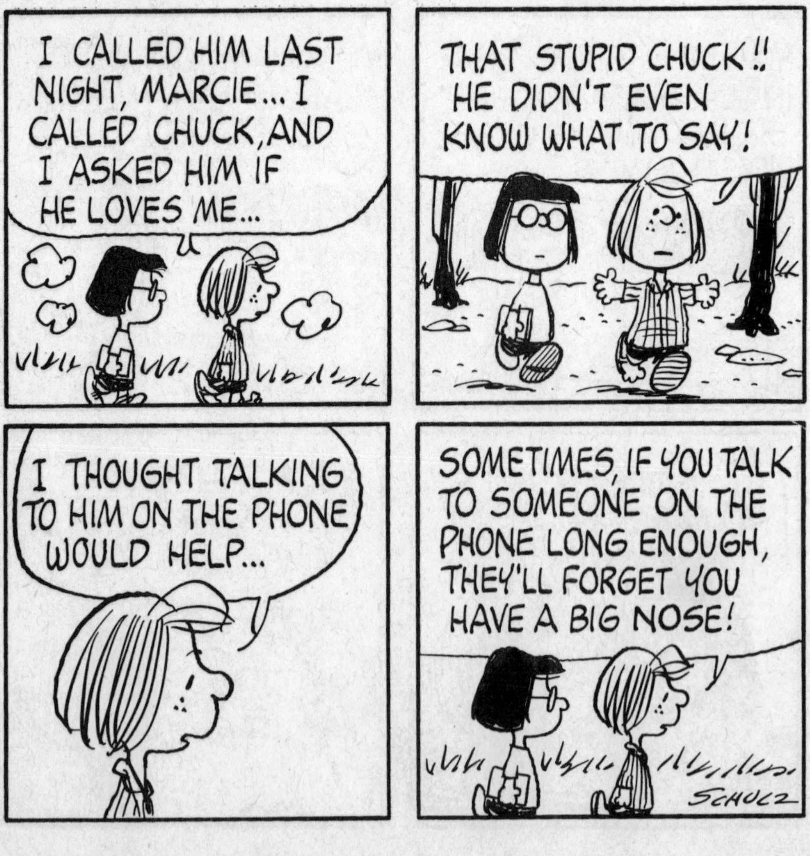
I CALLED HIM LAST NIGHT, MARCIE... I CALLED CHUCK, AND I ASKED HIM IF HE LOVES ME...
THAT STUPID CHUCK!! HE DIDN'T EVEN KNOW WHAT TO SAY!
I THOUGHT TALKING TO HIM ON THE PHONE WOULD HELP...
SOMETIMES, IF YOU TALK TO SOMEONE ON THE PHONE LONG ENOUGH, THEY'LL FORGET YOU HAVE A BIG NOSE!
SCHULZ

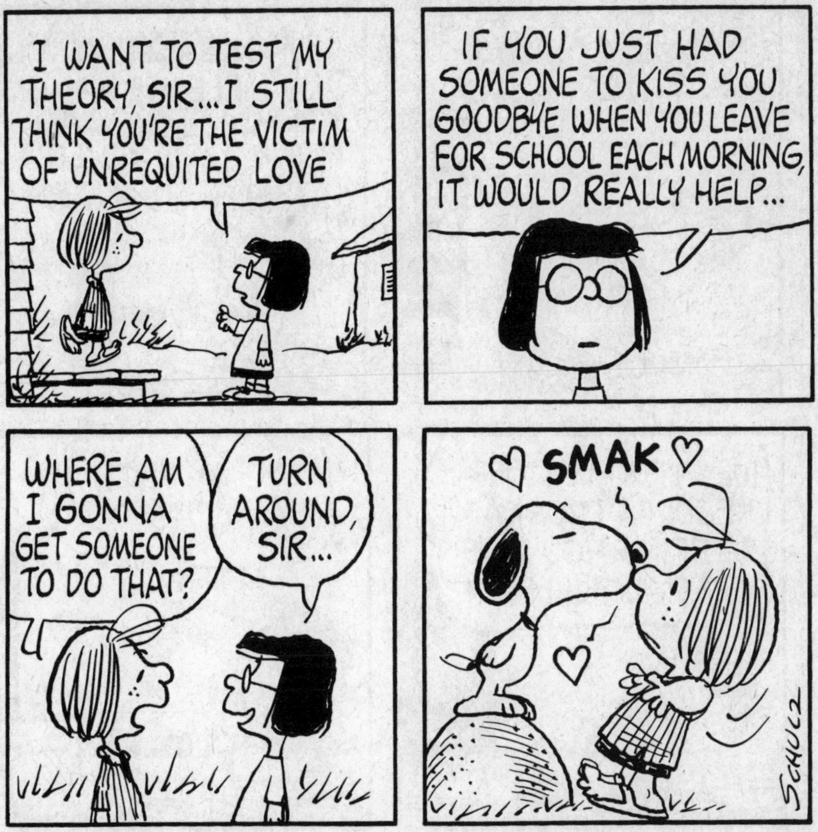
I WANT TO TEST MY THEORY, SIR...I STILL THINK YOU'RE THE VICTIM OF UNREQUITED LOVE
IF YOU JUST HAD SOMEONE TO KISS YOU GOODBYE WHEN YOU LEAVE FOR SCHOOL EACH MORNING, IT WOULD REALLY HELP...
WHERE AM I GONNA GET SOMEONE TO DO THAT?
TURN AROUND, SIR...
SMAK
SCHULZ

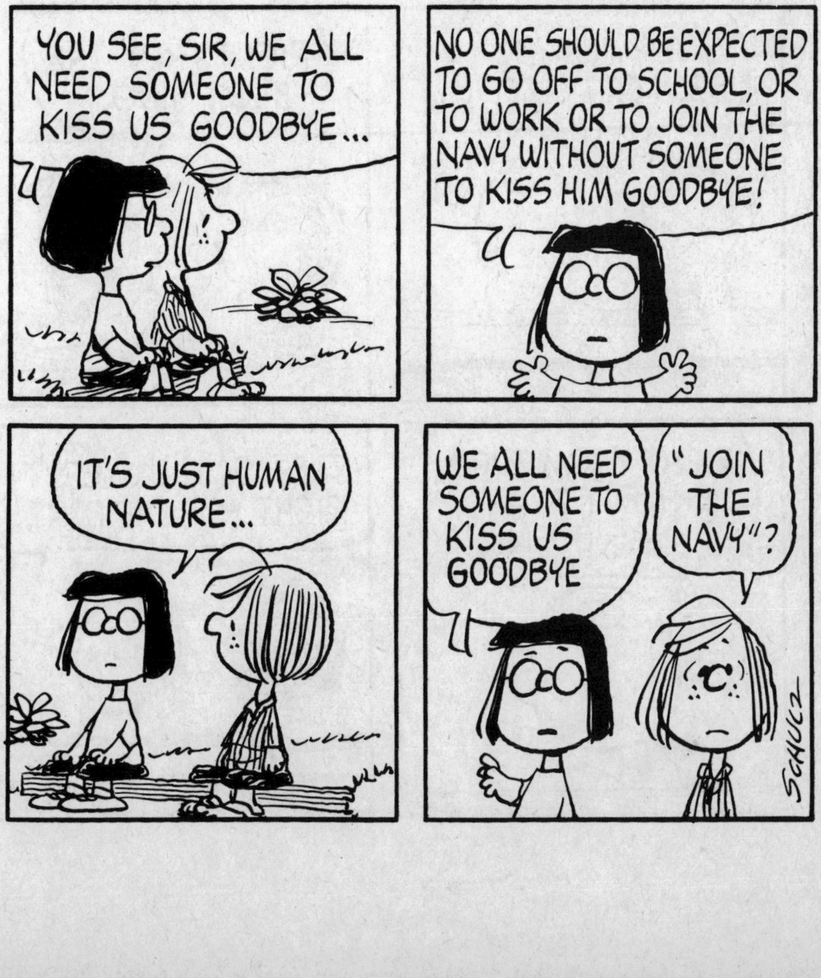
YOU SEE, SIR, WE ALL NEED SOMEONE TO KISS US GOODBYE...
NO ONE SHOULD BE EXPECTED TO GO OFF TO SCHOOL, OR TO WORK OR TO JOIN THE NAVY WITHOUT SOMEONE TO KISS HIM GOODBYE!
IT'S JUST HUMAN NATURE...
WE ALL NEED SOMEONE TO KISS US GOODBYE
"JOIN THE NAVY"?
SCHULZ

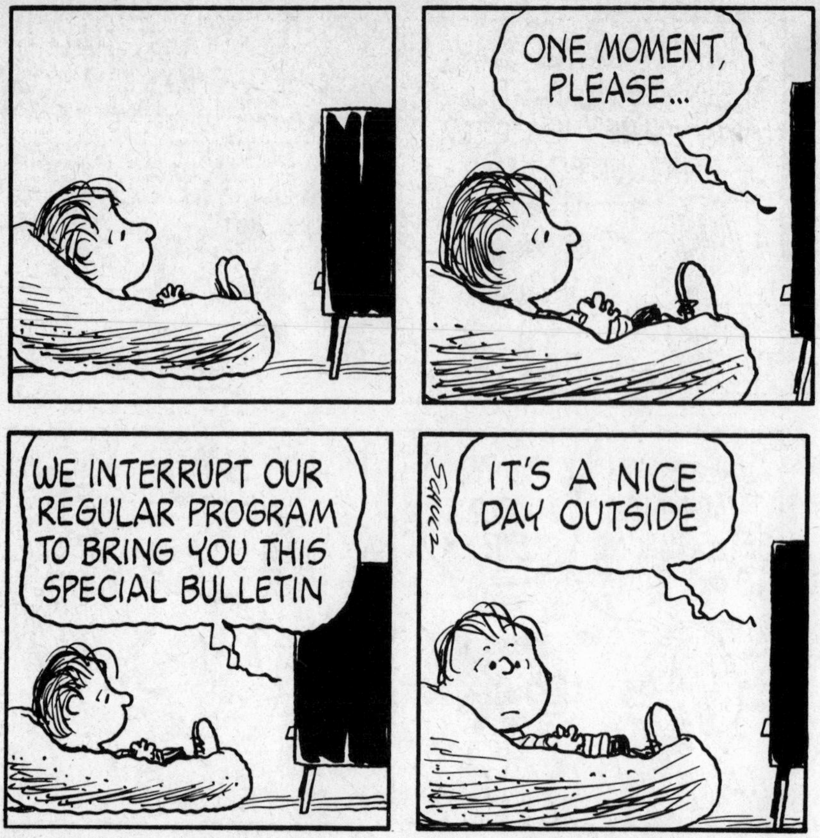
ONE MOMENT, PLEASE...
WE INTERRUPT OUR REGULAR PROGRAM TO BRING YOU THIS SPECIAL BULLETIN
SCHULZ
IT'S A NICE DAY OUTSIDE

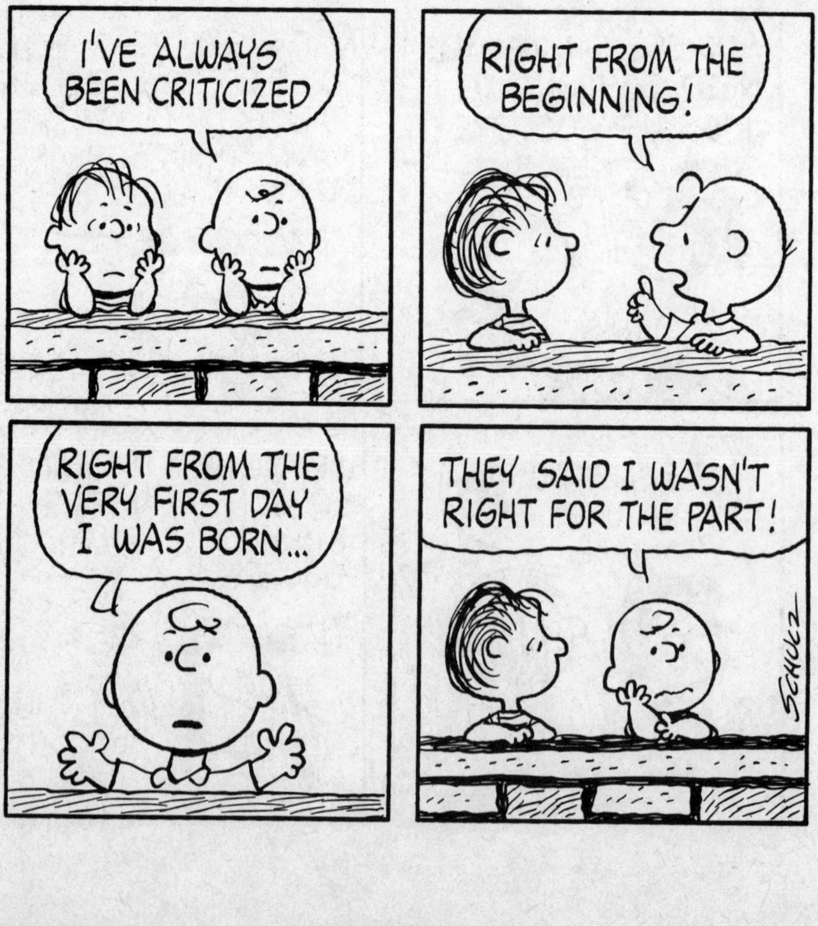
I'VE ALWAYS BEEN CRITICIZED
RIGHT FROM THE BEGINNING!
RIGHT FROM THE VERY FIRST DAY I WAS BORN...
THEY SAID I WASN'T RIGHT FOR THE PART!
SCHULZ

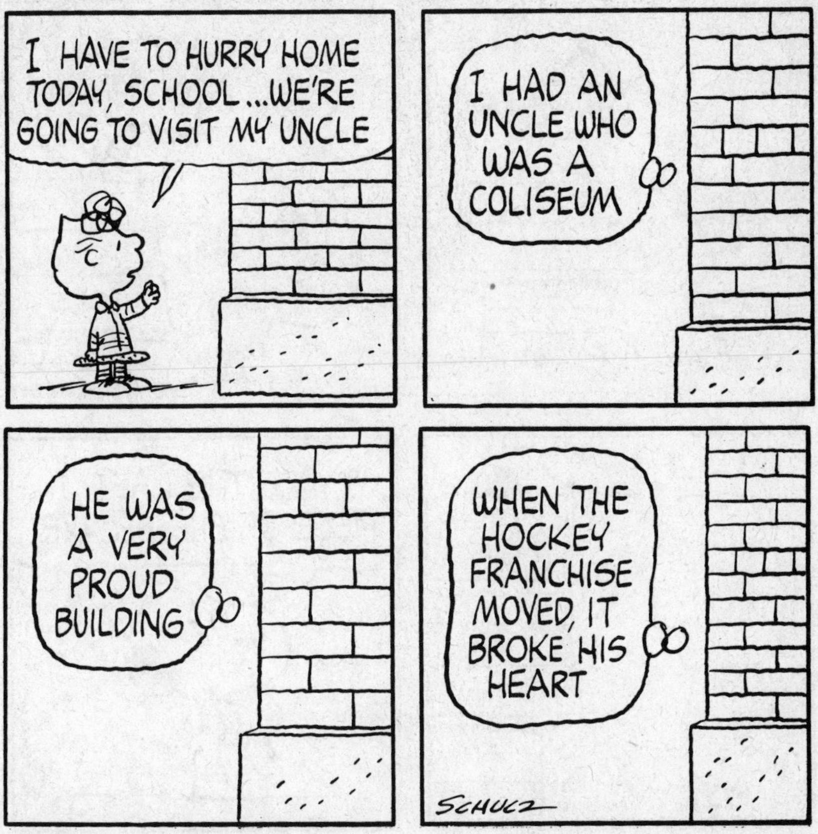
I HAVE TO HURRY HOME TODAY, SCHOOL...WE'RE GOING TO VISIT MY UNCLE
I HAD AN UNCLE WHO WAS A COLISEUM
HE WAS A VERY PROUD BUILDING
WHEN THE HOCKEY FRANCHISE MOVED, IT BROKE HIS HEART
SCHULZ

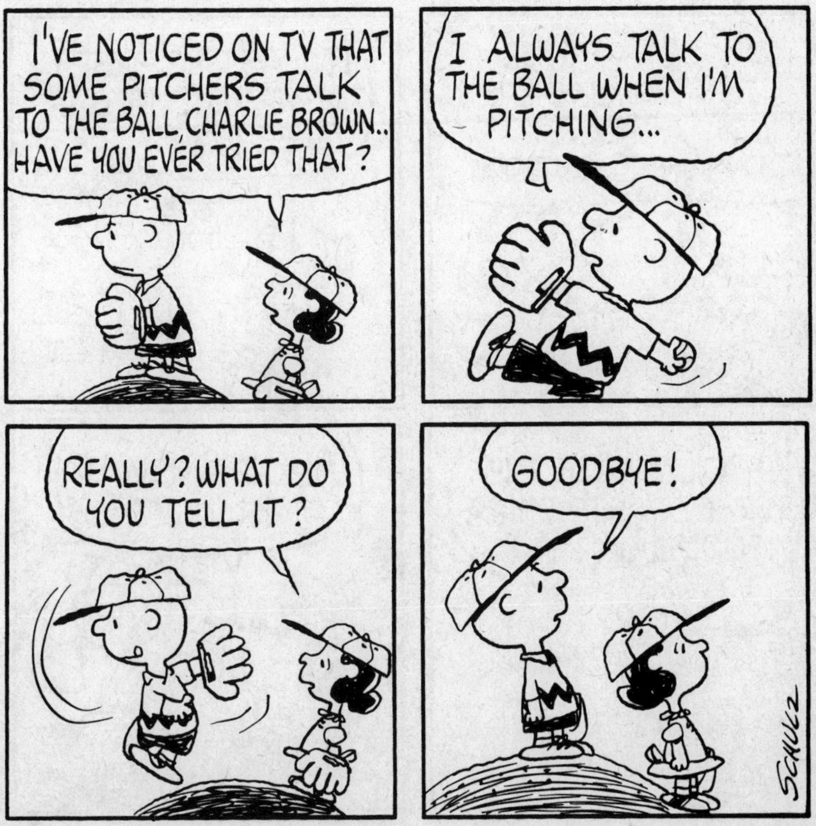
I'VE NOTICED ON TV THAT SOME PITCHERS TALK TO THE BALL, CHARLIE BROWN.. HAVE YOU EVER TRIED THAT?
I ALWAYS TALK TO THE BALL WHEN I'M PITCHING...
REALLY? WHAT DO YOU TELL IT?
GOODBYE!
SCHULZ

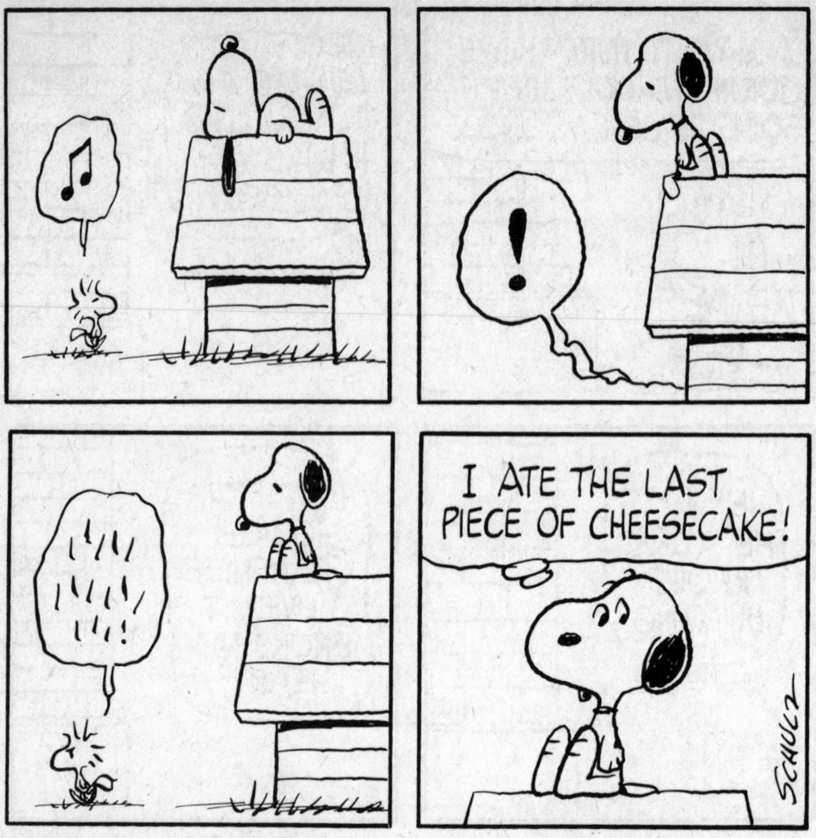
!
I ATE THE LAST PIECE OF CHEESECAKE!
SCHULZ

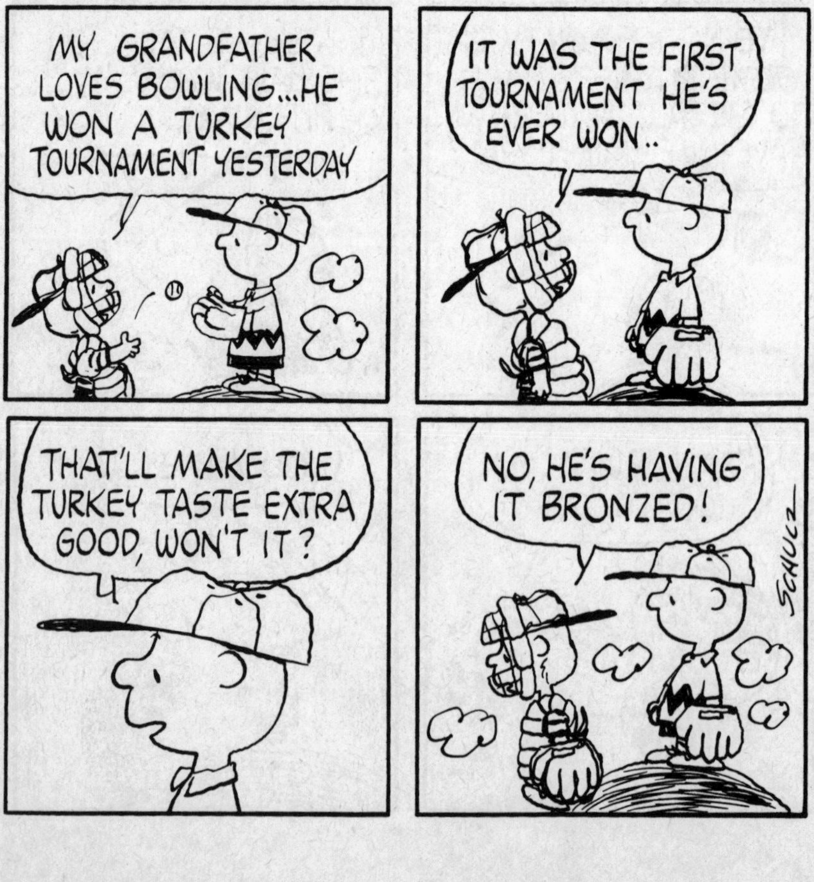
MY GRANDFATHER LOVES BOWLING...HE WON A TURKEY TOURNAMENT YESTERDAY
IT WAS THE FIRST TOURNAMENT HE'S EVER WON..
THAT'LL MAKE THE TURKEY TASTE EXTRA GOOD, WON'T IT?
NO, HE'S HAVING IT BRONZED!
SCHULZ

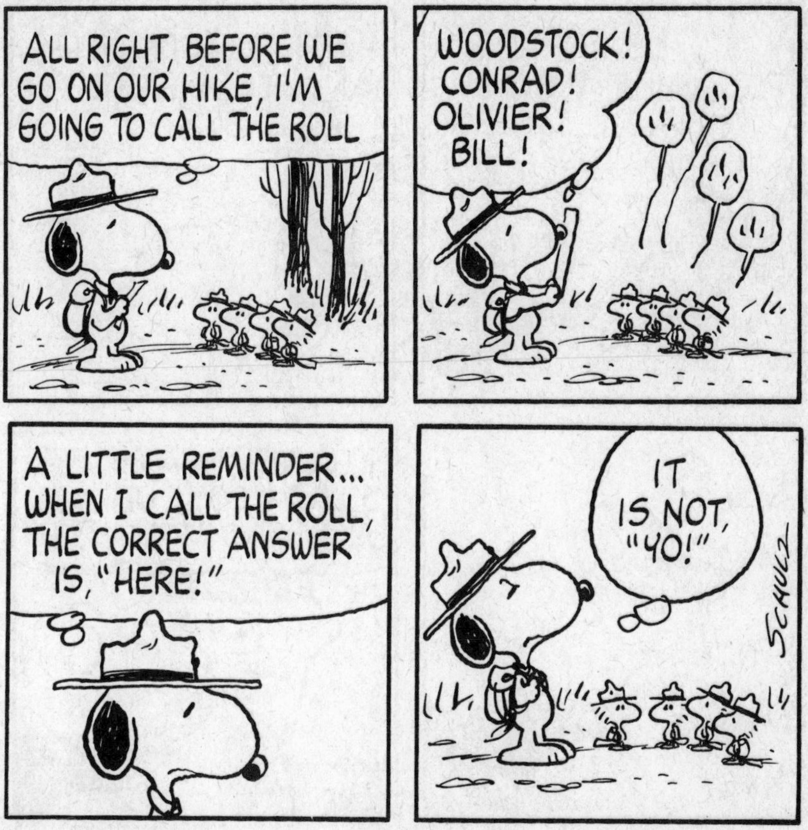
ALL RIGHT, BEFORE WE GO ON OUR HIKE, I'M GOING TO CALL THE ROLL
WOODSTOCK! CONRAD! OLIVIER! BILL!
A LITTLE REMINDER... WHEN I CALL THE ROLL, THE CORRECT ANSWER IS, "HERE!"
IT IS NOT, "YO!"
SCHULZ

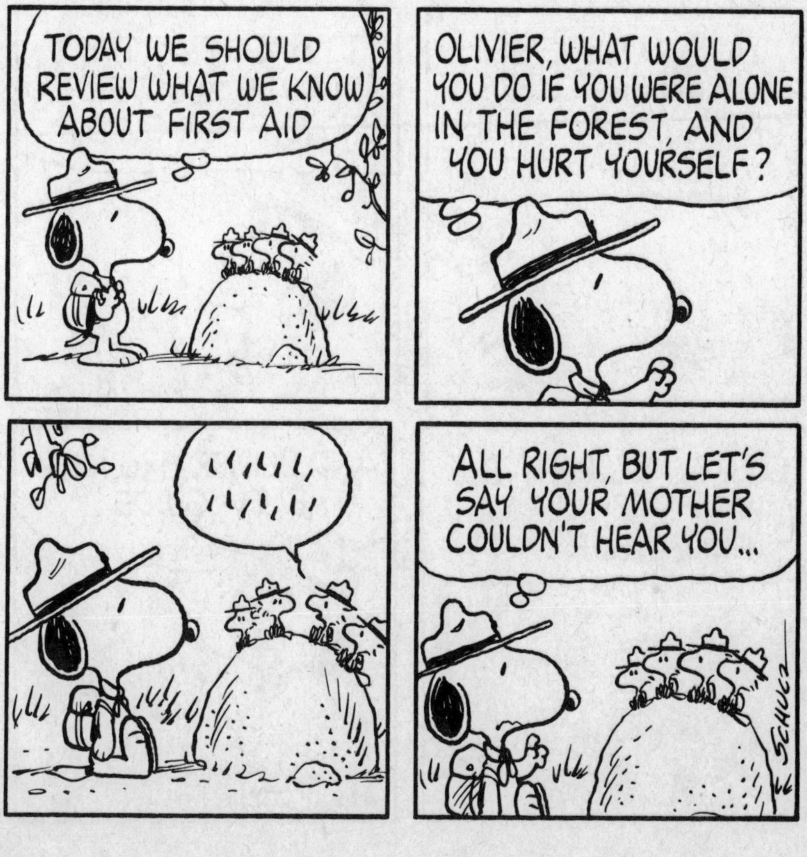
TODAY WE SHOULD REVIEW WHAT WE KNOW ABOUT FIRST AID
OLIVIER, WHAT WOULD YOU DO IF YOU WERE ALONE IN THE FOREST, AND YOU HURT YOURSELF?
ALL RIGHT, BUT LET'S SAY YOUR MOTHER COULDN'T HEAR YOU...
SCHULZ

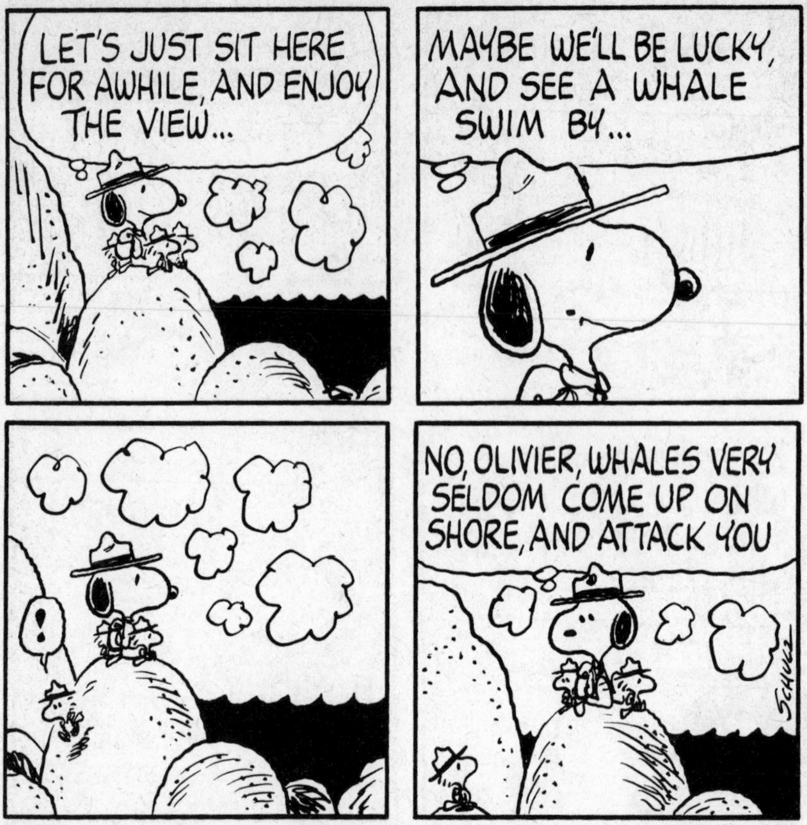
LET'S JUST SIT HERE FOR AWHILE, AND ENJOY THE VIEW...
MAYBE WE'LL BE LUCKY, AND SEE A WHALE SWIM BY...
!
NO, OLIVIER, WHALES VERY SELDOM COME UP ON SHORE, AND ATTACK YOU
SCHULZ

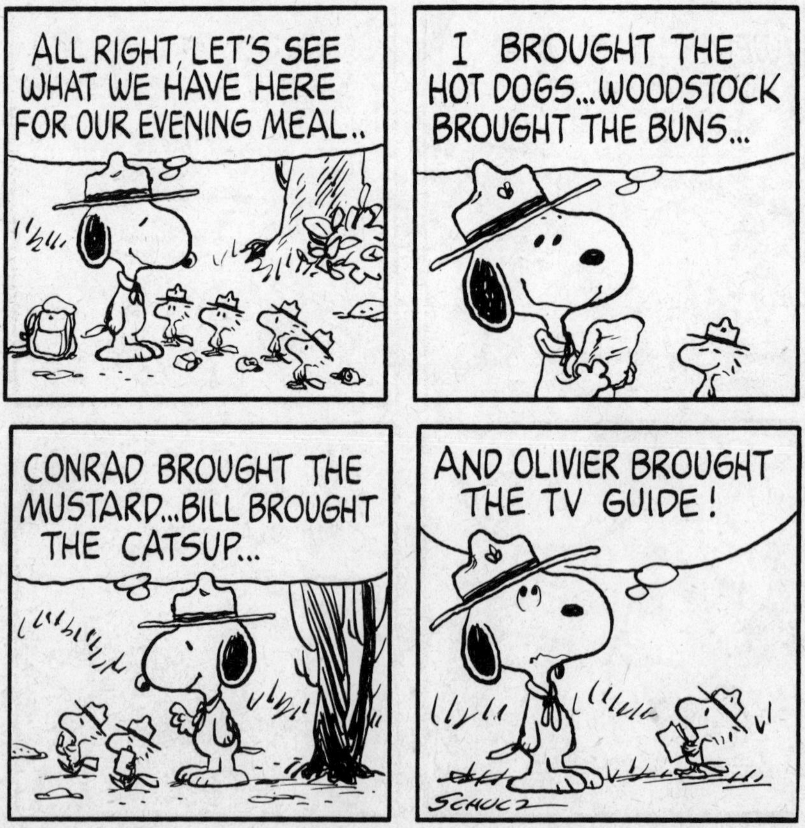
ALL RIGHT, LET'S SEE WHAT WE HAVE HERE FOR OUR EVENING MEAL..
I BROUGHT THE HOT DOGS...WOODSTOCK BROUGHT THE BUNS...
CONRAD BROUGHT THE MUSTARD...BILL BROUGHT THE CATSUP...
AND OLIVIER BROUGHT THE TV GUIDE!
SCHULZ

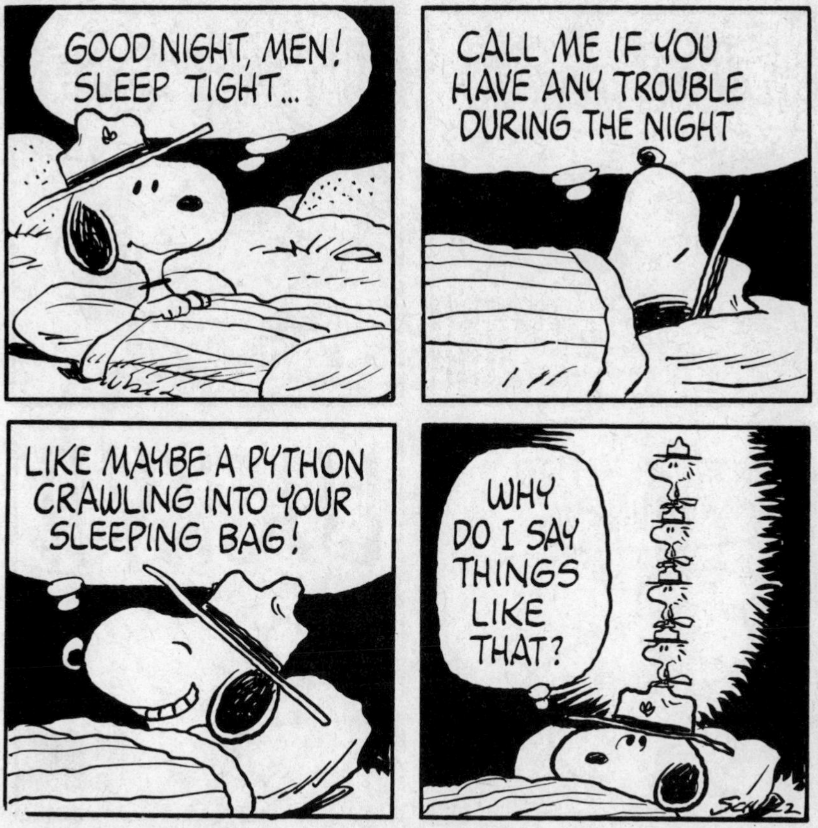
GOOD NIGHT, MEN! SLEEP TIGHT...
CALL ME IF YOU HAVE ANY TROUBLE DURING THE NIGHT
LIKE MAYBE A PYTHON CRAWLING INTO YOUR SLEEPING BAG!
WHY DO I SAY THINGS LIKE THAT?

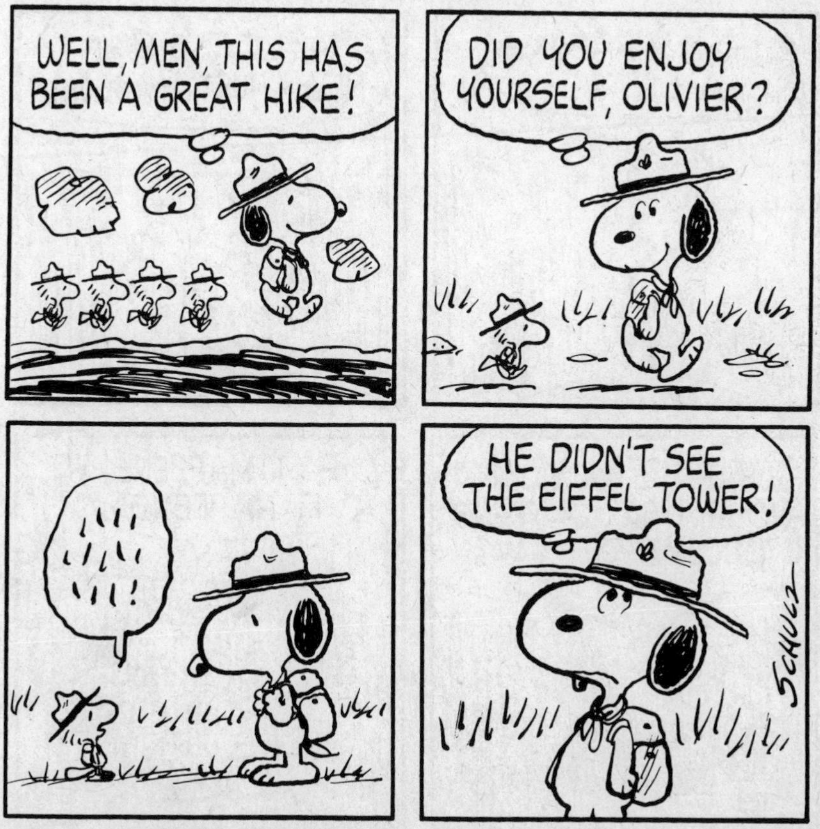
WELL, MEN, THIS HAS BEEN A GREAT HIKE!
DID YOU ENJOY YOURSELF, OLIVIER?
HE DIDN'T SEE THE EIFFEL TOWER!
SCHULZ

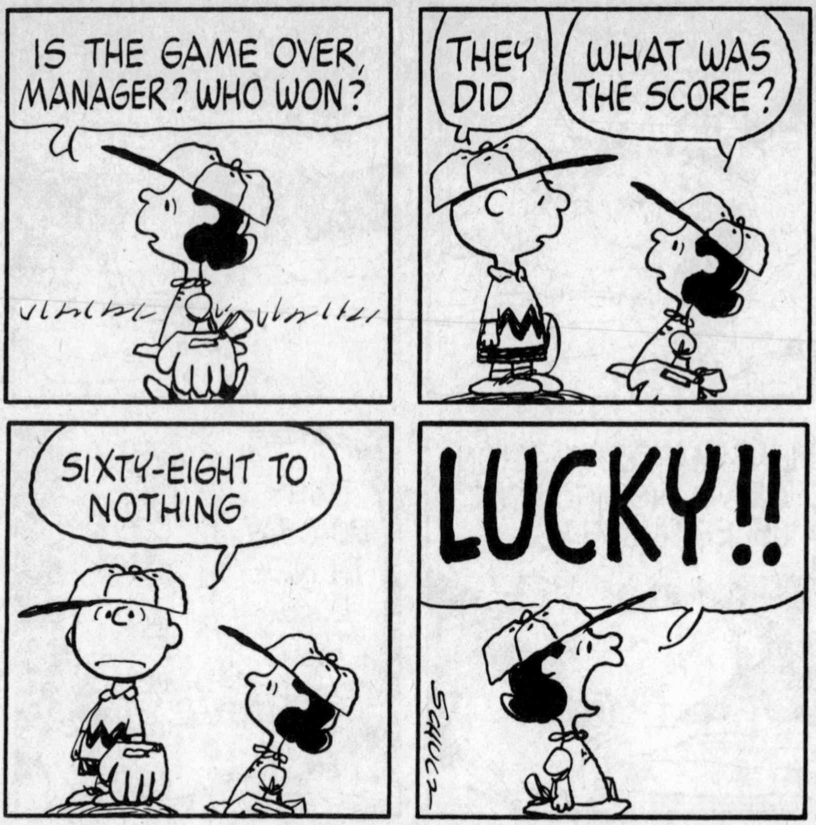
IS THE GAME OVER, MANAGER? WHO WON?
THEY DID
WHAT WAS THE SCORE?
SIXTY-EIGHT TO NOTHING
LUCKY!!

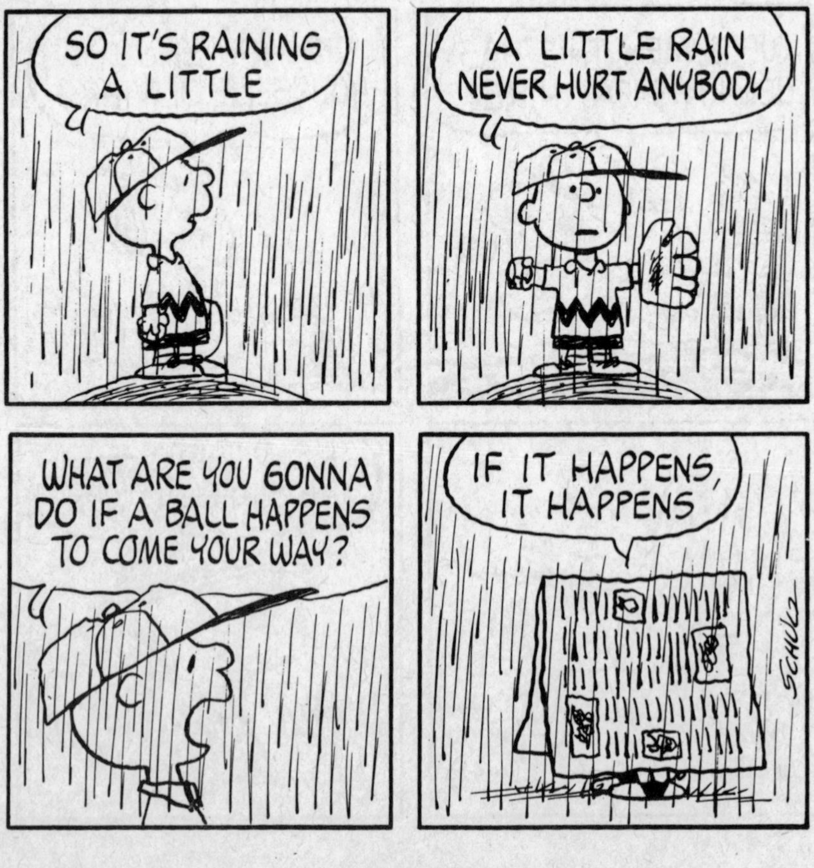
SO IT'S RAINING A LITTLE
A LITTLE RAIN NEVER HURT ANYBODY
WHAT ARE YOU GONNA DO IF A BALL HAPPENS TO COME YOUR WAY?
IF IT HAPPENS, IT HAPPENS

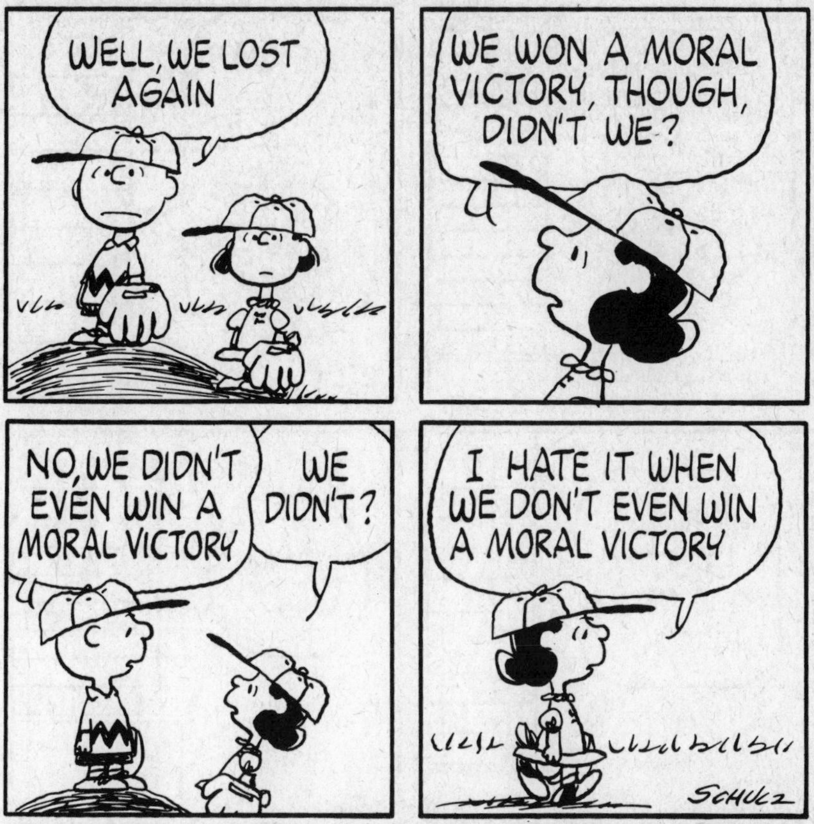
WELL, WE LOST AGAIN
WE WON A MORAL VICTORY, THOUGH, DIDN'T WE?
NO, WE DIDN'T EVEN WIN A MORAL VICTORY
WE DIDN'T?
I HATE IT WHEN WE DON'T EVEN WIN A MORAL VICTORY
SCHULZ

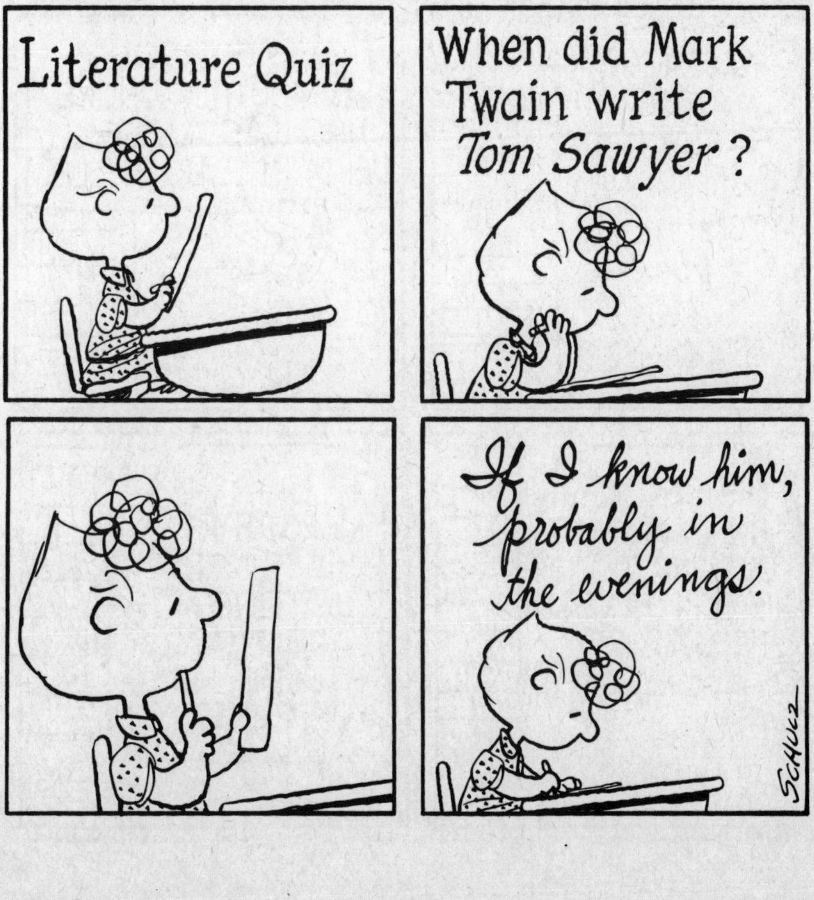
Literature Quiz
When did Mark Twain write *Tom Sawyer*?
If I know him, probably in the evenings.
SCHULZ

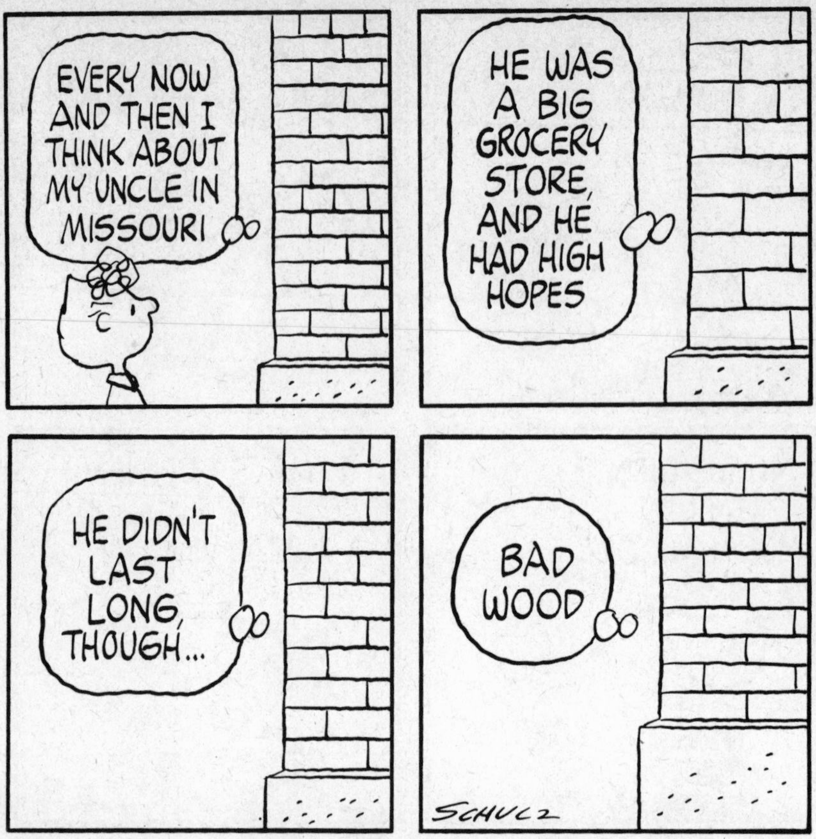
EVERY NOW AND THEN I THINK ABOUT MY UNCLE IN MISSOURI
HE WAS A BIG GROCERY STORE, AND HE HAD HIGH HOPES
HE DIDN'T LAST LONG, THOUGH...
BAD WOOD
SCHULZ

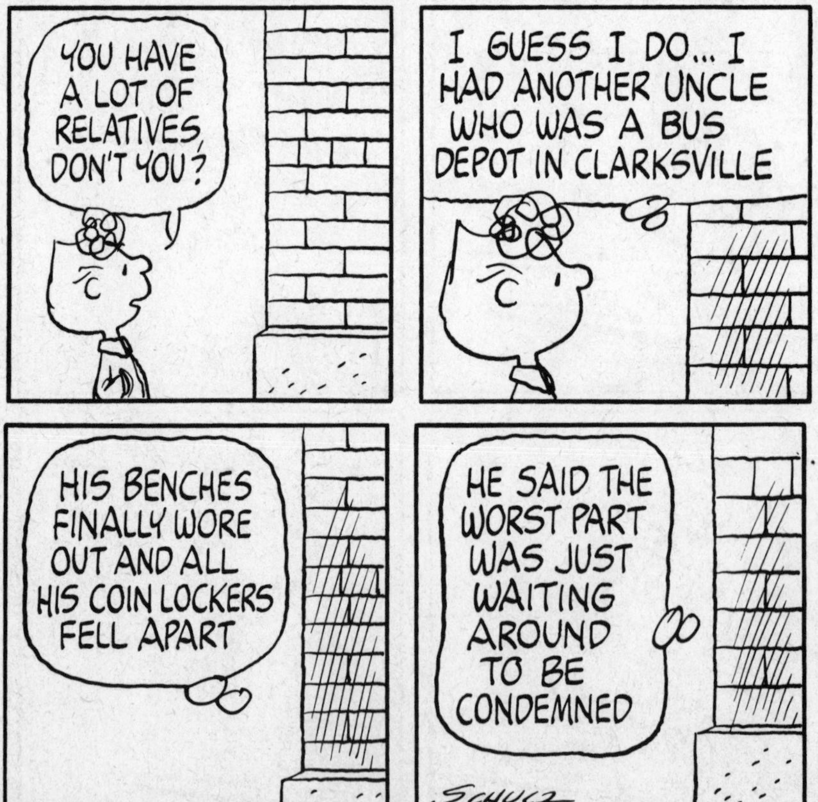
YOU HAVE A LOT OF RELATIVES, DON'T YOU?
I GUESS I DO... I HAD ANOTHER UNCLE WHO WAS A BUS DEPOT IN CLARKSVILLE
HIS BENCHES FINALLY WORE OUT AND ALL HIS COIN LOCKERS FELL APART
HE SAID THE WORST PART WAS JUST WAITING AROUND TO BE CONDEMNED
SCHULZ

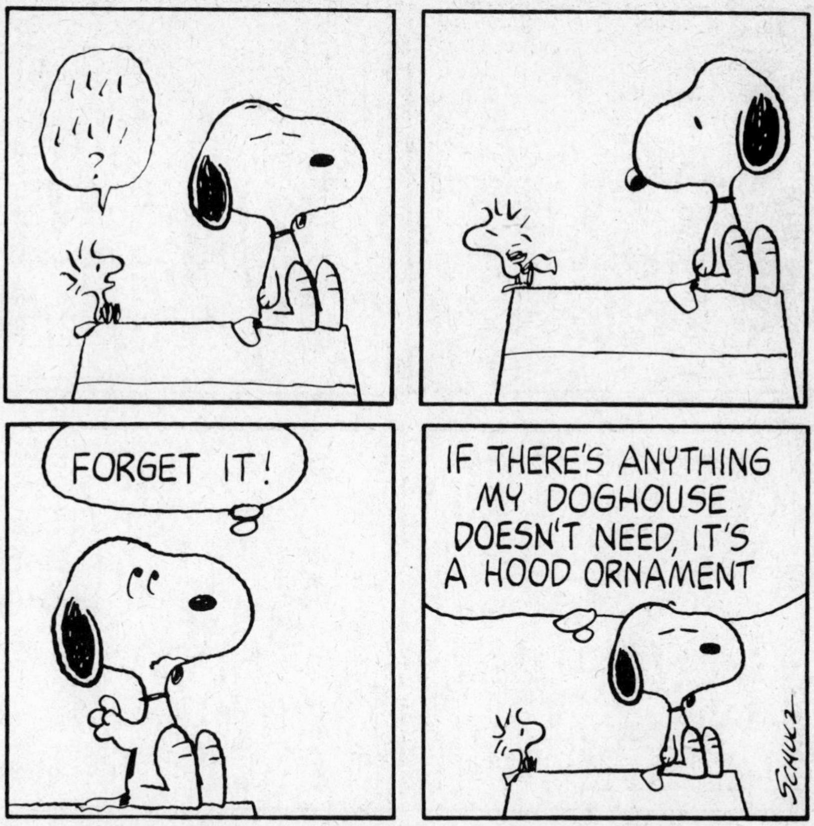
?
FORGET IT!
IF THERE'S ANYTHING MY DOGHOUSE DOESN'T NEED, IT'S A HOOD ORNAMENT
SCHULZ

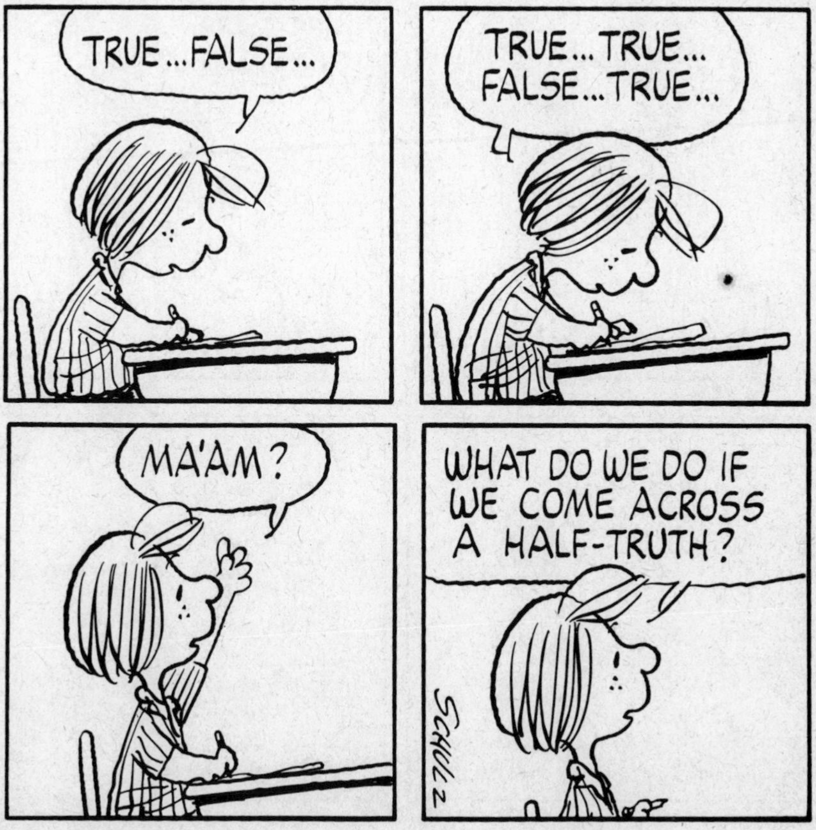
TRUE...FALSE...
TRUE...TRUE... FALSE...TRUE...
MA'AM?
WHAT DO WE DO IF WE COME ACROSS A HALF-TRUTH?
SCHULZ

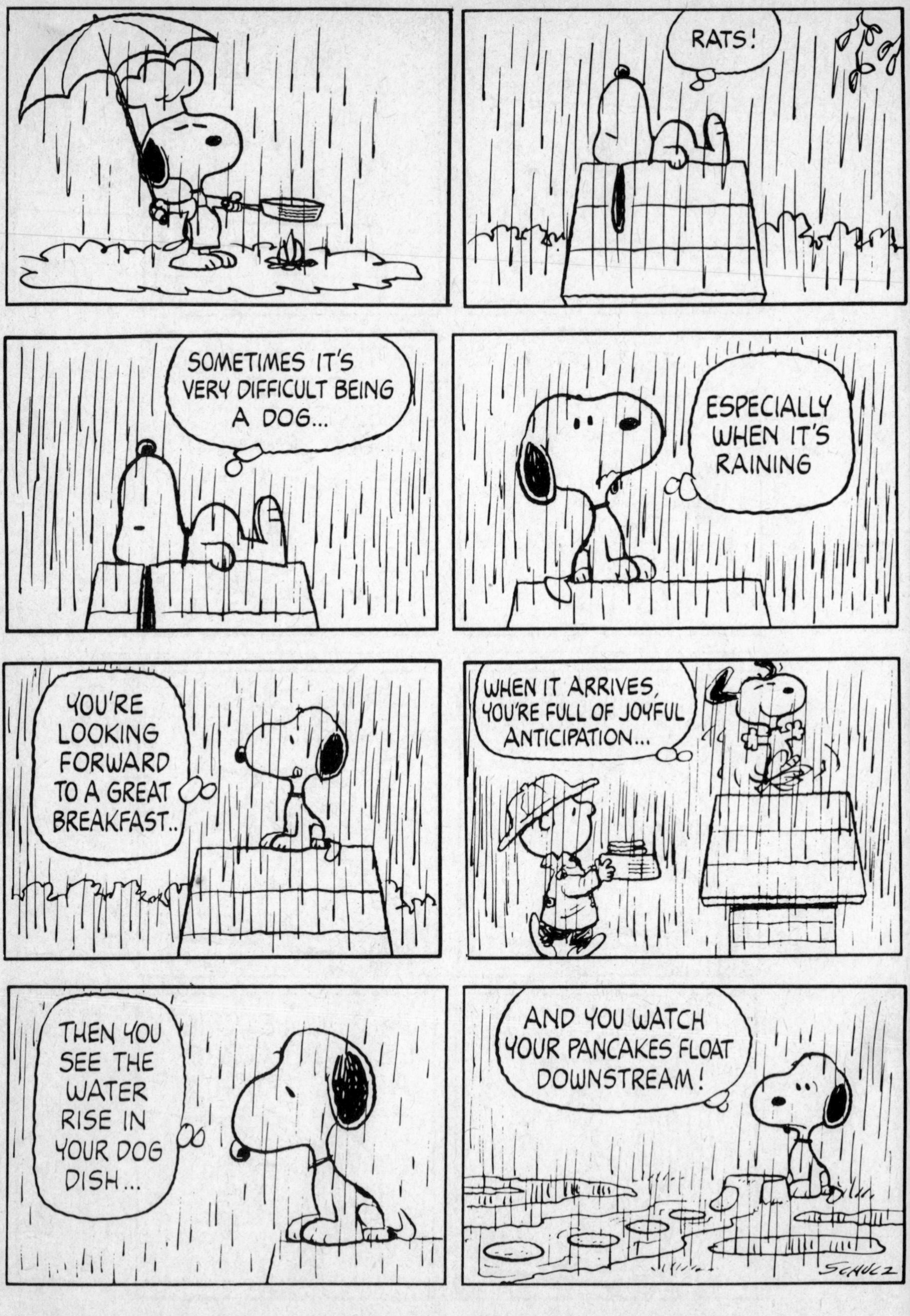
RATS!
SOMETIMES IT'S VERY DIFFICULT BEING A DOG...
ESPECIALLY WHEN IT'S RAINING
YOU'RE LOOKING FORWARD TO A GREAT BREAKFAST..
WHEN IT ARRIVES, YOU'RE FULL OF JOYFUL ANTICIPATION...
THEN YOU SEE THE WATER RISE IN YOUR DOG DISH...
AND YOU WATCH YOUR PANCAKES FLOAT DOWNSTREAM!
SCHULZ

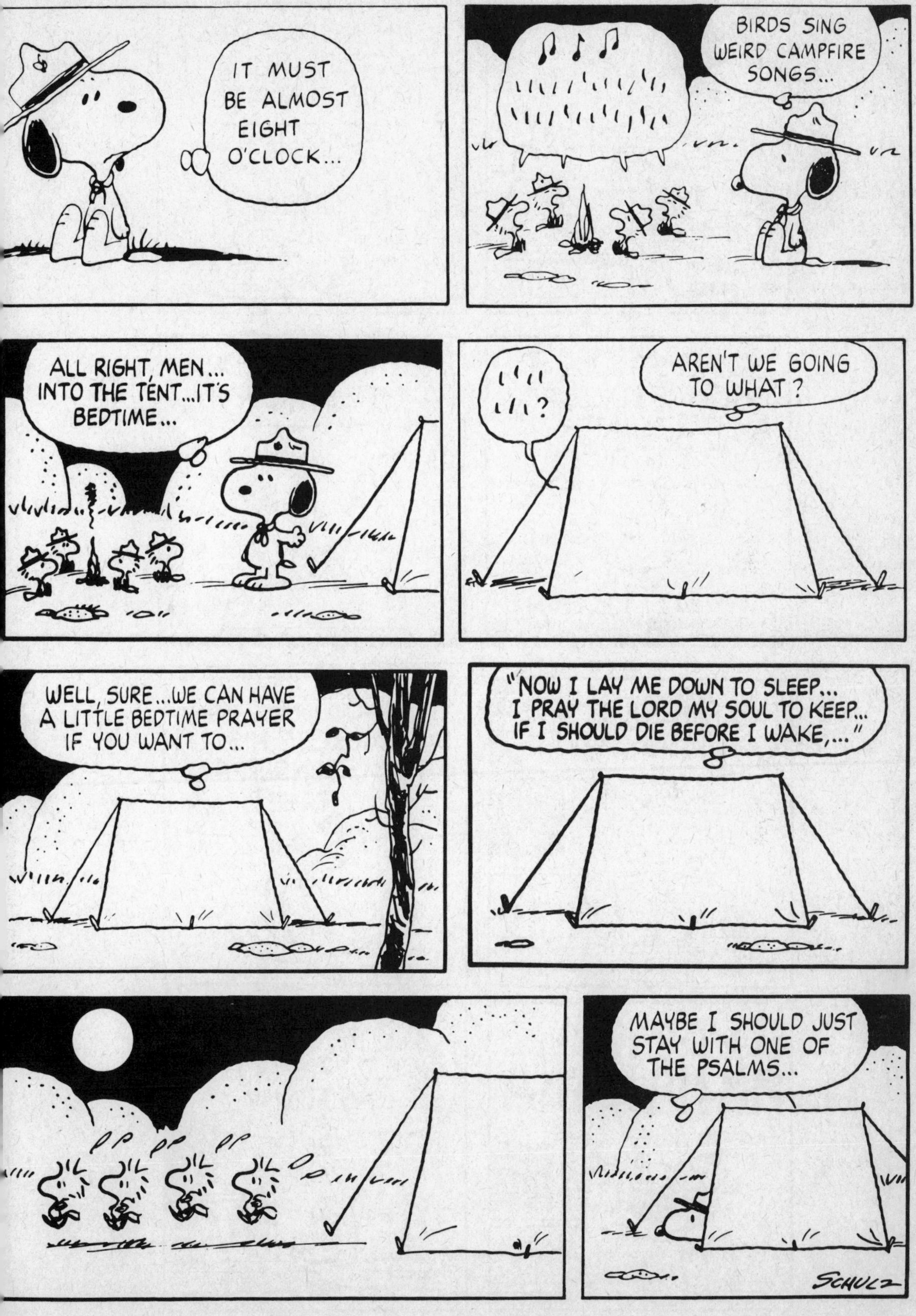
IT MUST BE ALMOST EIGHT O'CLOCK...
BIRDS SING WEIRD CAMPFIRE SONGS...
ALL RIGHT, MEN... INTO THE TENT...IT'S BEDTIME...
AREN'T WE GOING TO WHAT ?
WELL, SURE...WE CAN HAVE A LITTLE BEDTIME PRAYER IF YOU WANT TO...
"NOW I LAY ME DOWN TO SLEEP... I PRAY THE LORD MY SOUL TO KEEP... IF I SHOULD DIE BEFORE I WAKE,..."
MAYBE I SHOULD JUST STAY WITH ONE OF THE PSALMS...
SCHULZ

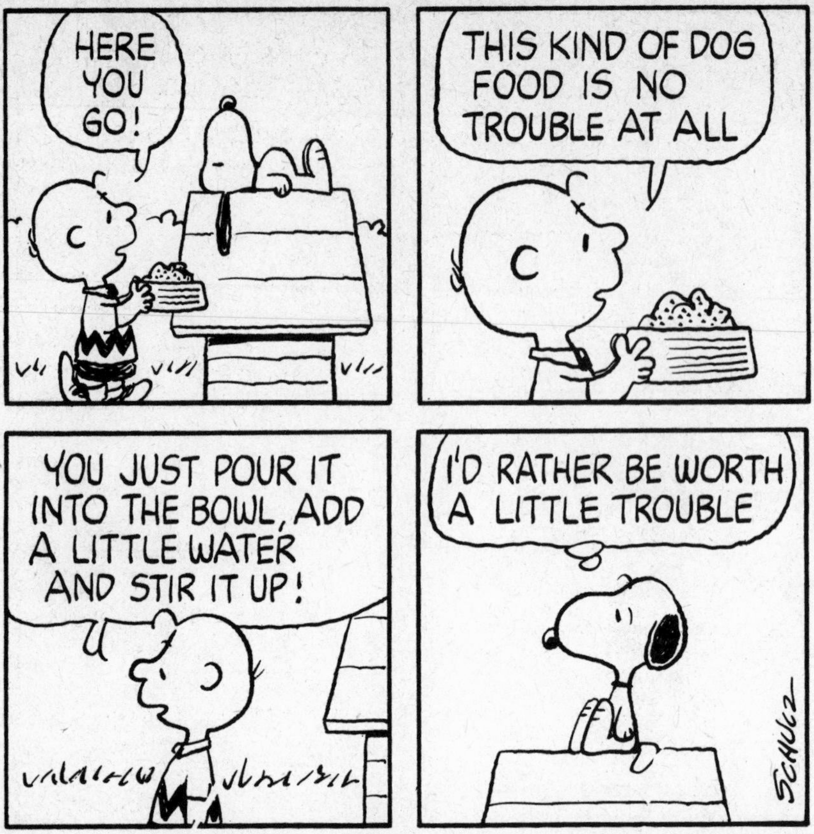
HERE YOU GO!
THIS KIND OF DOG FOOD IS NO TROUBLE AT ALL
YOU JUST POUR IT INTO THE BOWL, ADD A LITTLE WATER AND STIR IT UP!
I'D RATHER BE WORTH A LITTLE TROUBLE
SCHULZ

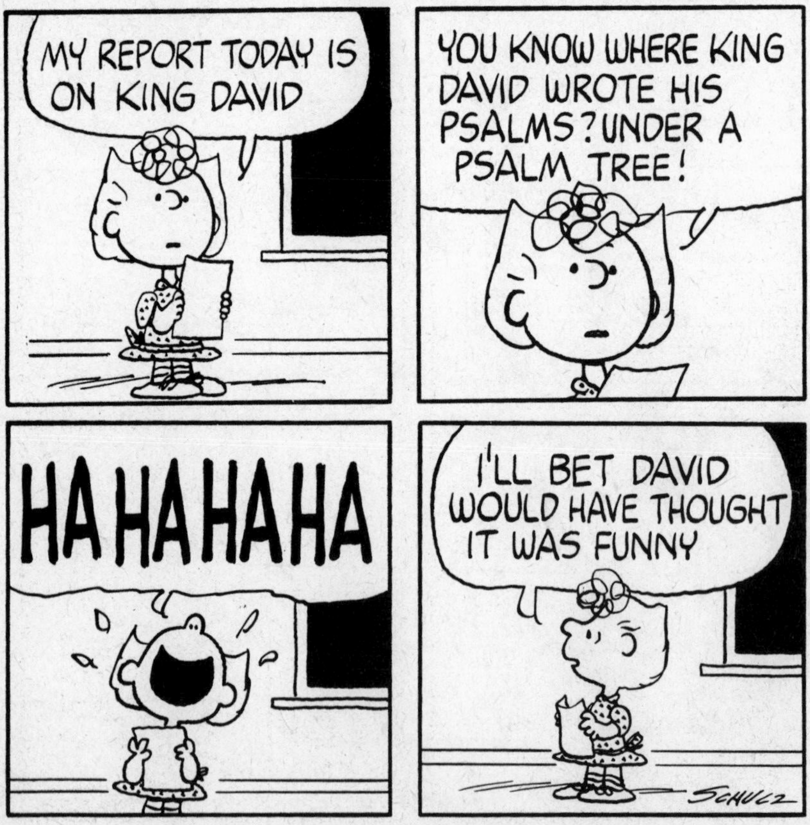
MY REPORT TODAY IS ON KING DAVID
YOU KNOW WHERE KING DAVID WROTE HIS PSALMS? UNDER A PSALM TREE!
HA HA HA HA
I'LL BET DAVID WOULD HAVE THOUGHT IT WAS FUNNY
SCHULZ

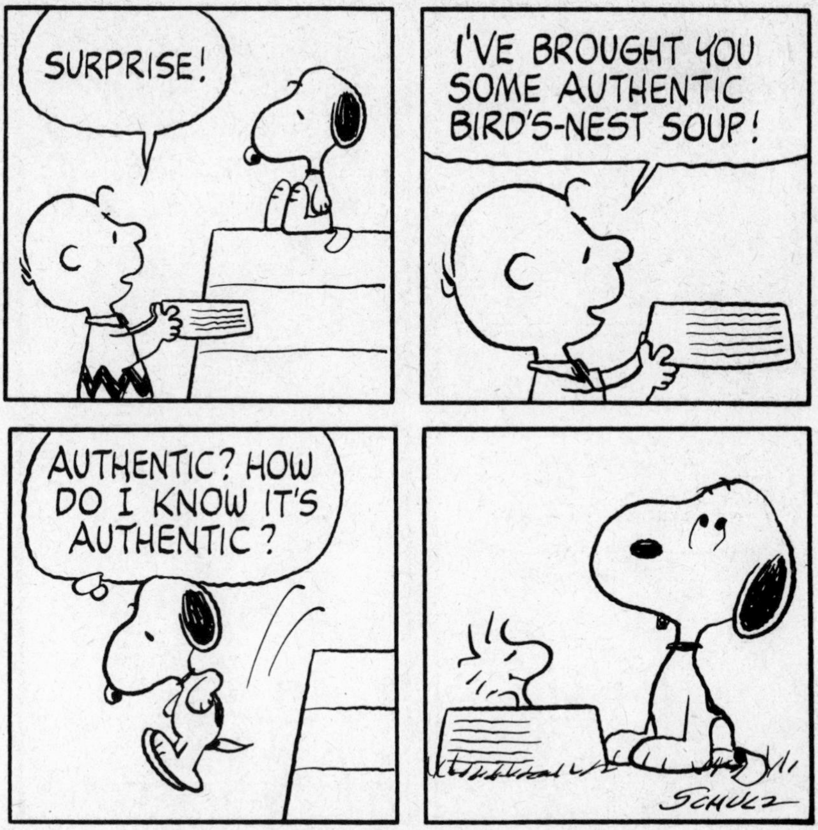
SURPRISE!
I'VE BROUGHT YOU SOME AUTHENTIC BIRD'S-NEST SOUP!
AUTHENTIC? HOW DO I KNOW IT'S AUTHENTIC?
SCHULZ

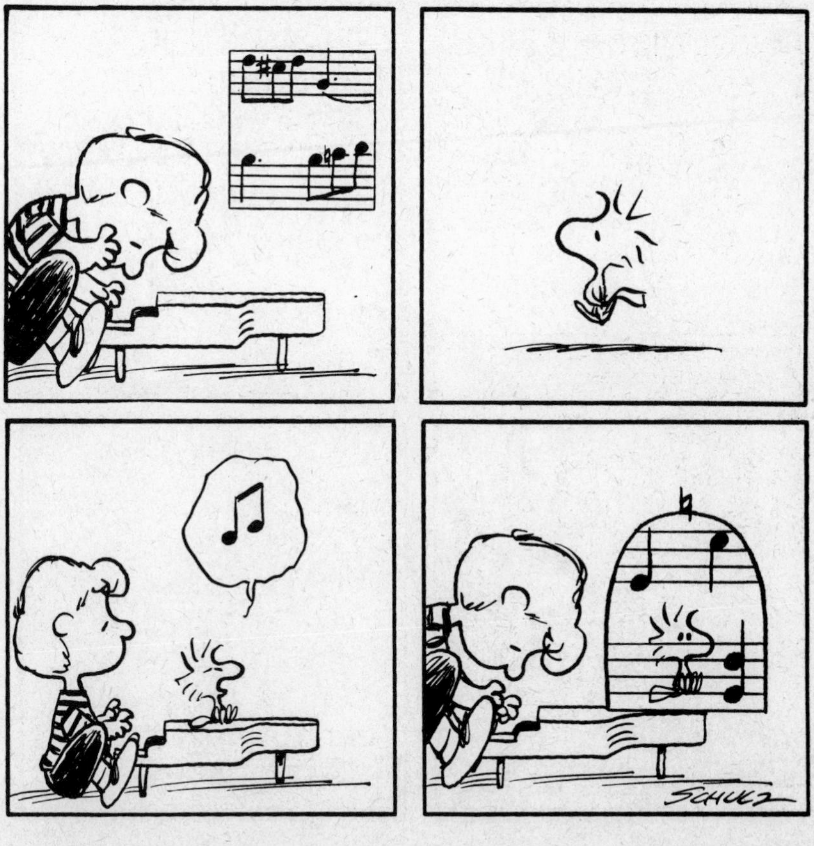
SCHULZ

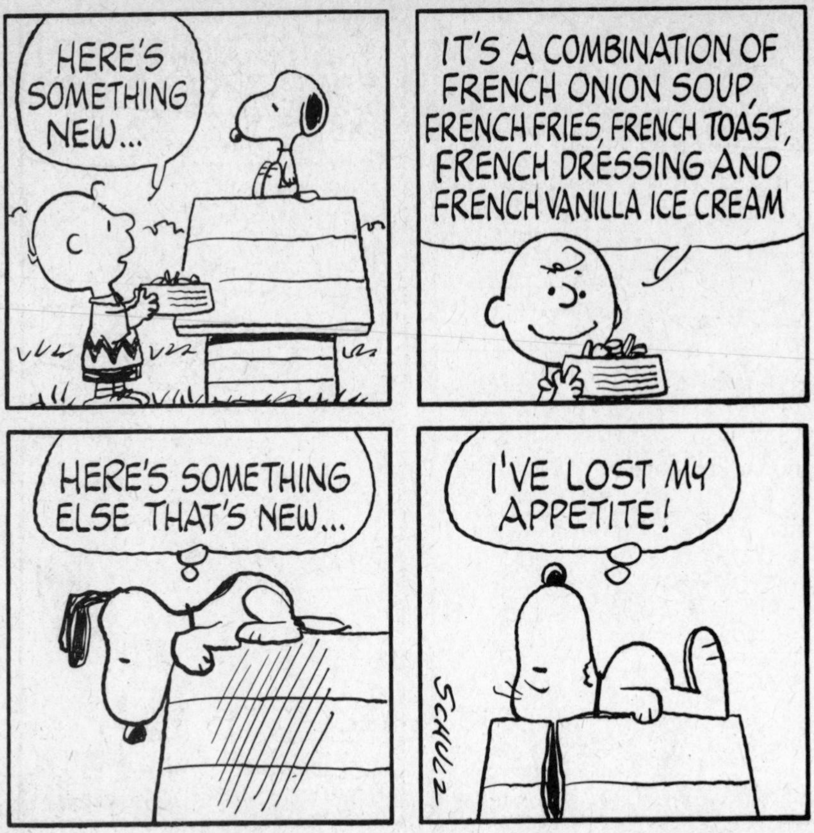
HERE'S SOMETHING NEW...
IT'S A COMBINATION OF FRENCH ONION SOUP, FRENCH FRIES, FRENCH TOAST, FRENCH DRESSING AND FRENCH VANILLA ICE CREAM
HERE'S SOMETHING ELSE THAT'S NEW...
I'VE LOST MY APPETITE!
SCHULZ

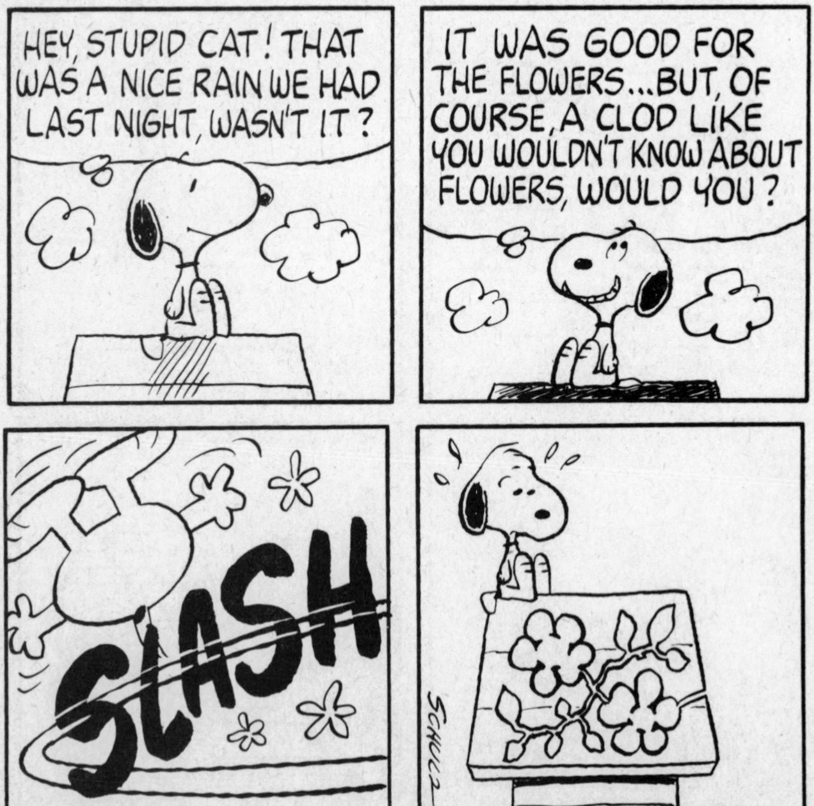
HEY, STUPID CAT! THAT WAS A NICE RAIN WE HAD LAST NIGHT, WASN'T IT?
IT WAS GOOD FOR THE FLOWERS...BUT, OF COURSE, A CLOD LIKE YOU WOULDN'T KNOW ABOUT FLOWERS, WOULD YOU?
SLASH
SCHULZ

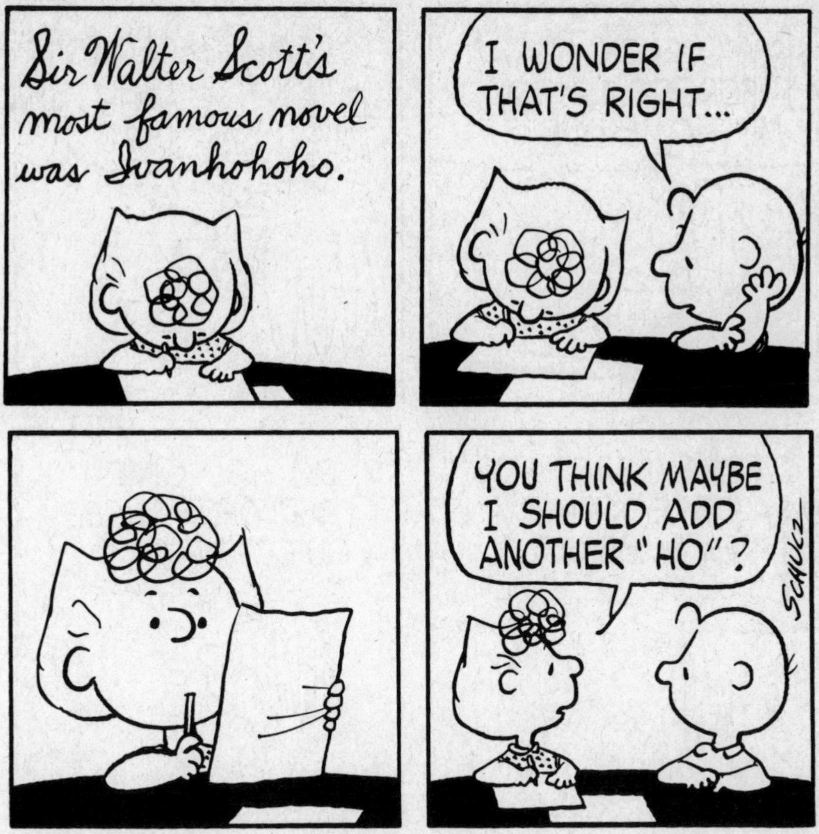
Sir Walter Scott's most famous novel was Ivanhohoho.
I WONDER IF THAT'S RIGHT...
YOU THINK MAYBE I SHOULD ADD ANOTHER "HO"?
SCHULZ

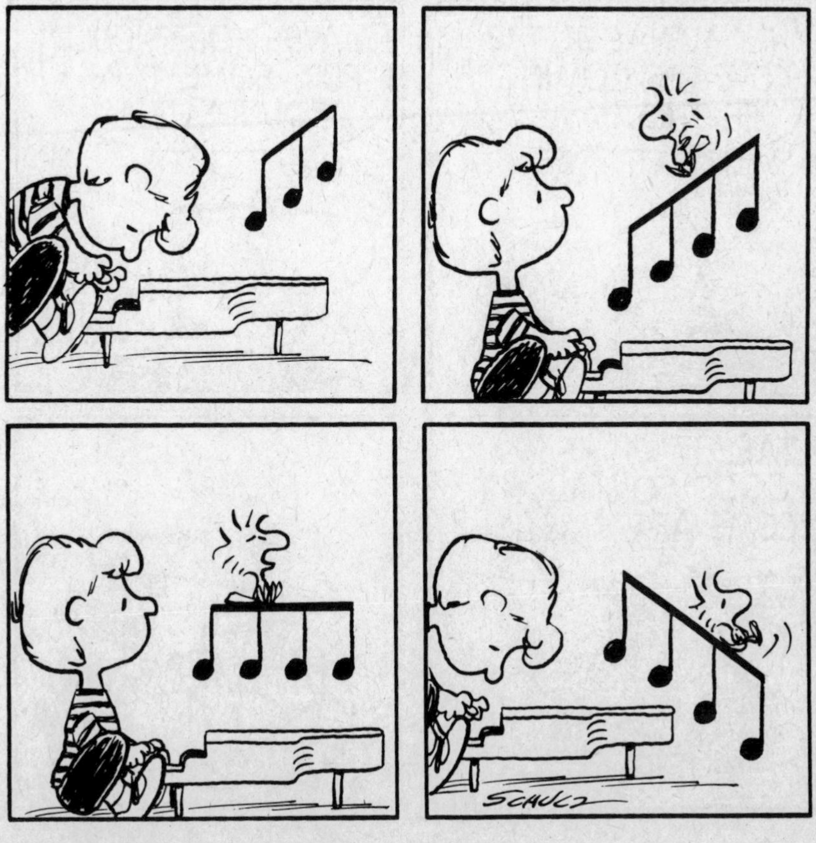
SCHULZ

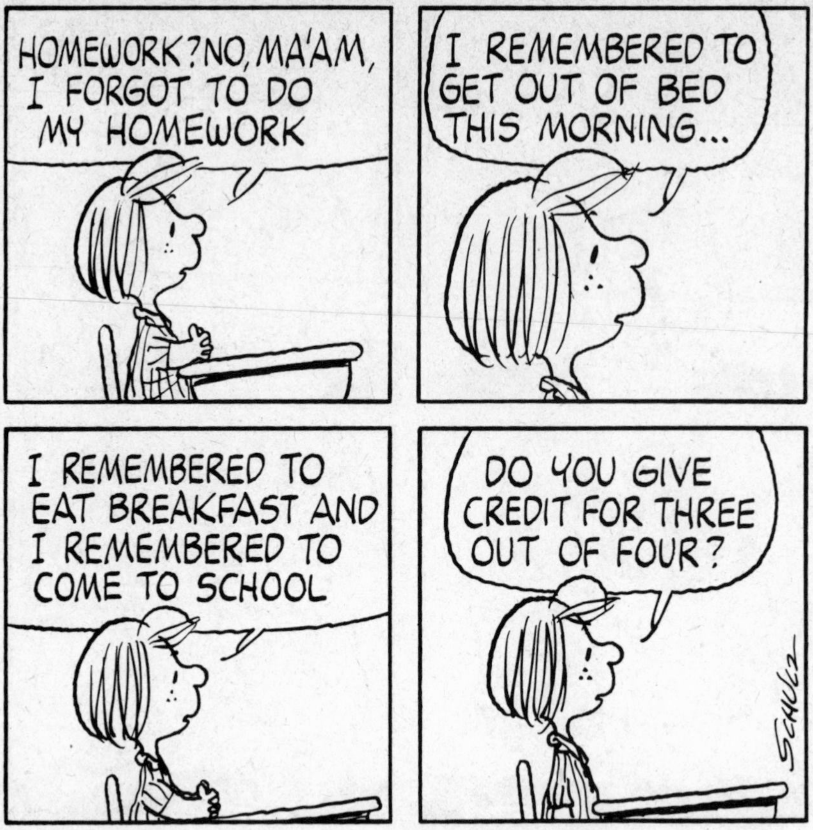
HOMEWORK? NO, MA'AM, I FORGOT TO DO MY HOMEWORK
I REMEMBERED TO GET OUT OF BED THIS MORNING...
I REMEMBERED TO EAT BREAKFAST AND I REMEMBERED TO COME TO SCHOOL
DO YOU GIVE CREDIT FOR THREE OUT OF FOUR?
SCHULZ

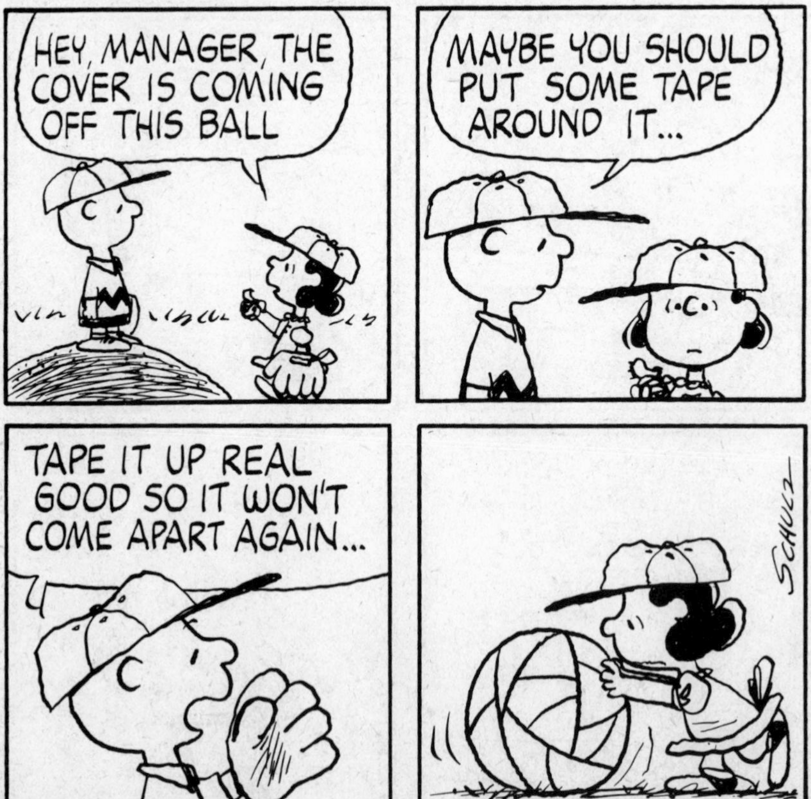
HEY, MANAGER, THE COVER IS COMING OFF THIS BALL
MAYBE YOU SHOULD PUT SOME TAPE AROUND IT...
TAPE IT UP REAL GOOD SO IT WON'T COME APART AGAIN...
SCHULZ

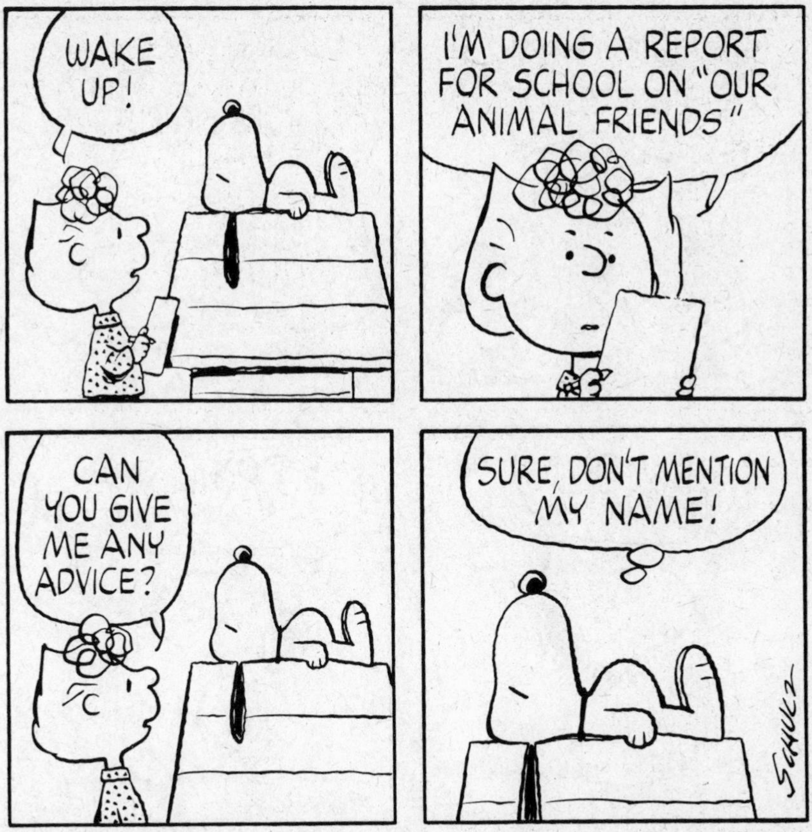
WAKE UP!
I'M DOING A REPORT FOR SCHOOL ON "OUR ANIMAL FRIENDS"
CAN YOU GIVE ME ANY ADVICE?
SURE, DON'T MENTION MY NAME!
SCHULZ

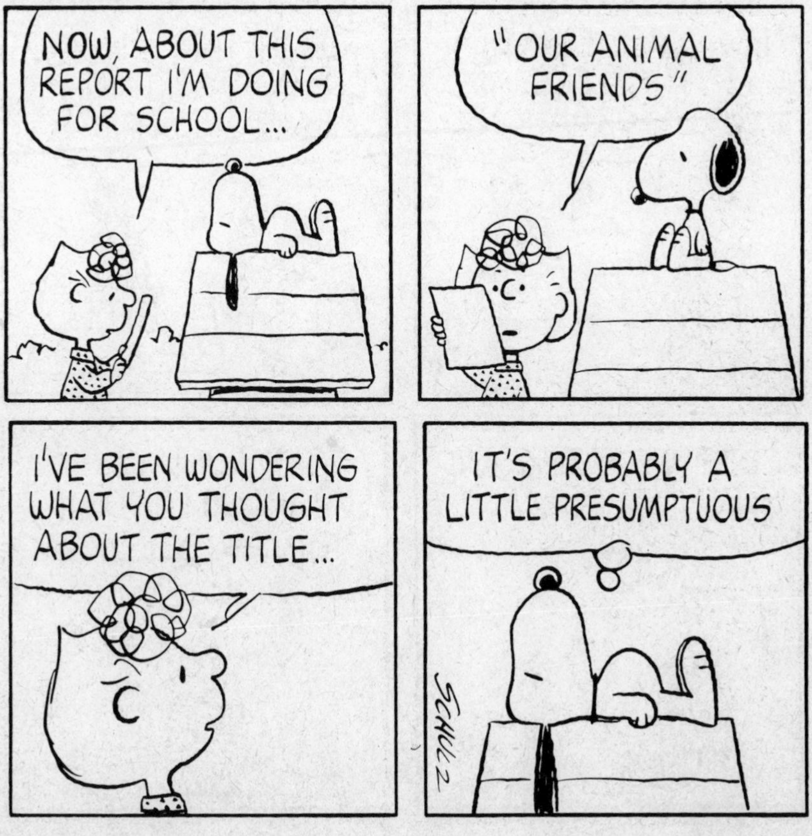
NOW, ABOUT THIS REPORT I'M DOING FOR SCHOOL...
"OUR ANIMAL FRIENDS"
I'VE BEEN WONDERING WHAT YOU THOUGHT ABOUT THE TITLE...
IT'S PROBABLY A LITTLE PRESUMPTUOUS
SCHULZ

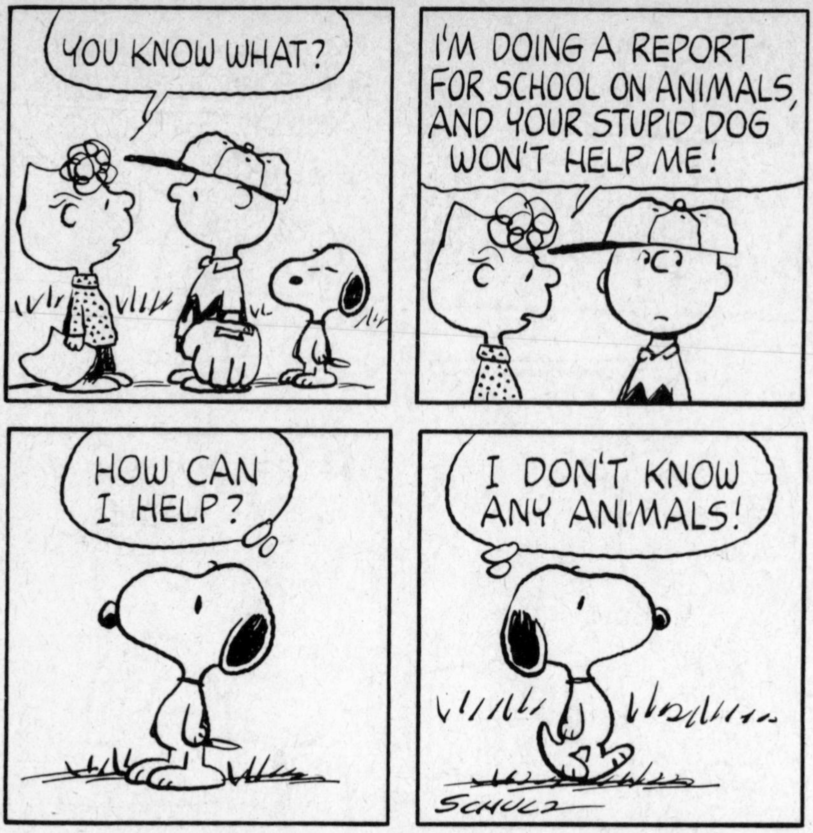
YOU KNOW WHAT?
I'M DOING A REPORT FOR SCHOOL ON ANIMALS, AND YOUR STUPID DOG WON'T HELP ME!
HOW CAN I HELP?
I DON'T KNOW ANY ANIMALS!
SCHULZ

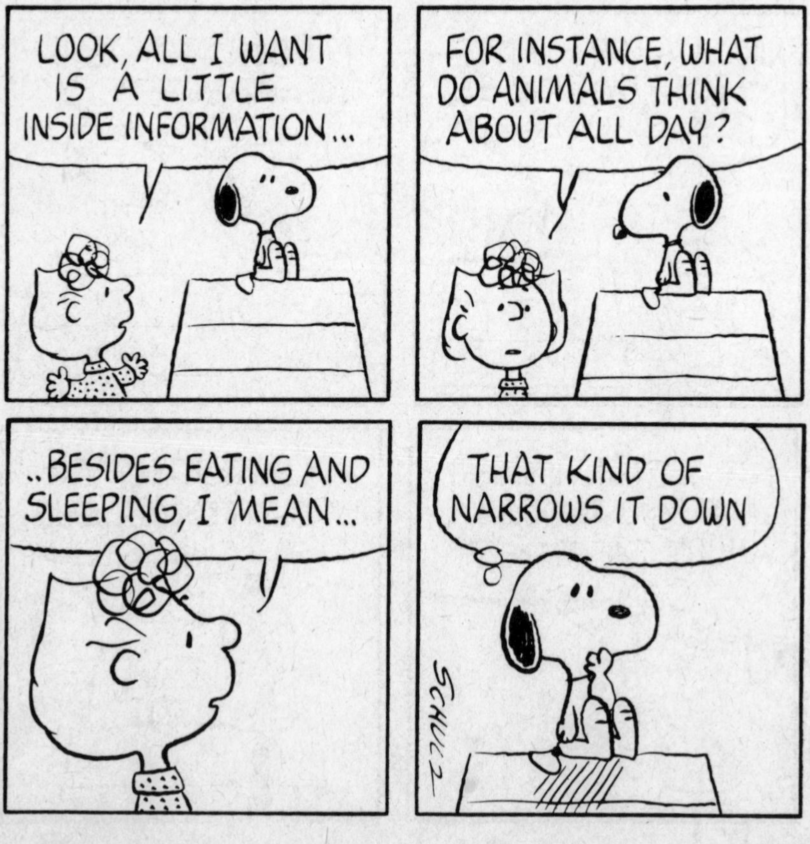
LOOK, ALL I WANT IS A LITTLE INSIDE INFORMATION...
FOR INSTANCE, WHAT DO ANIMALS THINK ABOUT ALL DAY?
..BESIDES EATING AND SLEEPING, I MEAN...
THAT KIND OF NARROWS IT DOWN
SCHULZ

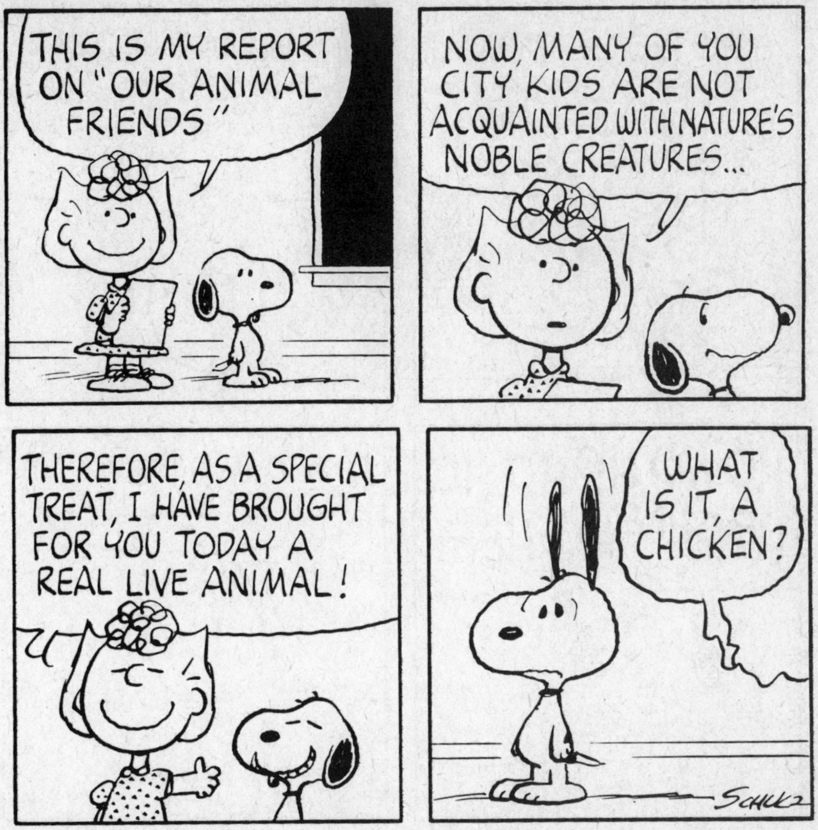
THIS IS MY REPORT ON "OUR ANIMAL FRIENDS"
NOW, MANY OF YOU CITY KIDS ARE NOT ACQUAINTED WITH NATURE'S NOBLE CREATURES...
THEREFORE, AS A SPECIAL TREAT, I HAVE BROUGHT FOR YOU TODAY A REAL LIVE ANIMAL!
WHAT IS IT, A CHICKEN?
SCHULZ

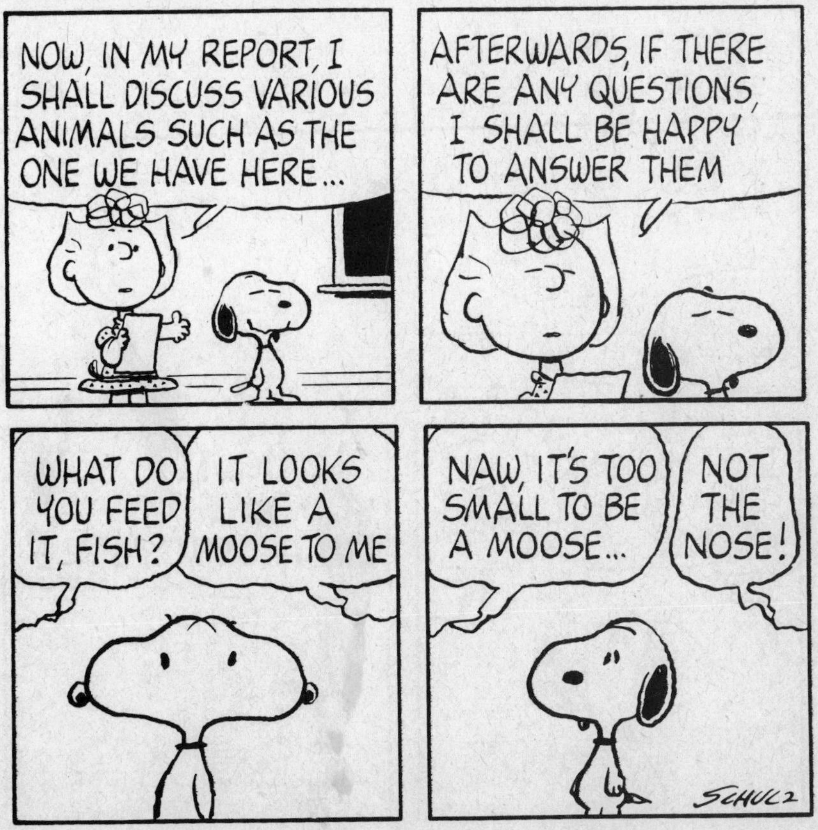
NOW, IN MY REPORT, I SHALL DISCUSS VARIOUS ANIMALS SUCH AS THE ONE WE HAVE HERE...
AFTERWARDS, IF THERE ARE ANY QUESTIONS, I SHALL BE HAPPY TO ANSWER THEM
WHAT DO YOU FEED IT, FISH?
IT LOOKS LIKE A MOOSE TO ME
NAW, IT'S TOO SMALL TO BE A MOOSE...
NOT THE NOSE!
SCHULZ

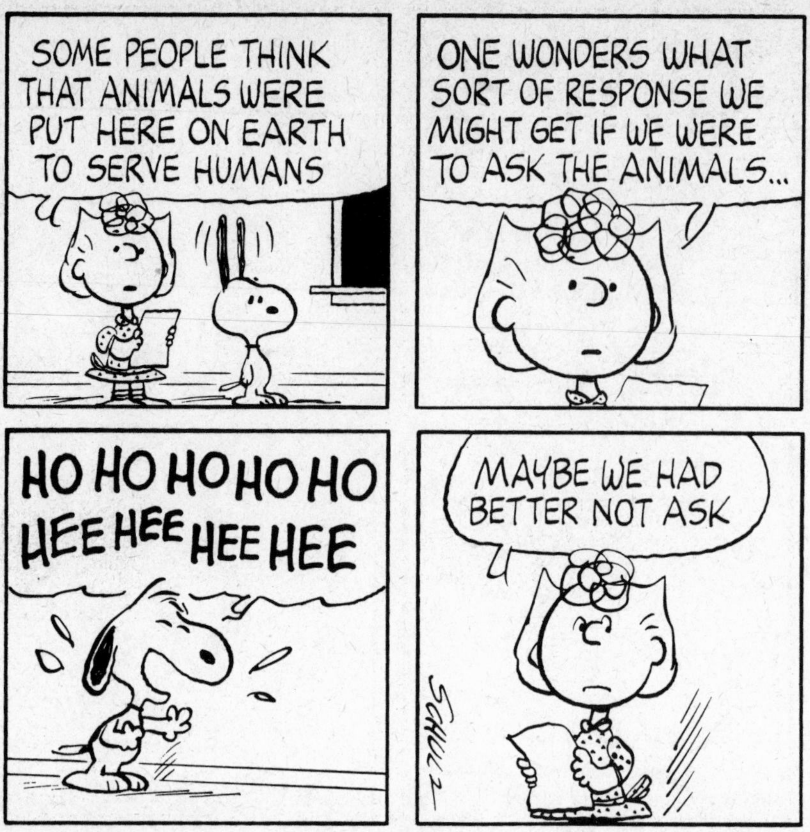
SOME PEOPLE THINK THAT ANIMALS WERE PUT HERE ON EARTH TO SERVE HUMANS
ONE WONDERS WHAT SORT OF RESPONSE WE MIGHT GET IF WE WERE TO ASK THE ANIMALS...
HO HO HO HO HO HEE HEE HEE HEE
MAYBE WE HAD BETTER NOT ASK
SCHULZ

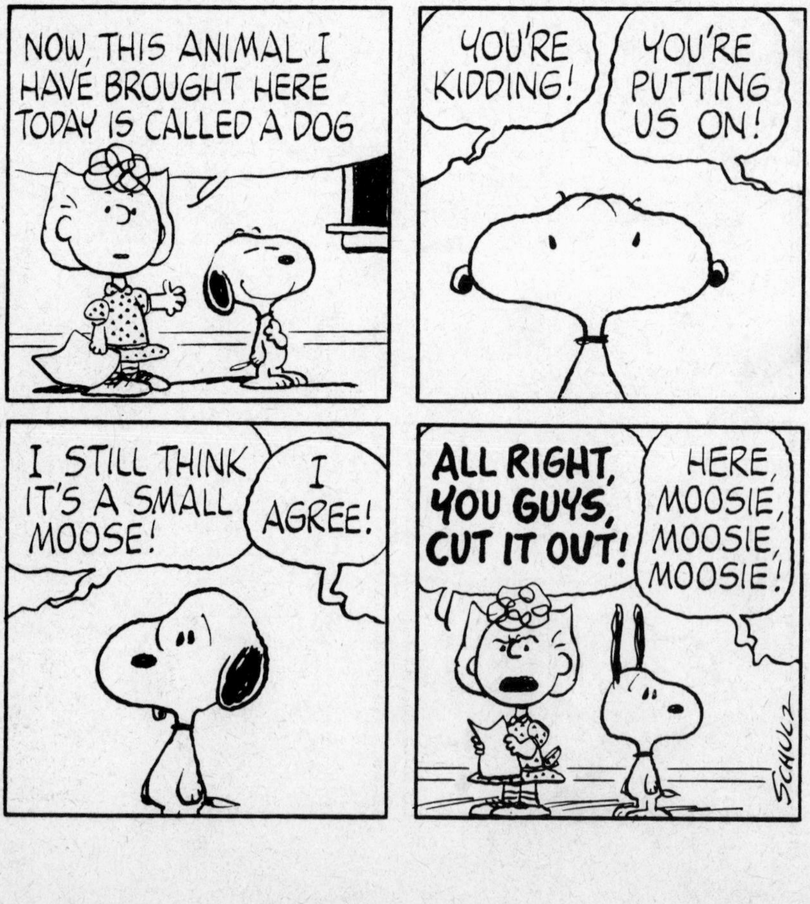
NOW, THIS ANIMAL I HAVE BROUGHT HERE TODAY IS CALLED A DOG
YOU'RE KIDDING!
YOU'RE PUTTING US ON!
I STILL THINK IT'S A SMALL MOOSE!
I AGREE!
ALL RIGHT, YOU GUYS, CUT IT OUT!
HERE, MOOSIE, MOOSIE, MOOSIE!
SCHULZ

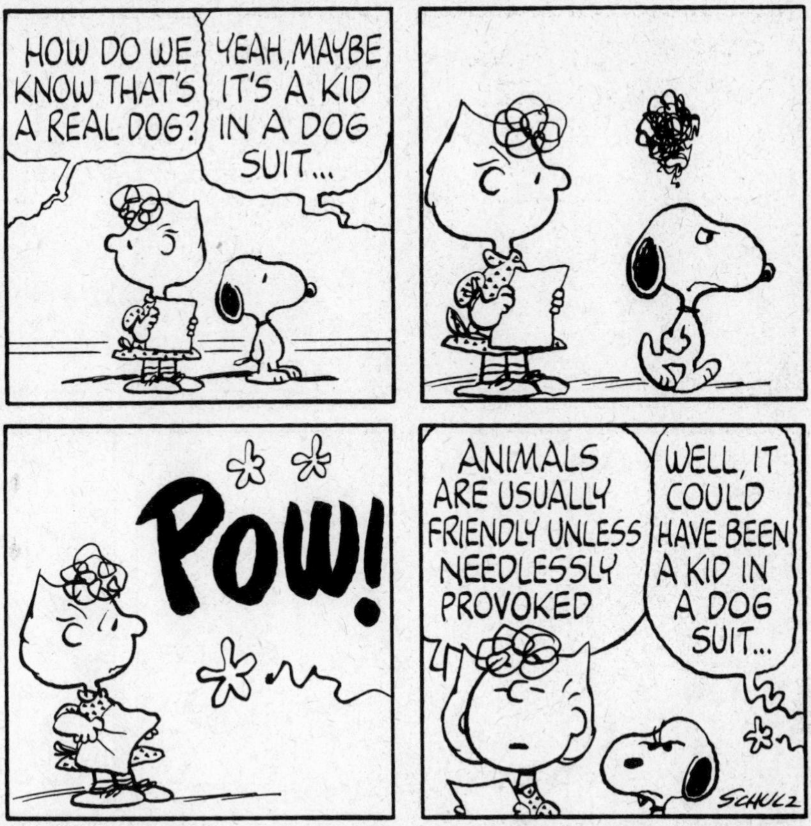
HOW DO WE KNOW THAT'S A REAL DOG?
YEAH, MAYBE IT'S A KID IN A DOG SUIT...
POW!
ANIMALS ARE USUALLY FRIENDLY UNLESS NEEDLESSLY PROVOKED
WELL, IT COULD HAVE BEEN A KID IN A DOG SUIT...
SCHULZ

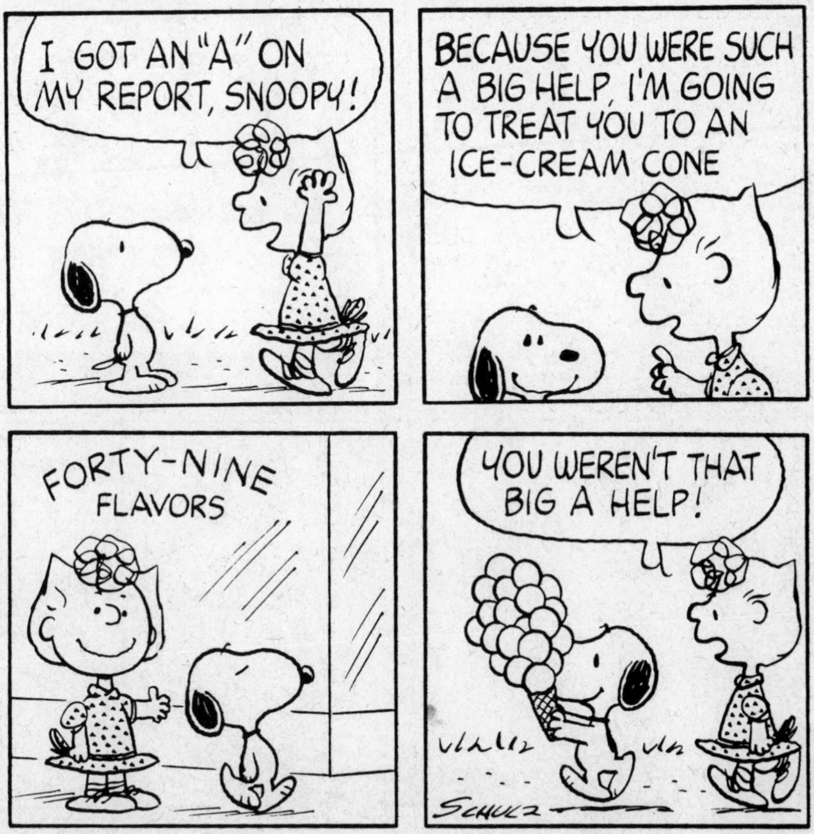
I GOT AN "A" ON MY REPORT, SNOOPY!
BECAUSE YOU WERE SUCH A BIG HELP, I'M GOING TO TREAT YOU TO AN ICE-CREAM CONE
FORTY-NINE FLAVORS
YOU WEREN'T THAT BIG A HELP!
SCHULZ

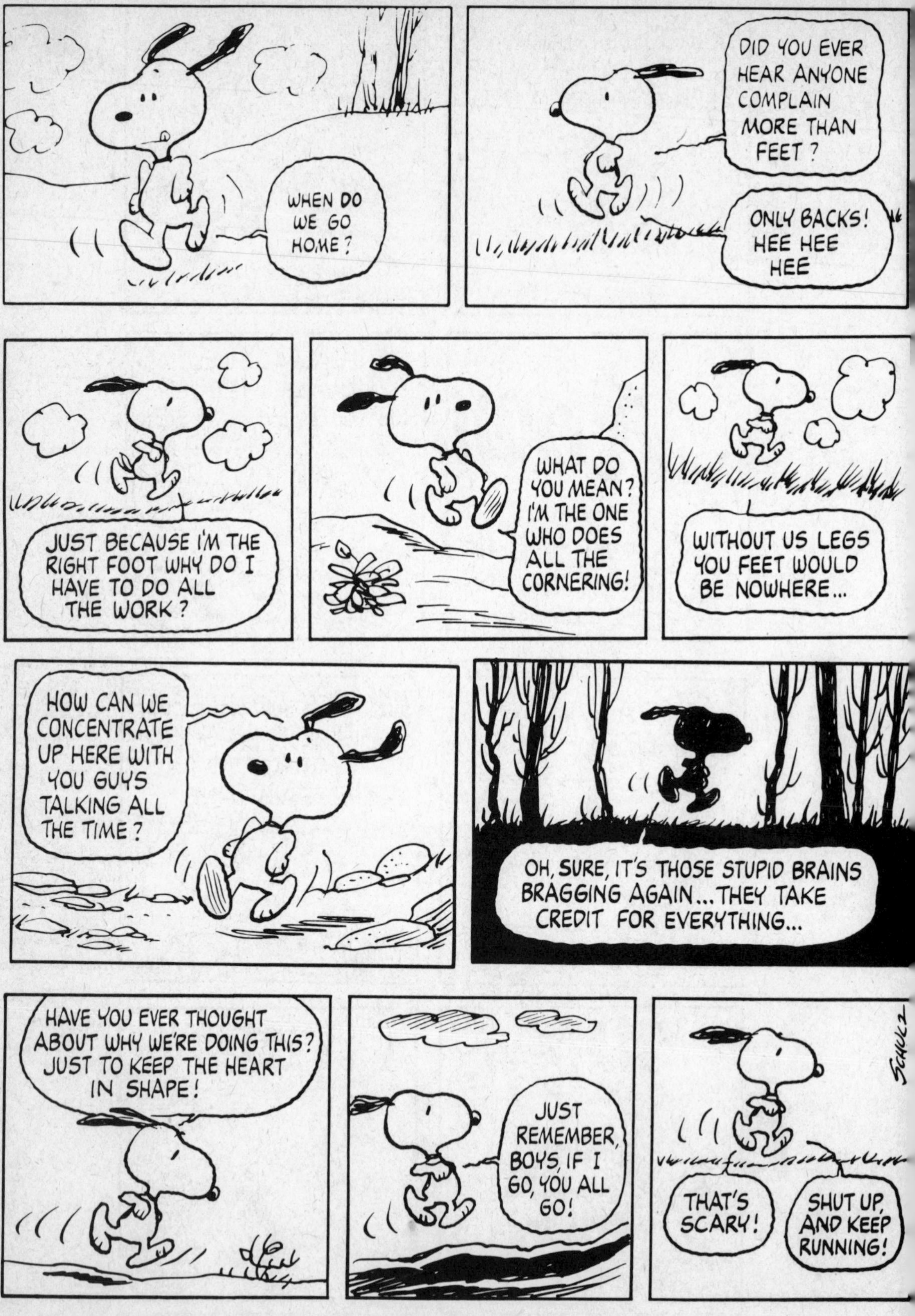
WHEN DO WE GO HOME?
DID YOU EVER HEAR ANYONE COMPLAIN MORE THAN FEET?
ONLY BACKS! HEE HEE HEE
JUST BECAUSE I'M THE RIGHT FOOT WHY DO I HAVE TO DO ALL THE WORK?
WHAT DO YOU MEAN? I'M THE ONE WHO DOES ALL THE CORNERING!
WITHOUT US LEGS YOU FEET WOULD BE NOWHERE...
HOW CAN WE CONCENTRATE UP HERE WITH YOU GUYS TALKING ALL THE TIME?
OH, SURE, IT'S THOSE STUPID BRAINS BRAGGING AGAIN... THEY TAKE CREDIT FOR EVERYTHING...
HAVE YOU EVER THOUGHT ABOUT WHY WE'RE DOING THIS? JUST TO KEEP THE HEART IN SHAPE!
JUST REMEMBER, BOYS, IF I GO, YOU ALL GO!
THAT'S SCARY!
SHUT UP, AND KEEP RUNNING!
SCHULZ

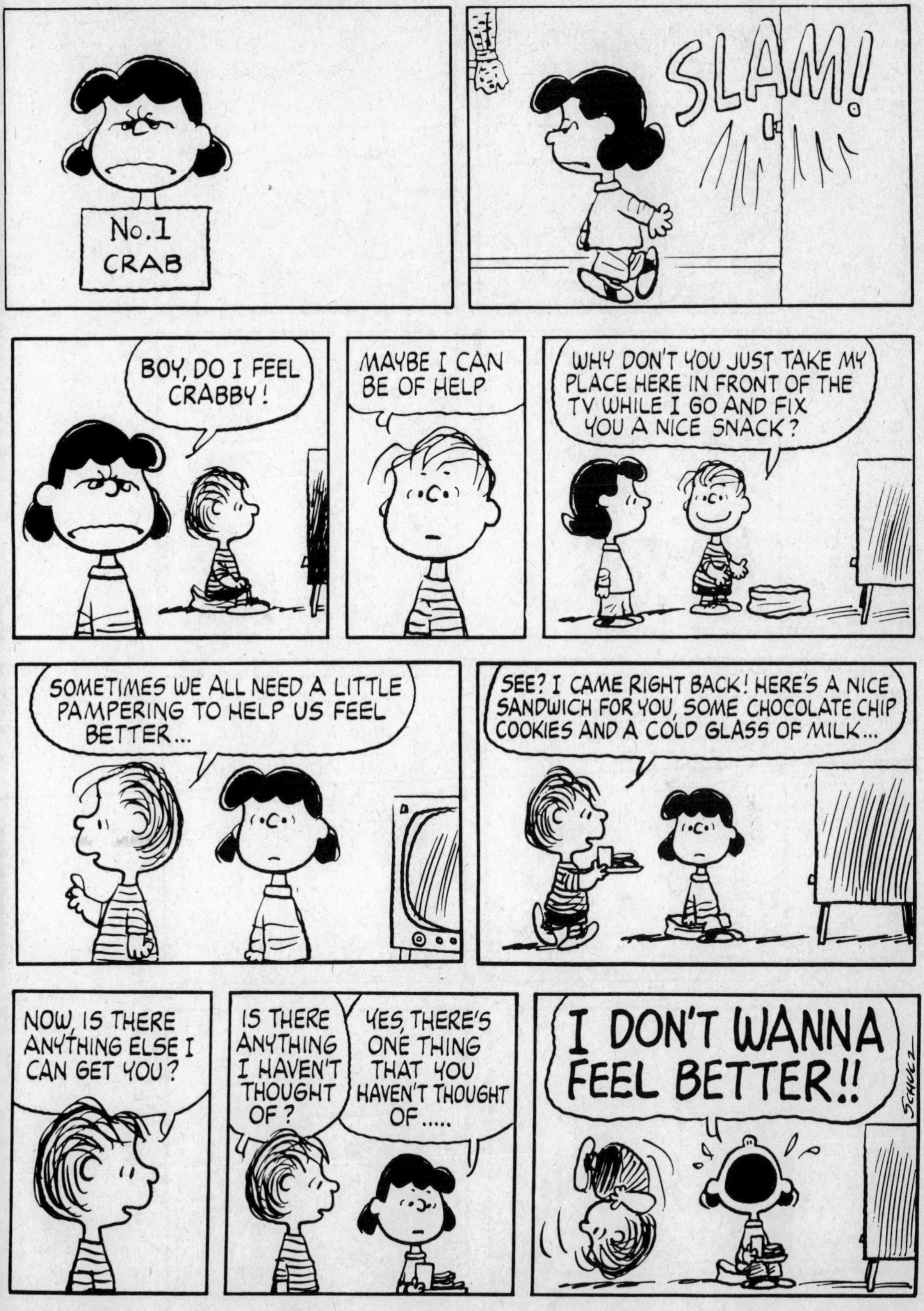
No.1
CRAB
SLAM!
BOY, DO I FEEL CRABBY!
MAYBE I CAN BE OF HELP
WHY DON'T YOU JUST TAKE MY PLACE HERE IN FRONT OF THE TV WHILE I GO AND FIX YOU A NICE SNACK?
SOMETIMES WE ALL NEED A LITTLE PAMPERING TO HELP US FEEL BETTER...
SEE? I CAME RIGHT BACK! HERE'S A NICE SANDWICH FOR YOU, SOME CHOCOLATE CHIP COOKIES AND A COLD GLASS OF MILK...
NOW, IS THERE ANYTHING ELSE I CAN GET YOU?
IS THERE ANYTHING I HAVEN'T THOUGHT OF?
YES, THERE'S ONE THING THAT YOU HAVEN'T THOUGHT OF.....
I DON'T WANNA FEEL BETTER!!
SCHULZ

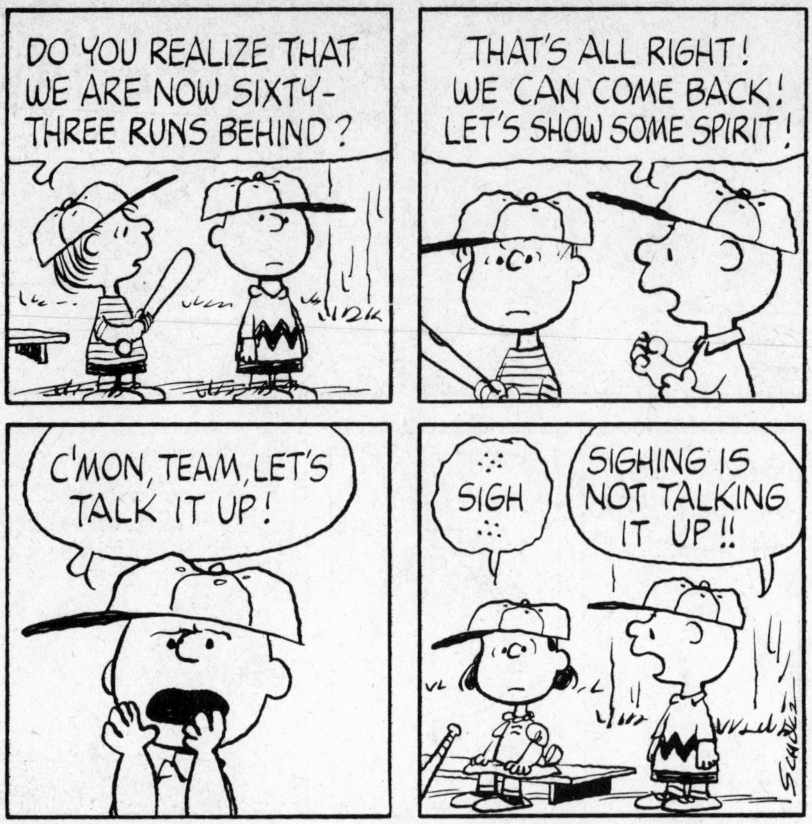
DO YOU REALIZE THAT WE ARE NOW SIXTY-THREE RUNS BEHIND?
THAT'S ALL RIGHT! WE CAN COME BACK! LET'S SHOW SOME SPIRIT!
C'MON, TEAM, LET'S TALK IT UP!
SIGH
SIGHING IS NOT TALKING IT UP!!
SCHULZ

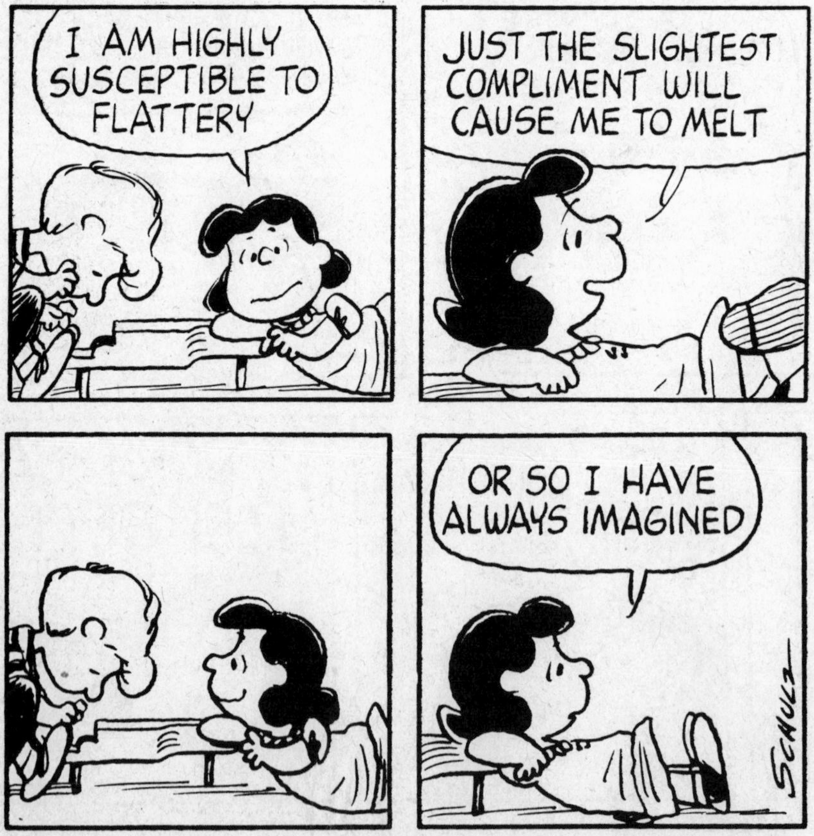
I AM HIGHLY SUSCEPTIBLE TO FLATTERY
JUST THE SLIGHTEST COMPLIMENT WILL CAUSE ME TO MELT
OR SO I HAVE ALWAYS IMAGINED
SCHULZ

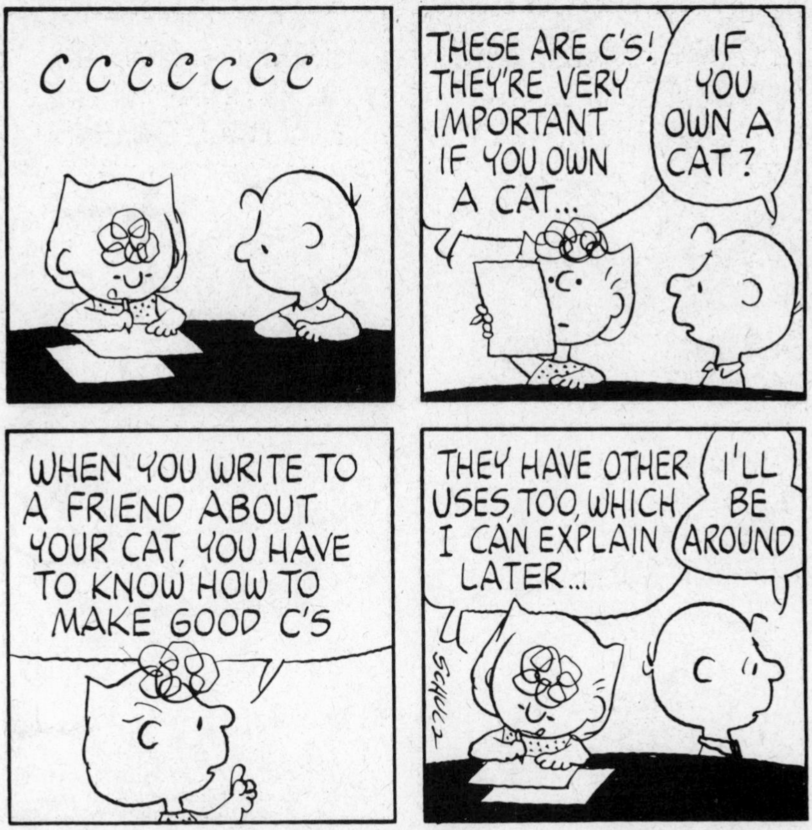
CCCCCCC
THESE ARE C'S! THEY'RE VERY IMPORTANT IF YOU OWN A CAT...
IF YOU OWN A CAT?
WHEN YOU WRITE TO A FRIEND ABOUT YOUR CAT, YOU HAVE TO KNOW HOW TO MAKE GOOD C'S
THEY HAVE OTHER USES, TOO, WHICH I CAN EXPLAIN LATER...
I'LL BE AROUND

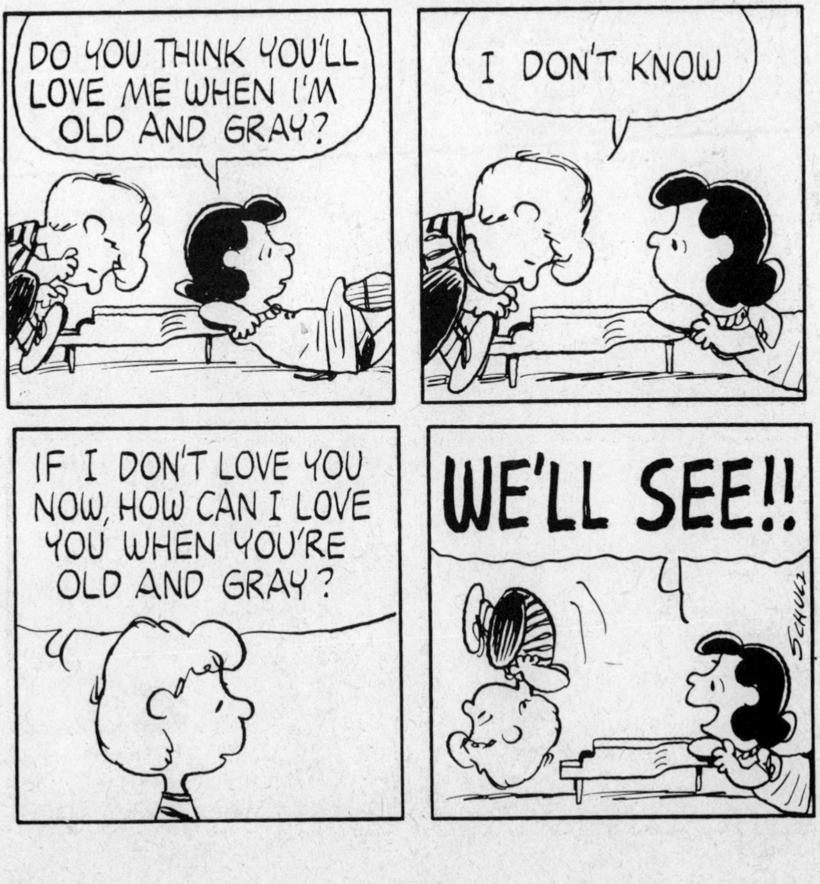
DO YOU THINK YOU'LL LOVE ME WHEN I'M OLD AND GRAY?
I DON'T KNOW
IF I DON'T LOVE YOU NOW, HOW CAN I LOVE YOU WHEN YOU'RE OLD AND GRAY?
WE'LL SEE!!

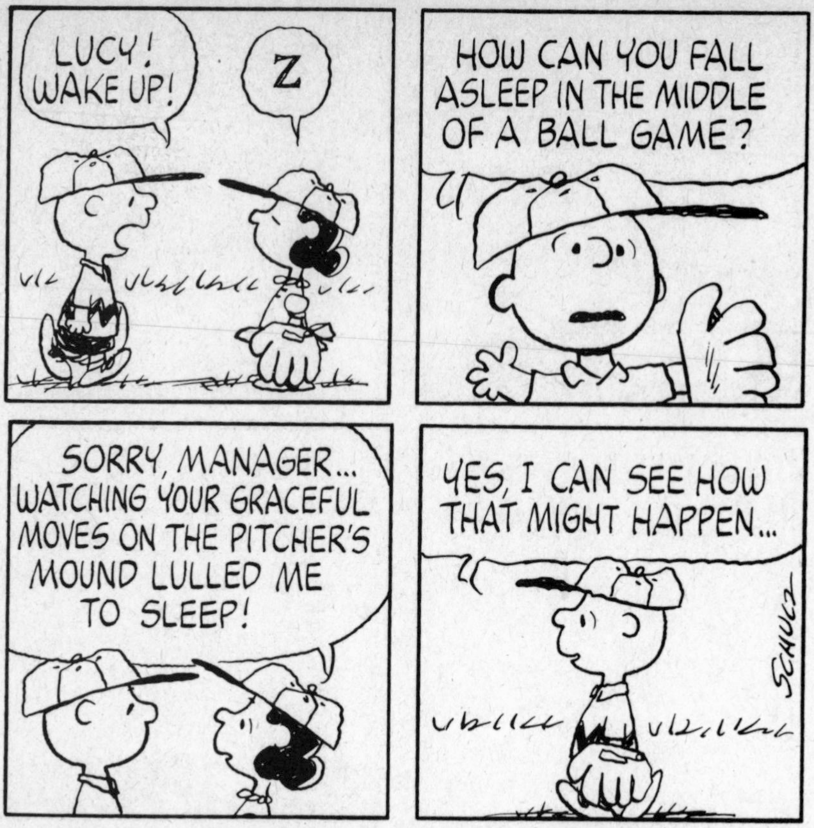

LUCY! WAKE UP!
Z
HOW CAN YOU FALL ASLEEP IN THE MIDDLE OF A BALL GAME?
SORRY, MANAGER... WATCHING YOUR GRACEFUL MOVES ON THE PITCHER'S MOUND LULLED ME TO SLEEP!
YES, I CAN SEE HOW THAT MIGHT HAPPEN...
SCHULZ

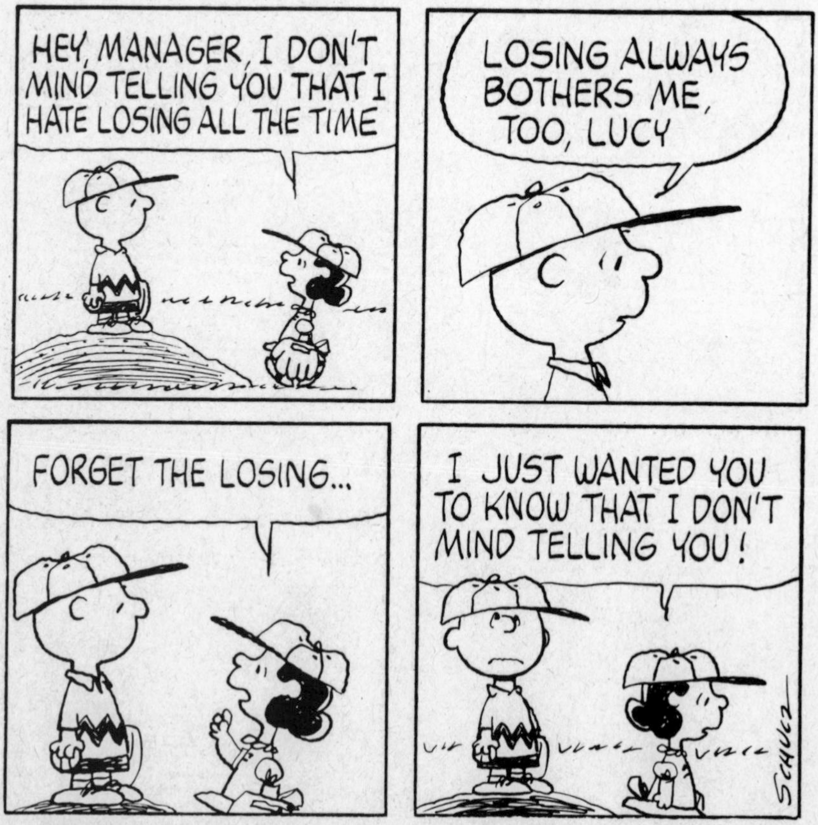

HEY, MANAGER, I DON'T MIND TELLING YOU THAT I HATE LOSING ALL THE TIME
LOSING ALWAYS BOTHERS ME, TOO, LUCY
FORGET THE LOSING...
I JUST WANTED YOU TO KNOW THAT I DON'T MIND TELLING YOU!
SCHULZ

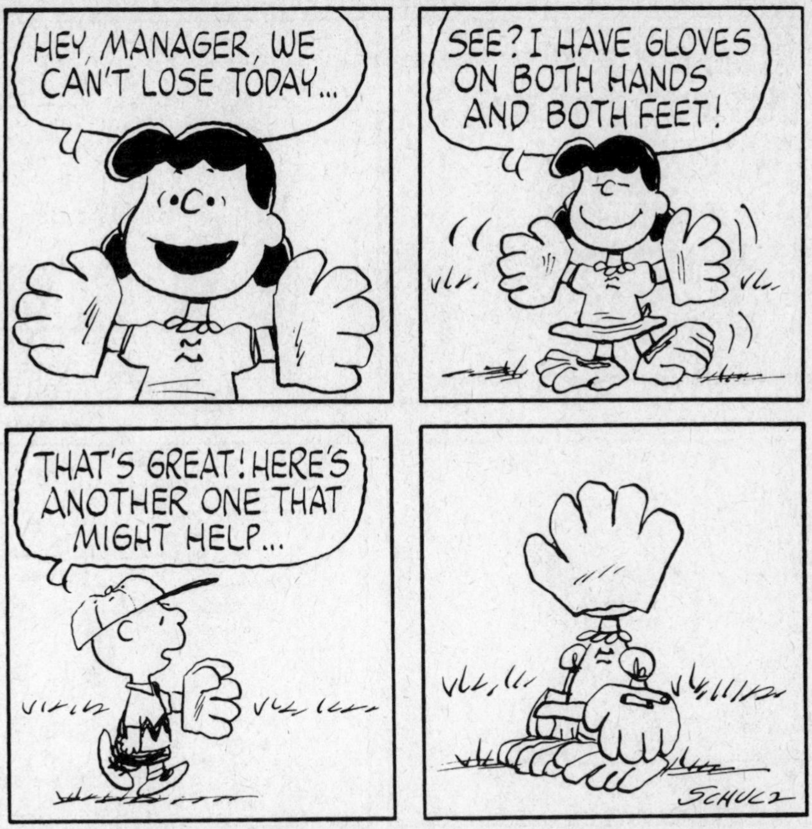
HEY, MANAGER, WE CAN'T LOSE TODAY...
SEE? I HAVE GLOVES ON BOTH HANDS AND BOTH FEET!
THAT'S GREAT! HERE'S ANOTHER ONE THAT MIGHT HELP...
SCHULZ

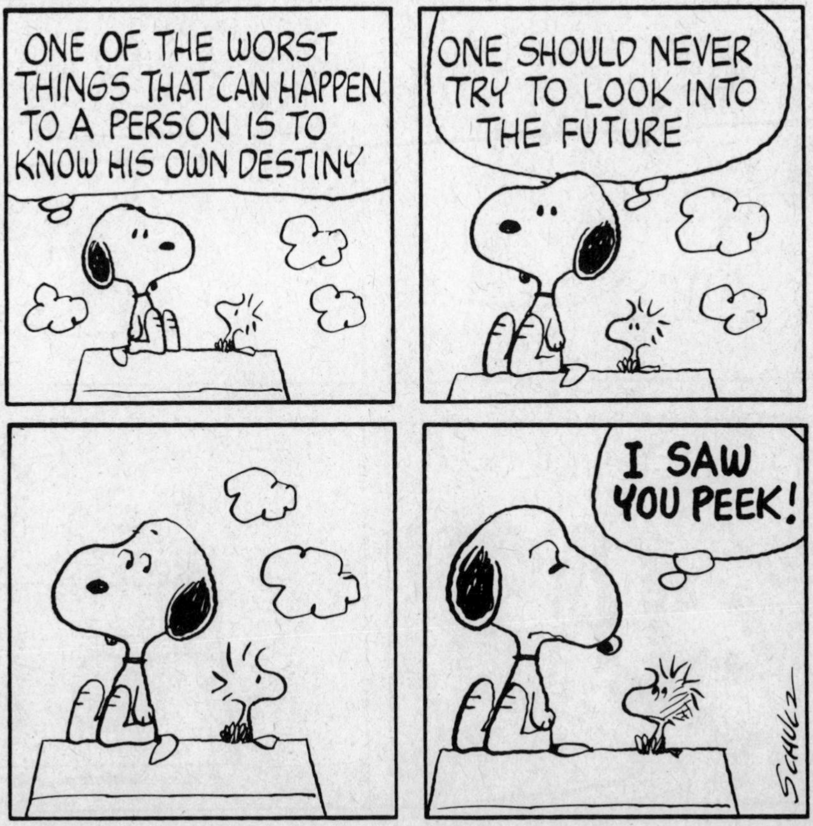
ONE OF THE WORST THINGS THAT CAN HAPPEN TO A PERSON IS TO KNOW HIS OWN DESTINY
ONE SHOULD NEVER TRY TO LOOK INTO THE FUTURE
I SAW YOU PEEK!
SCHULZ

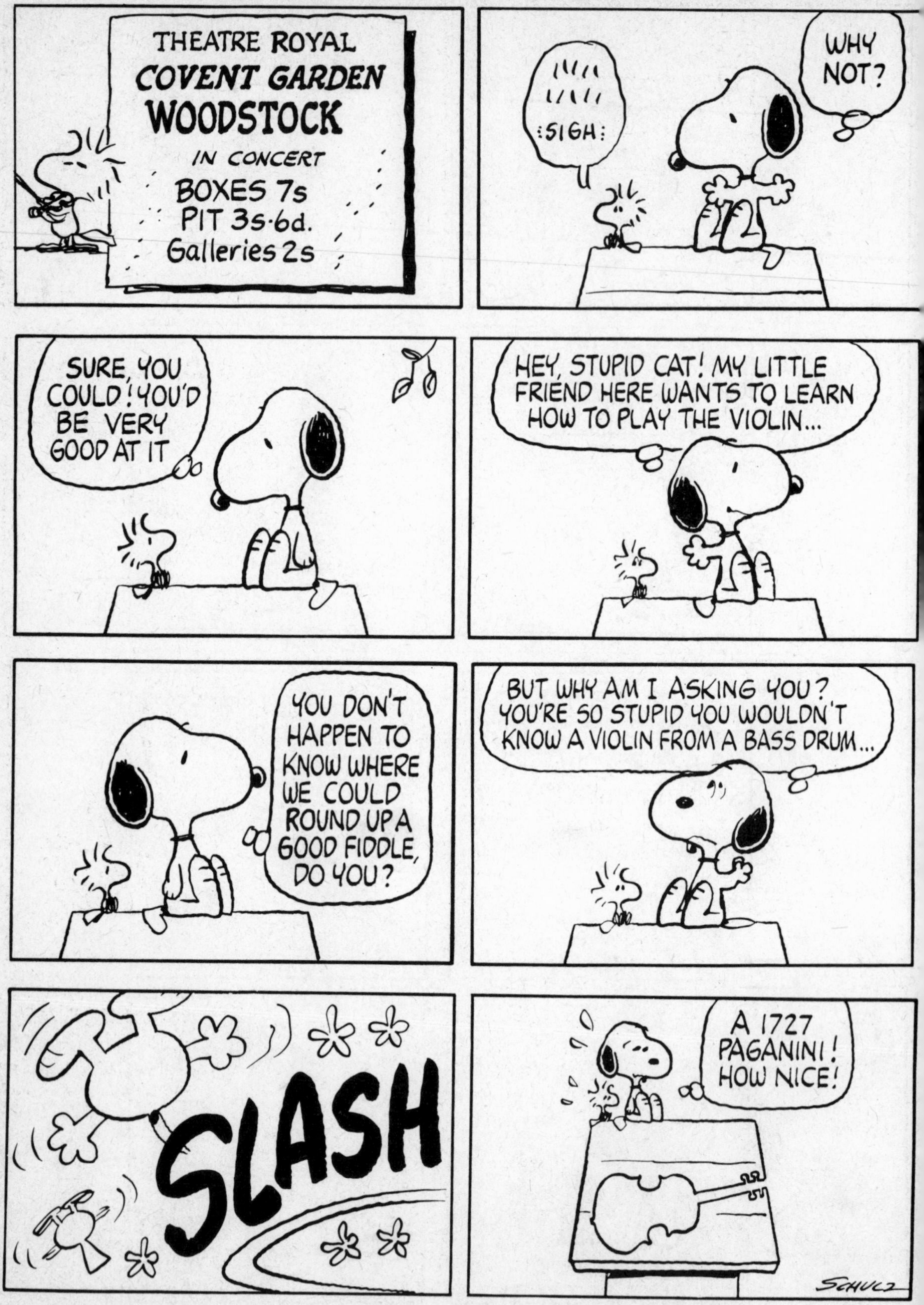
THEATRE ROYAL
COVENT GARDEN
WOODSTOCK
IN CONCERT
BOXES 7s
PIT 3s·6d.
Galleries 2s
SIGH
WHY NOT?
SURE, YOU COULD! YOU'D BE VERY GOOD AT IT
HEY, STUPID CAT! MY LITTLE FRIEND HERE WANTS TO LEARN HOW TO PLAY THE VIOLIN...
YOU DON'T HAPPEN TO KNOW WHERE WE COULD ROUND UP A GOOD FIDDLE, DO YOU?
BUT WHY AM I ASKING YOU? YOU'RE SO STUPID YOU WOULDN'T KNOW A VIOLIN FROM A BASS DRUM...
SLASH
A 1727 PAGANINI! HOW NICE!
SCHULZ

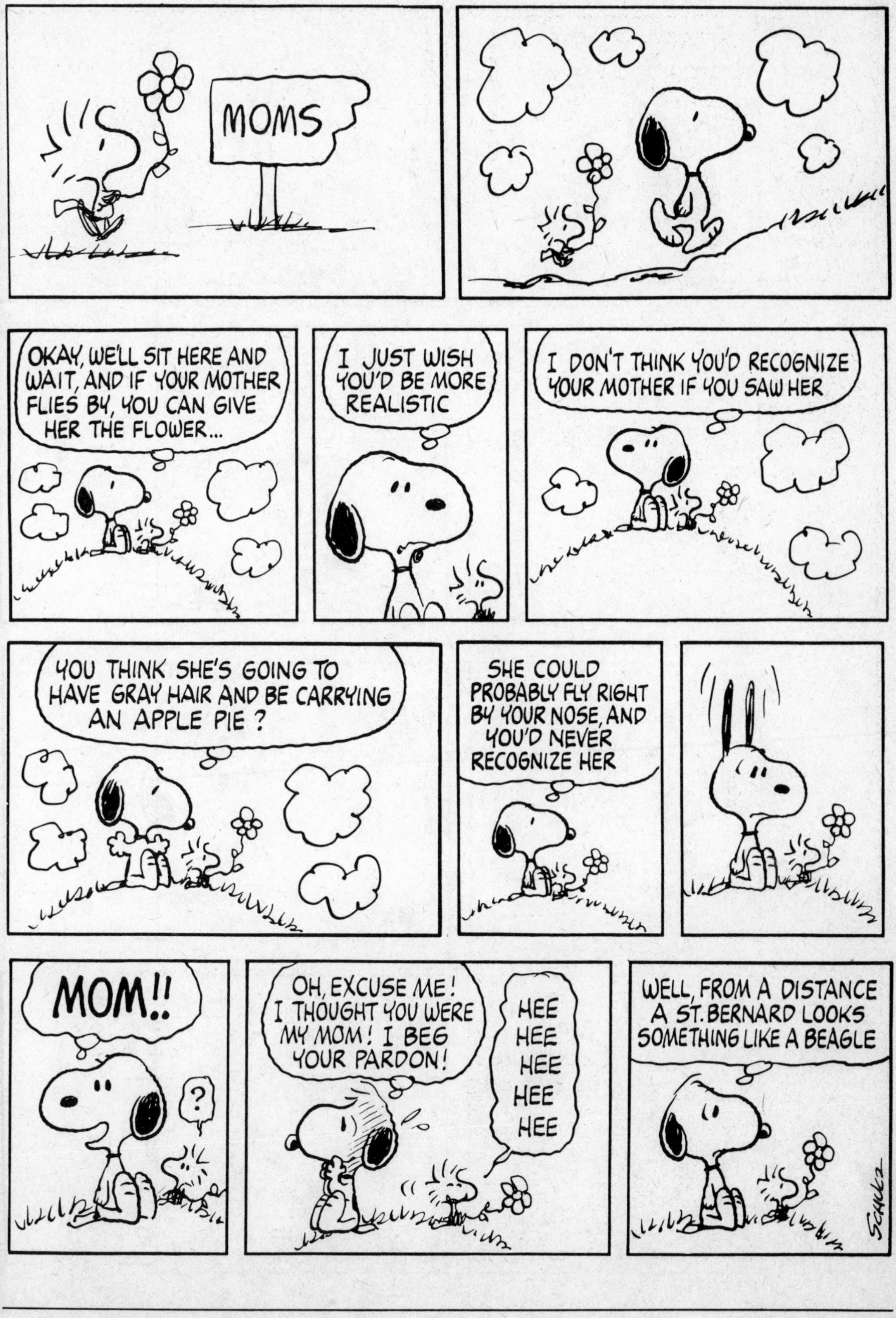
MOMS
OKAY, WE'LL SIT HERE AND WAIT, AND IF YOUR MOTHER FLIES BY, YOU CAN GIVE HER THE FLOWER...
I JUST WISH YOU'D BE MORE REALISTIC
I DON'T THINK YOU'D RECOGNIZE YOUR MOTHER IF YOU SAW HER
YOU THINK SHE'S GOING TO HAVE GRAY HAIR AND BE CARRYING AN APPLE PIE ?
SHE COULD PROBABLY FLY RIGHT BY YOUR NOSE, AND YOU'D NEVER RECOGNIZE HER
MOM!!
?
OH, EXCUSE ME! I THOUGHT YOU WERE MY MOM! I BEG YOUR PARDON!
HEE HEE HEE HEE HEE
WELL, FROM A DISTANCE A ST. BERNARD LOOKS SOMETHING LIKE A BEAGLE
SCHULZ

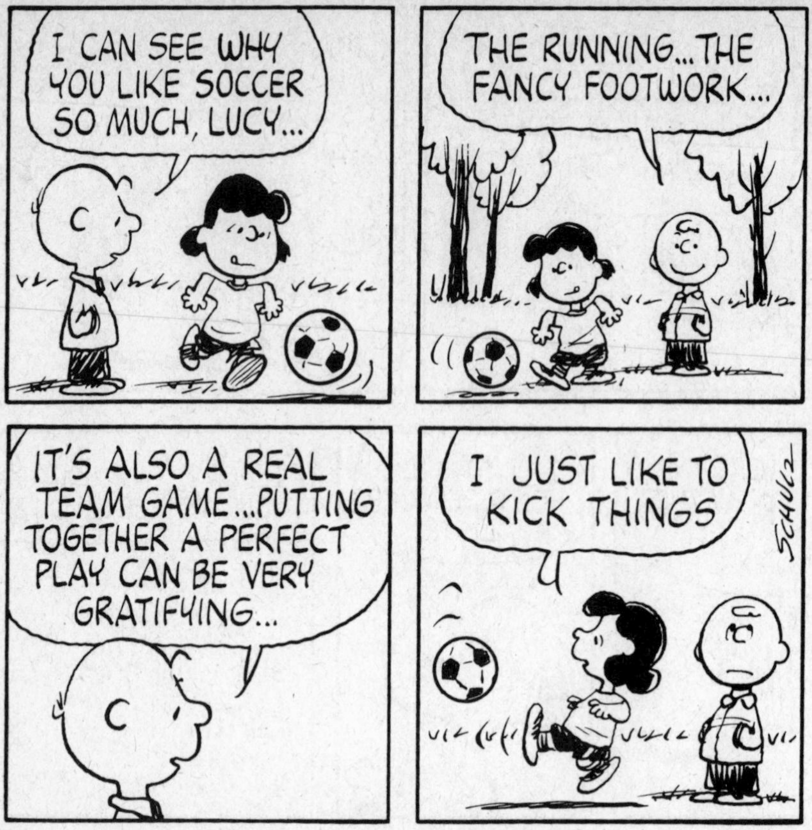
I CAN SEE WHY YOU LIKE SOCCER SO MUCH, LUCY...
THE RUNNING...THE FANCY FOOTWORK...
IT'S ALSO A REAL TEAM GAME...PUTTING TOGETHER A PERFECT PLAY CAN BE VERY GRATIFYING...
I JUST LIKE TO KICK THINGS
SCHULZ

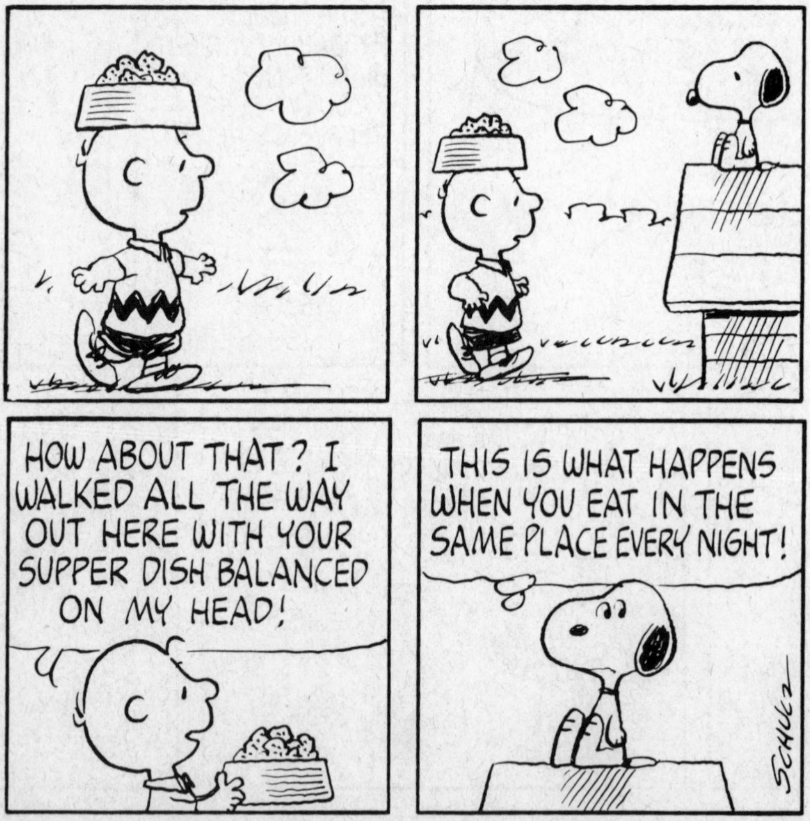
HOW ABOUT THAT? I WALKED ALL THE WAY OUT HERE WITH YOUR SUPPER DISH BALANCED ON MY HEAD!
THIS IS WHAT HAPPENS WHEN YOU EAT IN THE SAME PLACE EVERY NIGHT!
SCHULZ

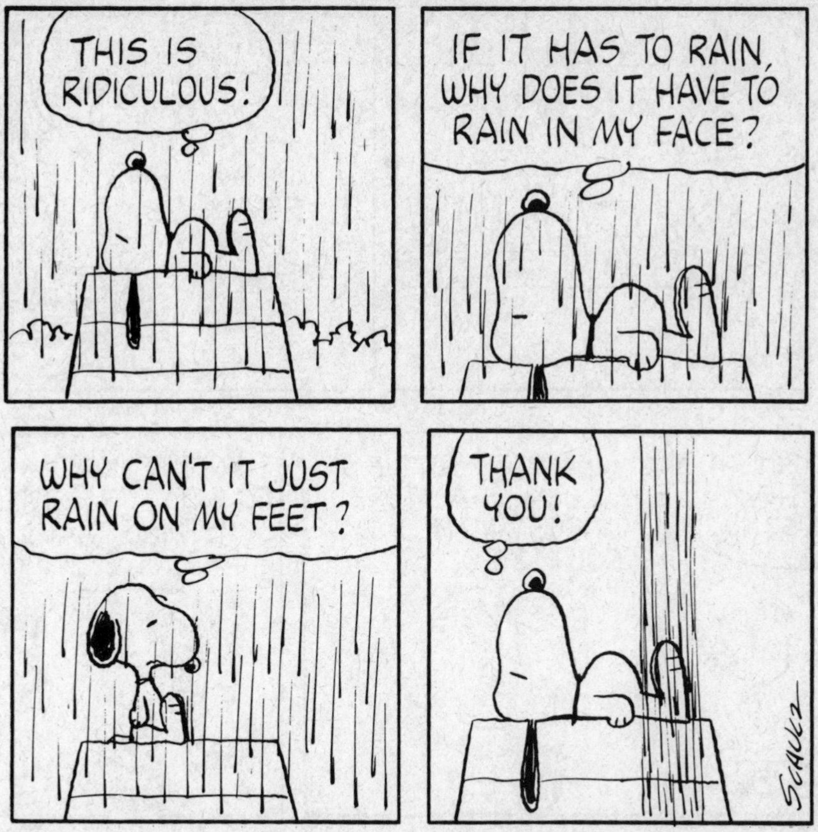
THIS IS RIDICULOUS!
IF IT HAS TO RAIN, WHY DOES IT HAVE TO RAIN IN MY FACE?
WHY CAN'T IT JUST RAIN ON MY FEET?
THANK YOU!
SCHULZ

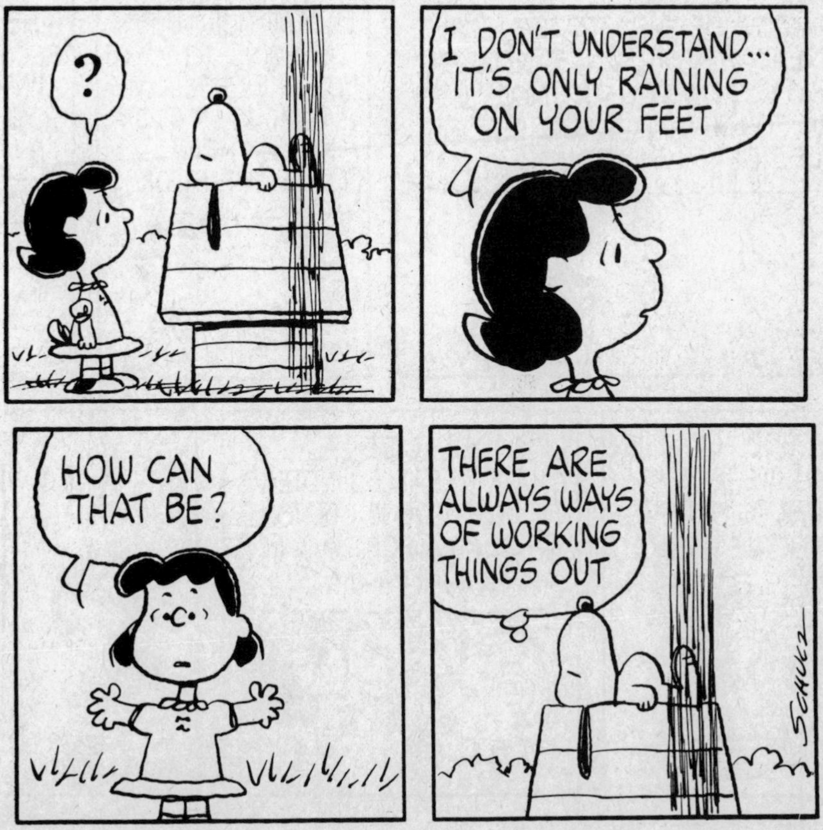
?
I DON'T UNDERSTAND... IT'S ONLY RAINING ON YOUR FEET
HOW CAN THAT BE?
THERE ARE ALWAYS WAYS OF WORKING THINGS OUT
SCHULZ

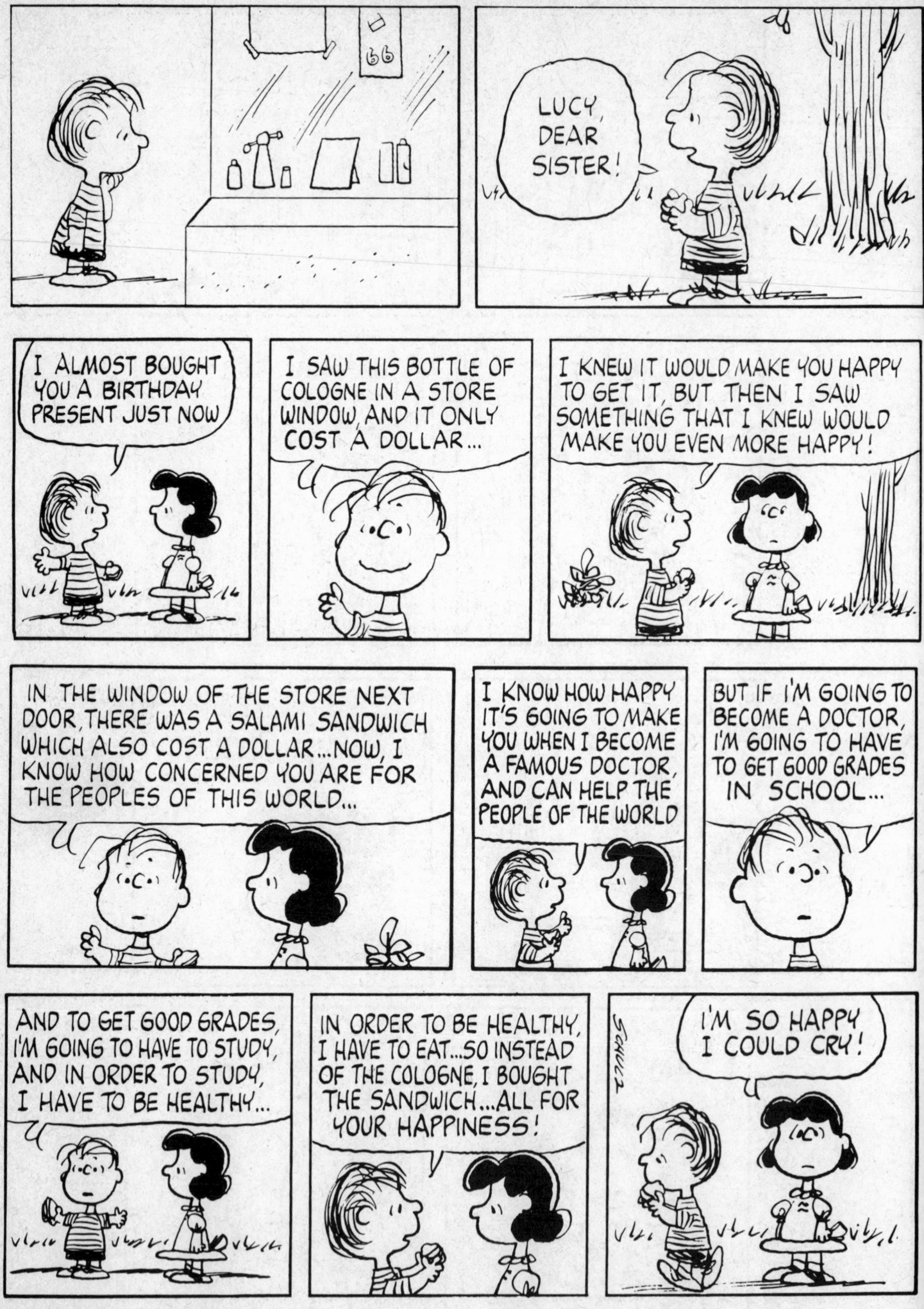

LUCY, DEAR SISTER!
I ALMOST BOUGHT YOU A BIRTHDAY PRESENT JUST NOW
I SAW THIS BOTTLE OF COLOGNE IN A STORE WINDOW, AND IT ONLY COST A DOLLAR...
I KNEW IT WOULD MAKE YOU HAPPY TO GET IT, BUT THEN I SAW SOMETHING THAT I KNEW WOULD MAKE YOU EVEN MORE HAPPY!
IN THE WINDOW OF THE STORE NEXT DOOR, THERE WAS A SALAMI SANDWICH WHICH ALSO COST A DOLLAR...NOW, I KNOW HOW CONCERNED YOU ARE FOR THE PEOPLES OF THIS WORLD...
I KNOW HOW HAPPY IT'S GOING TO MAKE YOU WHEN I BECOME A FAMOUS DOCTOR, AND CAN HELP THE PEOPLE OF THE WORLD
BUT IF I'M GOING TO BECOME A DOCTOR, I'M GOING TO HAVE TO GET GOOD GRADES IN SCHOOL...
AND TO GET GOOD GRADES, I'M GOING TO HAVE TO STUDY, AND IN ORDER TO STUDY, I HAVE TO BE HEALTHY...
IN ORDER TO BE HEALTHY, I HAVE TO EAT...SO INSTEAD OF THE COLOGNE, I BOUGHT THE SANDWICH...ALL FOR YOUR HAPPINESS!
SCHULZ
I'M SO HAPPY I COULD CRY!

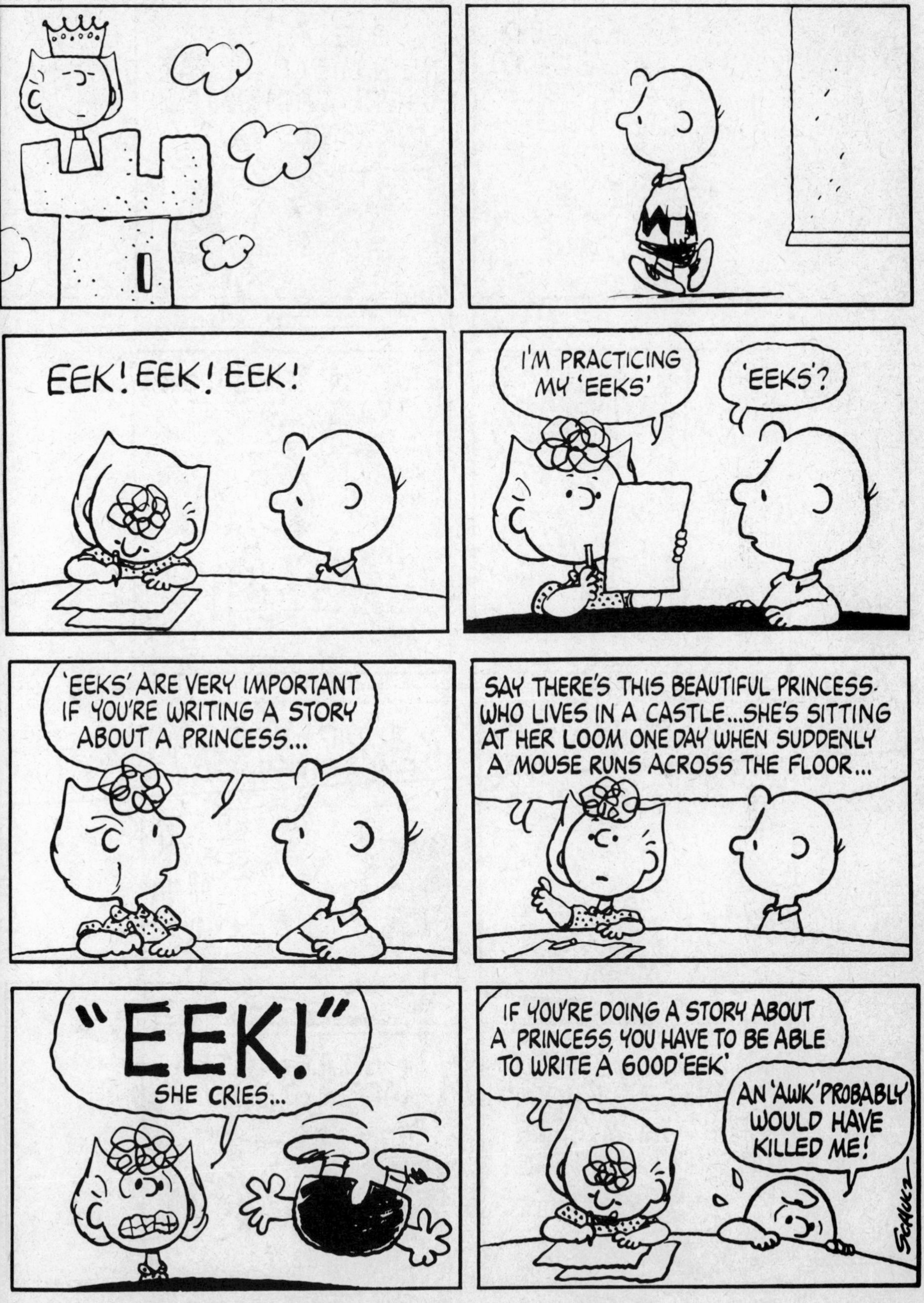
EEK! EEK! EEK!
I'M PRACTICING MY 'EEKS'
'EEKS'?
'EEKS' ARE VERY IMPORTANT IF YOU'RE WRITING A STORY ABOUT A PRINCESS...
SAY THERE'S THIS BEAUTIFUL PRINCESS WHO LIVES IN A CASTLE...SHE'S SITTING AT HER LOOM ONE DAY WHEN SUDDENLY A MOUSE RUNS ACROSS THE FLOOR...
"EEK!" SHE CRIES...
IF YOU'RE DOING A STORY ABOUT A PRINCESS, YOU HAVE TO BE ABLE TO WRITE A GOOD 'EEK'
AN 'AWK' PROBABLY WOULD HAVE KILLED ME!
SCHULZ

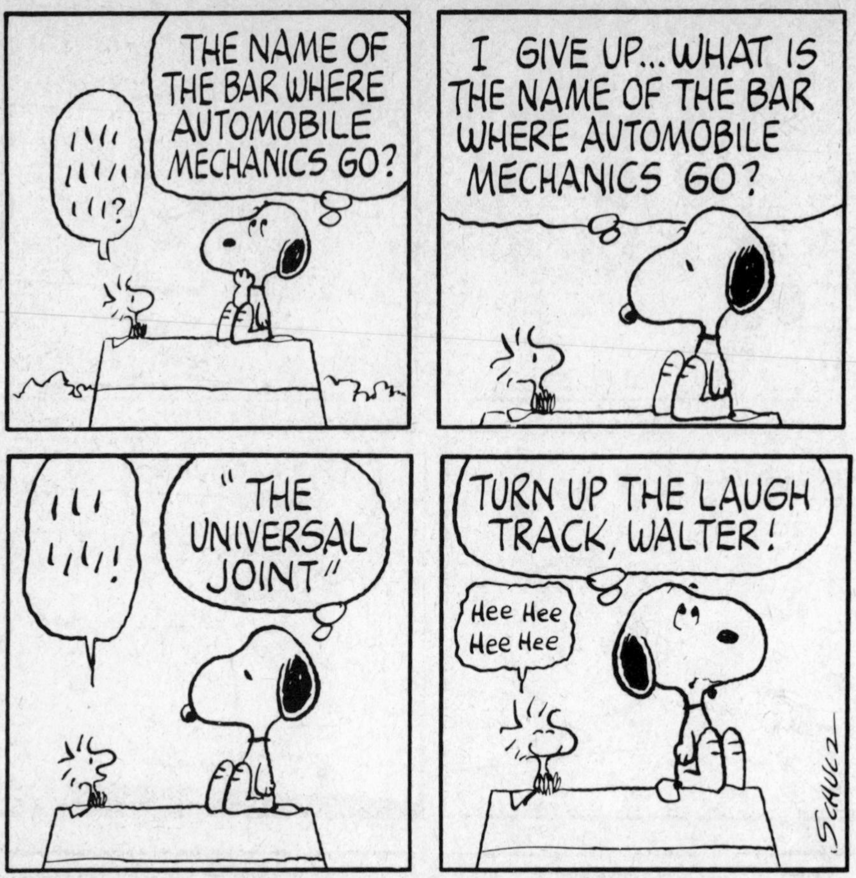
THE NAME OF THE BAR WHERE AUTOMOBILE MECHANICS GO?
I GIVE UP... WHAT IS THE NAME OF THE BAR WHERE AUTOMOBILE MECHANICS GO?
"THE UNIVERSAL JOINT"
TURN UP THE LAUGH TRACK, WALTER!
Hee Hee Hee Hee
SCHULZ

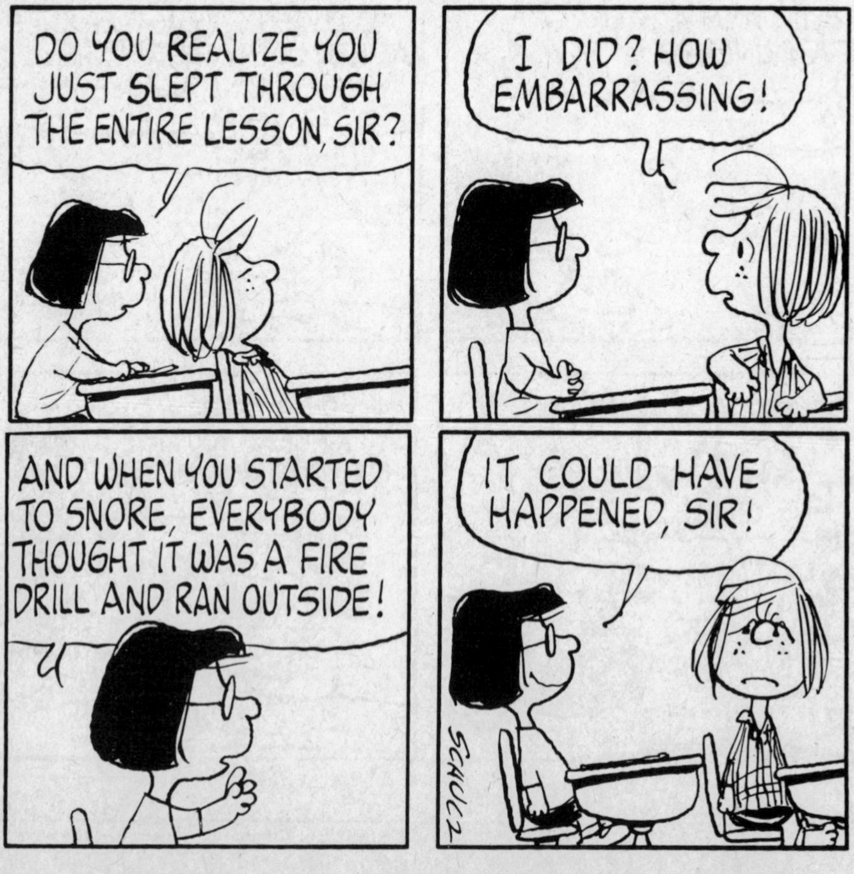
DO YOU REALIZE YOU JUST SLEPT THROUGH THE ENTIRE LESSON, SIR?
I DID? HOW EMBARRASSING!
AND WHEN YOU STARTED TO SNORE, EVERYBODY THOUGHT IT WAS A FIRE DRILL AND RAN OUTSIDE!
IT COULD HAVE HAPPENED, SIR!
SCHULZ

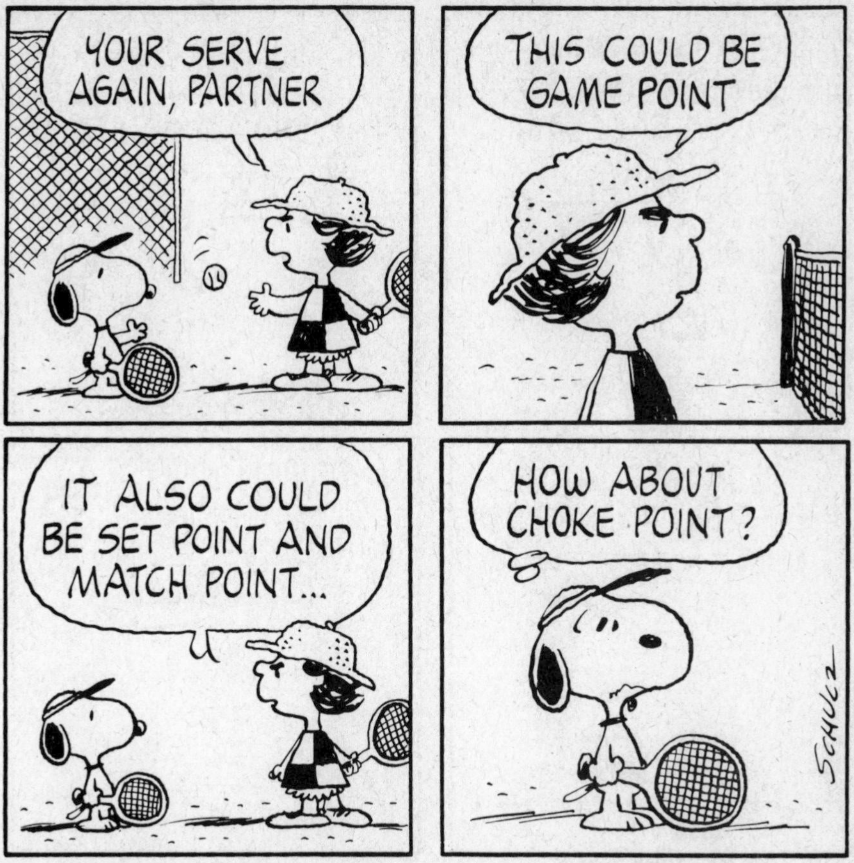
YOUR SERVE AGAIN, PARTNER
THIS COULD BE GAME POINT
IT ALSO COULD BE SET POINT AND MATCH POINT...
HOW ABOUT CHOKE POINT?
SCHULZ

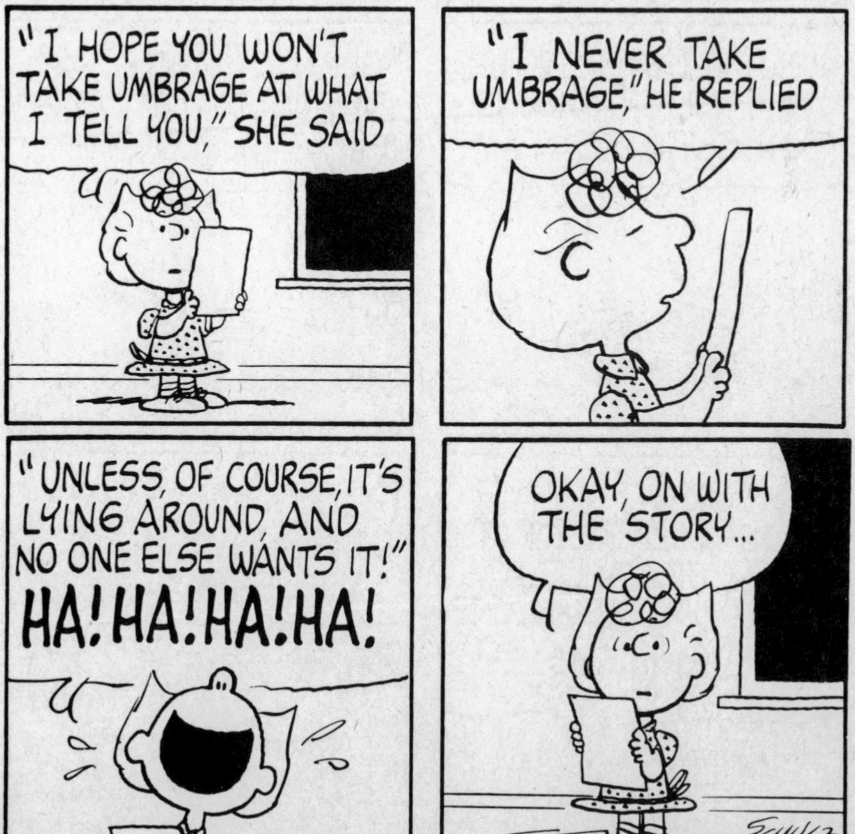
"I HOPE YOU WON'T TAKE UMBRAGE AT WHAT I TELL YOU," SHE SAID
"I NEVER TAKE UMBRAGE," HE REPLIED
"UNLESS, OF COURSE, IT'S LYING AROUND, AND NO ONE ELSE WANTS IT!"
HA! HA! HA! HA!
OKAY, ON WITH THE STORY...
SCHULZ

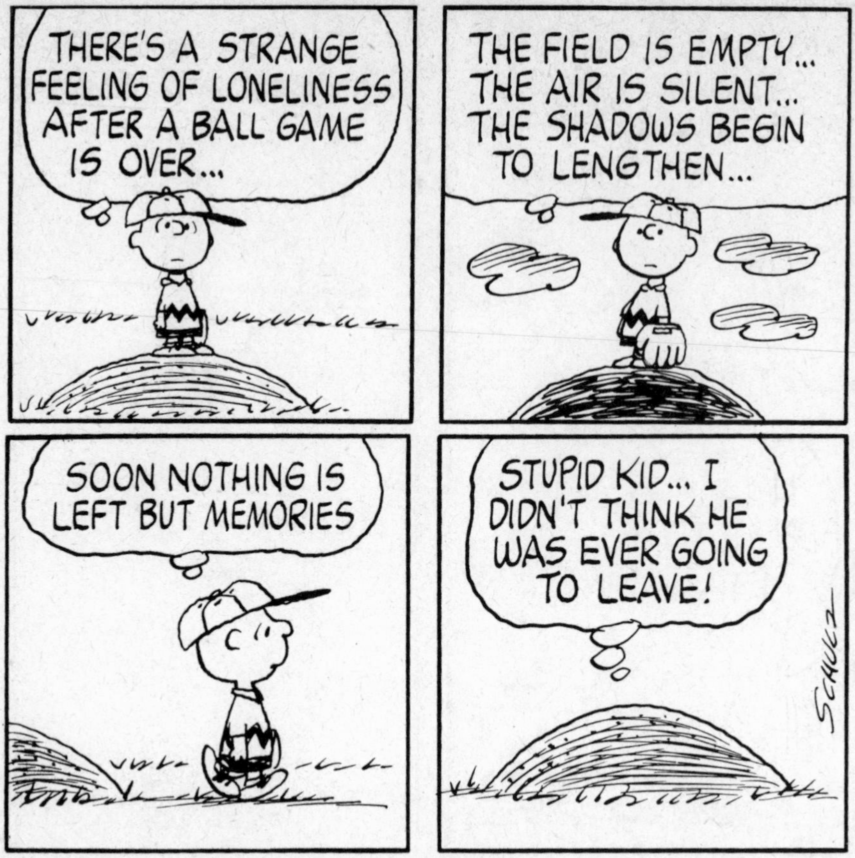
THERE'S A STRANGE FEELING OF LONELINESS AFTER A BALL GAME IS OVER...
THE FIELD IS EMPTY... THE AIR IS SILENT... THE SHADOWS BEGIN TO LENGTHEN...
SOON NOTHING IS LEFT BUT MEMORIES
STUPID KID... I DIDN'T THINK HE WAS EVER GOING TO LEAVE!
SCHULZ

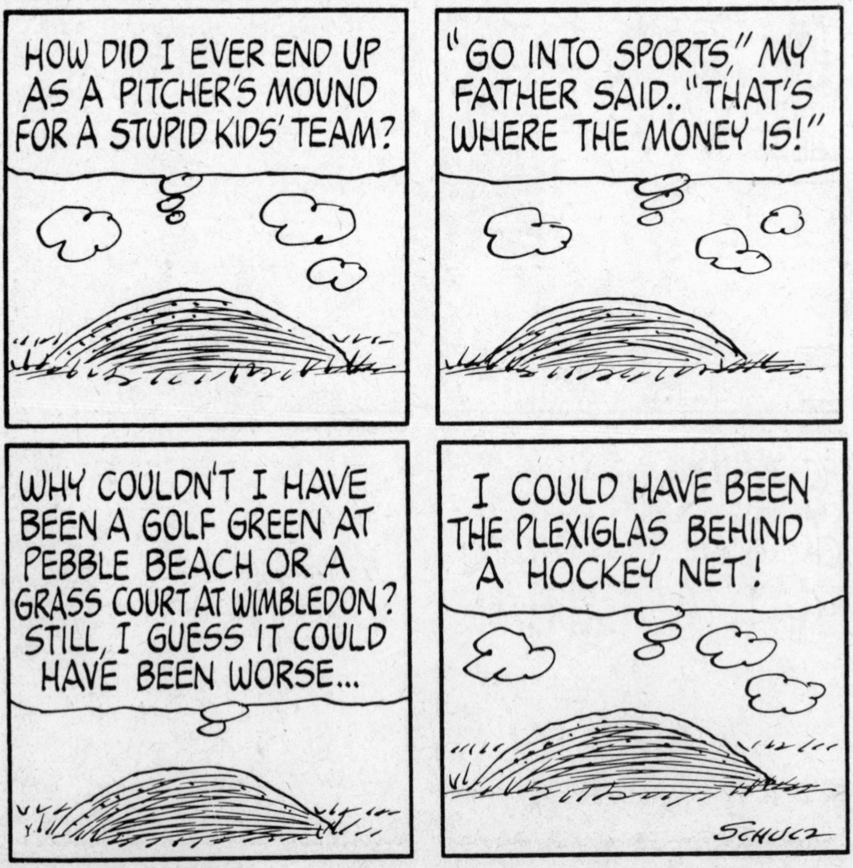
HOW DID I EVER END UP AS A PITCHER'S MOUND FOR A STUPID KIDS' TEAM?
"GO INTO SPORTS," MY FATHER SAID.. "THAT'S WHERE THE MONEY IS!"
WHY COULDN'T I HAVE BEEN A GOLF GREEN AT PEBBLE BEACH OR A GRASS COURT AT WIMBLEDON? STILL, I GUESS IT COULD HAVE BEEN WORSE...
I COULD HAVE BEEN THE PLEXIGLAS BEHIND A HOCKEY NET!
SCHULZ

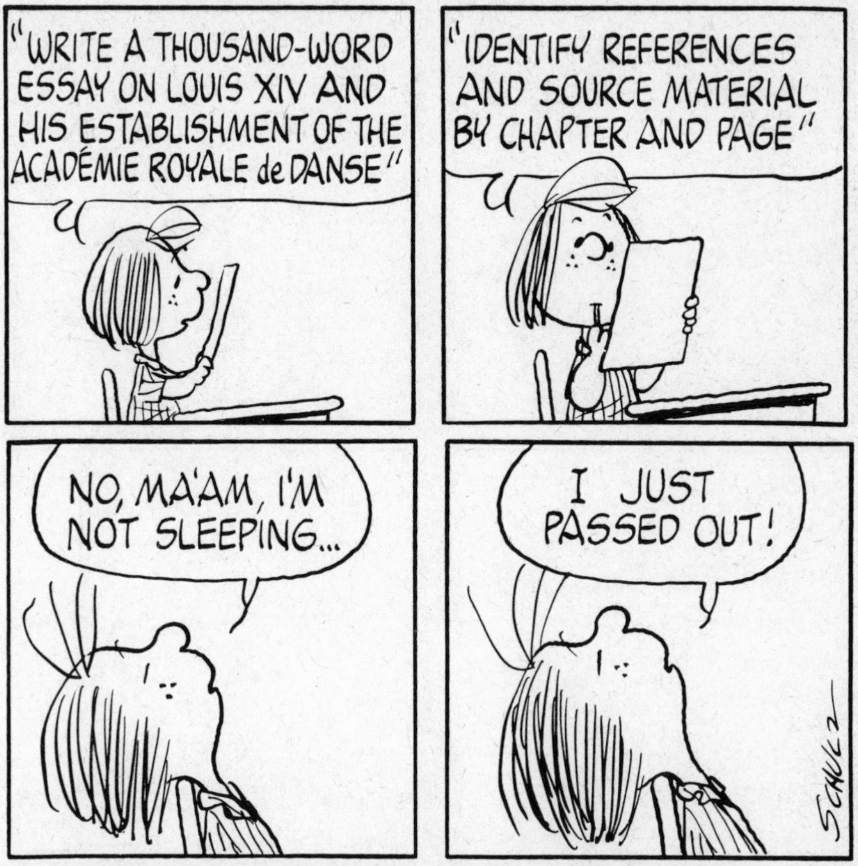
"WRITE A THOUSAND-WORD ESSAY ON LOUIS XIV AND HIS ESTABLISHMENT OF THE ACADÉMIE ROYALE de DANSE"
"IDENTIFY REFERENCES AND SOURCE MATERIAL BY CHAPTER AND PAGE"
NO, MA'AM, I'M NOT SLEEPING...
I JUST PASSED OUT!
SCHULZ

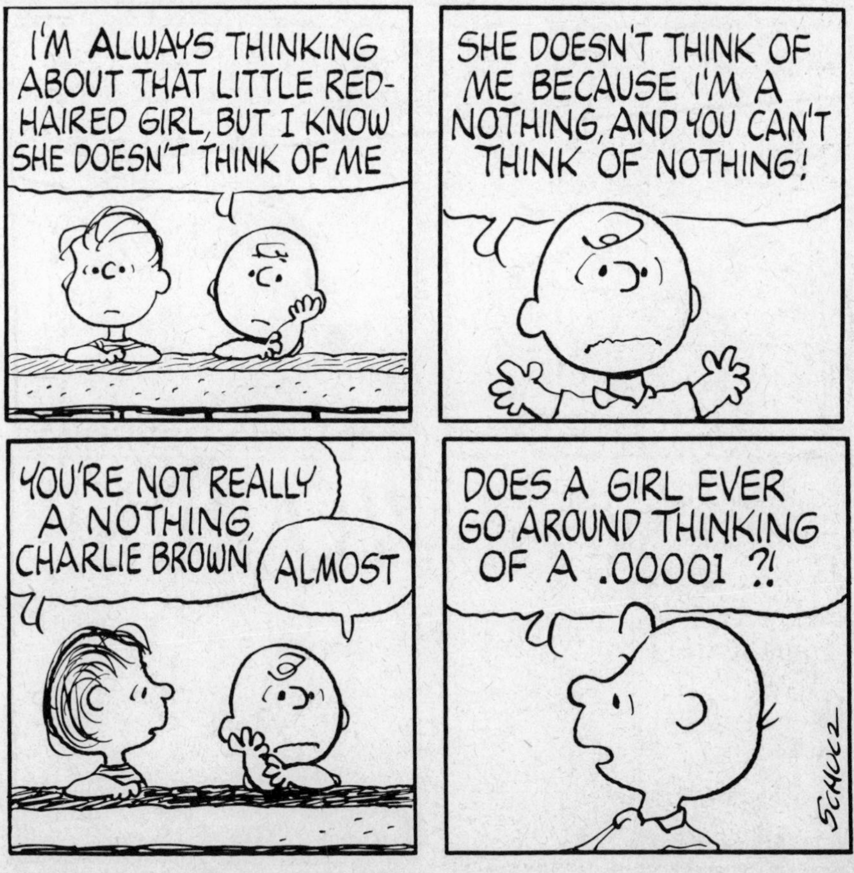
I'M ALWAYS THINKING ABOUT THAT LITTLE RED-HAIRED GIRL, BUT I KNOW SHE DOESN'T THINK OF ME
SHE DOESN'T THINK OF ME BECAUSE I'M A NOTHING, AND YOU CAN'T THINK OF NOTHING!
YOU'RE NOT REALLY A NOTHING, CHARLIE BROWN
ALMOST
DOES A GIRL EVER GO AROUND THINKING OF A .00001 ?!
SCHULZ

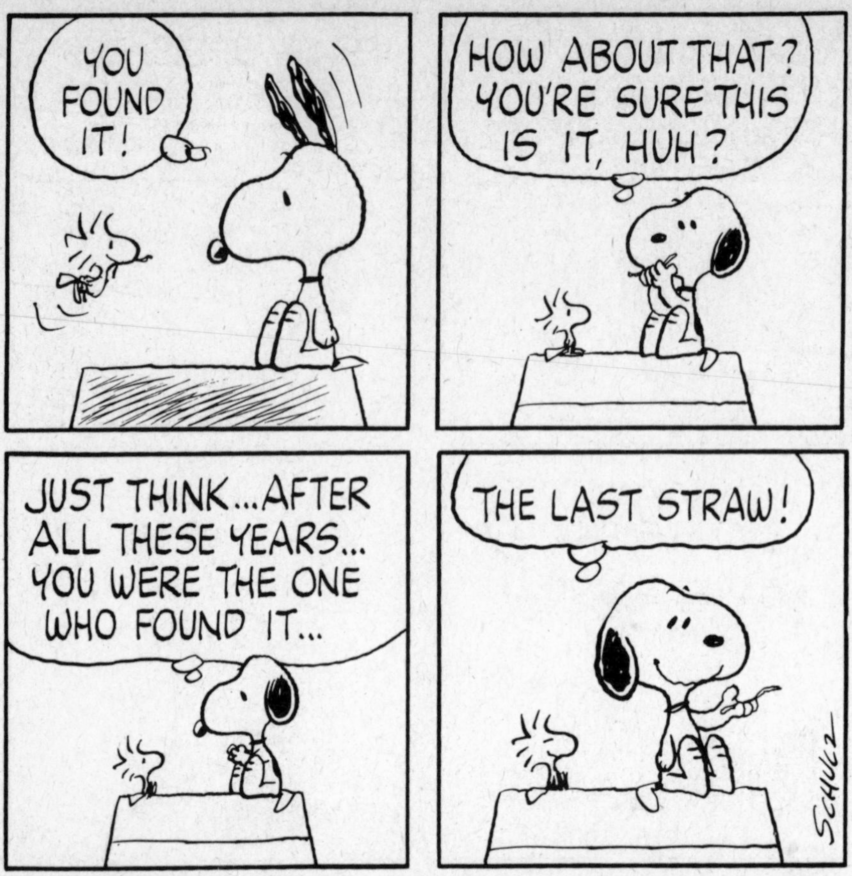
YOU FOUND IT!
HOW ABOUT THAT? YOU'RE SURE THIS IS IT, HUH?
JUST THINK...AFTER ALL THESE YEARS... YOU WERE THE ONE WHO FOUND IT...
THE LAST STRAW!
SCHULZ

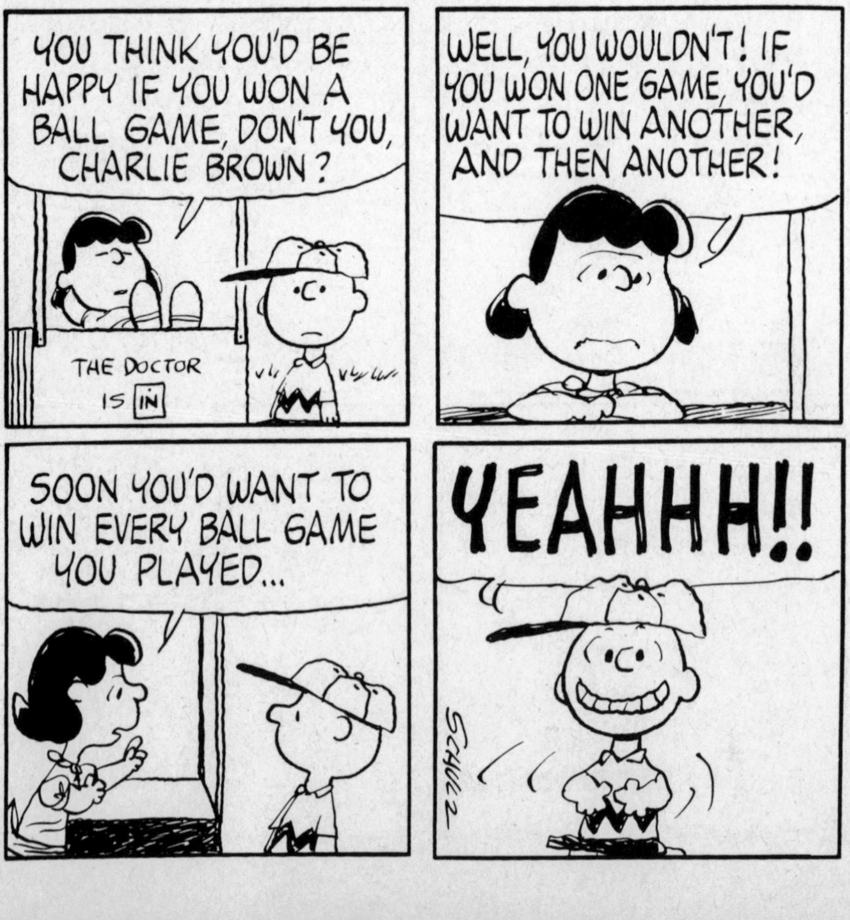
YOU THINK YOU'D BE HAPPY IF YOU WON A BALL GAME, DON'T YOU, CHARLIE BROWN?
THE DOCTOR IS IN
WELL, YOU WOULDN'T! IF YOU WON ONE GAME, YOU'D WANT TO WIN ANOTHER, AND THEN ANOTHER!
SOON YOU'D WANT TO WIN EVERY BALL GAME YOU PLAYED...
YEAHHH!!
SCHULZ

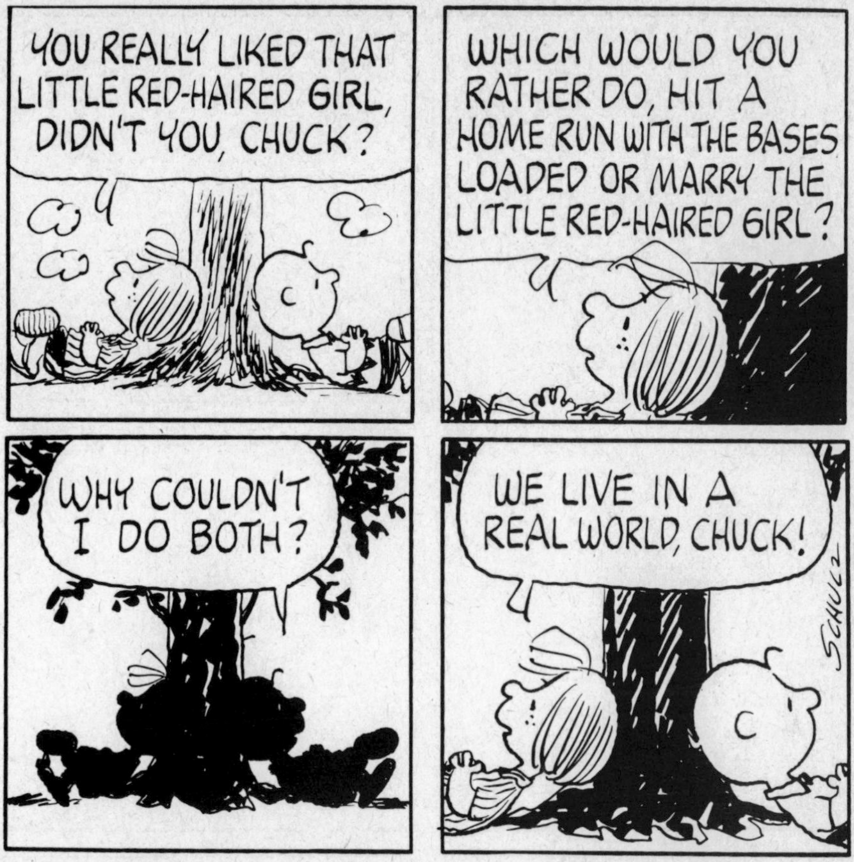
YOU REALLY LIKED THAT LITTLE RED-HAIRED GIRL, DIDN'T YOU, CHUCK?
WHICH WOULD YOU RATHER DO, HIT A HOME RUN WITH THE BASES LOADED OR MARRY THE LITTLE RED-HAIRED GIRL?
WHY COULDN'T I DO BOTH?
WE LIVE IN A REAL WORLD, CHUCK!
SCHULZ

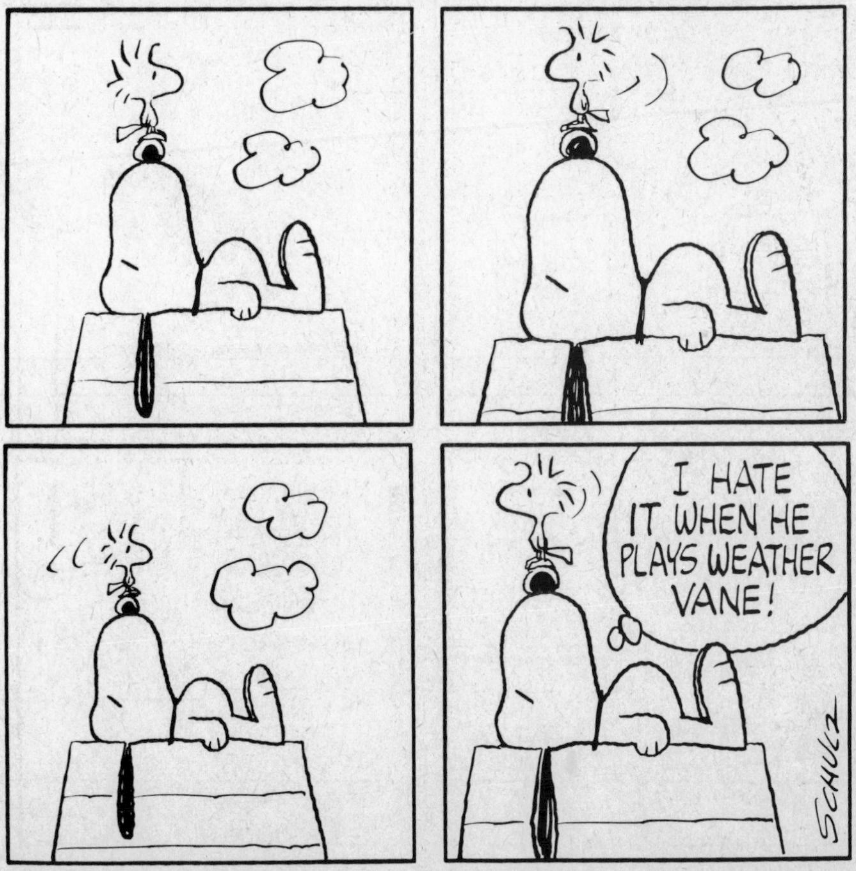
I HATE IT WHEN HE PLAYS WEATHER VANE!
SCHULZ

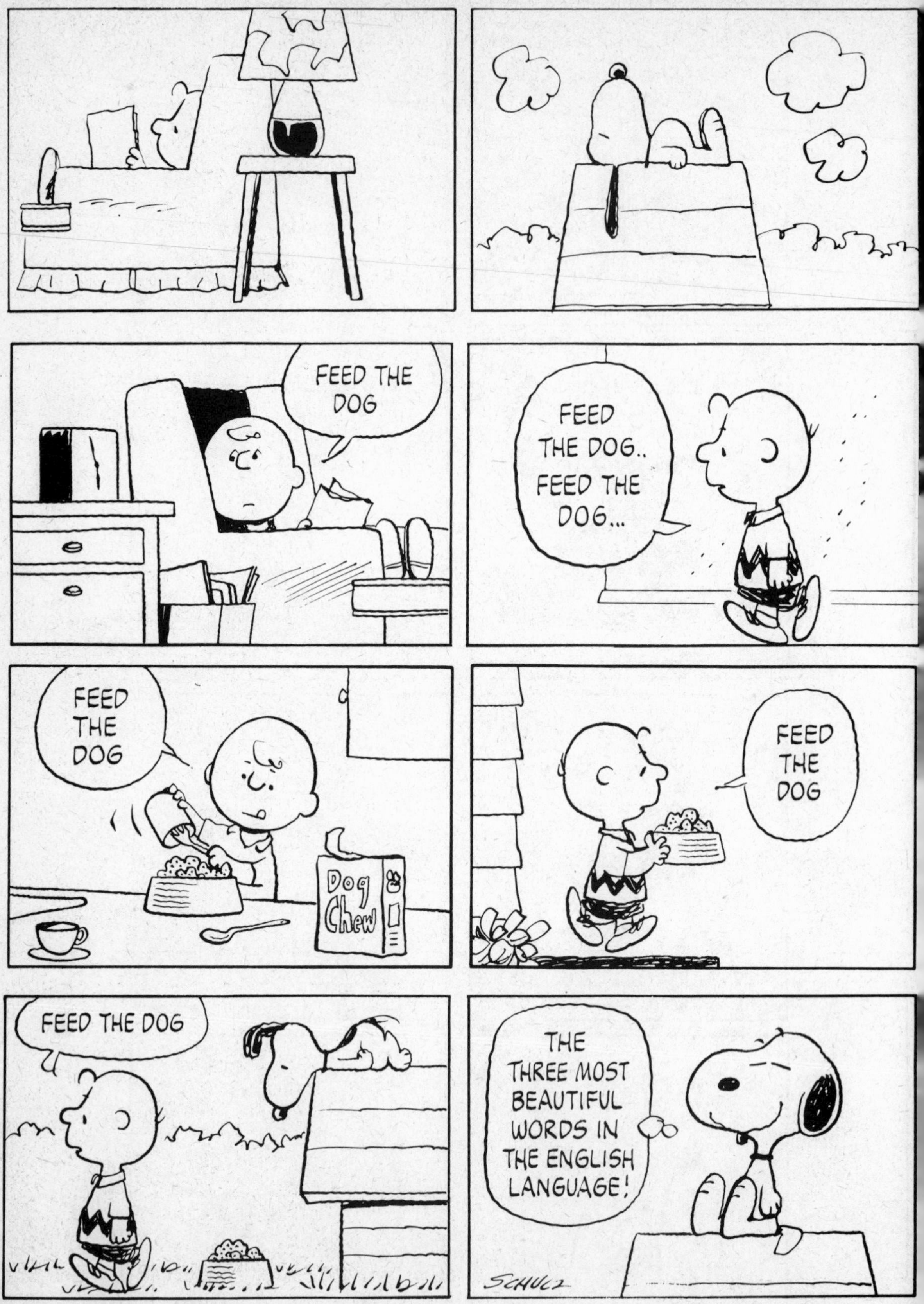
FEED THE DOG
FEED THE DOG.. FEED THE DOG...
FEED THE DOG
FEED THE DOG
FEED THE DOG
THE THREE MOST BEAUTIFUL WORDS IN THE ENGLISH LANGUAGE!
Dog Chew
SCHULZ

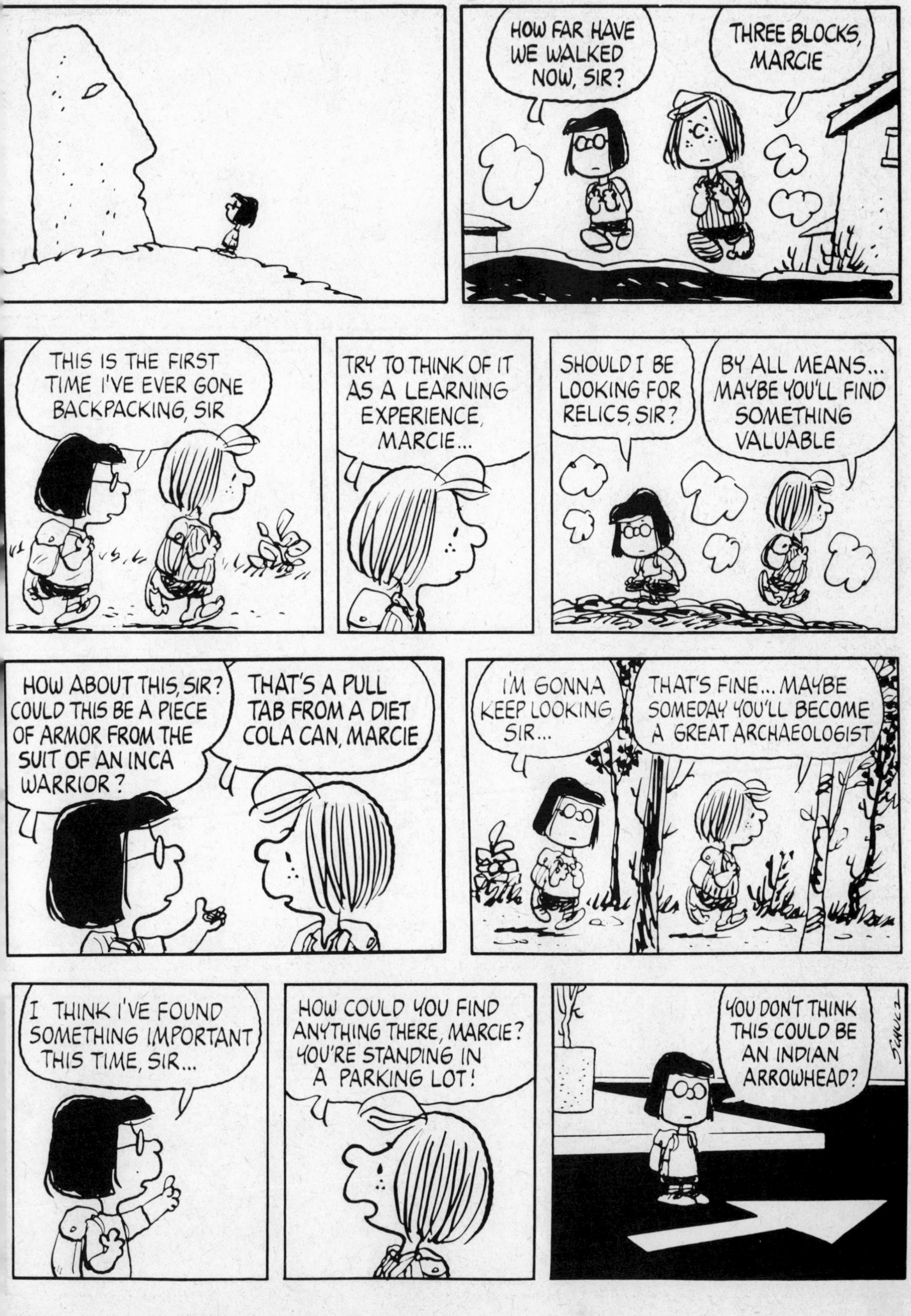
HOW FAR HAVE WE WALKED NOW, SIR?
THREE BLOCKS, MARCIE
THIS IS THE FIRST TIME I'VE EVER GONE BACKPACKING, SIR
TRY TO THINK OF IT AS A LEARNING EXPERIENCE, MARCIE...
SHOULD I BE LOOKING FOR RELICS, SIR?
BY ALL MEANS... MAYBE YOU'LL FIND SOMETHING VALUABLE
HOW ABOUT THIS, SIR? COULD THIS BE A PIECE OF ARMOR FROM THE SUIT OF AN INCA WARRIOR?
THAT'S A PULL TAB FROM A DIET COLA CAN, MARCIE
I'M GONNA KEEP LOOKING SIR...
THAT'S FINE... MAYBE SOMEDAY YOU'LL BECOME A GREAT ARCHAEOLOGIST
I THINK I'VE FOUND SOMETHING IMPORTANT THIS TIME, SIR...
HOW COULD YOU FIND ANYTHING THERE, MARCIE? YOU'RE STANDING IN A PARKING LOT!
YOU DON'T THINK THIS COULD BE AN INDIAN ARROWHEAD?
SCHULZ

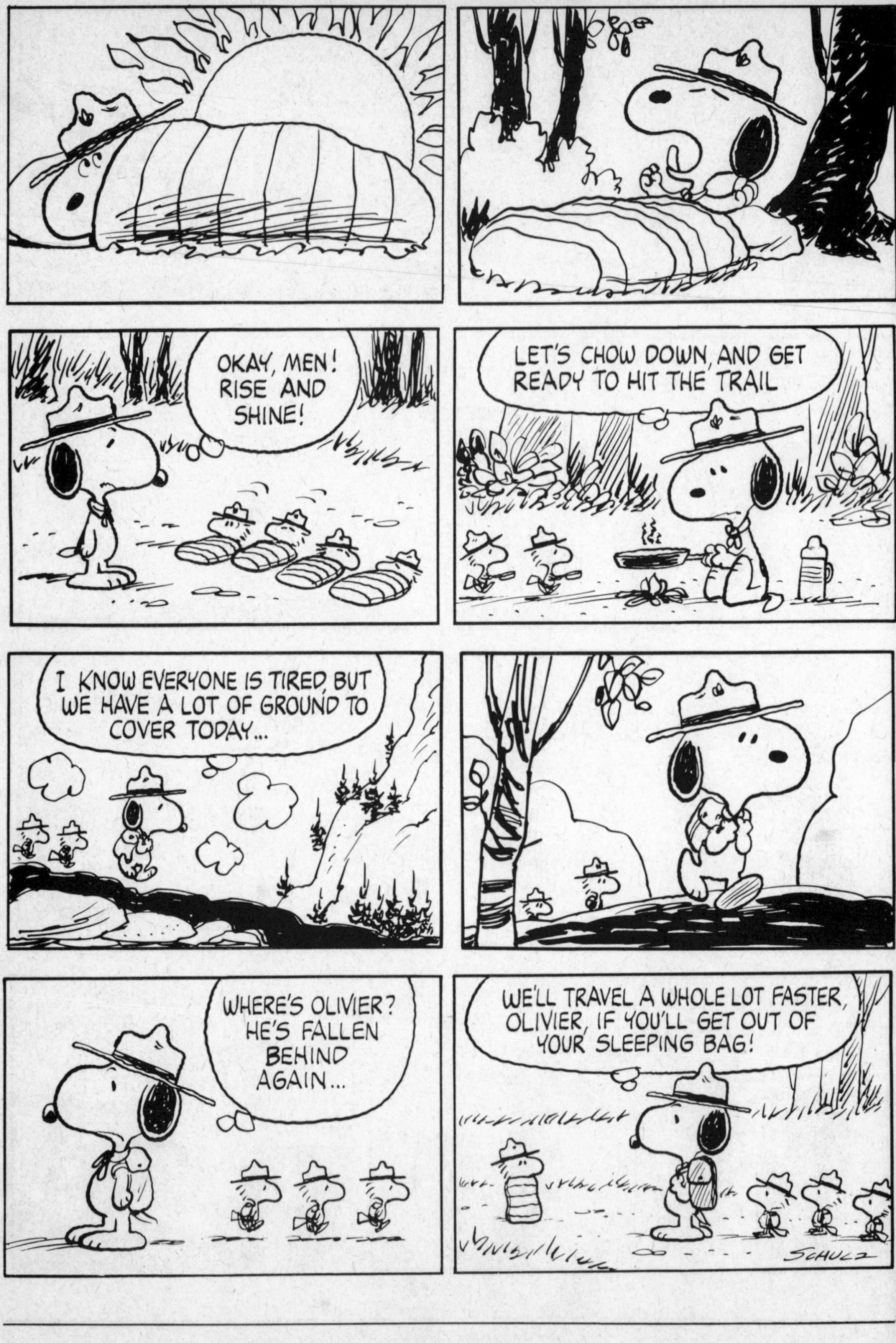
OKAY, MEN! RISE AND SHINE!
LET'S CHOW DOWN, AND GET READY TO HIT THE TRAIL
I KNOW EVERYONE IS TIRED, BUT WE HAVE A LOT OF GROUND TO COVER TODAY...
WHERE'S OLIVIER? HE'S FALLEN BEHIND AGAIN...
WE'LL TRAVEL A WHOLE LOT FASTER, OLIVIER, IF YOU'LL GET OUT OF YOUR SLEEPING BAG!
SCHULZ

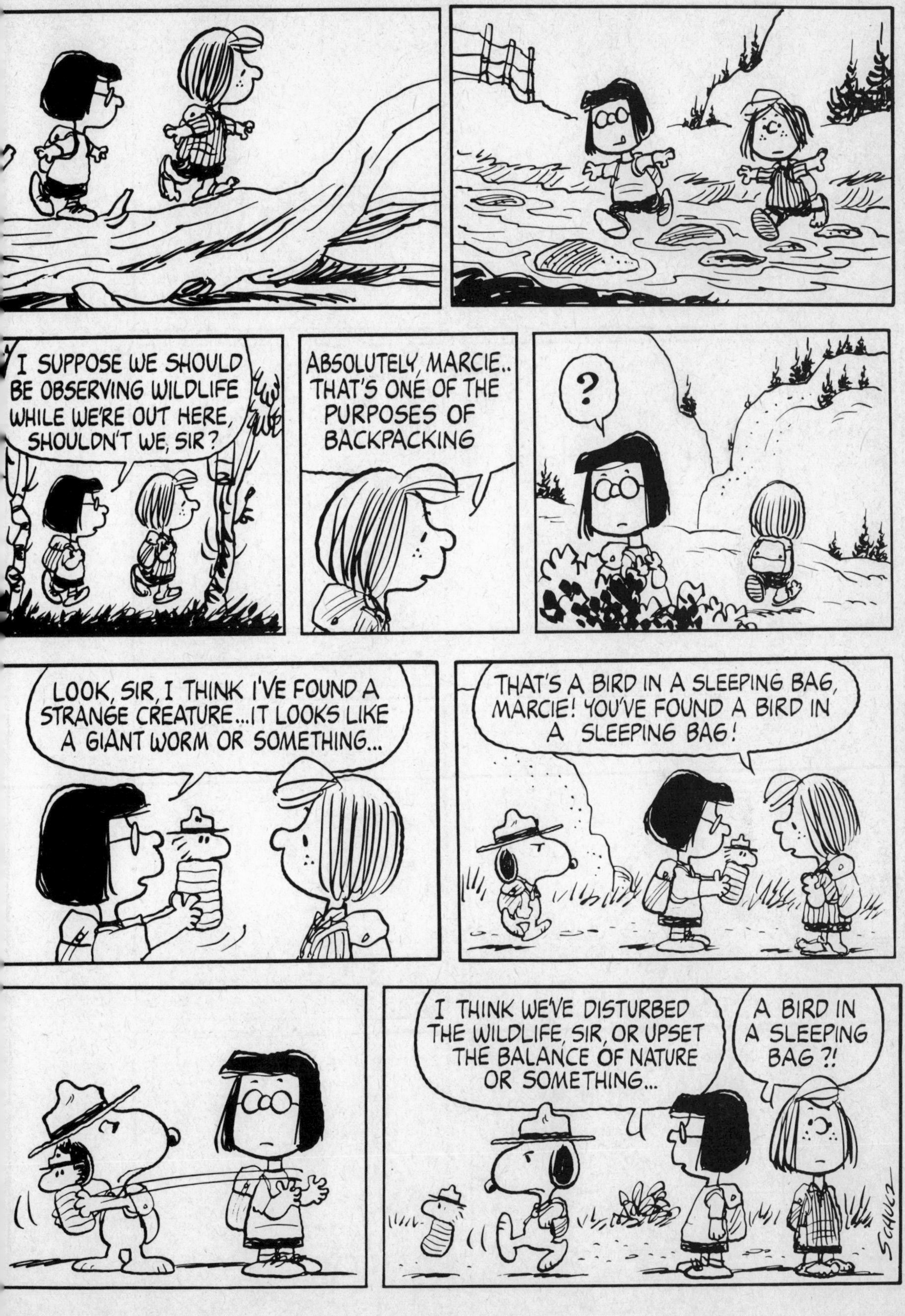
I SUPPOSE WE SHOULD BE OBSERVING WILDLIFE WHILE WE'RE OUT HERE, SHOULDN'T WE, SIR?
ABSOLUTELY, MARCIE.. THAT'S ONE OF THE PURPOSES OF BACKPACKING
?
LOOK, SIR, I THINK I'VE FOUND A STRANGE CREATURE...IT LOOKS LIKE A GIANT WORM OR SOMETHING...
THAT'S A BIRD IN A SLEEPING BAG, MARCIE! YOU'VE FOUND A BIRD IN A SLEEPING BAG!
I THINK WE'VE DISTURBED THE WILDLIFE, SIR, OR UPSET THE BALANCE OF NATURE OR SOMETHING...
A BIRD IN A SLEEPING BAG ?!
SCHULZ

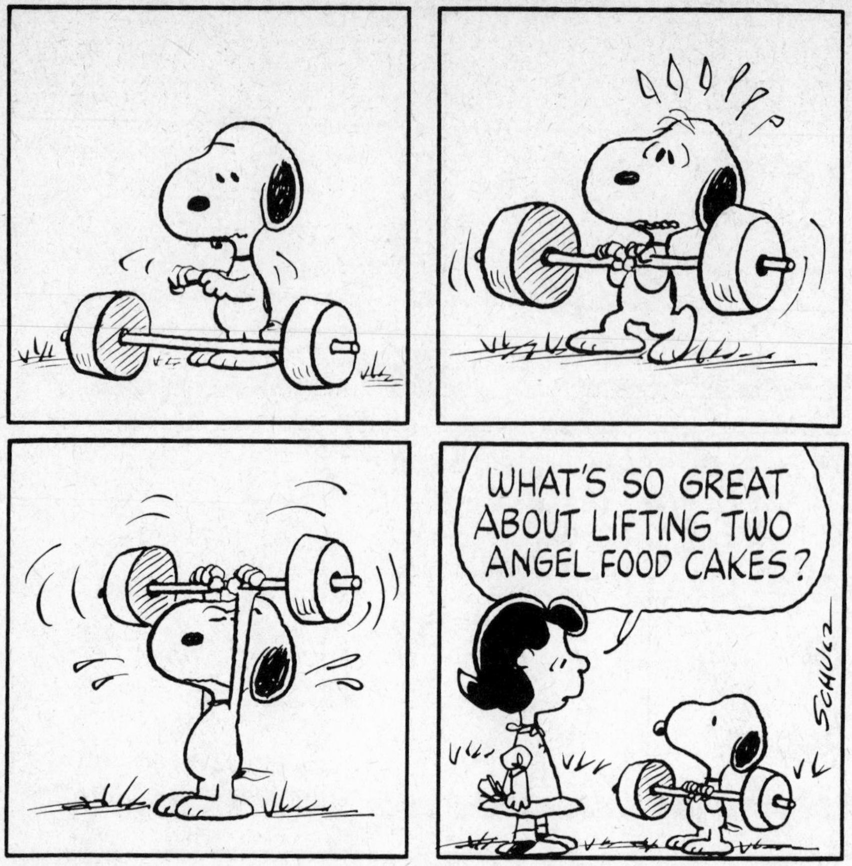
WHAT'S SO GREAT ABOUT LIFTING TWO ANGEL FOOD CAKES?
SCHULZ

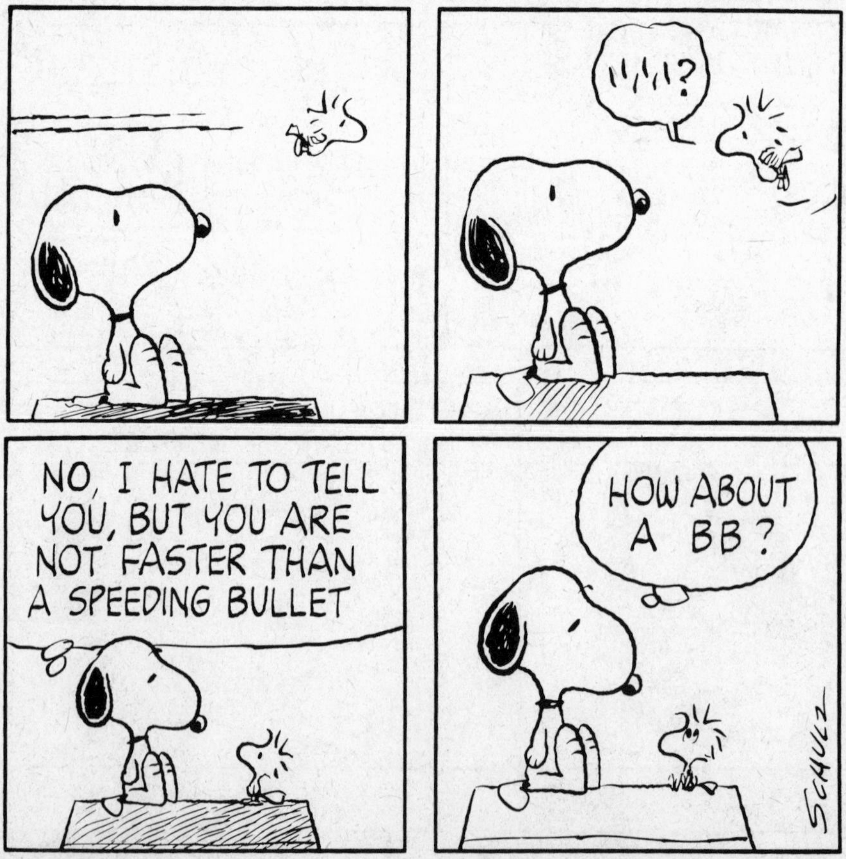
NO, I HATE TO TELL YOU, BUT YOU ARE NOT FASTER THAN A SPEEDING BULLET
HOW ABOUT A BB?
SCHULZ

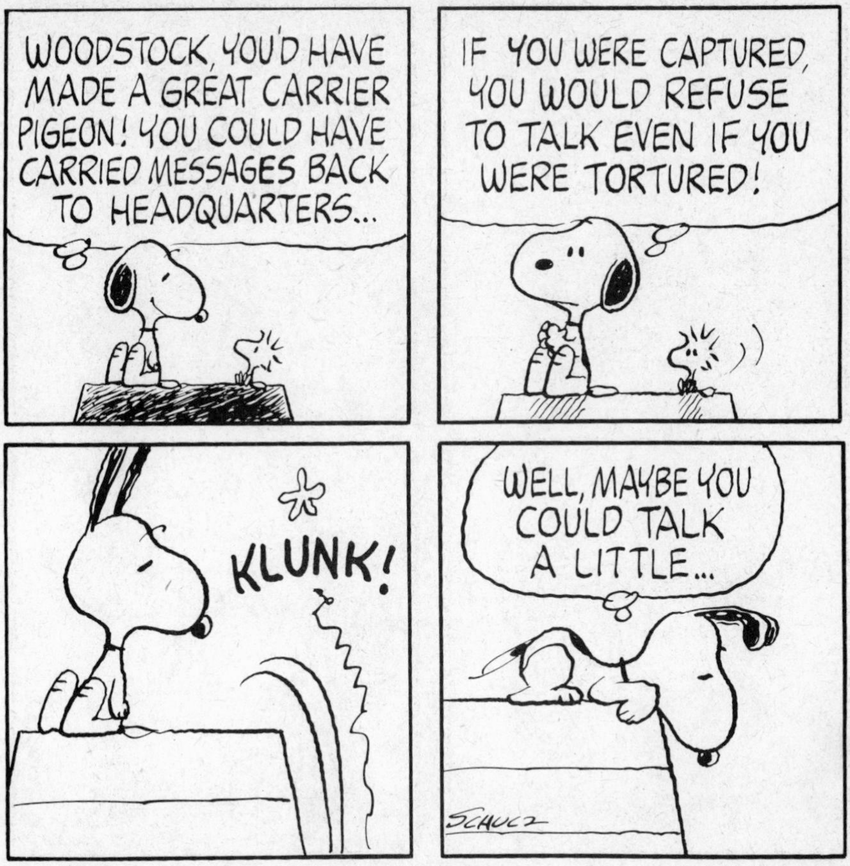
WOODSTOCK, YOU'D HAVE MADE A GREAT CARRIER PIGEON! YOU COULD HAVE CARRIED MESSAGES BACK TO HEADQUARTERS...
IF YOU WERE CAPTURED, YOU WOULD REFUSE TO TALK EVEN IF YOU WERE TORTURED!
KLUNK!
WELL, MAYBE YOU COULD TALK A LITTLE...
SCHULZ

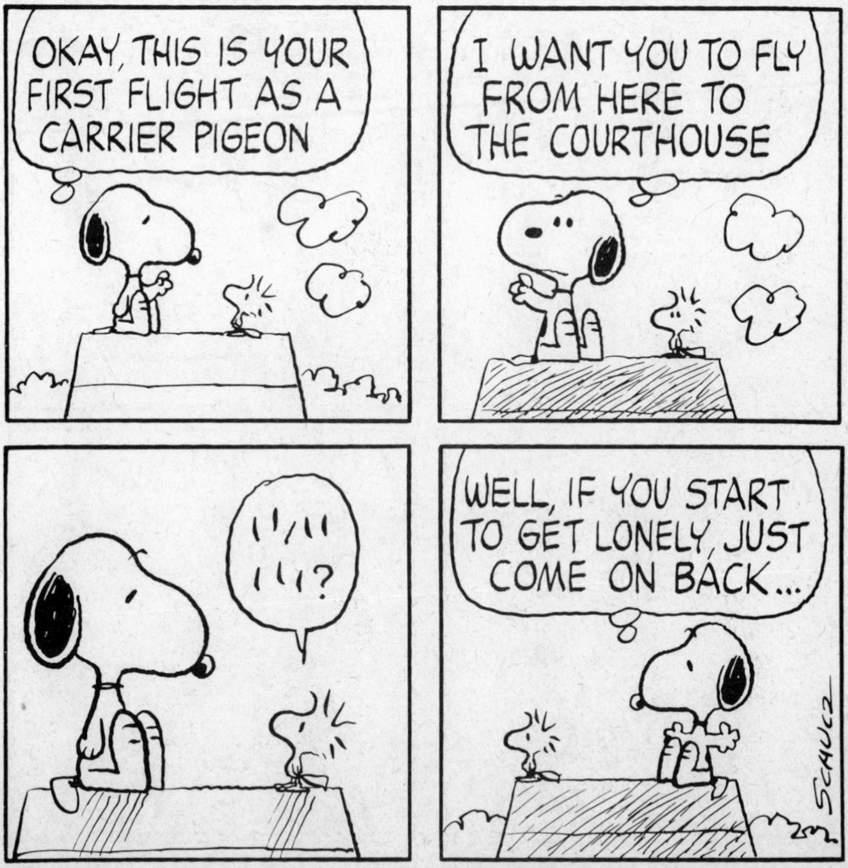
OKAY, THIS IS YOUR FIRST FLIGHT AS A CARRIER PIGEON
I WANT YOU TO FLY FROM HERE TO THE COURTHOUSE
WELL, IF YOU START TO GET LONELY, JUST COME ON BACK...
SCHULZ

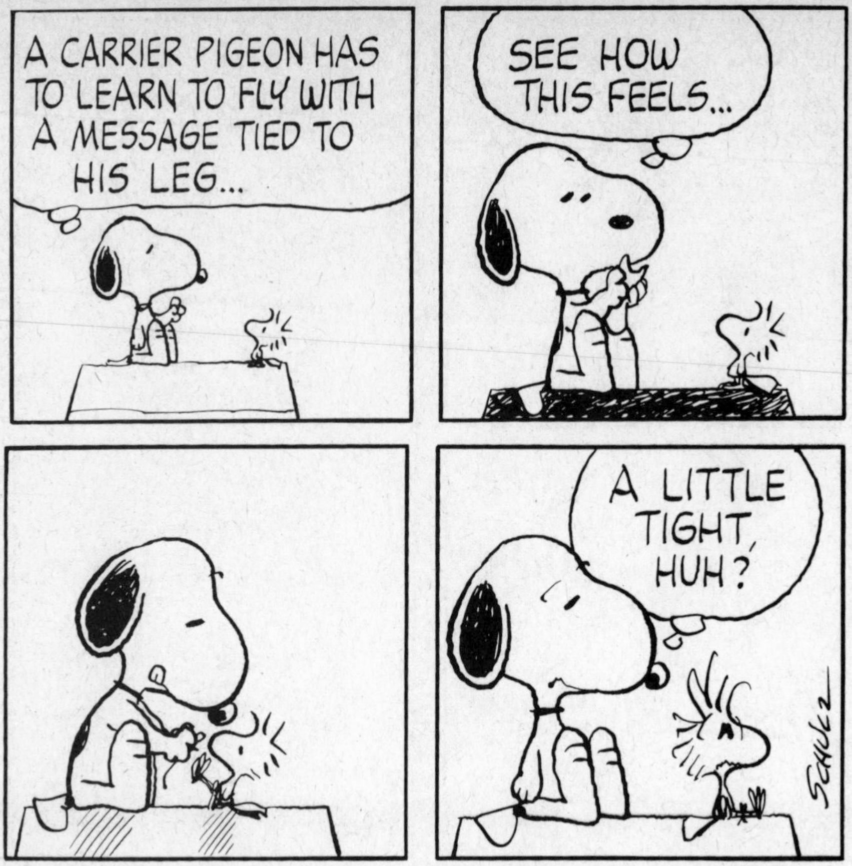
A CARRIER PIGEON HAS TO LEARN TO FLY WITH A MESSAGE TIED TO HIS LEG...
SEE HOW THIS FEELS...
A LITTLE TIGHT, HUH?
SCHULZ

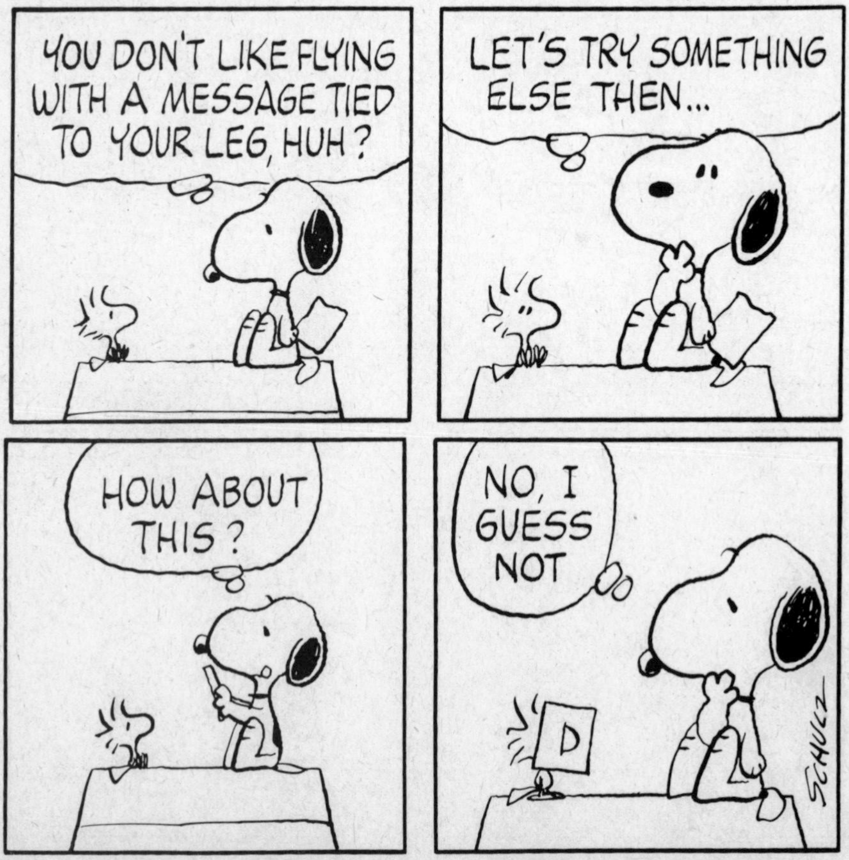
YOU DON'T LIKE FLYING WITH A MESSAGE TIED TO YOUR LEG, HUH?
LET'S TRY SOMETHING ELSE THEN...
HOW ABOUT THIS?
NO, I GUESS NOT
D
SCHULZ

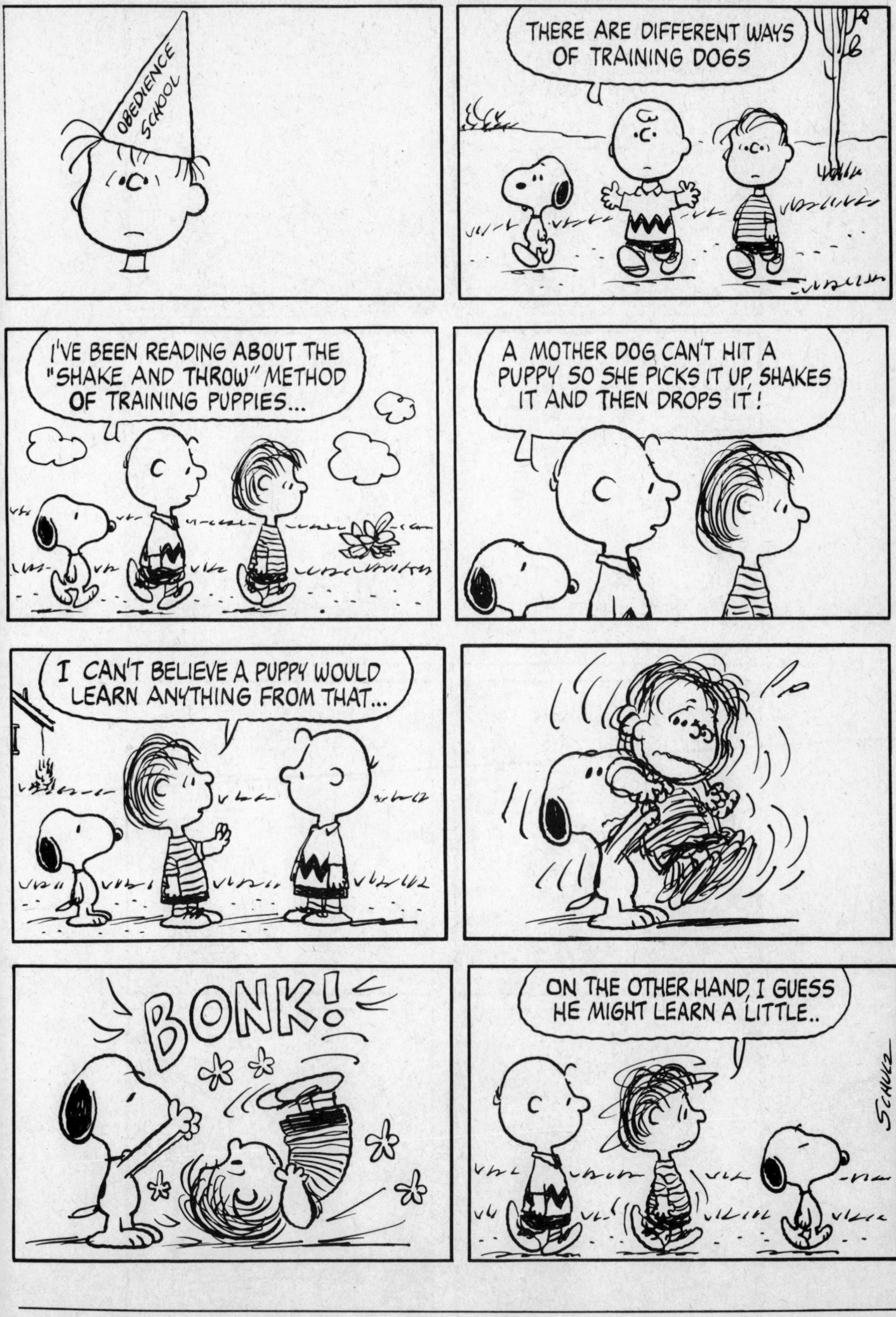
OBEDIENCE SCHOOL
THERE ARE DIFFERENT WAYS OF TRAINING DOGS
I'VE BEEN READING ABOUT THE "SHAKE AND THROW" METHOD OF TRAINING PUPPIES...
A MOTHER DOG CAN'T HIT A PUPPY SO SHE PICKS IT UP, SHAKES IT AND THEN DROPS IT!
I CAN'T BELIEVE A PUPPY WOULD LEARN ANYTHING FROM THAT...
BONK!
ON THE OTHER HAND, I GUESS HE MIGHT LEARN A LITTLE..
SCHULZ

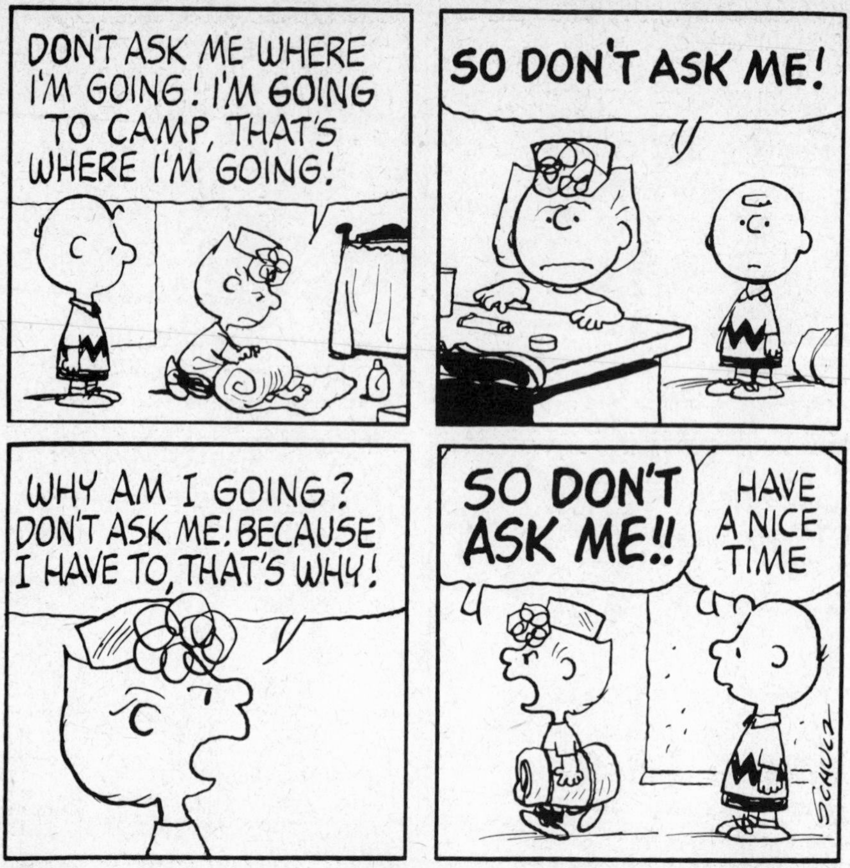
DON'T ASK ME WHERE I'M GOING! I'M GOING TO CAMP, THAT'S WHERE I'M GOING!
SO DON'T ASK ME!
WHY AM I GOING? DON'T ASK ME! BECAUSE I HAVE TO, THAT'S WHY!
SO DON'T ASK ME!!
HAVE A NICE TIME
SCHULZ

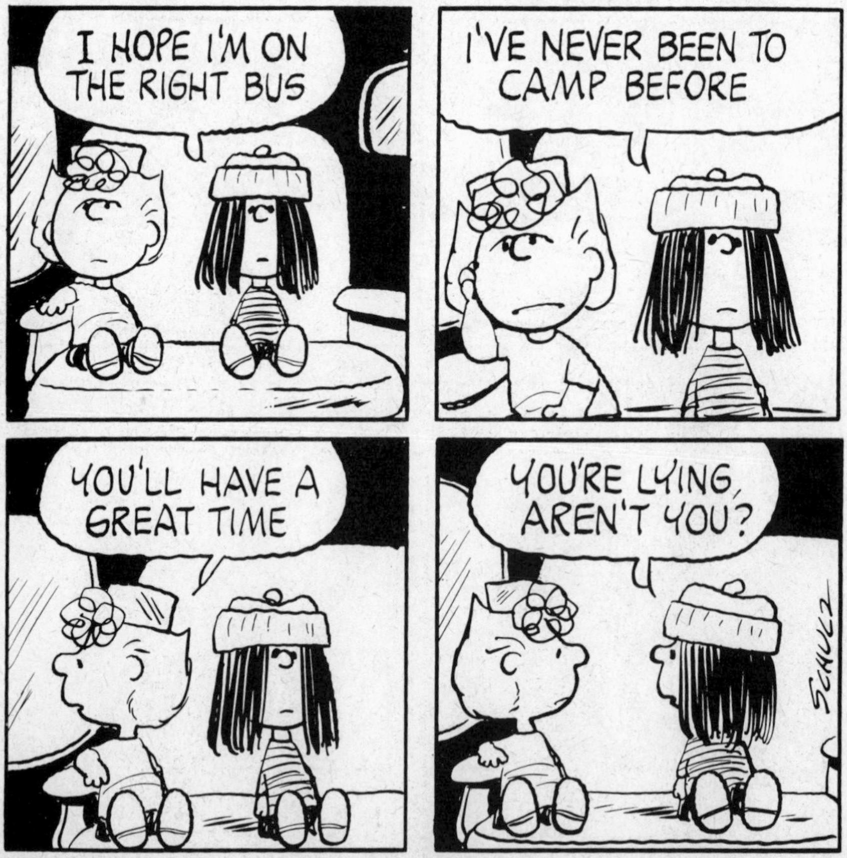
I HOPE I'M ON THE RIGHT BUS
I'VE NEVER BEEN TO CAMP BEFORE
YOU'LL HAVE A GREAT TIME
YOU'RE LYING, AREN'T YOU?
SCHULZ

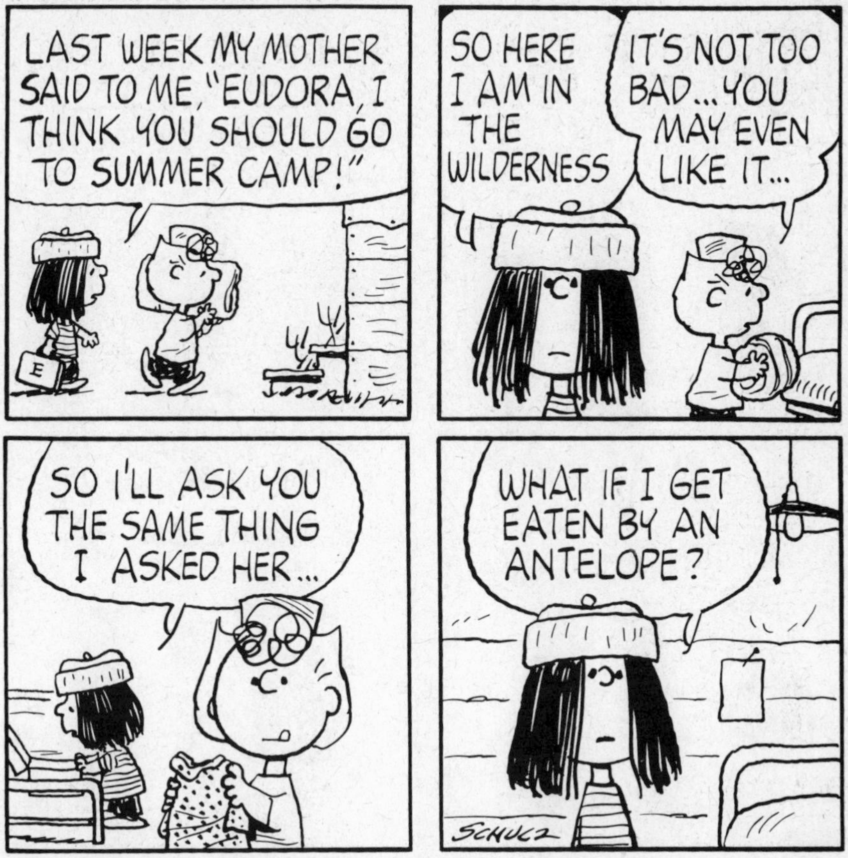
LAST WEEK MY MOTHER SAID TO ME, "EUDORA, I THINK YOU SHOULD GO TO SUMMER CAMP!"
SO HERE I AM IN THE WILDERNESS
IT'S NOT TOO BAD... YOU MAY EVEN LIKE IT...
SO I'LL ASK YOU THE SAME THING I ASKED HER...
WHAT IF I GET EATEN BY AN ANTELOPE?
SCHULZ

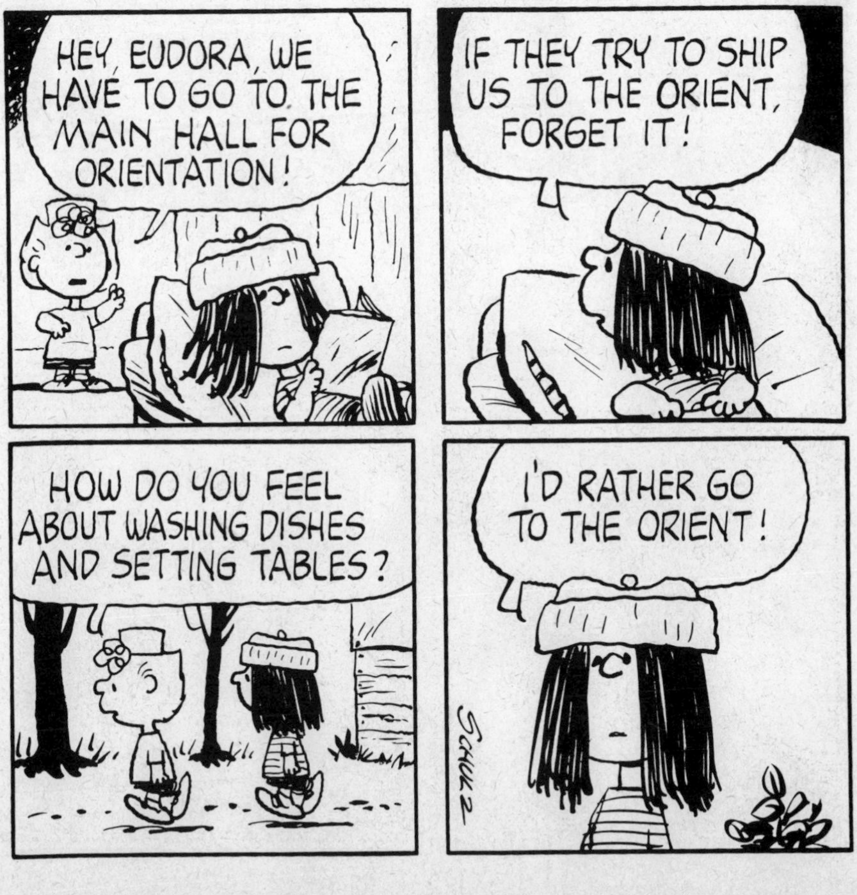
HEY, EUDORA, WE HAVE TO GO TO THE MAIN HALL FOR ORIENTATION!
IF THEY TRY TO SHIP US TO THE ORIENT, FORGET IT!
HOW DO YOU FEEL ABOUT WASHING DISHES AND SETTING TABLES?
I'D RATHER GO TO THE ORIENT!
SCHULZ

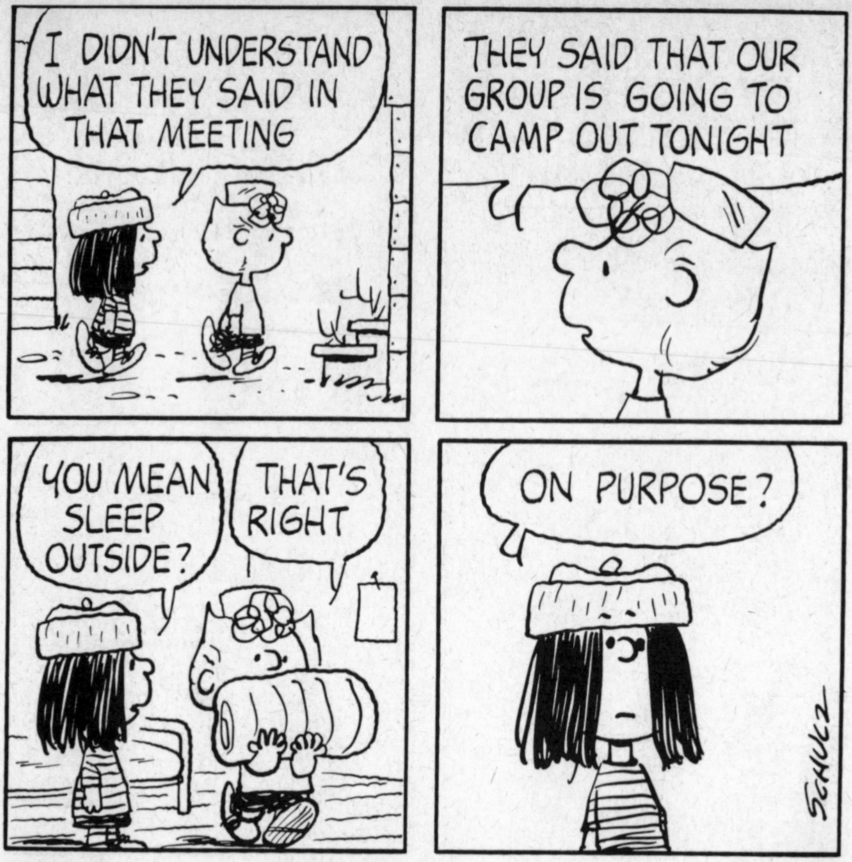
I DIDN'T UNDERSTAND WHAT THEY SAID IN THAT MEETING
THEY SAID THAT OUR GROUP IS GOING TO CAMP OUT TONIGHT
YOU MEAN SLEEP OUTSIDE?
THAT'S RIGHT
ON PURPOSE?
SCHULZ

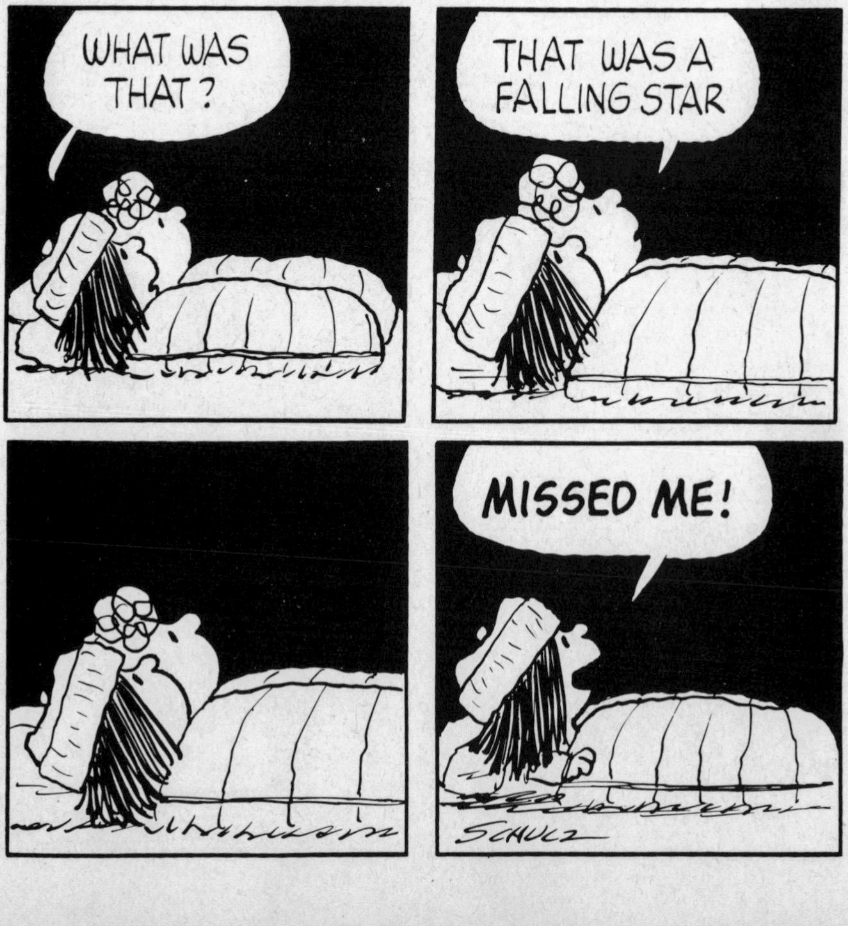
WHAT WAS THAT?
THAT WAS A FALLING STAR
MISSED ME!
SCHULZ

SALLY, DO YOU BELIEVE IN UFO'S?
NO!
I THINK THE WHOLE IDEA OF CREATURES OF SUPERIOR INTELLIGENCE TRYING TO CONTACT US IS STUPID!
MY MOTHER TRIED TO CALL ME ON THE PHONE THIS MORNING
SCHULZ

IF WE BECAME LOST IN THE WOODS, HOW LONG COULD WE GO WITHOUT REAL FOOD?
I'LL BET WE COULD GO FOR A MONTH WITHOUT REAL FOOD
HOW ABOUT JUNK FOOD?
ELEVEN MINUTES!
SCHULZ

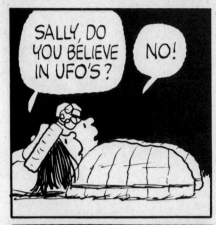

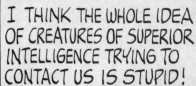

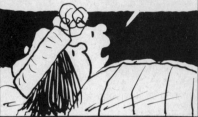

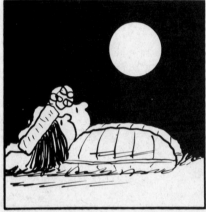

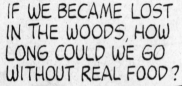

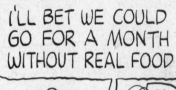

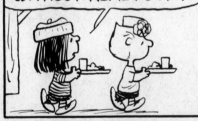

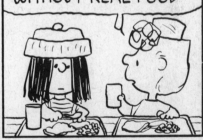

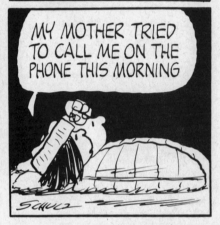

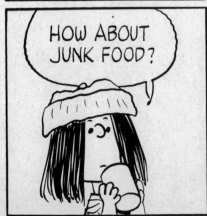

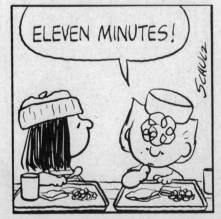

EUDORA, ARE YOU CRYING? WHAT'S THE MATTER?
I NEVER WANTED TO COME TO THIS CAMP
BUT I'M NOT AS LONELY AS I THOUGHT I WAS GOING TO BE
I'M ONLY CRYING WITH ONE EYE
SCHULZ

YOU'RE GOING TO TAKE ME FISHING? THAT'S GREAT! I DON'T KNOW ANYTHING ABOUT FISHING
WELL, WHAT WE'LL DO IS, WE'LL GO DOWN ON THE DOCK, AND SEE IF THERE ARE ANY FISH IN THE LAKE, AND THEN...
I SEE ONE!
YOU JUST PADDLE AROUND THERE AWHILE, AND I'LL EXPLAIN ABOUT THESE POLES...
SCHULZ

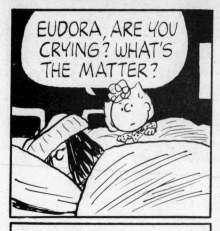

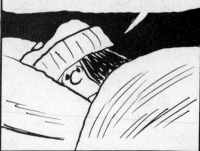

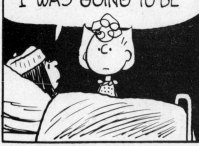

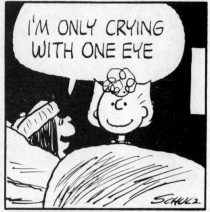

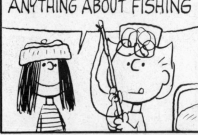

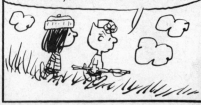

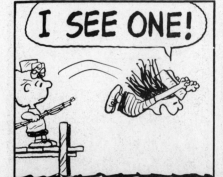

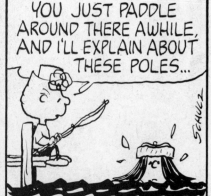

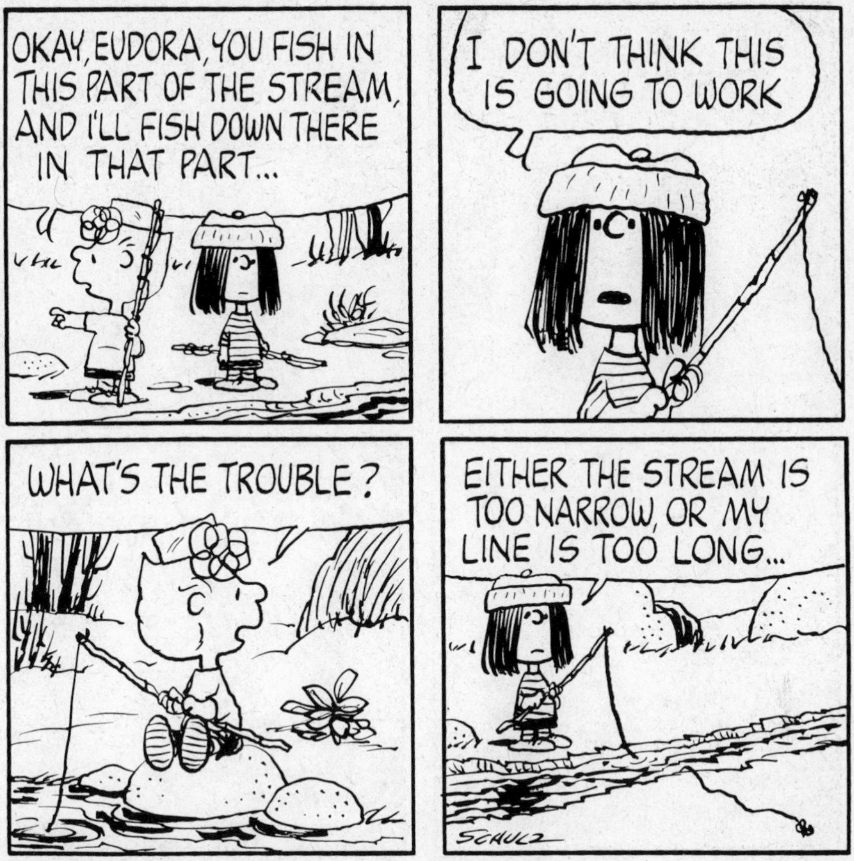
OKAY, EUDORA, YOU FISH IN THIS PART OF THE STREAM, AND I'LL FISH DOWN THERE IN THAT PART...
I DON'T THINK THIS IS GOING TO WORK
WHAT'S THE TROUBLE?
EITHER THE STREAM IS TOO NARROW, OR MY LINE IS TOO LONG...
SCHULZ

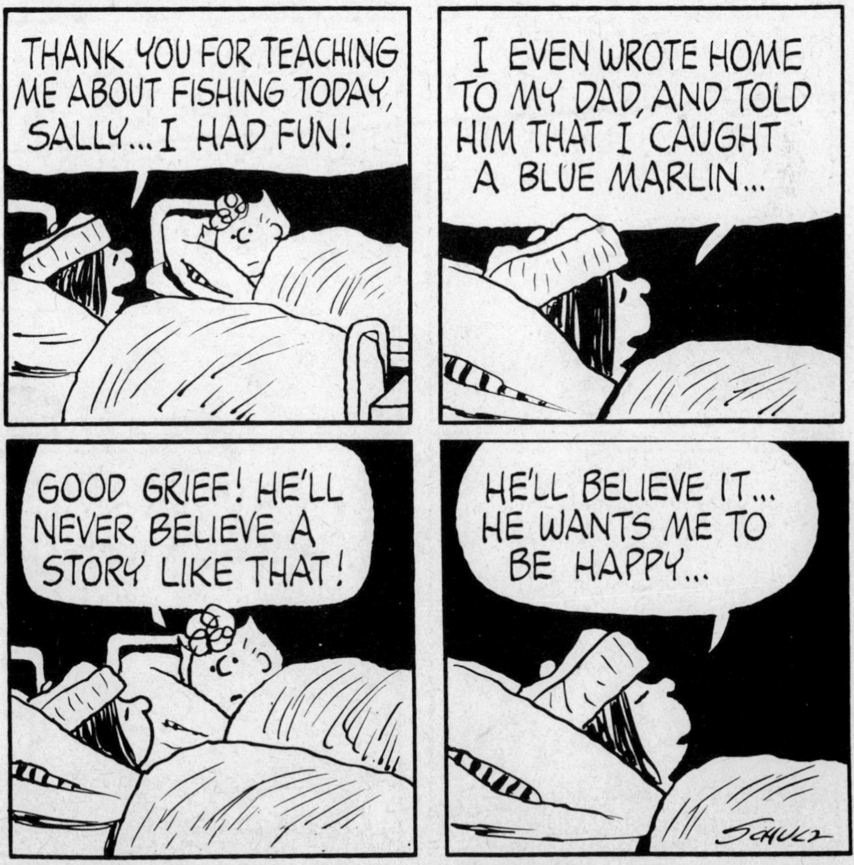
THANK YOU FOR TEACHING ME ABOUT FISHING TODAY, SALLY... I HAD FUN!
I EVEN WROTE HOME TO MY DAD, AND TOLD HIM THAT I CAUGHT A BLUE MARLIN...
GOOD GRIEF! HE'LL NEVER BELIEVE A STORY LIKE THAT!
HE'LL BELIEVE IT... HE WANTS ME TO BE HAPPY...
SCHULZ

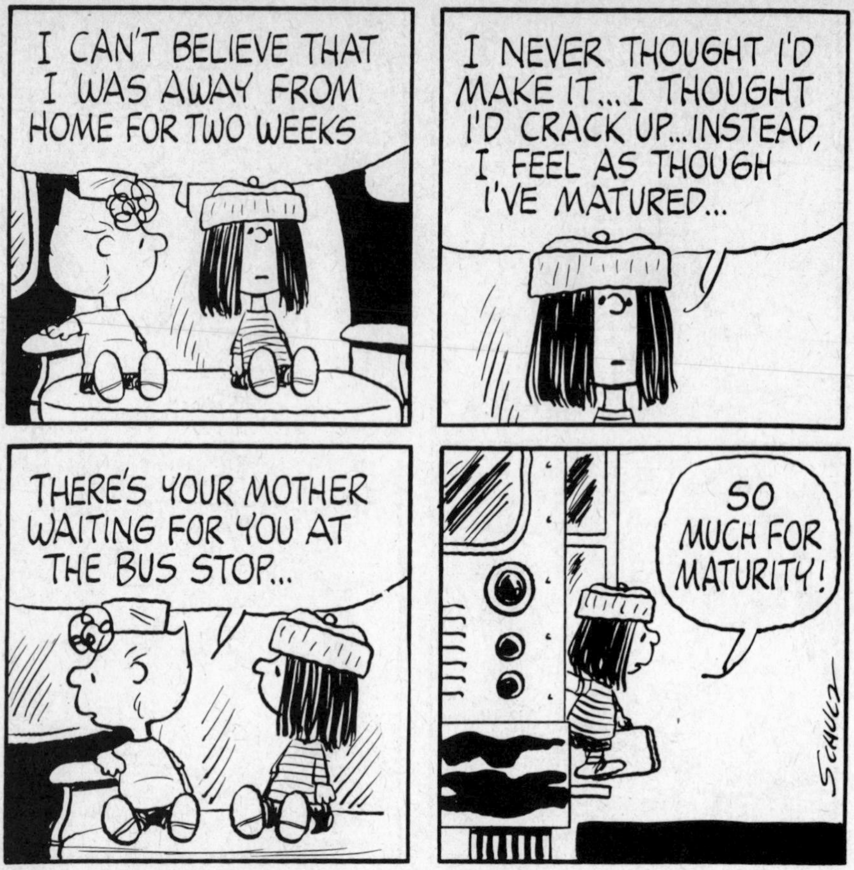
I CAN'T BELIEVE THAT I WAS AWAY FROM HOME FOR TWO WEEKS
I NEVER THOUGHT I'D MAKE IT... I THOUGHT I'D CRACK UP...INSTEAD, I FEEL AS THOUGH I'VE MATURED...
THERE'S YOUR MOTHER WAITING FOR YOU AT THE BUS STOP...
SO MUCH FOR MATURITY!
SCHULZ

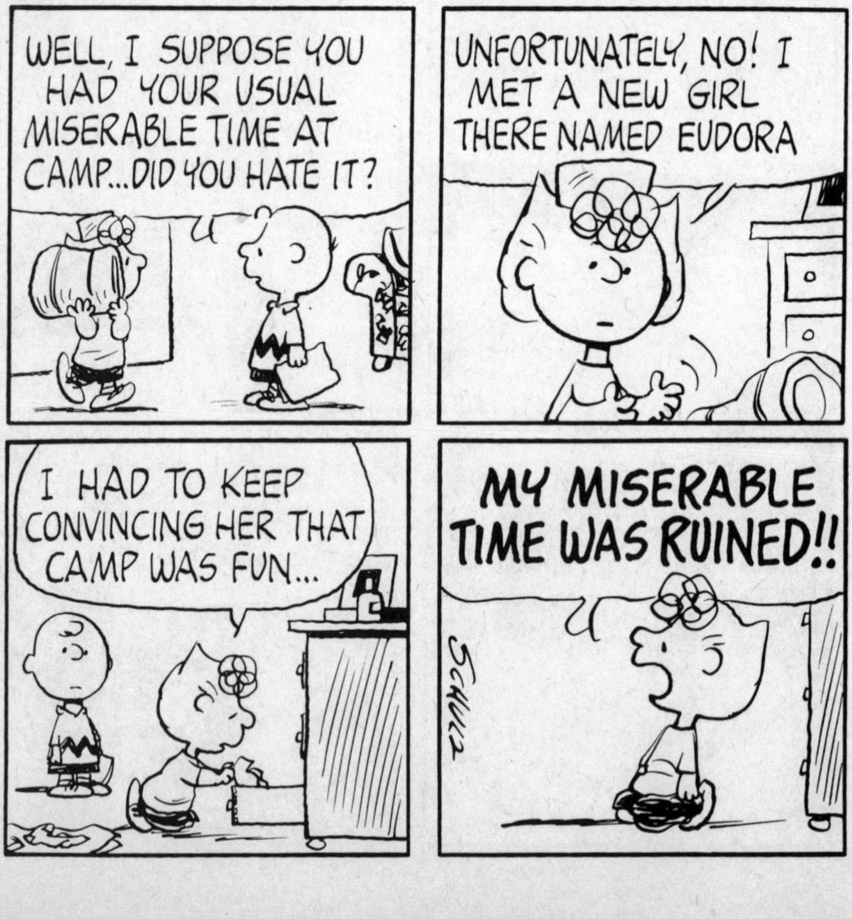
WELL, I SUPPOSE YOU HAD YOUR USUAL MISERABLE TIME AT CAMP...DID YOU HATE IT?
UNFORTUNATELY, NO! I MET A NEW GIRL THERE NAMED EUDORA
I HAD TO KEEP CONVINCING HER THAT CAMP WAS FUN...
MY MISERABLE TIME WAS RUINED!!
SCHULZ

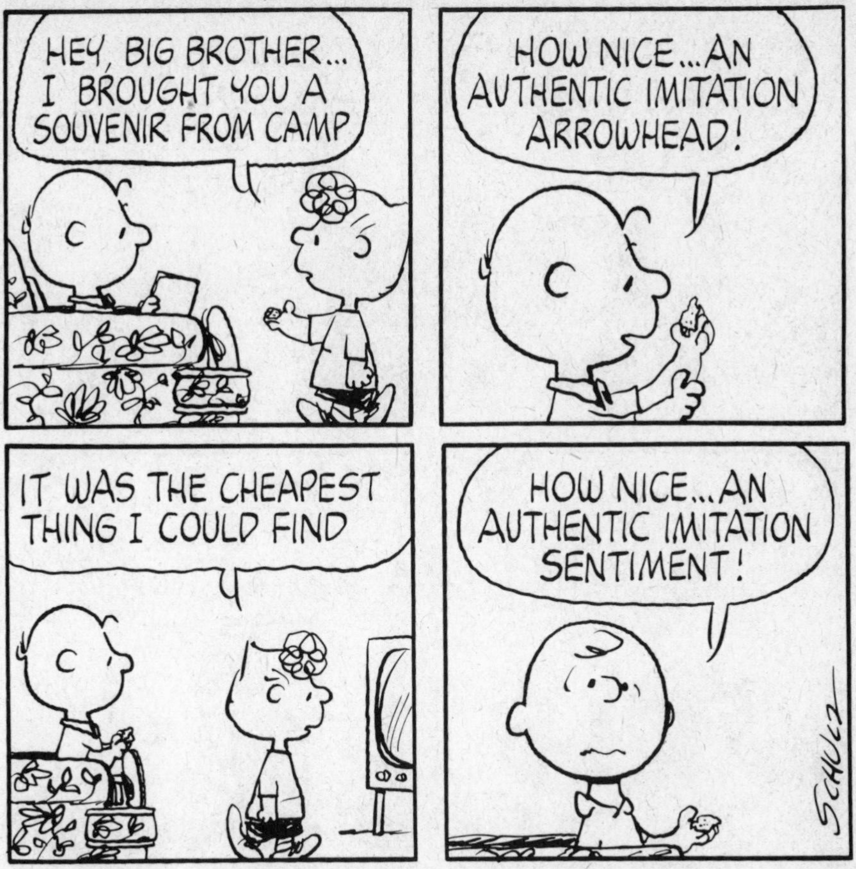
HEY, BIG BROTHER... I BROUGHT YOU A SOUVENIR FROM CAMP
HOW NICE...AN AUTHENTIC IMITATION ARROWHEAD!
IT WAS THE CHEAPEST THING I COULD FIND
HOW NICE...AN AUTHENTIC IMITATION SENTIMENT!
SCHULZ

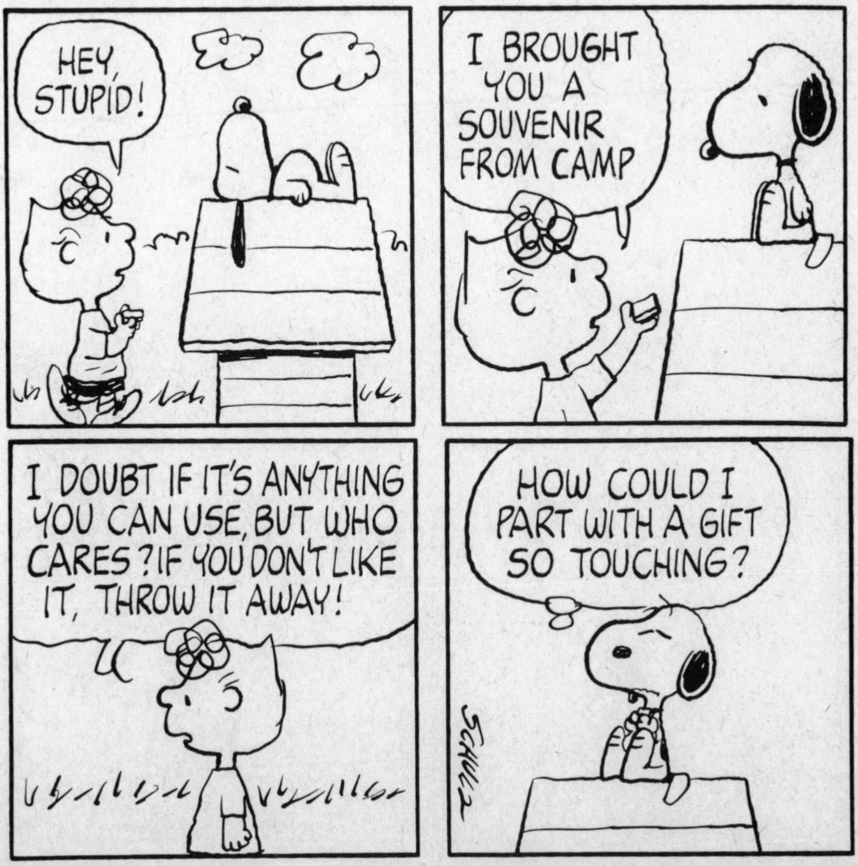
HEY, STUPID!
I BROUGHT YOU A SOUVENIR FROM CAMP
I DOUBT IF IT'S ANYTHING YOU CAN USE, BUT WHO CARES? IF YOU DON'T LIKE IT, THROW IT AWAY!
HOW COULD I PART WITH A GIFT SO TOUCHING?
SCHULZ

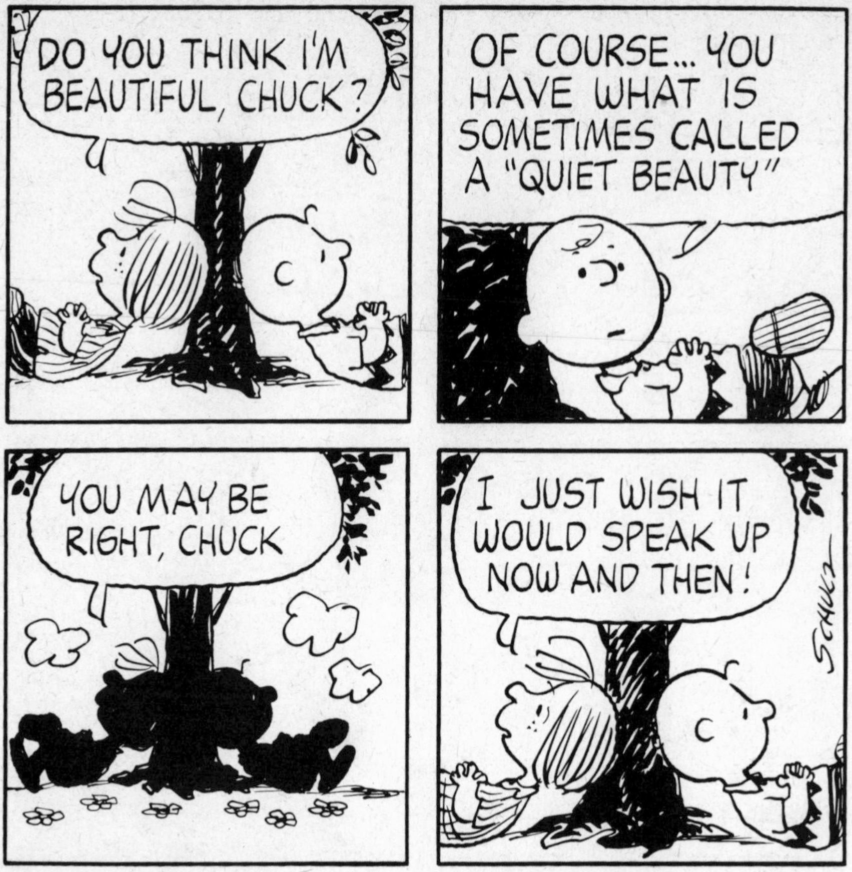
DO YOU THINK I'M BEAUTIFUL, CHUCK?
OF COURSE... YOU HAVE WHAT IS SOMETIMES CALLED A "QUIET BEAUTY"
YOU MAY BE RIGHT, CHUCK
I JUST WISH IT WOULD SPEAK UP NOW AND THEN!
SCHULZ

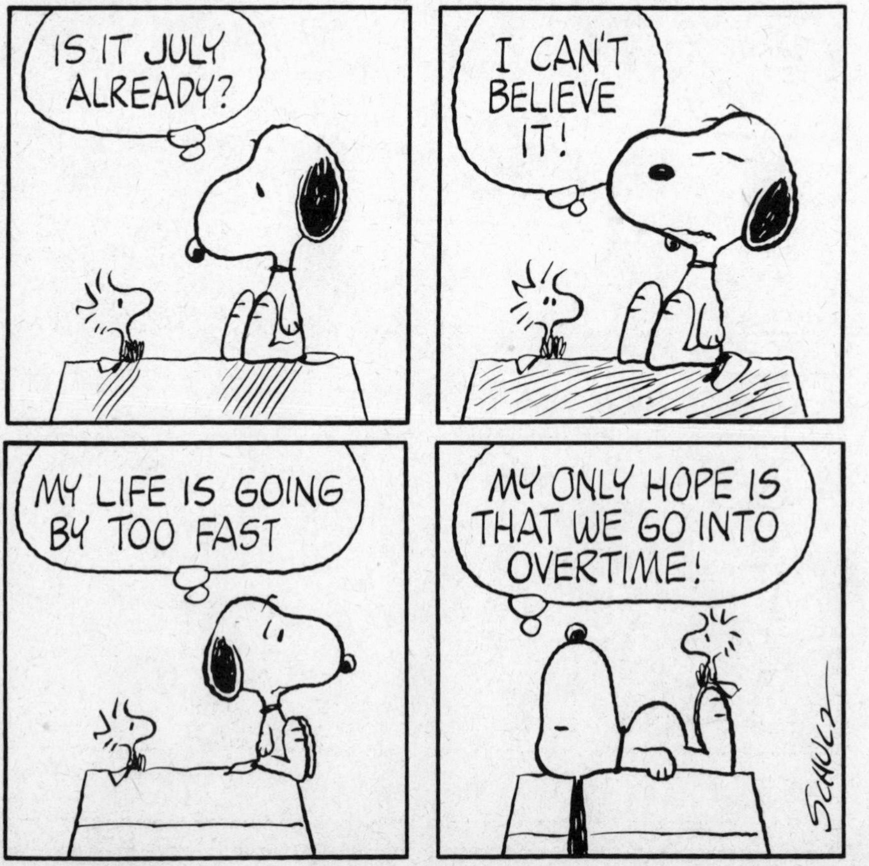
IS IT JULY ALREADY?
I CAN'T BELIEVE IT!
MY LIFE IS GOING BY TOO FAST
MY ONLY HOPE IS THAT WE GO INTO OVERTIME!
SCHULZ

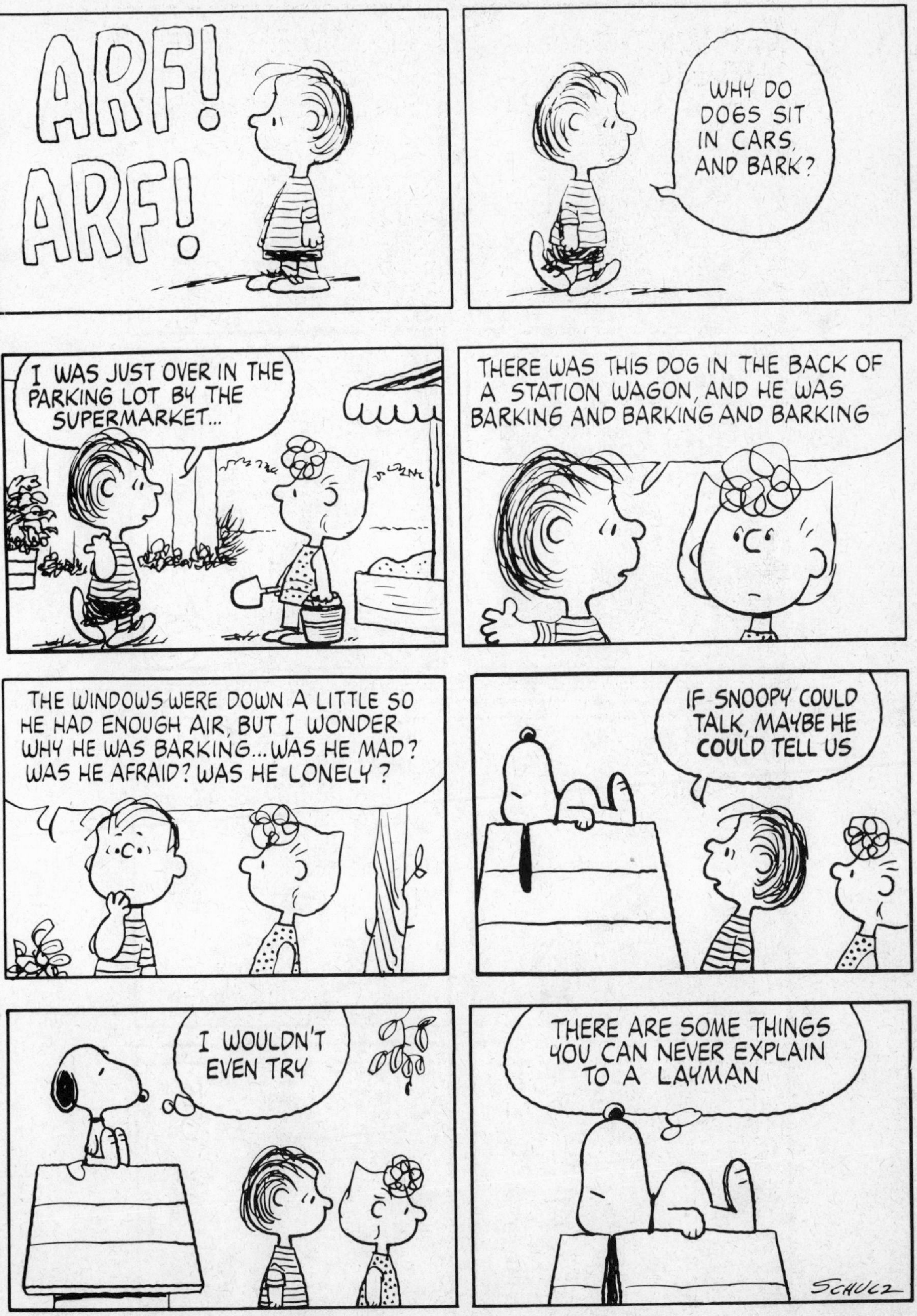
ARF! ARF!
WHY DO DOGS SIT IN CARS, AND BARK?
I WAS JUST OVER IN THE PARKING LOT BY THE SUPERMARKET...
THERE WAS THIS DOG IN THE BACK OF A STATION WAGON, AND HE WAS BARKING AND BARKING AND BARKING
THE WINDOWS WERE DOWN A LITTLE SO HE HAD ENOUGH AIR, BUT I WONDER WHY HE WAS BARKING...WAS HE MAD? WAS HE AFRAID? WAS HE LONELY?
IF SNOOPY COULD TALK, MAYBE HE COULD TELL US
I WOULDN'T EVEN TRY
THERE ARE SOME THINGS YOU CAN NEVER EXPLAIN TO A LAYMAN
SCHULZ

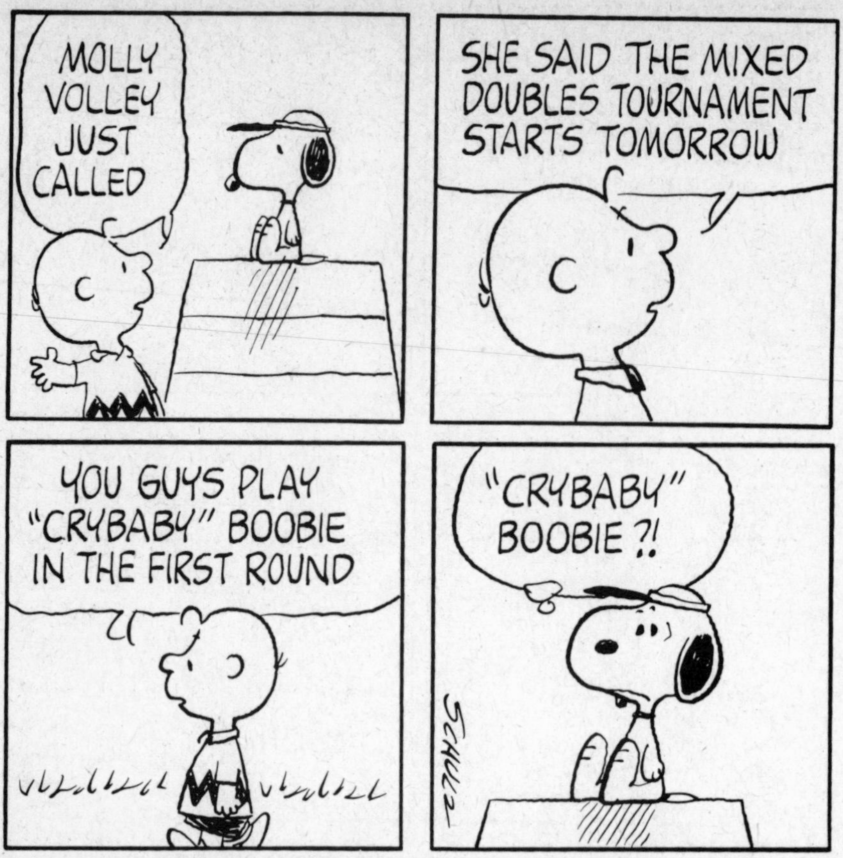
MOLLY VOLLEY JUST CALLED
SHE SAID THE MIXED DOUBLES TOURNAMENT STARTS TOMORROW
YOU GUYS PLAY "CRYBABY" BOOBIE IN THE FIRST ROUND
"CRYBABY" BOOBIE ?!
SCHULZ

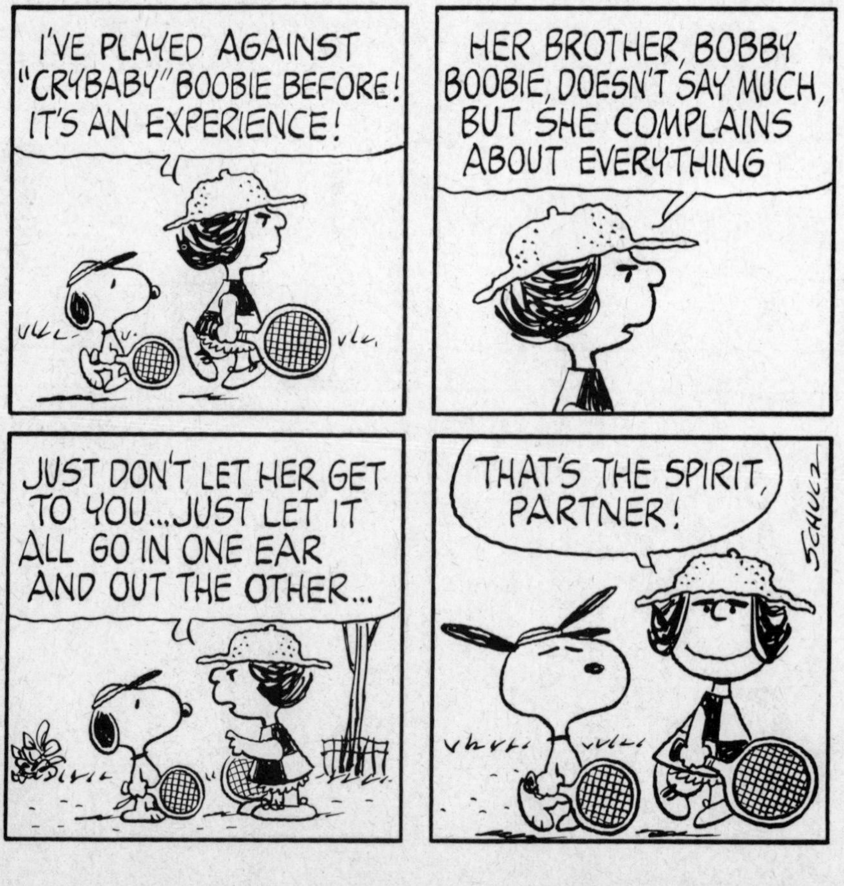
I'VE PLAYED AGAINST "CRYBABY" BOOBIE BEFORE! IT'S AN EXPERIENCE!
HER BROTHER, BOBBY BOOBIE, DOESN'T SAY MUCH, BUT SHE COMPLAINS ABOUT EVERYTHING
JUST DON'T LET HER GET TO YOU...JUST LET IT ALL GO IN ONE EAR AND OUT THE OTHER...
THAT'S THE SPIRIT, PARTNER!
SCHULZ

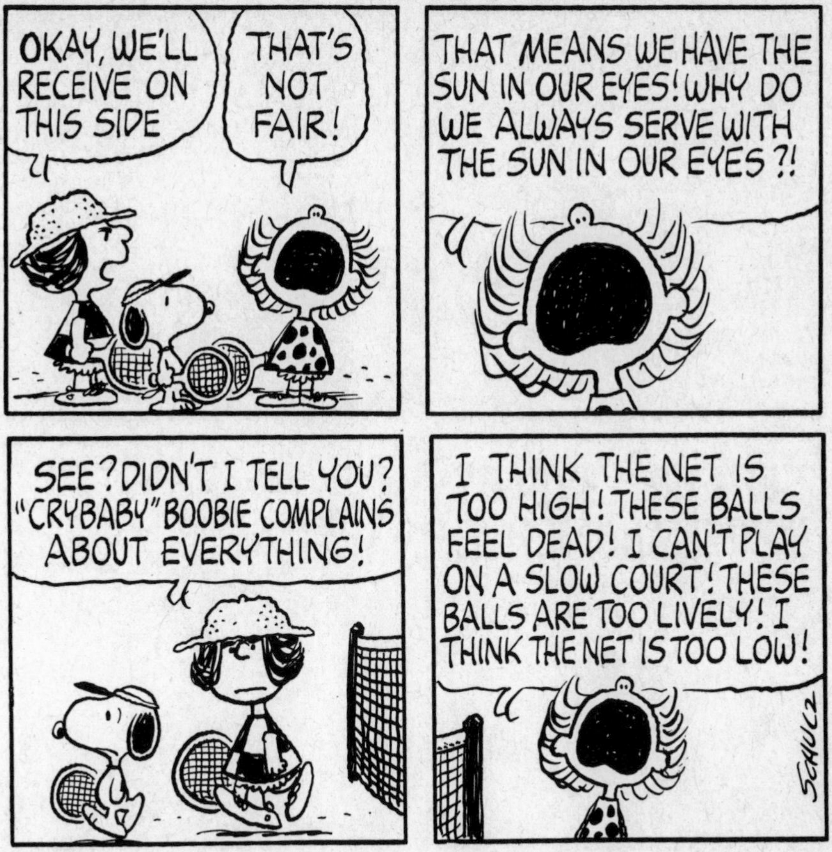
OKAY, WE'LL RECEIVE ON THIS SIDE
THAT'S NOT FAIR!
THAT MEANS WE HAVE THE SUN IN OUR EYES! WHY DO WE ALWAYS SERVE WITH THE SUN IN OUR EYES?!
SEE? DIDN'T I TELL YOU? "CRYBABY" BOOBIE COMPLAINS ABOUT EVERYTHING!
I THINK THE NET IS TOO HIGH! THESE BALLS FEEL DEAD! I CAN'T PLAY ON A SLOW COURT! THESE BALLS ARE TOO LIVELY! I THINK THE NET IS TOO LOW!
SCHULZ

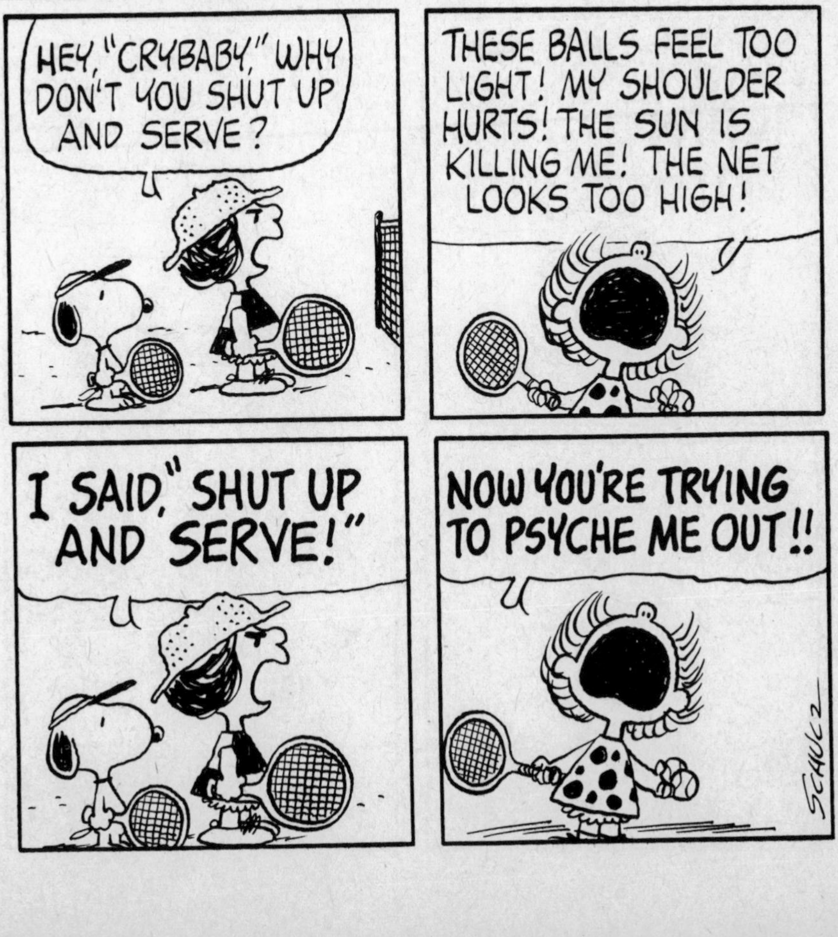
HEY, "CRYBABY," WHY DON'T YOU SHUT UP AND SERVE?
THESE BALLS FEEL TOO LIGHT! MY SHOULDER HURTS! THE SUN IS KILLING ME! THE NET LOOKS TOO HIGH!
I SAID, "SHUT UP AND SERVE!"
NOW YOU'RE TRYING TO PSYCHE ME OUT!!
SCHULZ

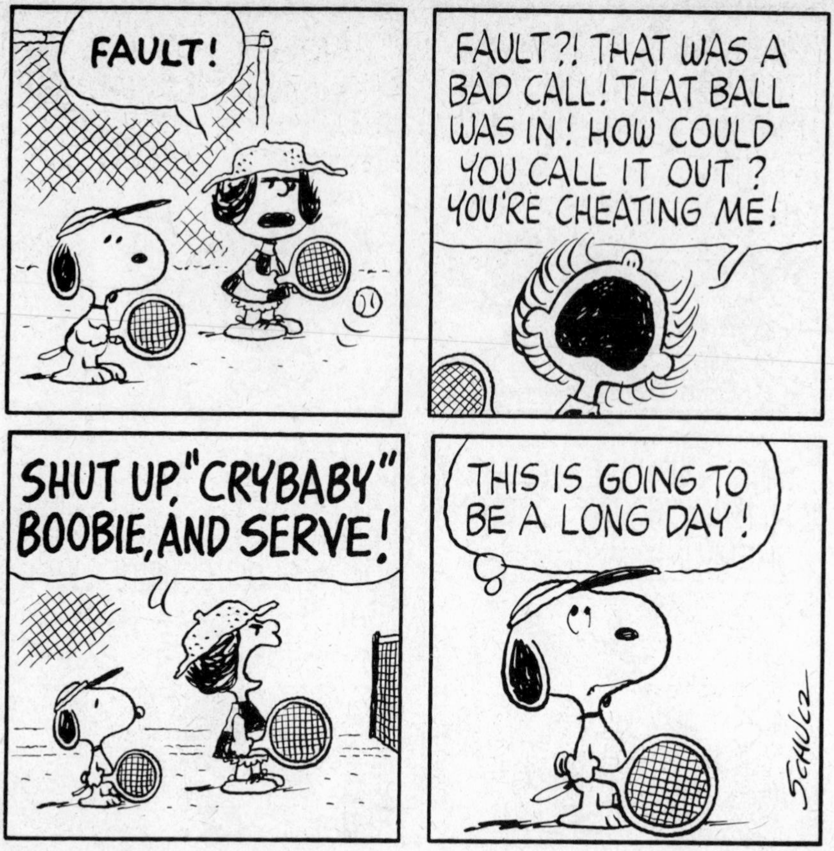
FAULT!
FAULT?! THAT WAS A BAD CALL! THAT BALL WAS IN! HOW COULD YOU CALL IT OUT? YOU'RE CHEATING ME!
SHUT UP, "CRYBABY" BOOBIE, AND SERVE!
THIS IS GOING TO BE A LONG DAY!
SCHULZ

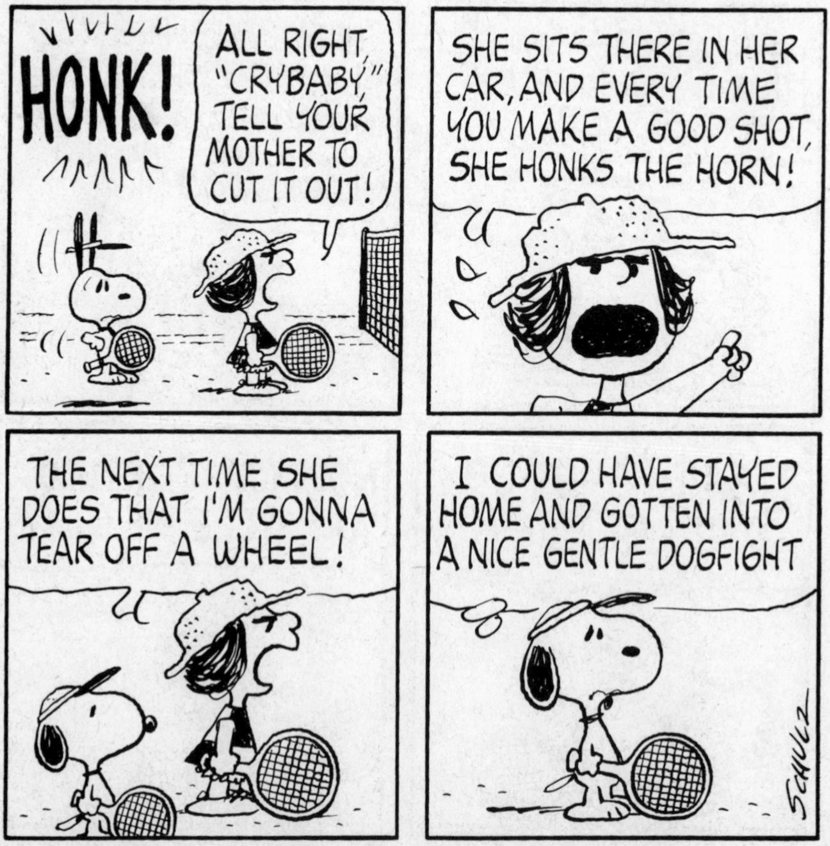
HONK!
ALL RIGHT, "CRYBABY," TELL YOUR MOTHER TO CUT IT OUT!
SHE SITS THERE IN HER CAR, AND EVERY TIME YOU MAKE A GOOD SHOT, SHE HONKS THE HORN!
THE NEXT TIME SHE DOES THAT I'M GONNA TEAR OFF A WHEEL!
I COULD HAVE STAYED HOME AND GOTTEN INTO A NICE GENTLE DOGFIGHT
SCHULZ

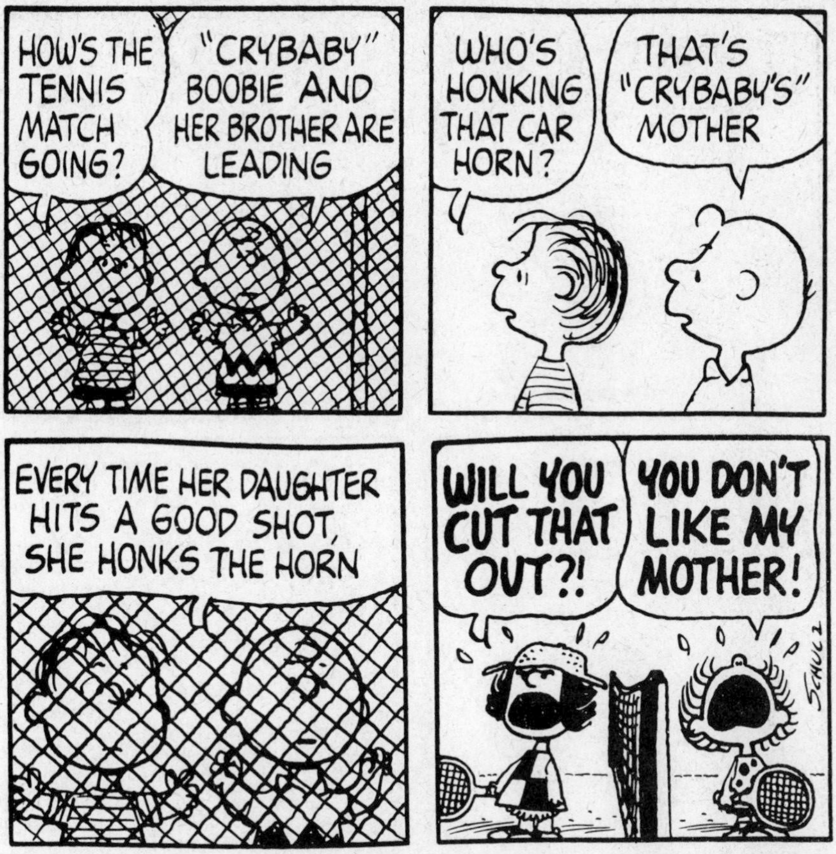
HOW'S THE TENNIS MATCH GOING?
"CRYBABY" BOOBIE AND HER BROTHER ARE LEADING
WHO'S HONKING THAT CAR HORN?
THAT'S "CRYBABY'S" MOTHER
EVERY TIME HER DAUGHTER HITS A GOOD SHOT, SHE HONKS THE HORN
WILL YOU CUT THAT OUT?!
YOU DON'T LIKE MY MOTHER!
SCHULZ

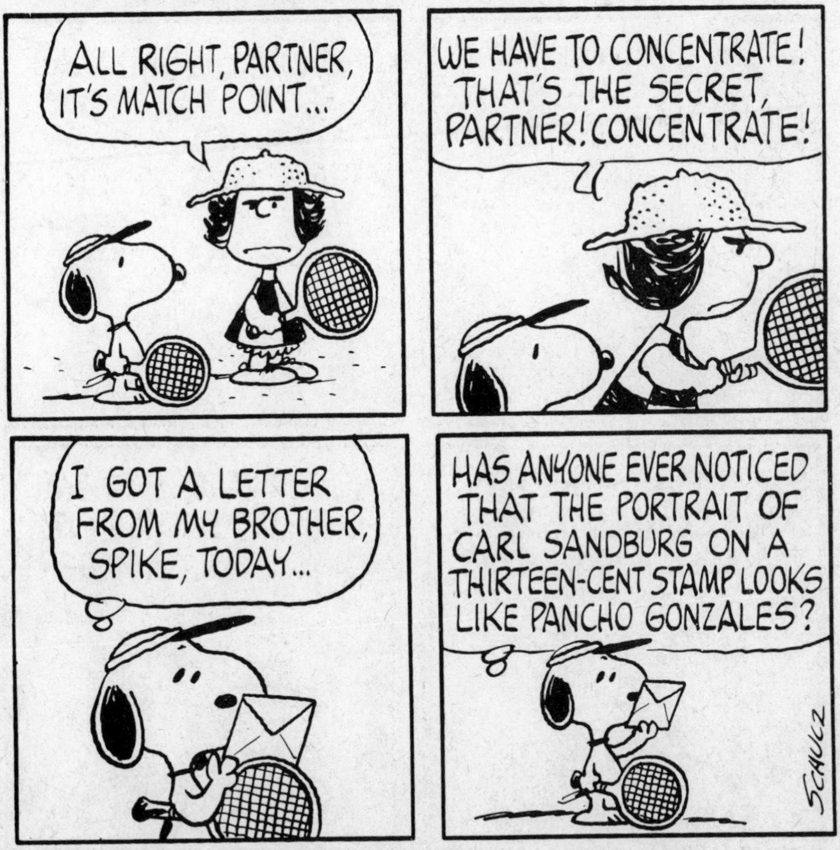
ALL RIGHT, PARTNER, IT'S MATCH POINT...
WE HAVE TO CONCENTRATE! THAT'S THE SECRET, PARTNER! CONCENTRATE!
I GOT A LETTER FROM MY BROTHER, SPIKE, TODAY...
HAS ANYONE EVER NOTICED THAT THE PORTRAIT OF CARL SANDBURG ON A THIRTEEN-CENT STAMP LOOKS LIKE PANCHO GONZALES?
SCHULZ

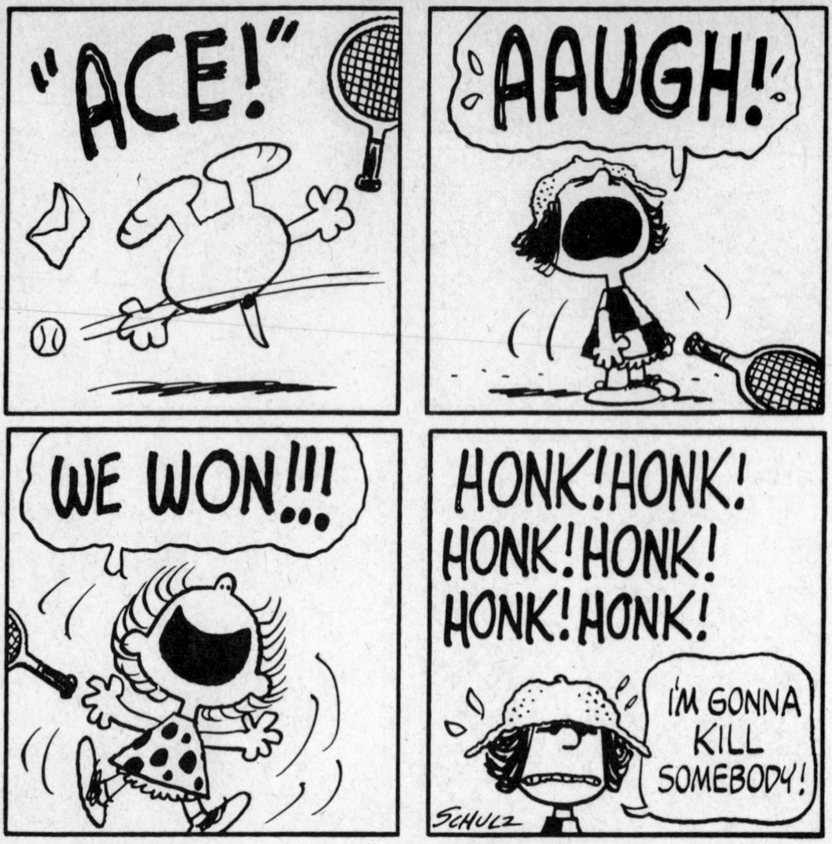
"ACE!"
AAUGH!
WE WON!!!...
HONK! HONK! HONK! HONK! HONK! HONK!
I'M GONNA KILL SOMEBODY!
SCHULZ

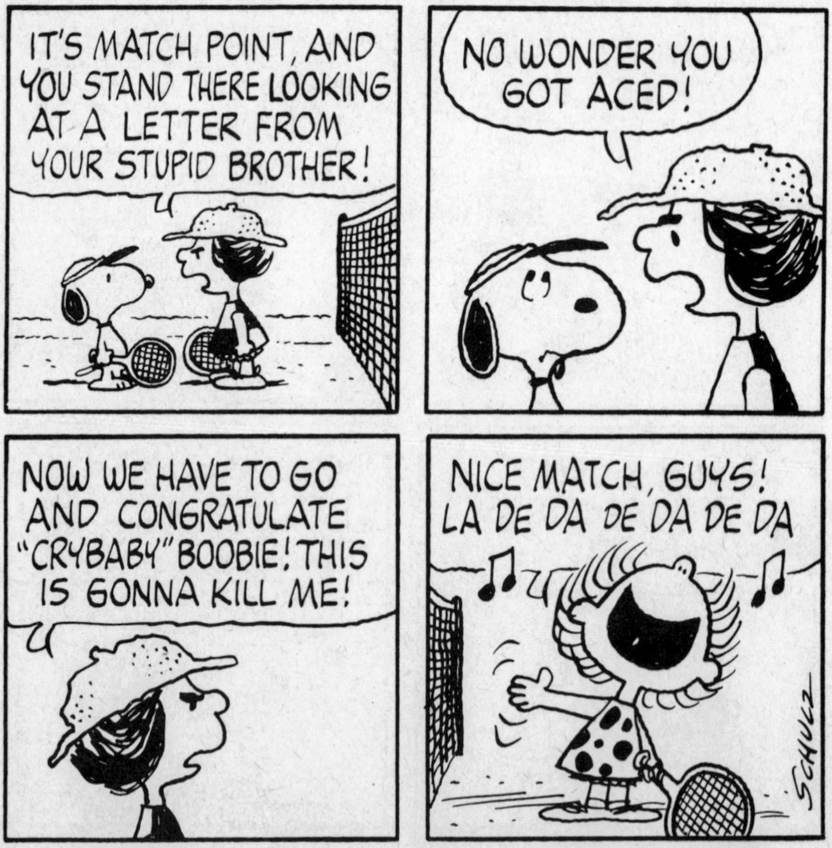
IT'S MATCH POINT, AND YOU STAND THERE LOOKING AT A LETTER FROM YOUR STUPID BROTHER!
NO WONDER YOU GOT ACED!
NOW WE HAVE TO GO AND CONGRATULATE "CRYBABY" BOOBIE! THIS IS GONNA KILL ME!
NICE MATCH, GUYS! LA DE DA DE DA DE DA
SCHULZ

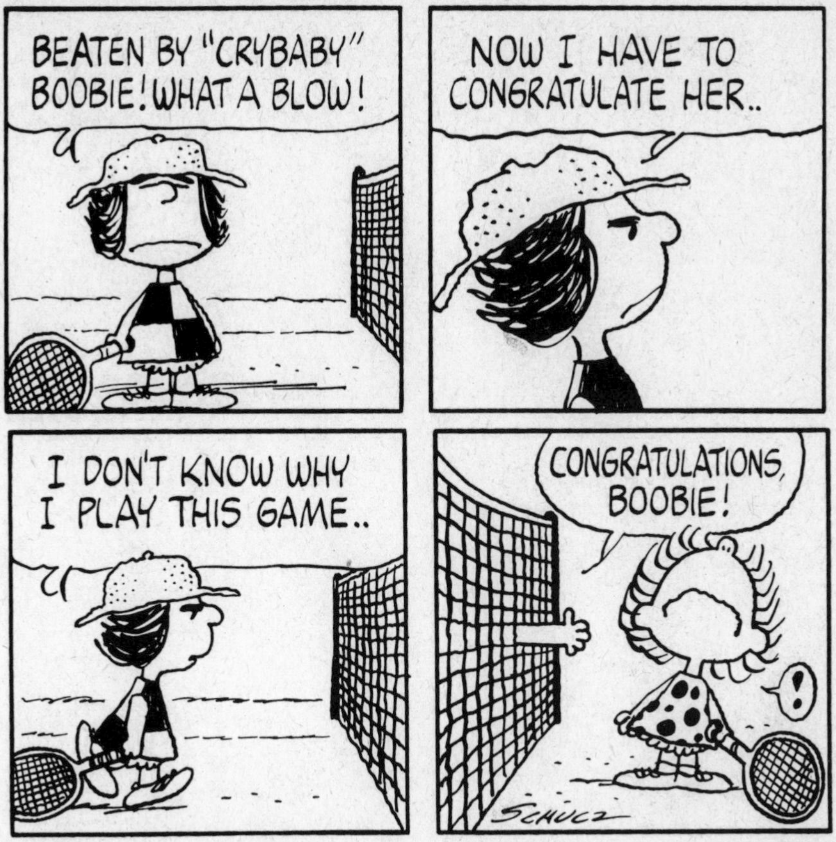
BEATEN BY "CRYBABY" BOOBIE! WHAT A BLOW!
NOW I HAVE TO CONGRATULATE HER..
I DON'T KNOW WHY I PLAY THIS GAME..
CONGRATULATIONS, BOOBIE!
!

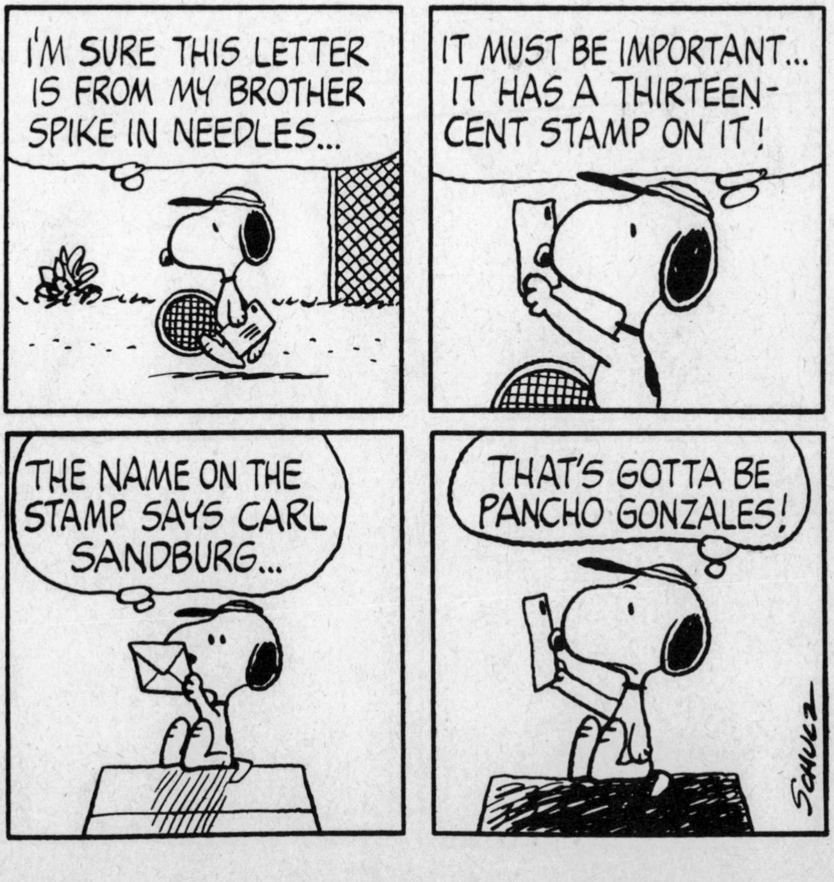
I'M SURE THIS LETTER IS FROM MY BROTHER SPIKE IN NEEDLES...
IT MUST BE IMPORTANT... IT HAS A THIRTEEN-CENT STAMP ON IT!
THE NAME ON THE STAMP SAYS CARL SANDBURG...
THAT'S GOTTA BE PANCHO GONZALES!

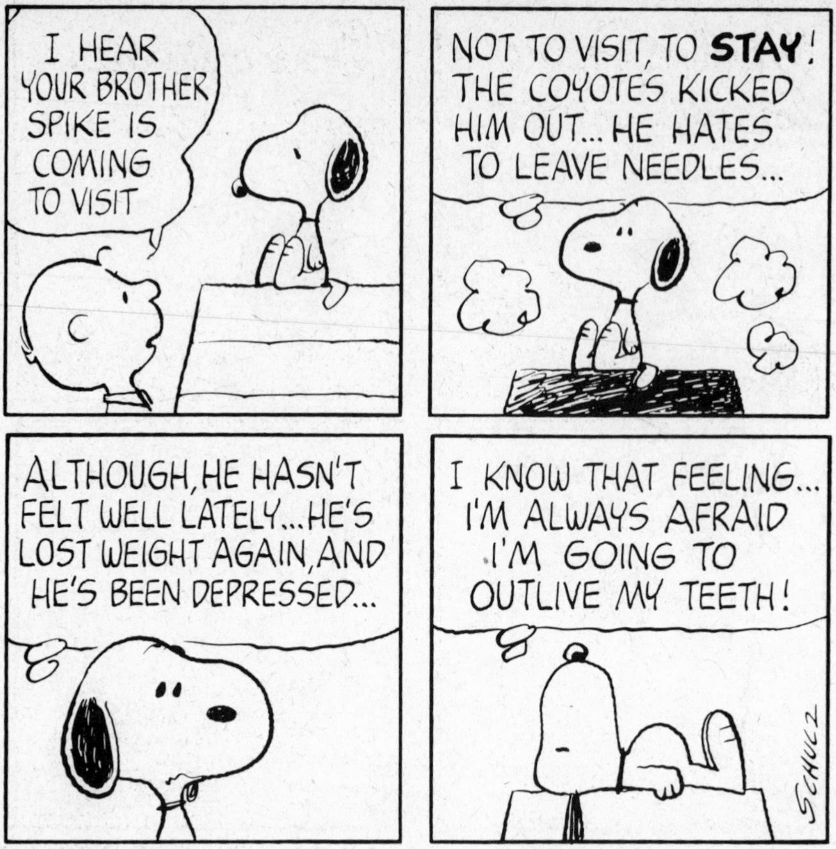
I HEAR YOUR BROTHER SPIKE IS COMING TO VISIT
NOT TO VISIT, TO **STAY**! THE COYOTES KICKED HIM OUT... HE HATES TO LEAVE NEEDLES...
ALTHOUGH, HE HASN'T FELT WELL LATELY...HE'S LOST WEIGHT AGAIN, AND HE'S BEEN DEPRESSED...
I KNOW THAT FEELING... I'M ALWAYS AFRAID I'M GOING TO OUTLIVE MY TEETH!
SCHULZ

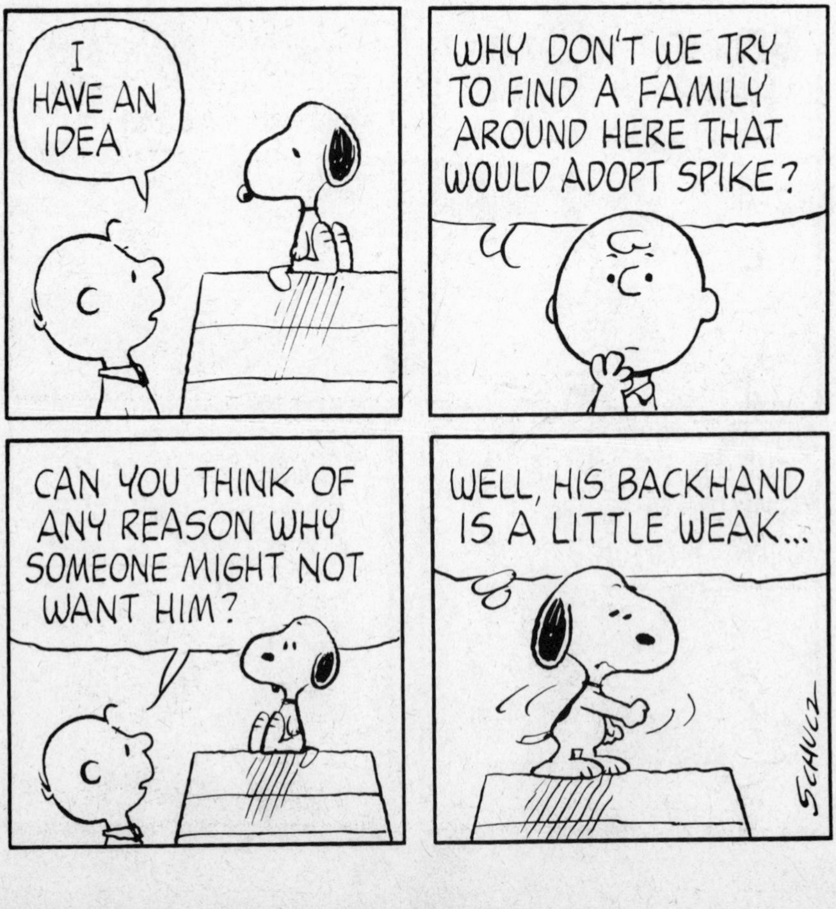
I HAVE AN IDEA
WHY DON'T WE TRY TO FIND A FAMILY AROUND HERE THAT WOULD ADOPT SPIKE?
CAN YOU THINK OF ANY REASON WHY SOMEONE MIGHT NOT WANT HIM?
WELL, HIS BACKHAND IS A LITTLE WEAK...
SCHULZ

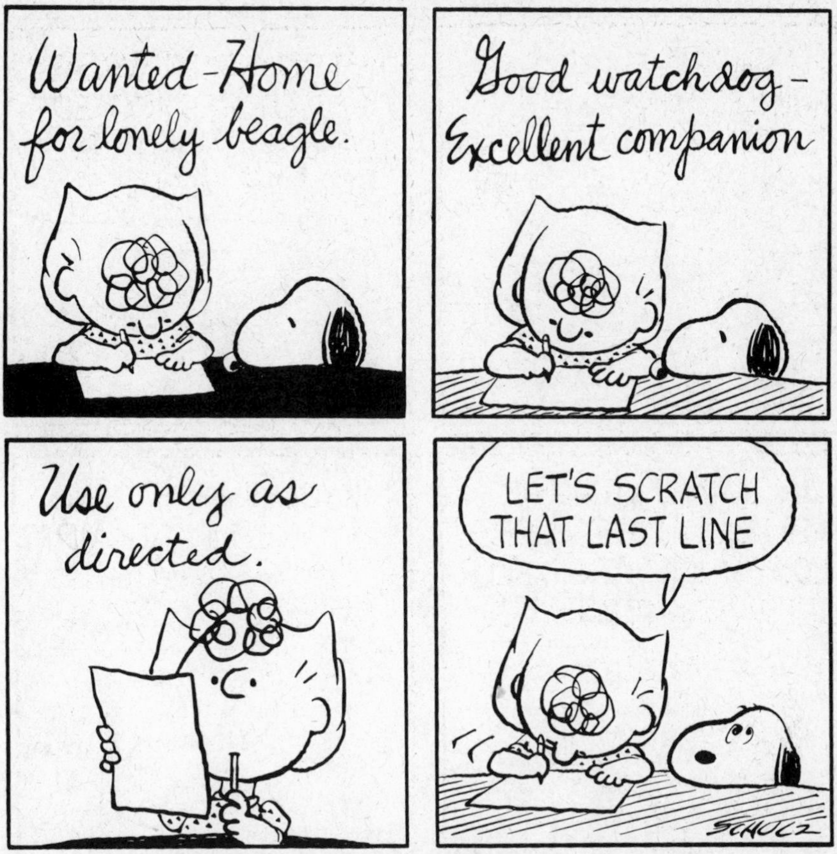
Wanted-Home for lonely beagle.
Good watchdog-Excellent companion
Use only as directed.
LET'S SCRATCH THAT LAST LINE

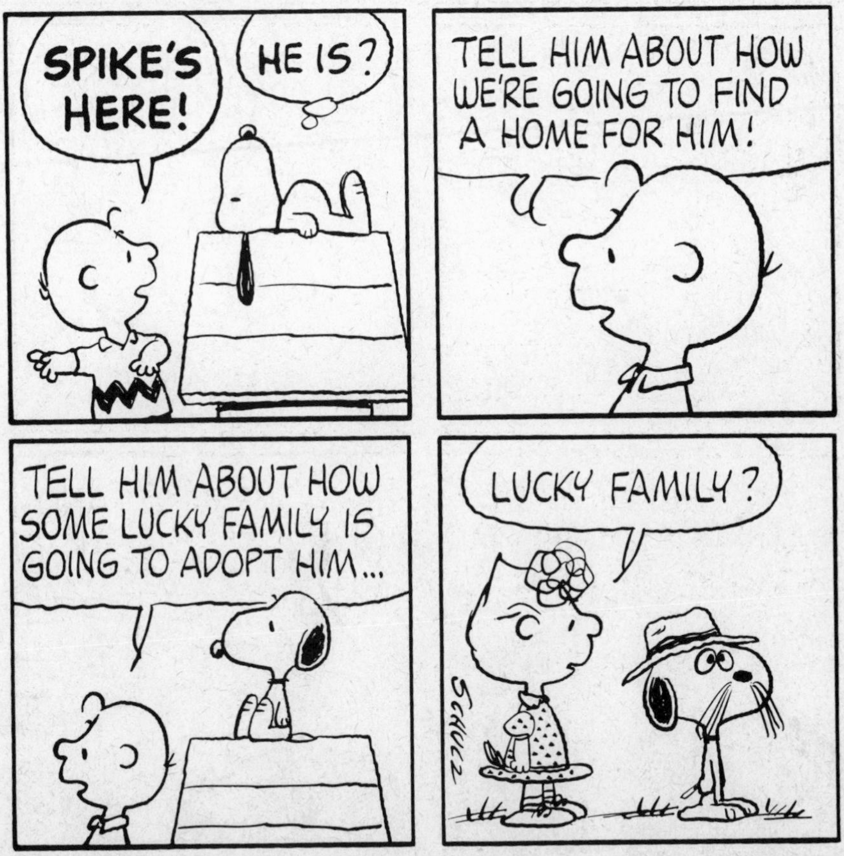
SPIKE'S HERE!
HE IS?
TELL HIM ABOUT HOW WE'RE GOING TO FIND A HOME FOR HIM!
TELL HIM ABOUT HOW SOME LUCKY FAMILY IS GOING TO ADOPT HIM...
LUCKY FAMILY?

YES, WE'RE THE PARTY THAT RAN THE AD IN THE NEWSPAPER...

YES, WE'RE TRYING TO FIND A NICE HOME FOR A DOG..ACTUALLY, HE'S THE BROTHER OF OUR OWN DOG...

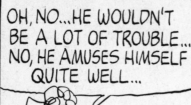

OH, NO...HE WOULDN'T BE A LOT OF TROUBLE... NO, HE AMUSES HIMSELF QUITE WELL...

AH, COLONEL HOGAN!

YOU'RE ASKING OUR FAMILY TO ADOPT THIS DOG?!

WHY NOT? HE'S SNOOPY'S BROTHER! HE'S A GOOD DOG

HE'S A FULL-BLOODED BEAGLE

THAT'S WHAT YOU SAY

I SAY HE'S PART BEAGLE AND PART DISASTER!

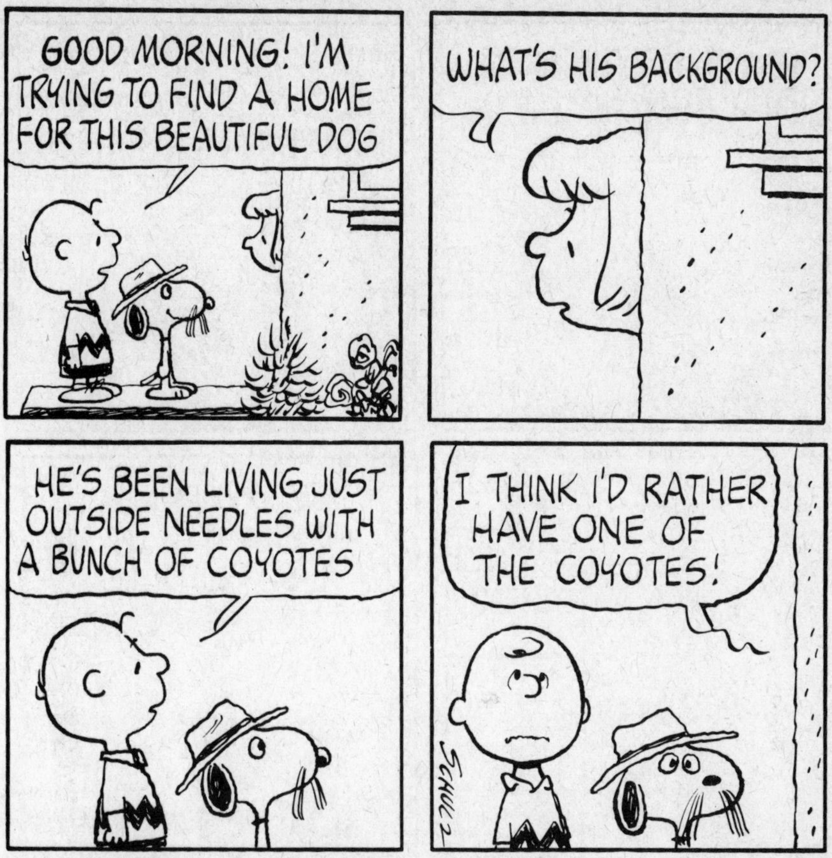
GOOD MORNING! I'M TRYING TO FIND A HOME FOR THIS BEAUTIFUL DOG
WHAT'S HIS BACKGROUND?
HE'S BEEN LIVING JUST OUTSIDE NEEDLES WITH A BUNCH OF COYOTES
I THINK I'D RATHER HAVE ONE OF THE COYOTES!

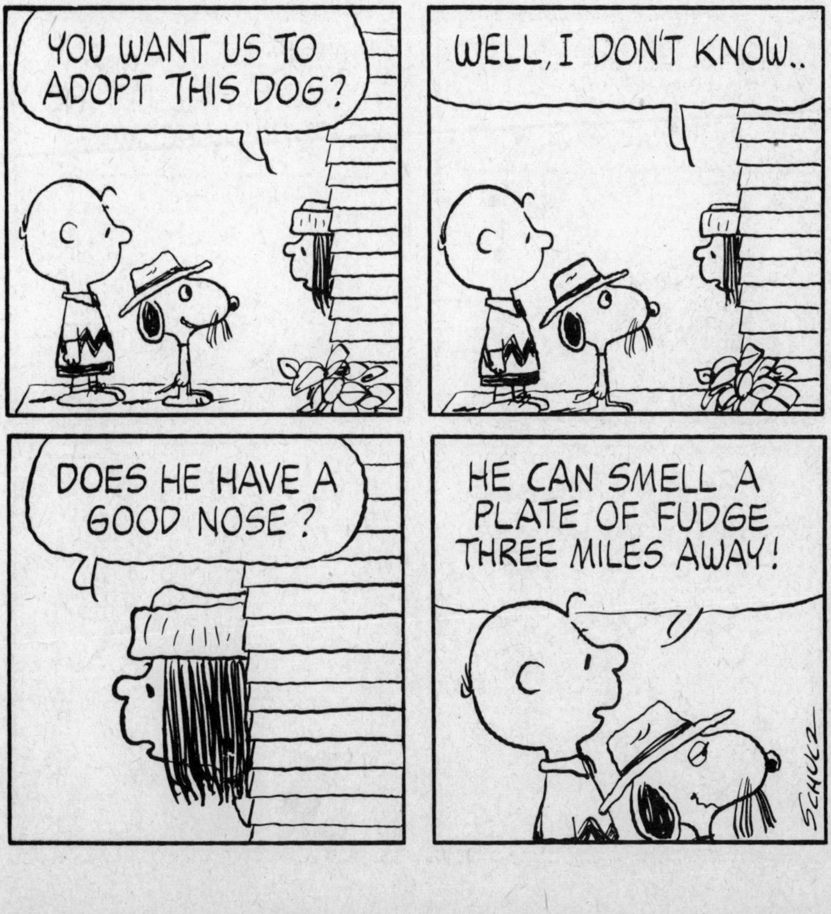
YOU WANT US TO ADOPT THIS DOG?
WELL, I DON'T KNOW..
DOES HE HAVE A GOOD NOSE?
HE CAN SMELL A PLATE OF FUDGE THREE MILES AWAY!

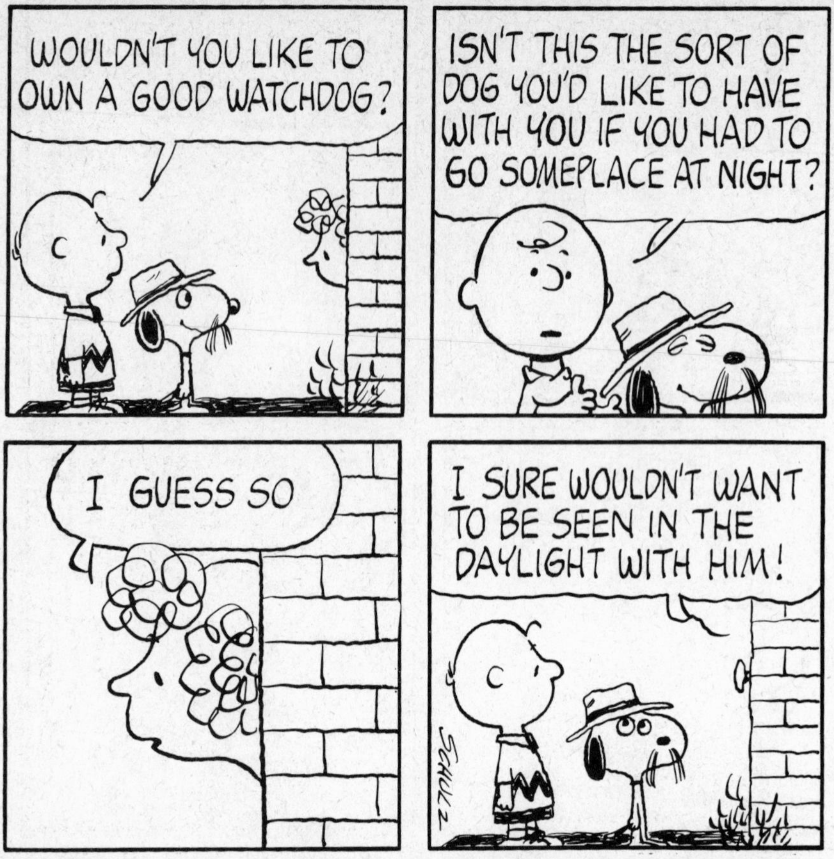
WOULDN'T YOU LIKE TO OWN A GOOD WATCHDOG?
ISN'T THIS THE SORT OF DOG YOU'D LIKE TO HAVE WITH YOU IF YOU HAD TO GO SOMEPLACE AT NIGHT?
I GUESS SO
I SURE WOULDN'T WANT TO BE SEEN IN THE DAYLIGHT WITH HIM!
SCHULZ

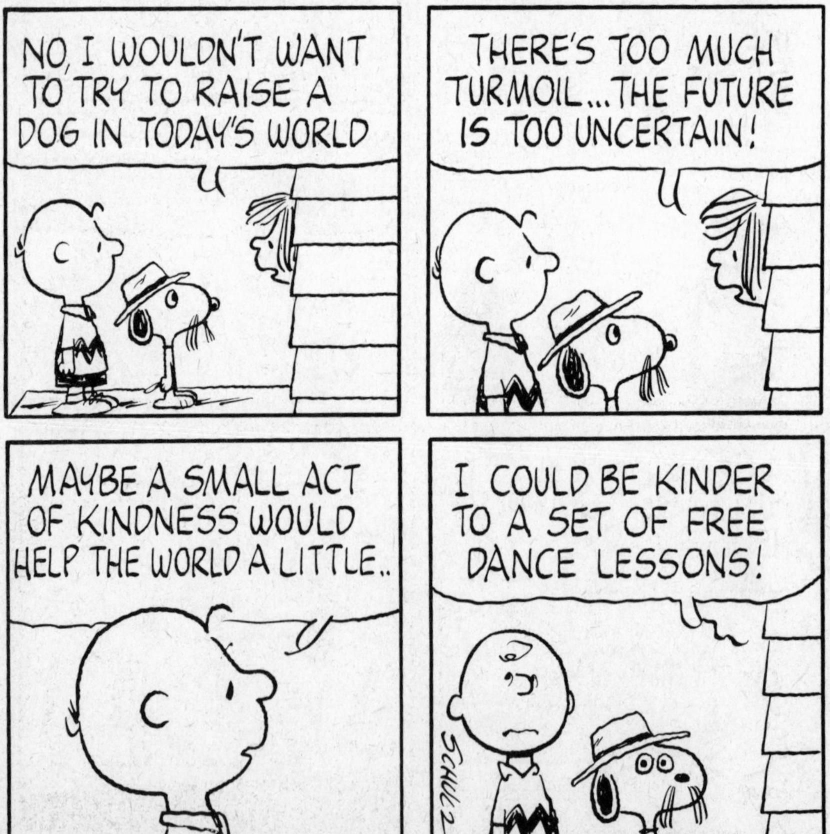
NO, I WOULDN'T WANT TO TRY TO RAISE A DOG IN TODAY'S WORLD
THERE'S TOO MUCH TURMOIL...THE FUTURE IS TOO UNCERTAIN!
MAYBE A SMALL ACT OF KINDNESS WOULD HELP THE WORLD A LITTLE..
I COULD BE KINDER TO A SET OF FREE DANCE LESSONS!
SCHULZ

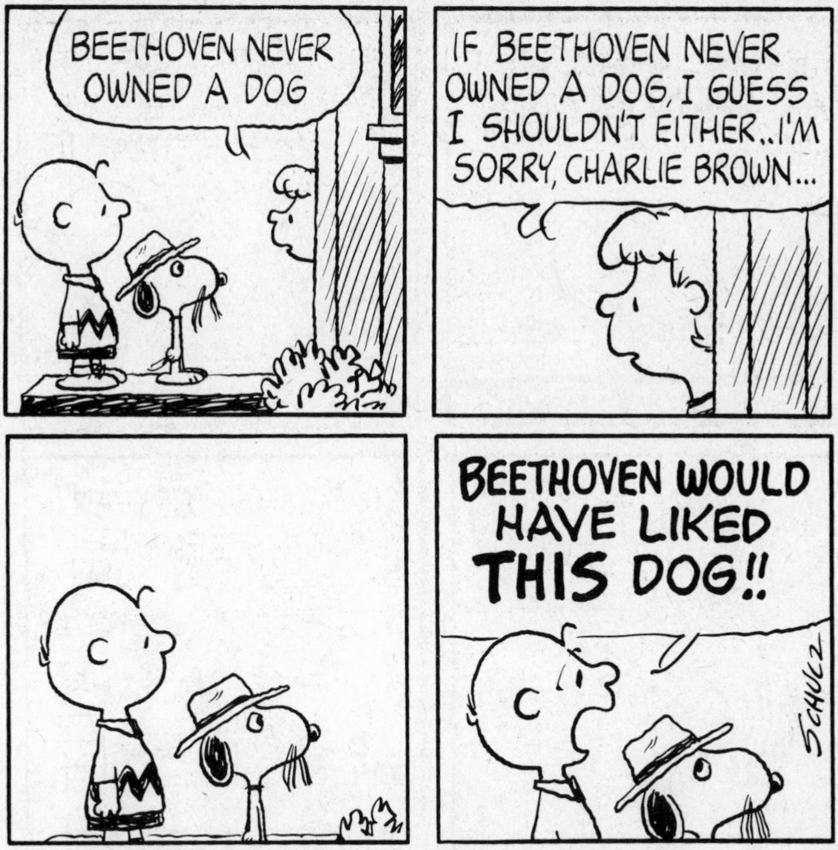
BEETHOVEN NEVER OWNED A DOG
IF BEETHOVEN NEVER OWNED A DOG, I GUESS I SHOULDN'T EITHER..I'M SORRY, CHARLIE BROWN...
BEETHOVEN WOULD HAVE LIKED THIS DOG!!
SCHULZ

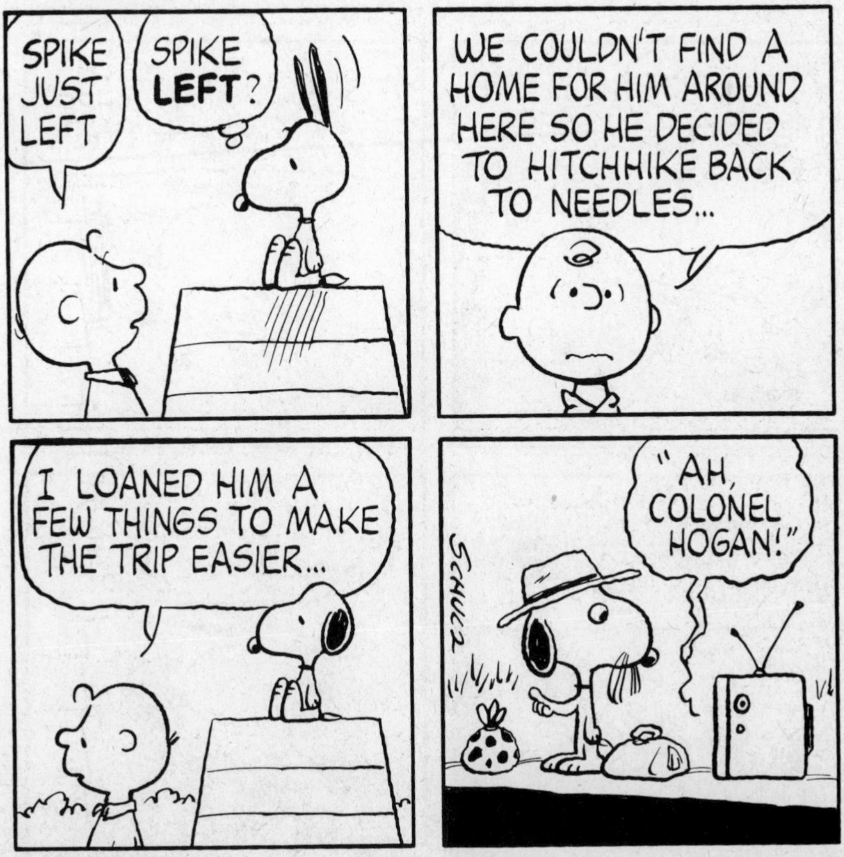
SPIKE JUST LEFT
SPIKE LEFT?
WE COULDN'T FIND A HOME FOR HIM AROUND HERE SO HE DECIDED TO HITCHHIKE BACK TO NEEDLES...
I LOANED HIM A FEW THINGS TO MAKE THE TRIP EASIER...
SCHULZ
"AH, COLONEL HOGAN!"

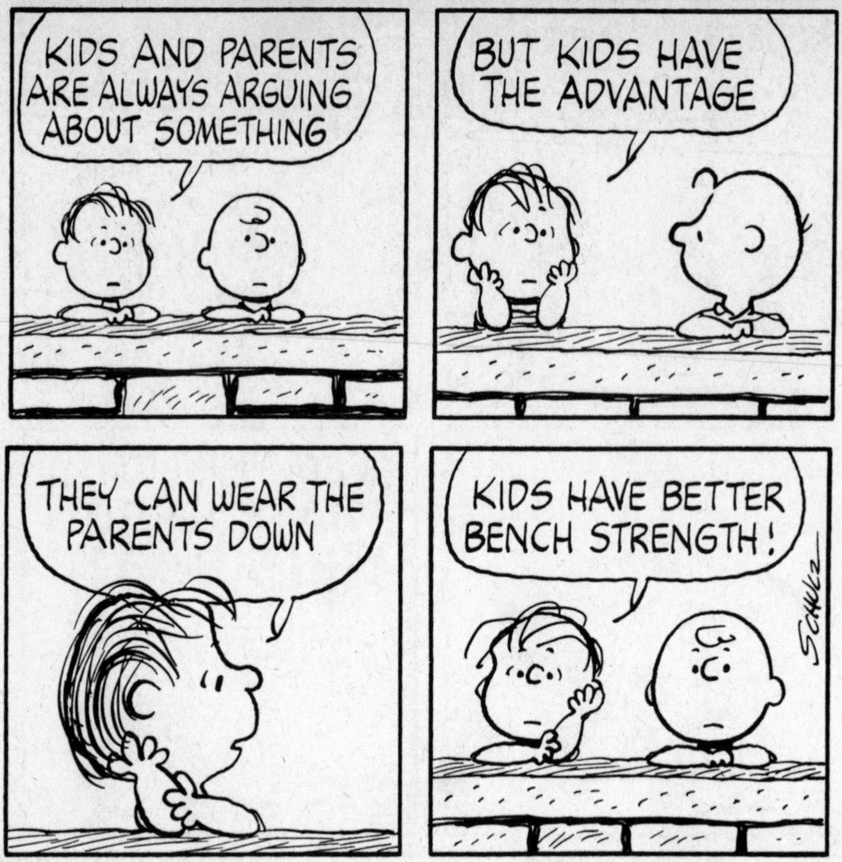
KIDS AND PARENTS ARE ALWAYS ARGUING ABOUT SOMETHING
BUT KIDS HAVE THE ADVANTAGE
THEY CAN WEAR THE PARENTS DOWN
KIDS HAVE BETTER BENCH STRENGTH!
SCHULZ

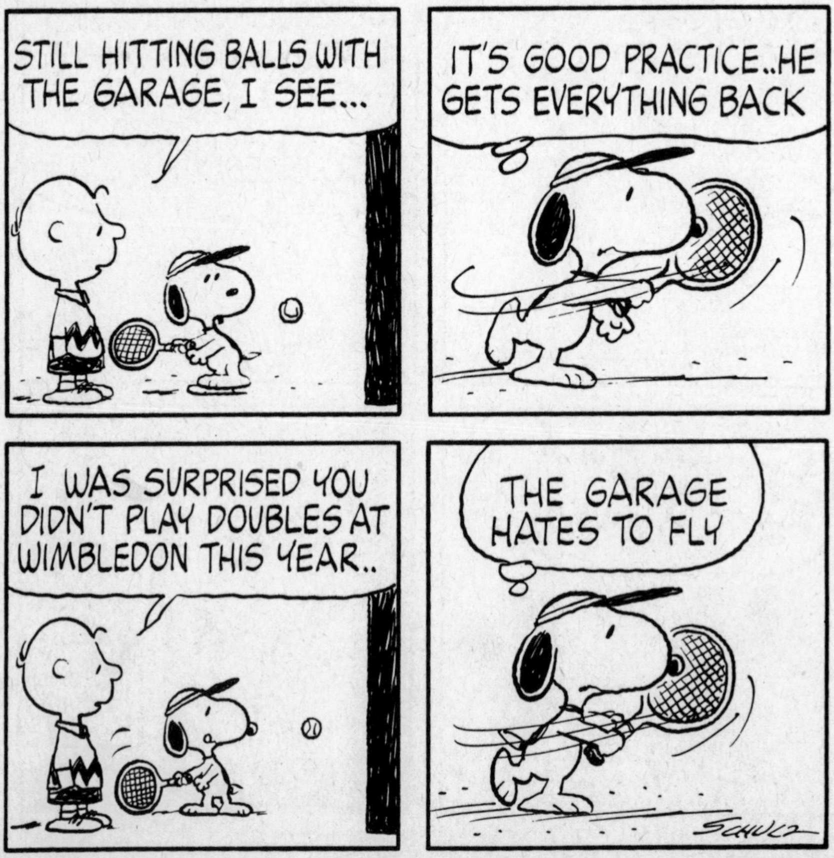
STILL HITTING BALLS WITH THE GARAGE, I SEE...
IT'S GOOD PRACTICE..HE GETS EVERYTHING BACK
I WAS SURPRISED YOU DIDN'T PLAY DOUBLES AT WIMBLEDON THIS YEAR..
THE GARAGE HATES TO FLY
SCHULZ

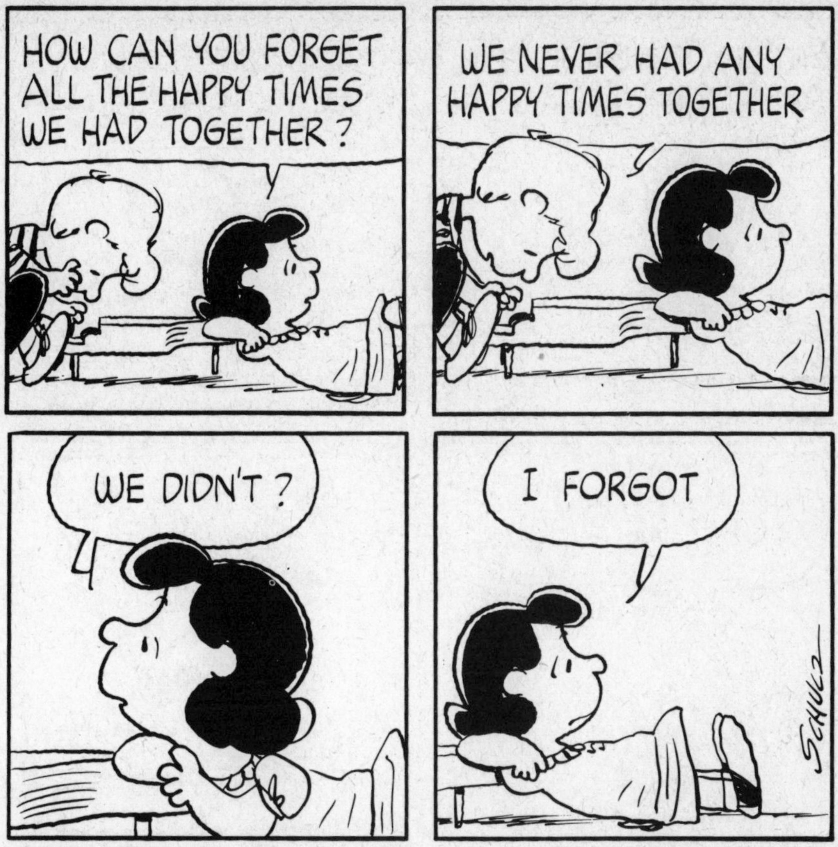
HOW CAN YOU FORGET ALL THE HAPPY TIMES WE HAD TOGETHER?
WE NEVER HAD ANY HAPPY TIMES TOGETHER
WE DIDN'T?
I FORGOT
SCHULZ

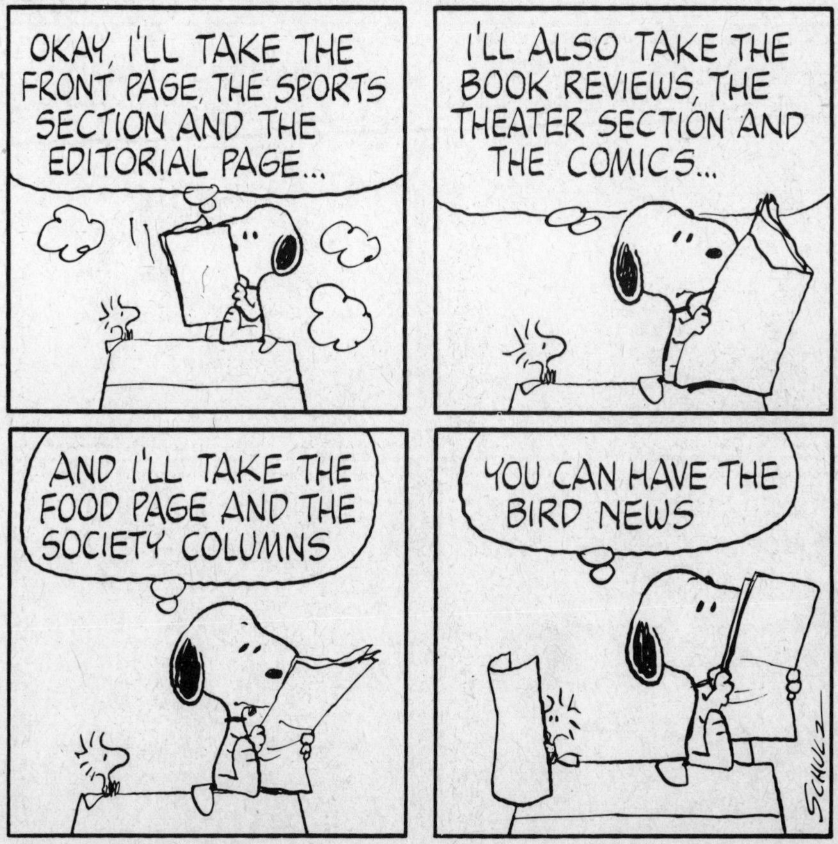
OKAY, I'LL TAKE THE FRONT PAGE, THE SPORTS SECTION AND THE EDITORIAL PAGE...
I'LL ALSO TAKE THE BOOK REVIEWS, THE THEATER SECTION AND THE COMICS...
AND I'LL TAKE THE FOOD PAGE AND THE SOCIETY COLUMNS
YOU CAN HAVE THE BIRD NEWS
SCHULZ

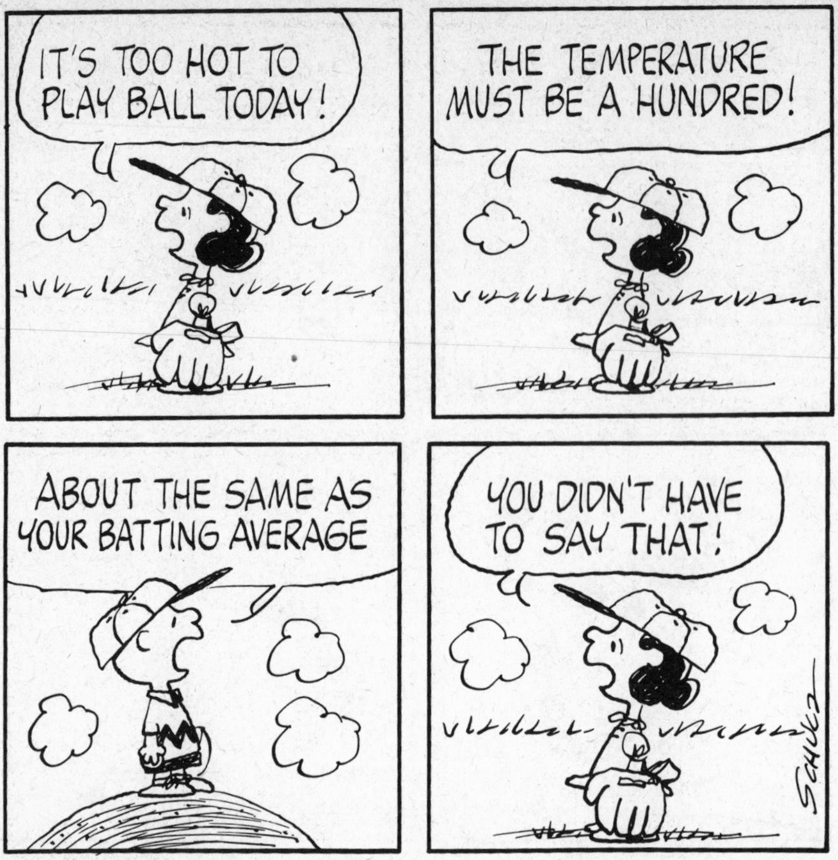
IT'S TOO HOT TO PLAY BALL TODAY!
THE TEMPERATURE MUST BE A HUNDRED!
ABOUT THE SAME AS YOUR BATTING AVERAGE
YOU DIDN'T HAVE TO SAY THAT!
SCHULZ

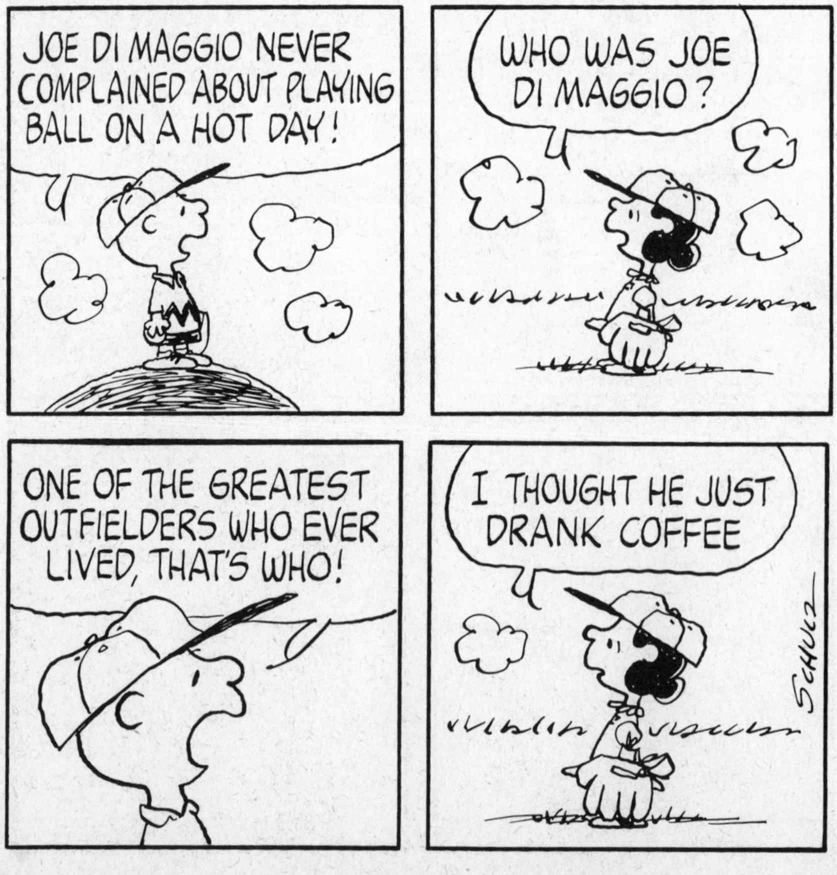
JOE DI MAGGIO NEVER COMPLAINED ABOUT PLAYING BALL ON A HOT DAY!
WHO WAS JOE DI MAGGIO?
ONE OF THE GREATEST OUTFIELDERS WHO EVER LIVED, THAT'S WHO!
I THOUGHT HE JUST DRANK COFFEE
SCHULZ

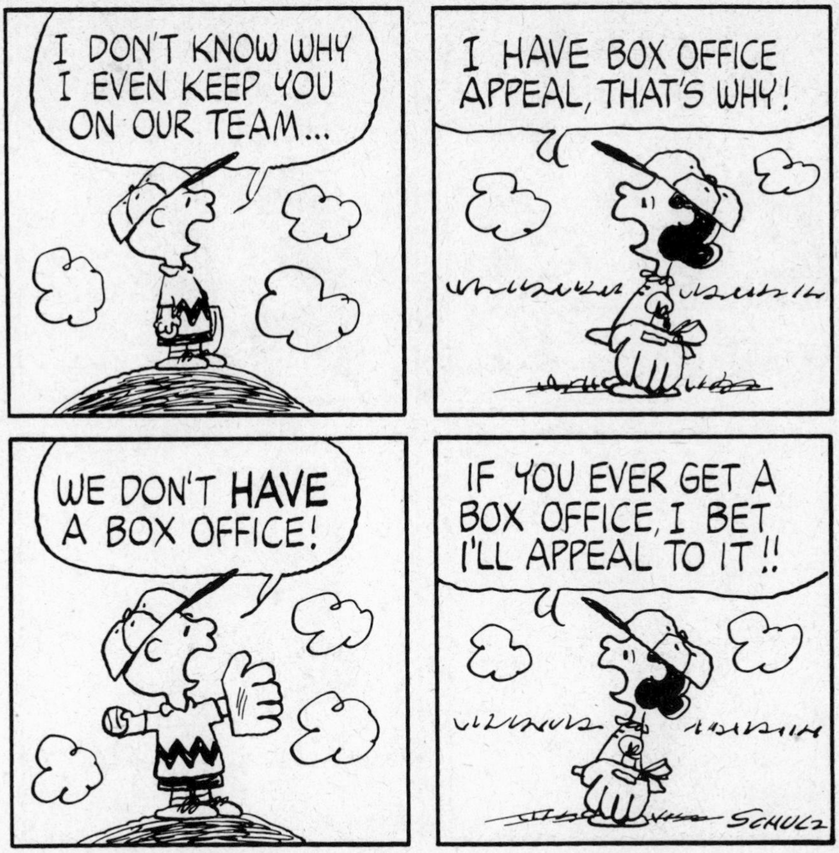
I DON'T KNOW WHY I EVEN KEEP YOU ON OUR TEAM...
I HAVE BOX OFFICE APPEAL, THAT'S WHY!
WE DON'T **HAVE** A BOX OFFICE!
IF YOU EVER GET A BOX OFFICE, I BET I'LL APPEAL TO IT!!
SCHULZ

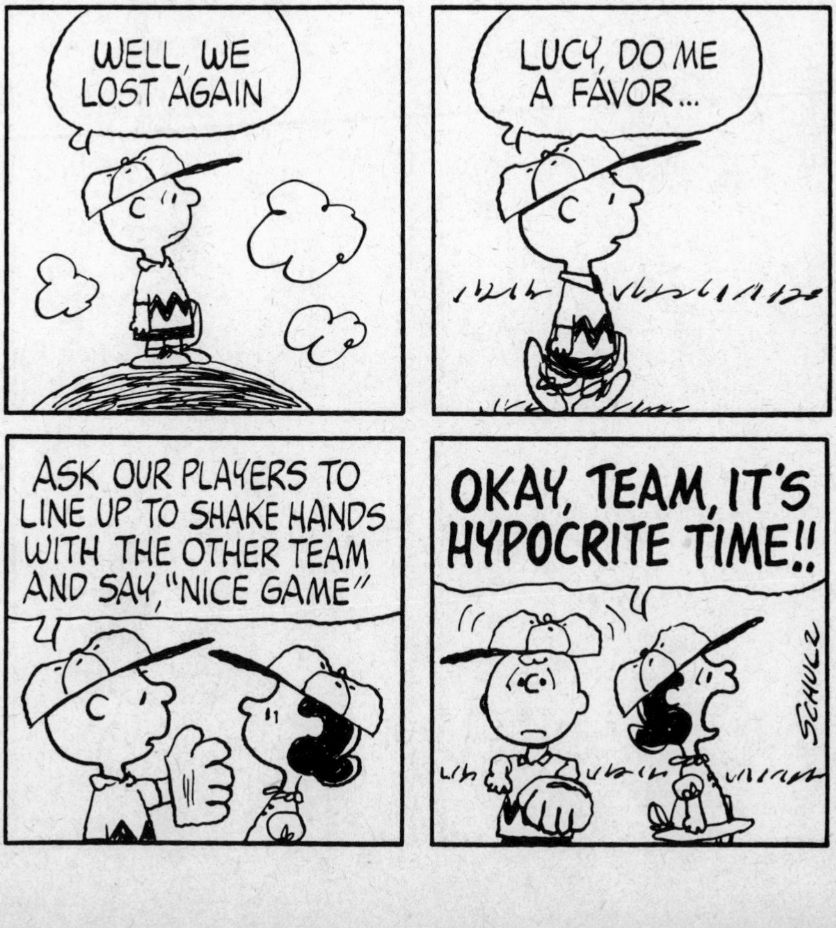
WELL, WE LOST AGAIN
LUCY, DO ME A FAVOR...
ASK OUR PLAYERS TO LINE UP TO SHAKE HANDS WITH THE OTHER TEAM AND SAY, "NICE GAME"
OKAY, TEAM, IT'S HYPOCRITE TIME!!
SCHULZ

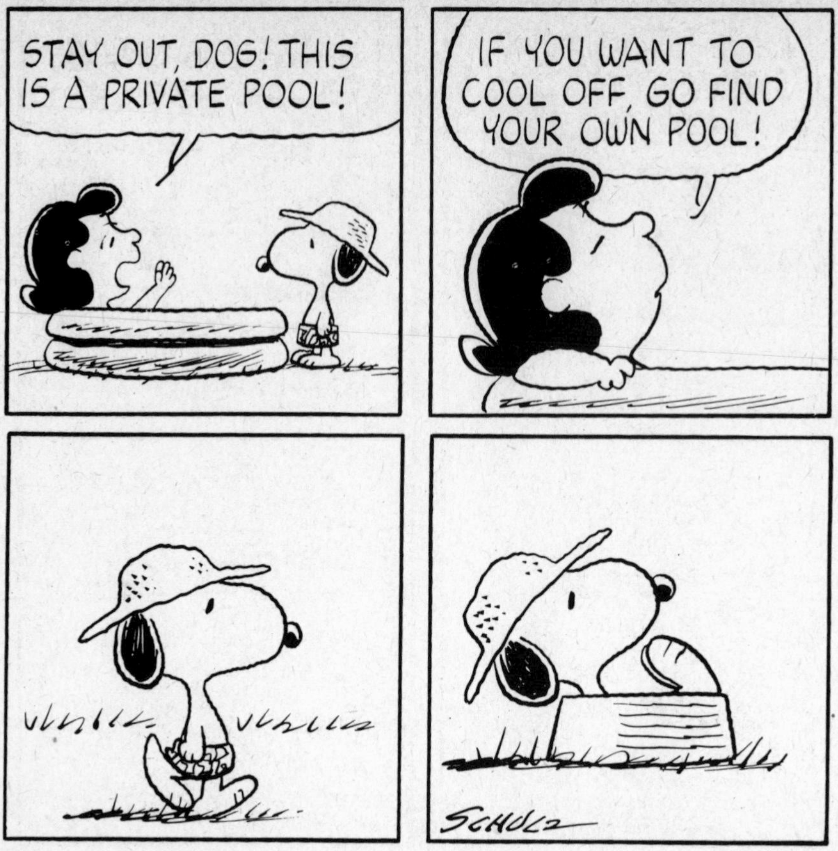
STAY OUT, DOG! THIS IS A PRIVATE POOL!
IF YOU WANT TO COOL OFF, GO FIND YOUR OWN POOL!
SCHULZ

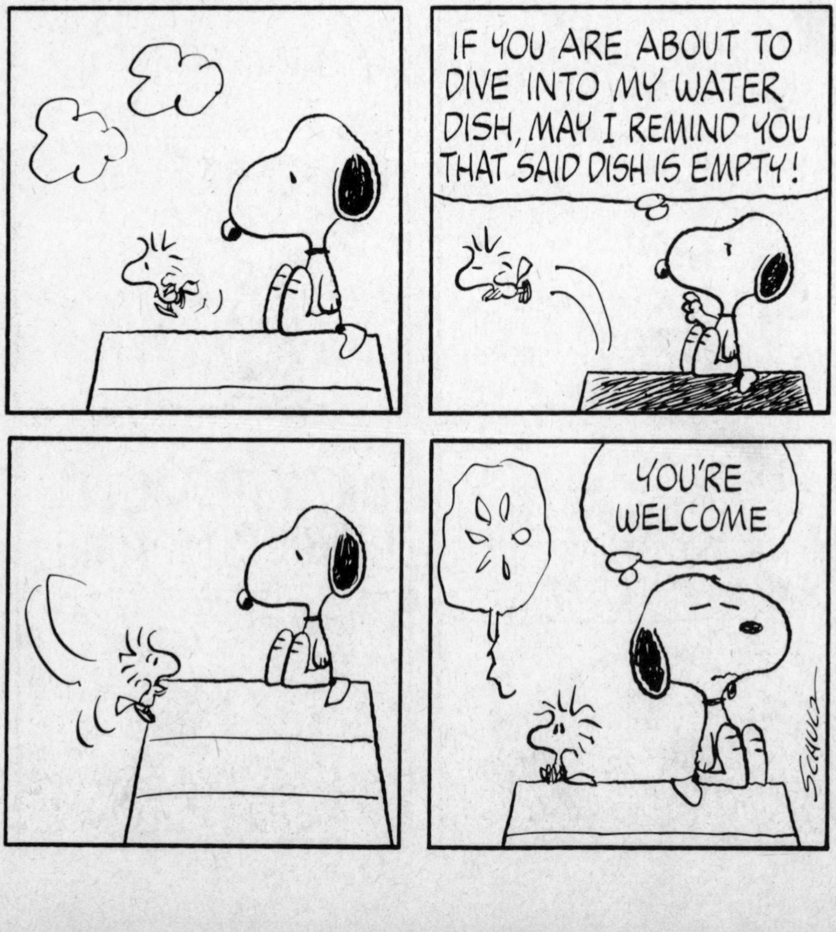
IF YOU ARE ABOUT TO DIVE INTO MY WATER DISH, MAY I REMIND YOU THAT SAID DISH IS EMPTY!
YOU'RE WELCOME
SCHULZ

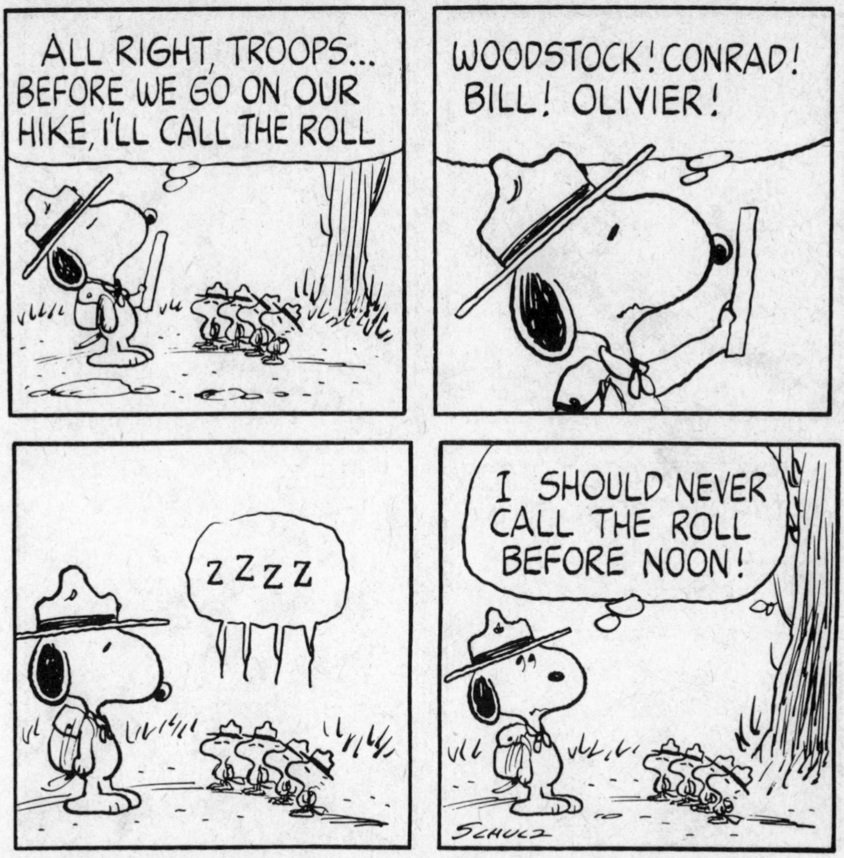
ALL RIGHT, TROOPS... BEFORE WE GO ON OUR HIKE, I'LL CALL THE ROLL
WOODSTOCK! CONRAD! BILL! OLIVIER!
Z Z Z Z
I SHOULD NEVER CALL THE ROLL BEFORE NOON!
SCHULZ

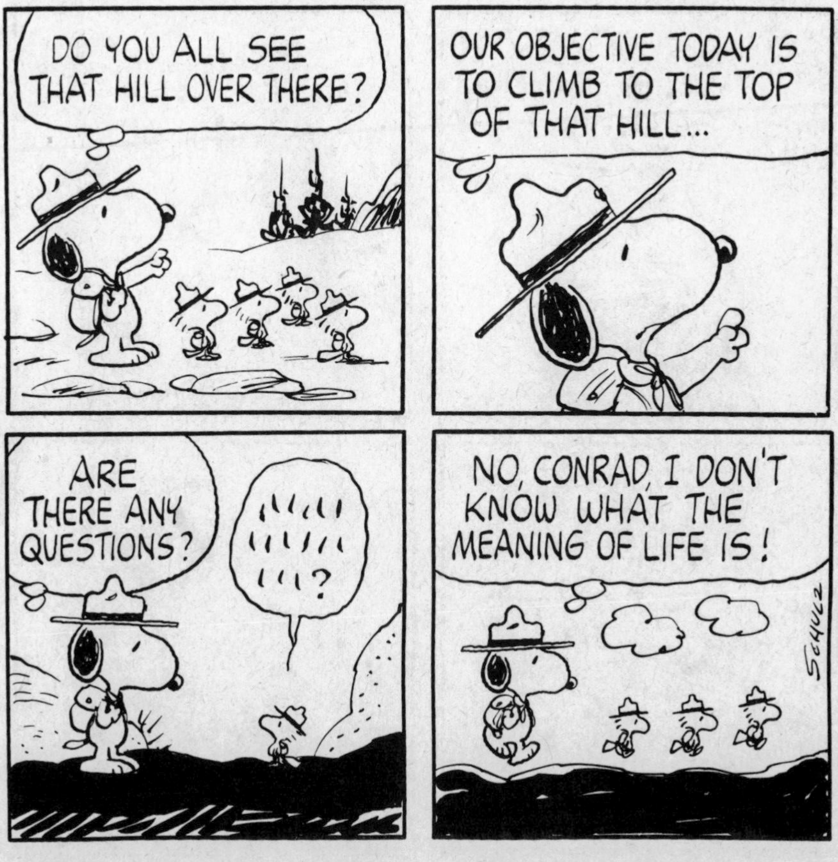
DO YOU ALL SEE THAT HILL OVER THERE?
OUR OBJECTIVE TODAY IS TO CLIMB TO THE TOP OF THAT HILL...
ARE THERE ANY QUESTIONS?
NO, CONRAD, I DON'T KNOW WHAT THE MEANING OF LIFE IS!
SCHULZ

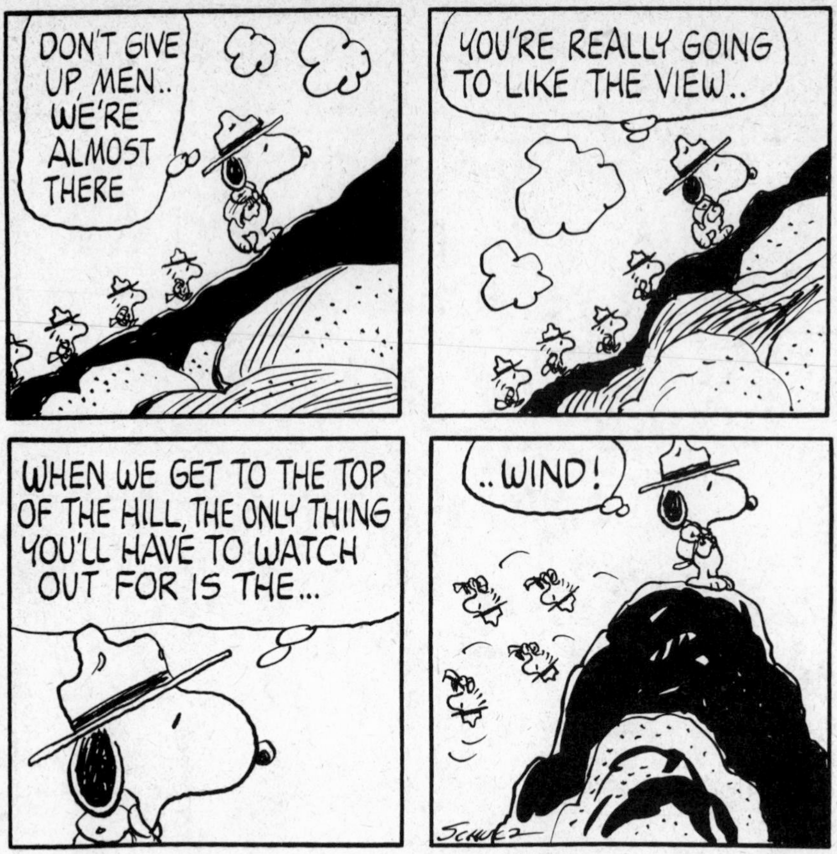
DON'T GIVE UP, MEN.. WE'RE ALMOST THERE
YOU'RE REALLY GOING TO LIKE THE VIEW..
WHEN WE GET TO THE TOP OF THE HILL, THE ONLY THING YOU'LL HAVE TO WATCH OUT FOR IS THE...
..WIND!
SCHULZ

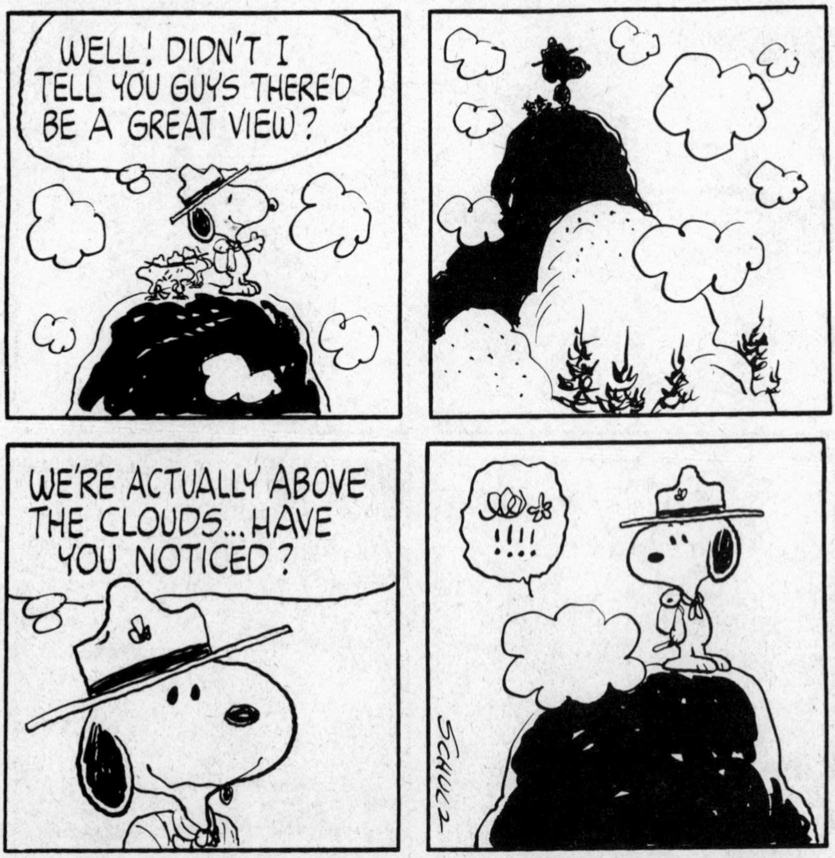
WELL! DIDN'T I TELL YOU GUYS THERE'D BE A GREAT VIEW?
WE'RE ACTUALLY ABOVE THE CLOUDS...HAVE YOU NOTICED?
!!!!
SCHULZ

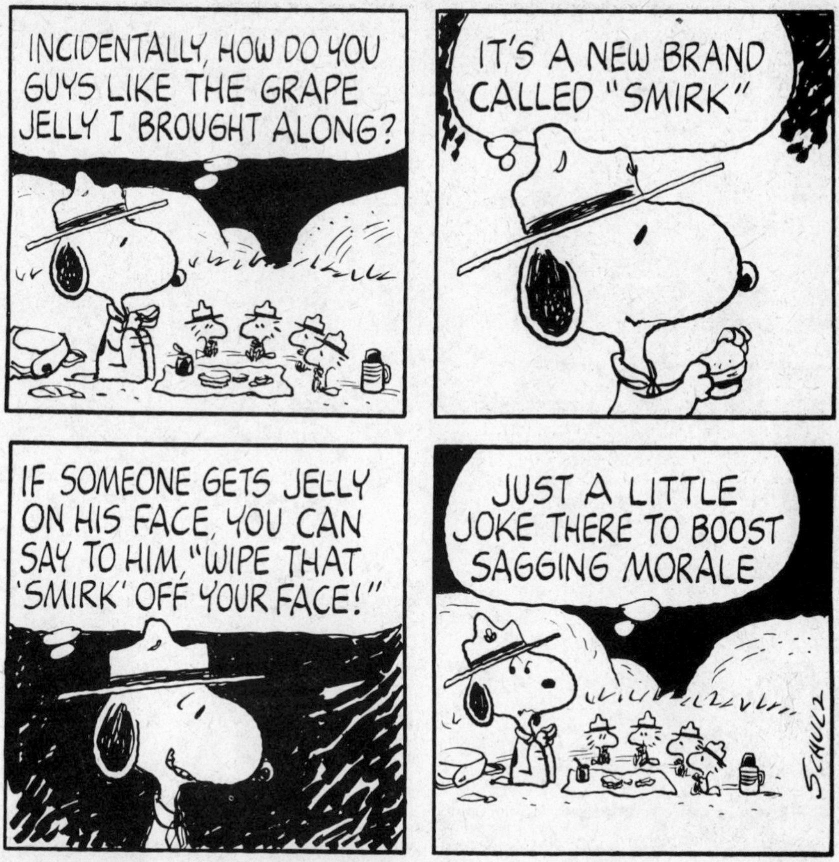
INCIDENTALLY, HOW DO YOU GUYS LIKE THE GRAPE JELLY I BROUGHT ALONG?
IT'S A NEW BRAND CALLED "SMIRK"
IF SOMEONE GETS JELLY ON HIS FACE, YOU CAN SAY TO HIM, "WIPE THAT 'SMIRK' OFF YOUR FACE!"
JUST A LITTLE JOKE THERE TO BOOST SAGGING MORALE
SCHULZ

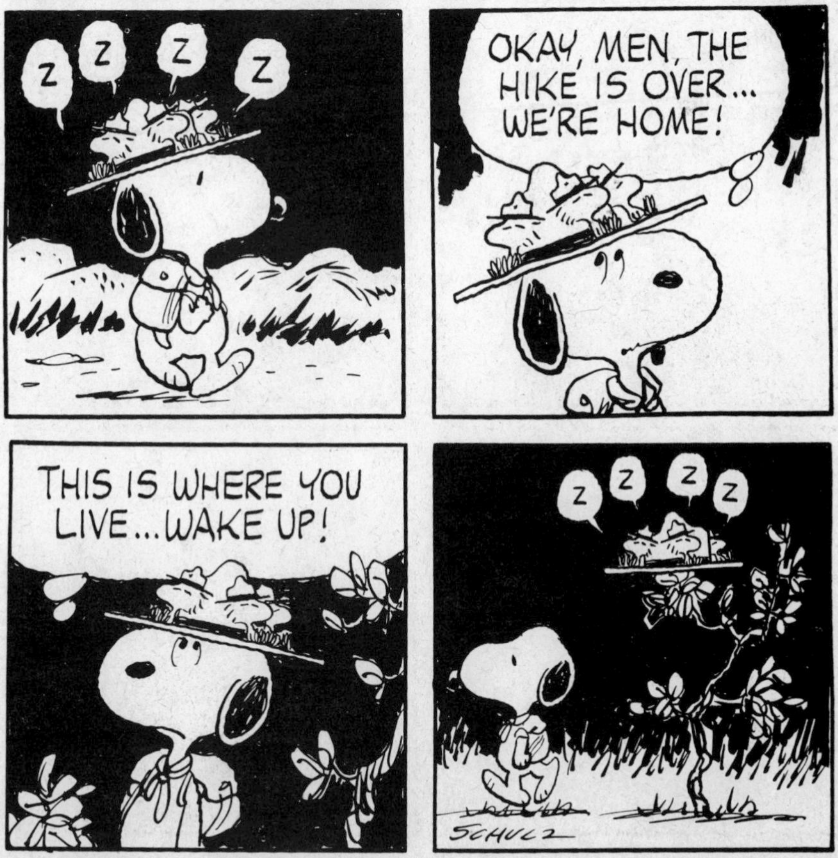
Z Z Z Z
OKAY, MEN, THE HIKE IS OVER... WE'RE HOME!
THIS IS WHERE YOU LIVE...WAKE UP!
Z Z Z Z
SCHULZ

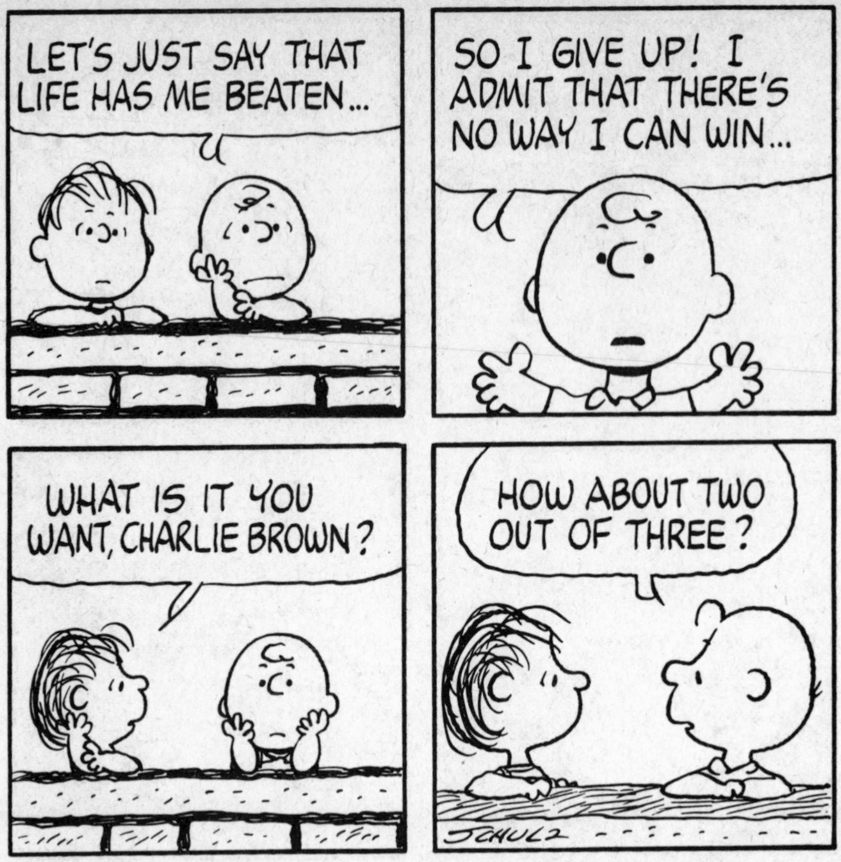
LET'S JUST SAY THAT LIFE HAS ME BEATEN...
SO I GIVE UP! I ADMIT THAT THERE'S NO WAY I CAN WIN...
WHAT IS IT YOU WANT, CHARLIE BROWN?
HOW ABOUT TWO OUT OF THREE?
SCHULZ

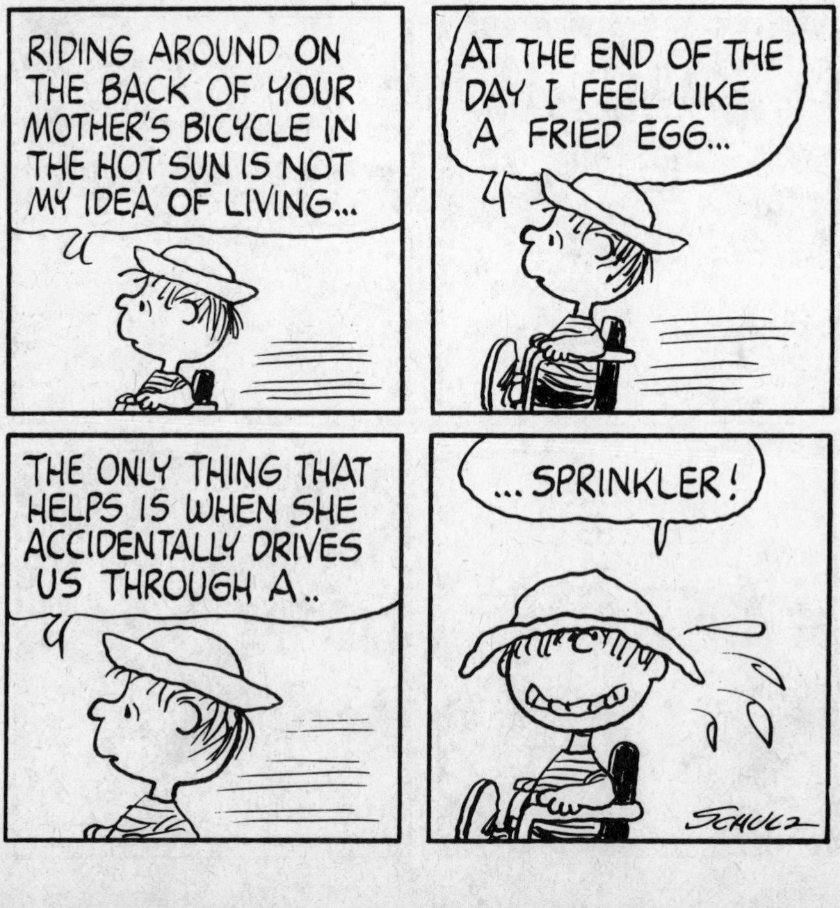
RIDING AROUND ON THE BACK OF YOUR MOTHER'S BICYCLE IN THE HOT SUN IS NOT MY IDEA OF LIVING...
AT THE END OF THE DAY I FEEL LIKE A FRIED EGG...
THE ONLY THING THAT HELPS IS WHEN SHE ACCIDENTALLY DRIVES US THROUGH A..
...SPRINKLER!
SCHULZ

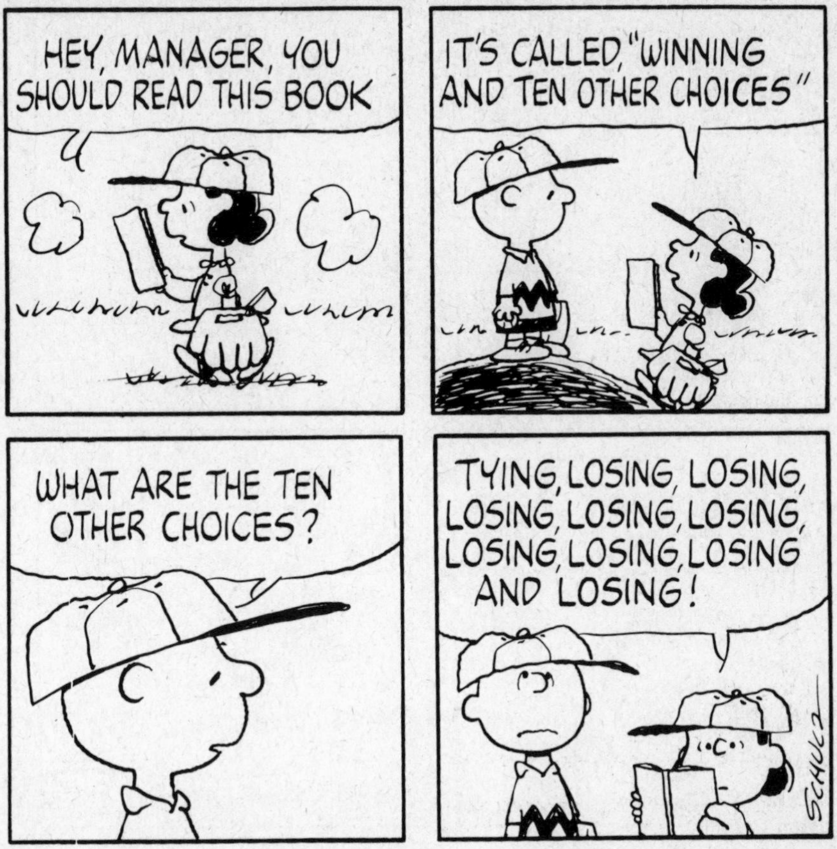
HEY, MANAGER, YOU SHOULD READ THIS BOOK
IT'S CALLED, "WINNING AND TEN OTHER CHOICES"
WHAT ARE THE TEN OTHER CHOICES?
TYING, LOSING, LOSING, LOSING, LOSING, LOSING, LOSING, LOSING, LOSING, LOSING AND LOSING!
SCHULZ

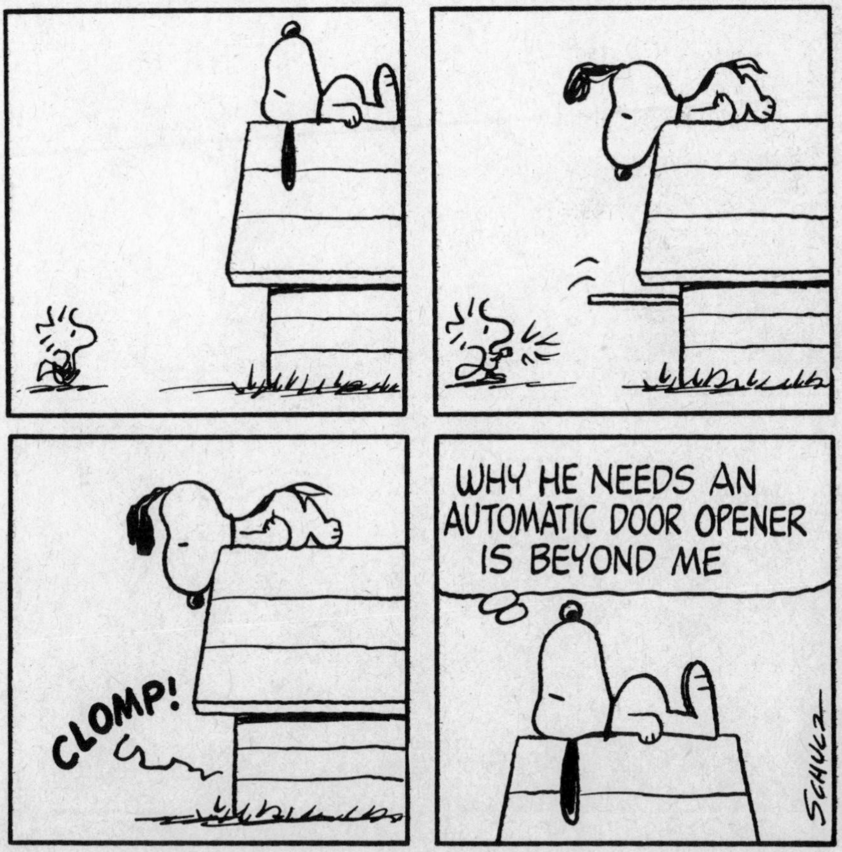
CLOMP!
WHY HE NEEDS AN AUTOMATIC DOOR OPENER IS BEYOND ME
SCHULZ

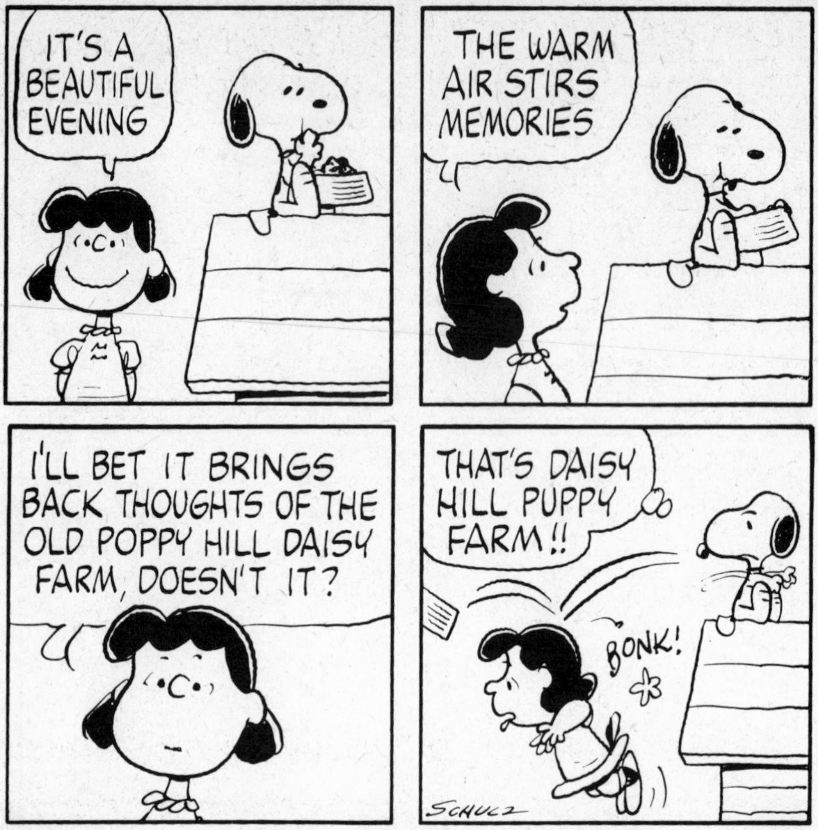
IT'S A BEAUTIFUL EVENING
THE WARM AIR STIRS MEMORIES
I'LL BET IT BRINGS BACK THOUGHTS OF THE OLD POPPY HILL DAISY FARM, DOESN'T IT?
THAT'S DAISY HILL PUPPY FARM!!
BONK!
SCHULZ

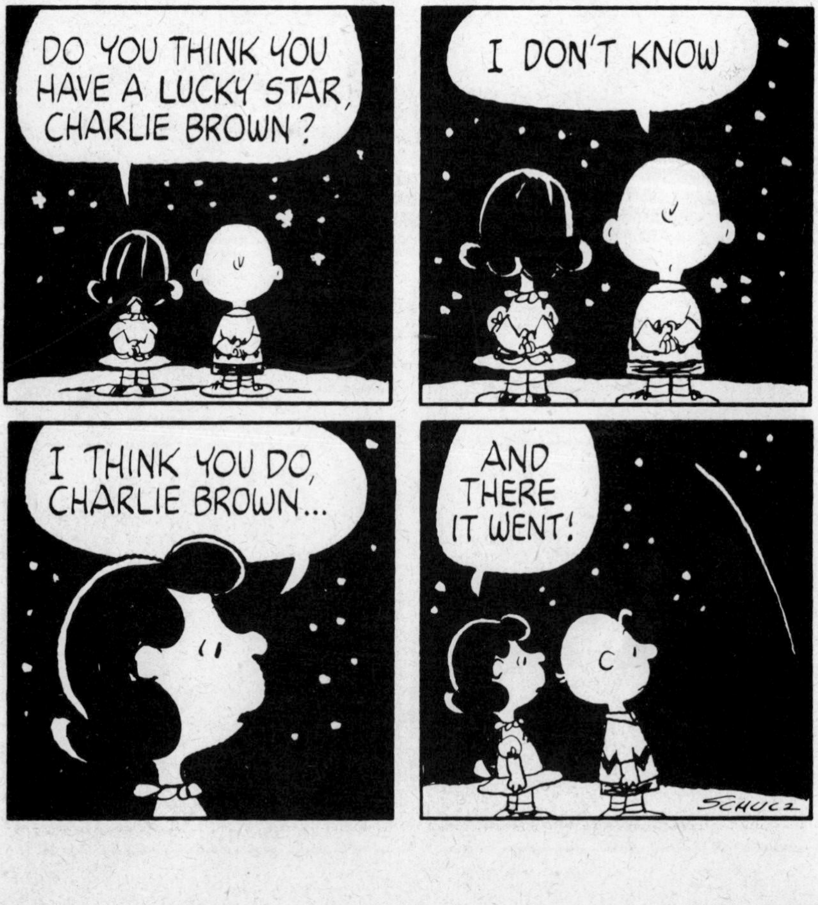
DO YOU THINK YOU HAVE A LUCKY STAR, CHARLIE BROWN?
I DON'T KNOW
I THINK YOU DO, CHARLIE BROWN...
AND THERE IT WENT!
SCHULZ

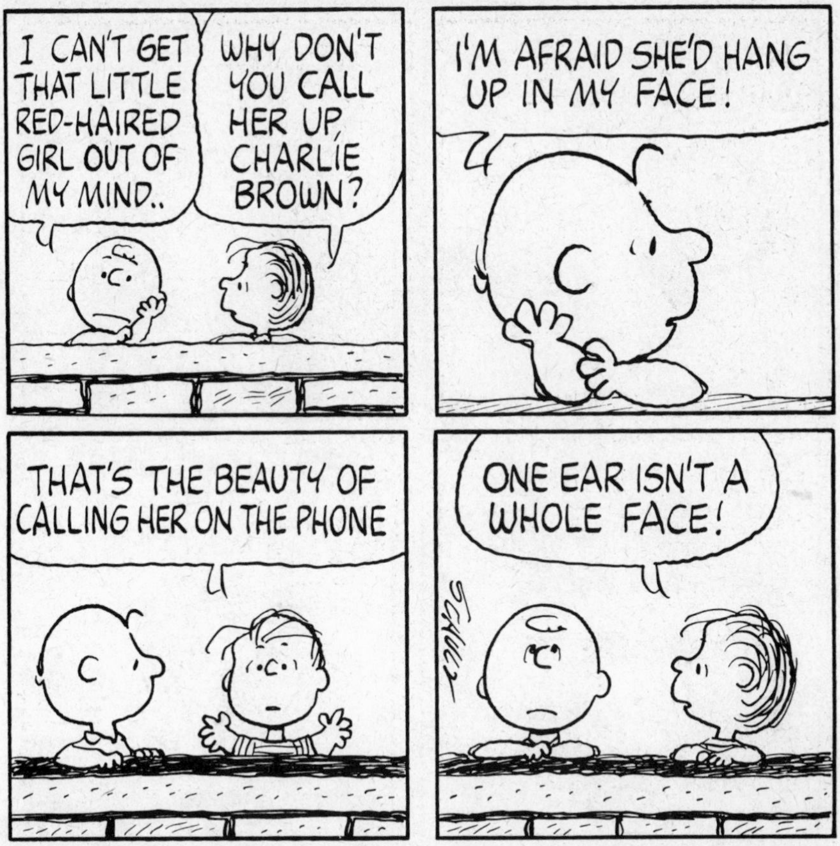
I CAN'T GET THAT LITTLE RED-HAIRED GIRL OUT OF MY MIND..
WHY DON'T YOU CALL HER UP, CHARLIE BROWN?
I'M AFRAID SHE'D HANG UP IN MY FACE!
THAT'S THE BEAUTY OF CALLING HER ON THE PHONE
ONE EAR ISN'T A WHOLE FACE!
SCHULZ

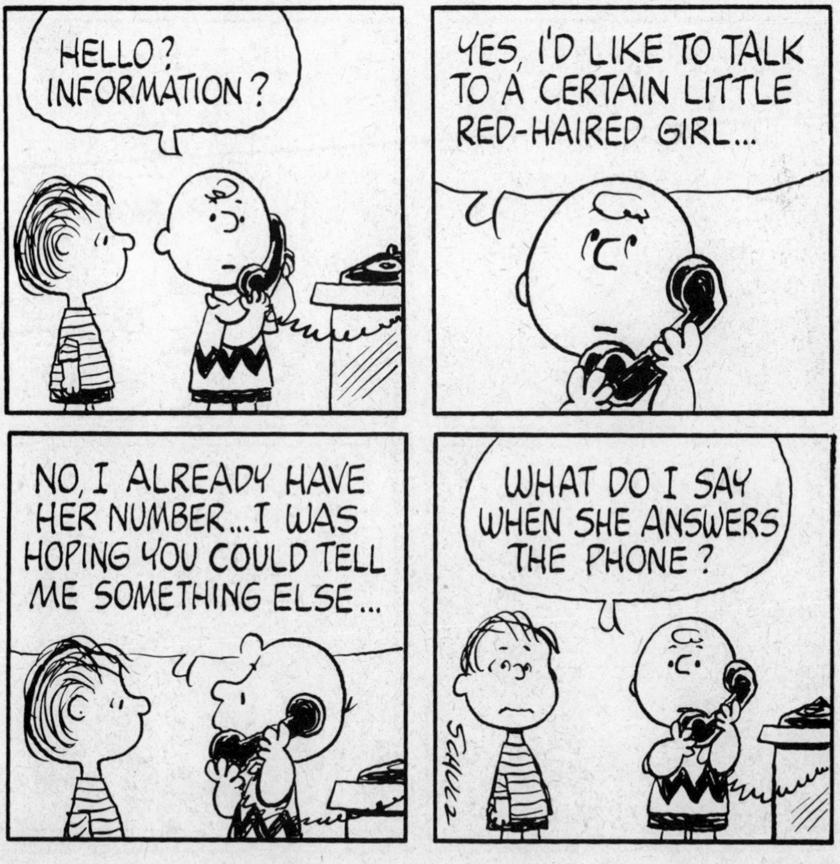
HELLO? INFORMATION?
YES, I'D LIKE TO TALK TO A CERTAIN LITTLE RED-HAIRED GIRL...
NO, I ALREADY HAVE HER NUMBER...I WAS HOPING YOU COULD TELL ME SOMETHING ELSE...
WHAT DO I SAY WHEN SHE ANSWERS THE PHONE?
SCHULZ

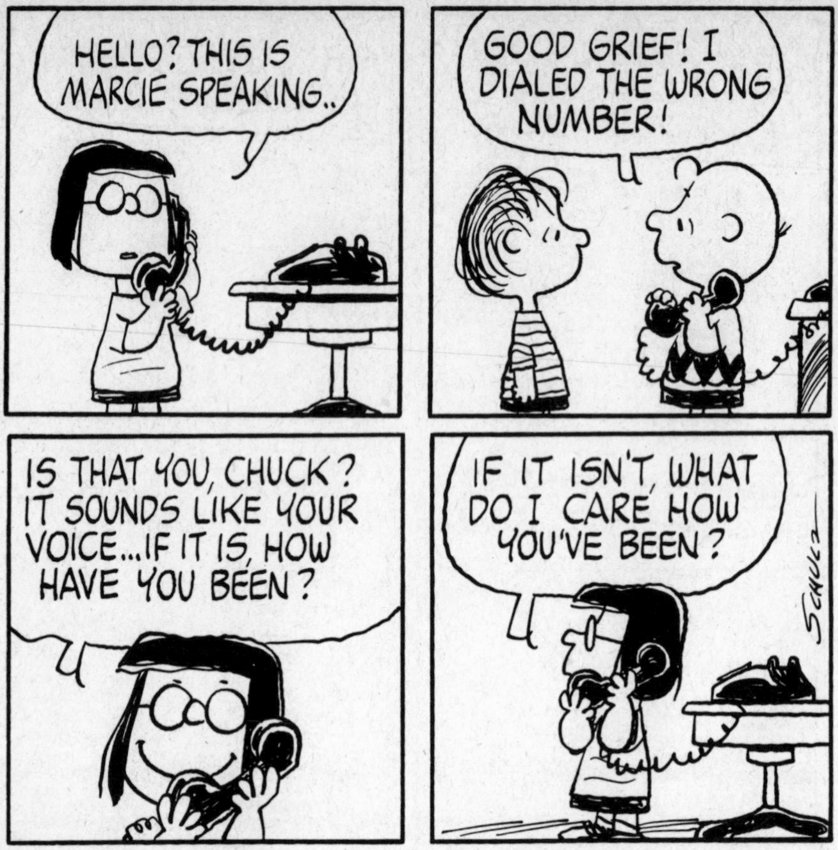
HELLO? THIS IS MARCIE SPEAKING..
GOOD GRIEF! I DIALED THE WRONG NUMBER!
IS THAT YOU, CHUCK? IT SOUNDS LIKE YOUR VOICE...IF IT IS, HOW HAVE YOU BEEN?
IF IT ISN'T, WHAT DO I CARE HOW YOU'VE BEEN?
SCHULZ

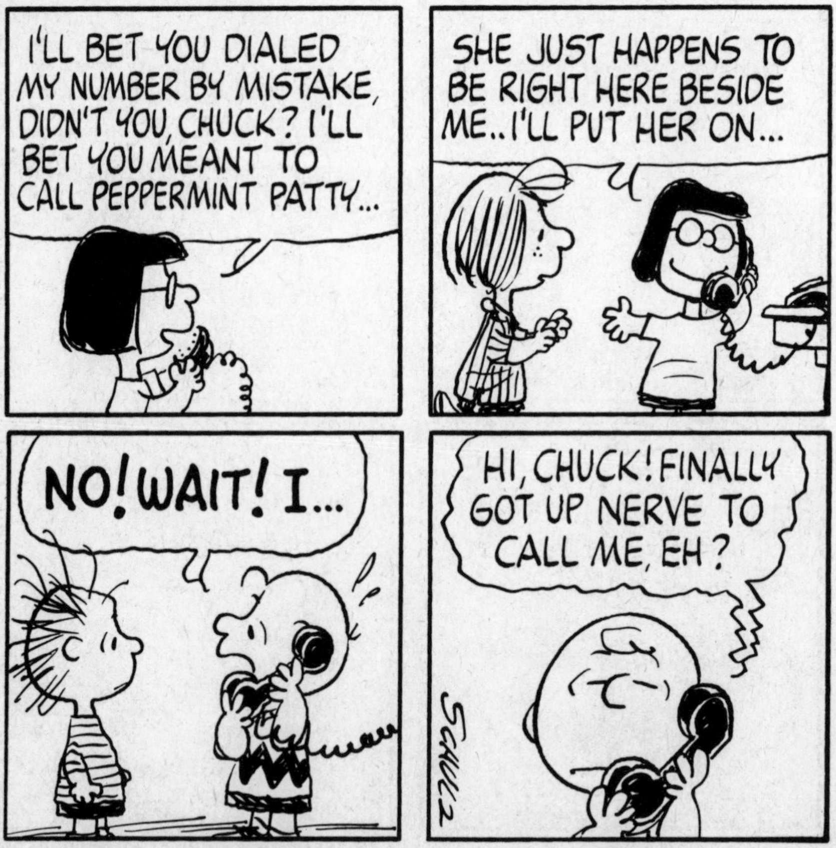
I'LL BET YOU DIALED MY NUMBER BY MISTAKE, DIDN'T YOU, CHUCK? I'LL BET YOU MEANT TO CALL PEPPERMINT PATTY...
SHE JUST HAPPENS TO BE RIGHT HERE BESIDE ME..I'LL PUT HER ON...
NO! WAIT! I...
HI, CHUCK! FINALLY GOT UP NERVE TO CALL ME, EH?
SCHULZ

WHAT DID YOU WANT TO TALK TO ME ABOUT, CHUCK?

IF IT'S ABOUT GOING TO THE SHOW, WHY DON'T WE JUST MEET THERE AROUND ONE? THAT'LL SAVE YOU COMIN' CLEAR OVER HERE!

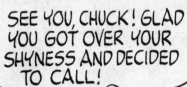

SEE YOU, CHUCK! GLAD YOU GOT OVER YOUR SHYNESS AND DECIDED TO CALL!

I CAN'T STAND IT...

WHERE ARE YOU GOING, BIG BROTHER?

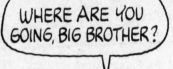

WELL, I FINALLY GOT UP NERVE TO CALL THAT LITTLE RED-HAIRED GIRL, BUT I DIALED MARCIE BY MISTAKE, AND GOT A DATE WITH PEPPERMINT PATTY...

I THINK YOU'RE TOO WISHY-WASHY, BIG BROTHER

IT'S NOT A LOST ART!

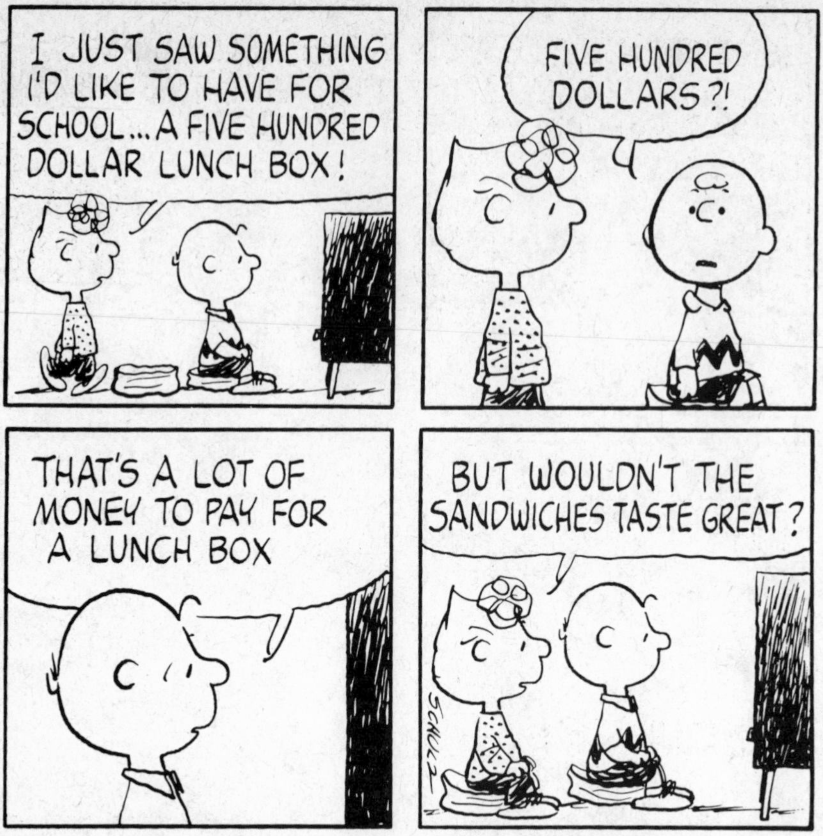
I JUST SAW SOMETHING I'D LIKE TO HAVE FOR SCHOOL...A FIVE HUNDRED DOLLAR LUNCH BOX!
FIVE HUNDRED DOLLARS?!
THAT'S A LOT OF MONEY TO PAY FOR A LUNCH BOX
BUT WOULDN'T THE SANDWICHES TASTE GREAT?
SCHULZ

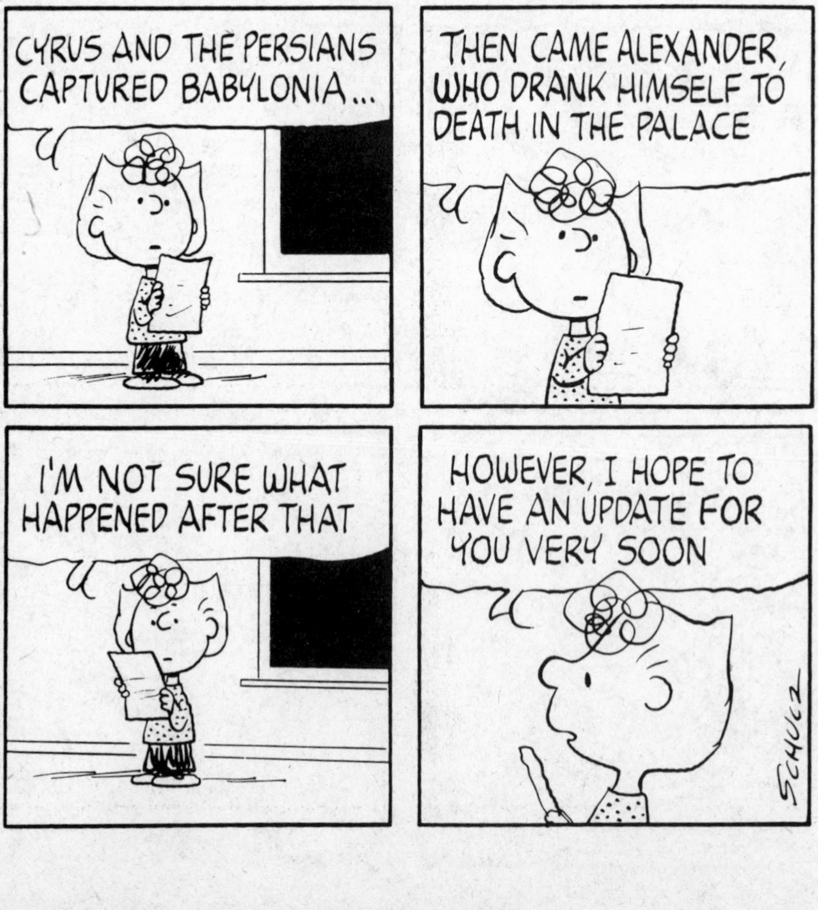
CYRUS AND THE PERSIANS CAPTURED BABYLONIA...
THEN CAME ALEXANDER, WHO DRANK HIMSELF TO DEATH IN THE PALACE
I'M NOT SURE WHAT HAPPENED AFTER THAT
HOWEVER, I HOPE TO HAVE AN UPDATE FOR YOU VERY SOON
SCHULZ

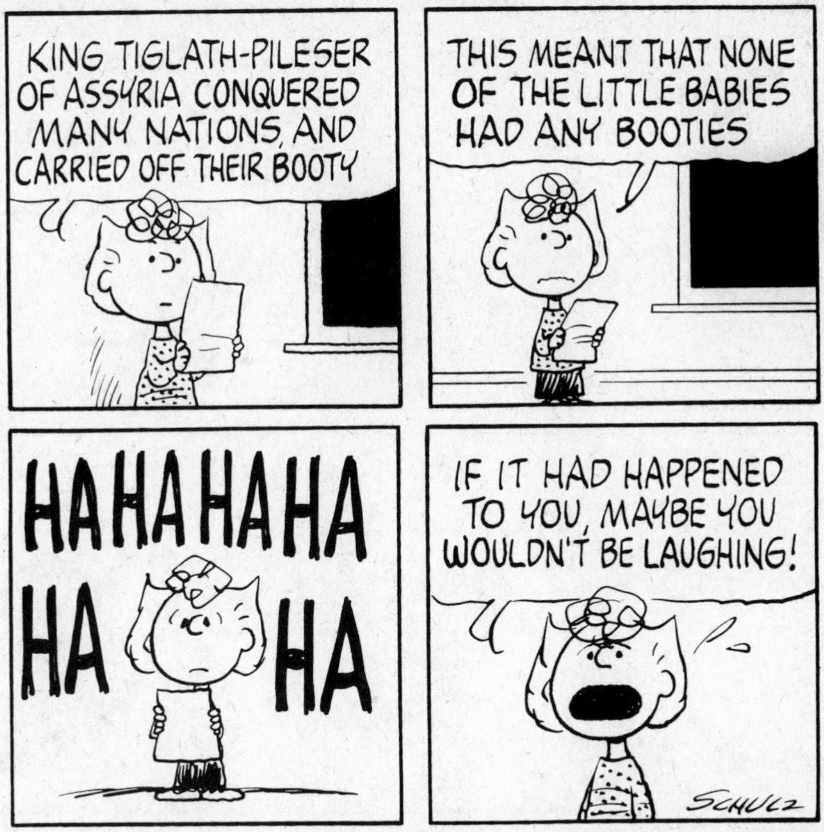
KING TIGLATH-PILESER OF ASSYRIA CONQUERED MANY NATIONS, AND CARRIED OFF THEIR BOOTY
THIS MEANT THAT NONE OF THE LITTLE BABIES HAD ANY BOOTIES
HAHAHAHAHA HA HA
IF IT HAD HAPPENED TO YOU, MAYBE YOU WOULDN'T BE LAUGHING!
SCHULZ

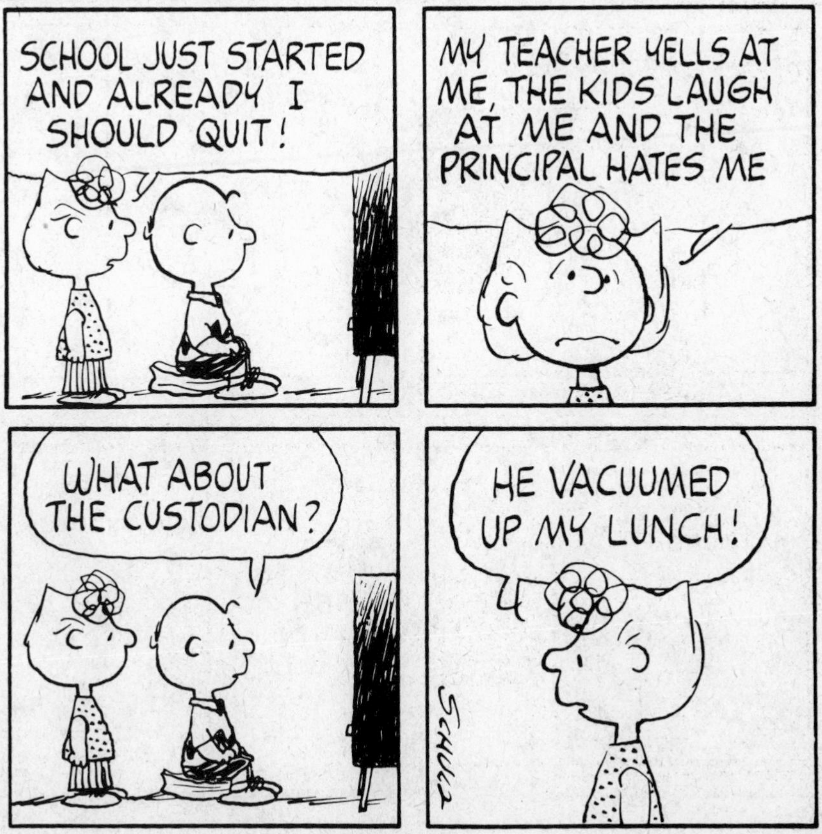
SCHOOL JUST STARTED AND ALREADY I SHOULD QUIT!
MY TEACHER YELLS AT ME, THE KIDS LAUGH AT ME AND THE PRINCIPAL HATES ME
WHAT ABOUT THE CUSTODIAN?
HE VACUUMED UP MY LUNCH!
SCHULZ

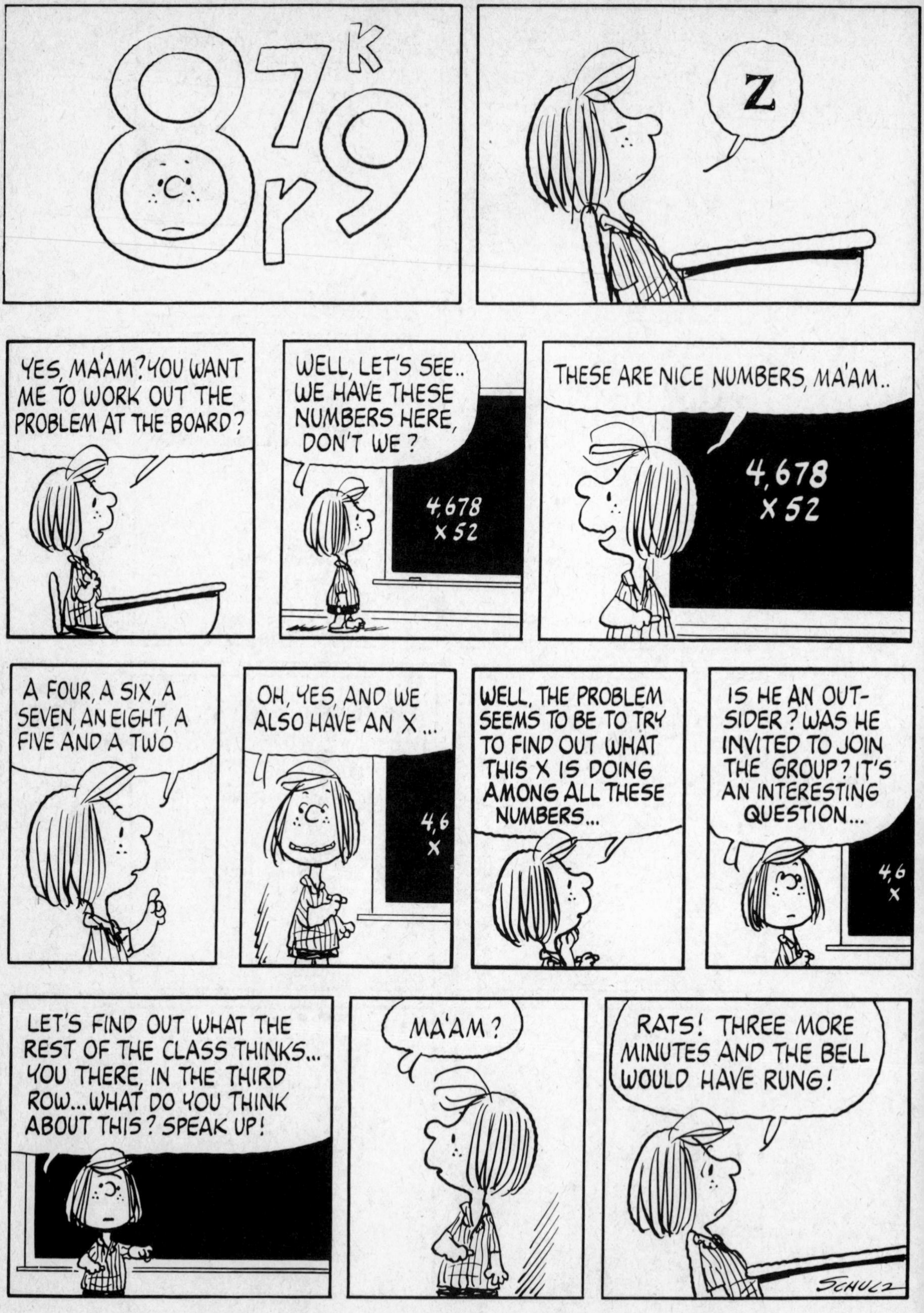

8
7
K
9
r
Z
YES, MA'AM? YOU WANT ME TO WORK OUT THE PROBLEM AT THE BOARD?
WELL, LET'S SEE.. WE HAVE THESE NUMBERS HERE, DON'T WE?
4,678 x 52
THESE ARE NICE NUMBERS, MA'AM..
4,678 x 52
A FOUR, A SIX, A SEVEN, AN EIGHT, A FIVE AND A TWO
OH, YES, AND WE ALSO HAVE AN X ...
WELL, THE PROBLEM SEEMS TO BE TO TRY TO FIND OUT WHAT THIS X IS DOING AMONG ALL THESE NUMBERS...
IS HE AN OUT-SIDER? WAS HE INVITED TO JOIN THE GROUP? IT'S AN INTERESTING QUESTION...
LET'S FIND OUT WHAT THE REST OF THE CLASS THINKS... YOU THERE, IN THE THIRD ROW...WHAT DO YOU THINK ABOUT THIS? SPEAK UP!
MA'AM?
RATS! THREE MORE MINUTES AND THE BELL WOULD HAVE RUNG!
SCHULZ

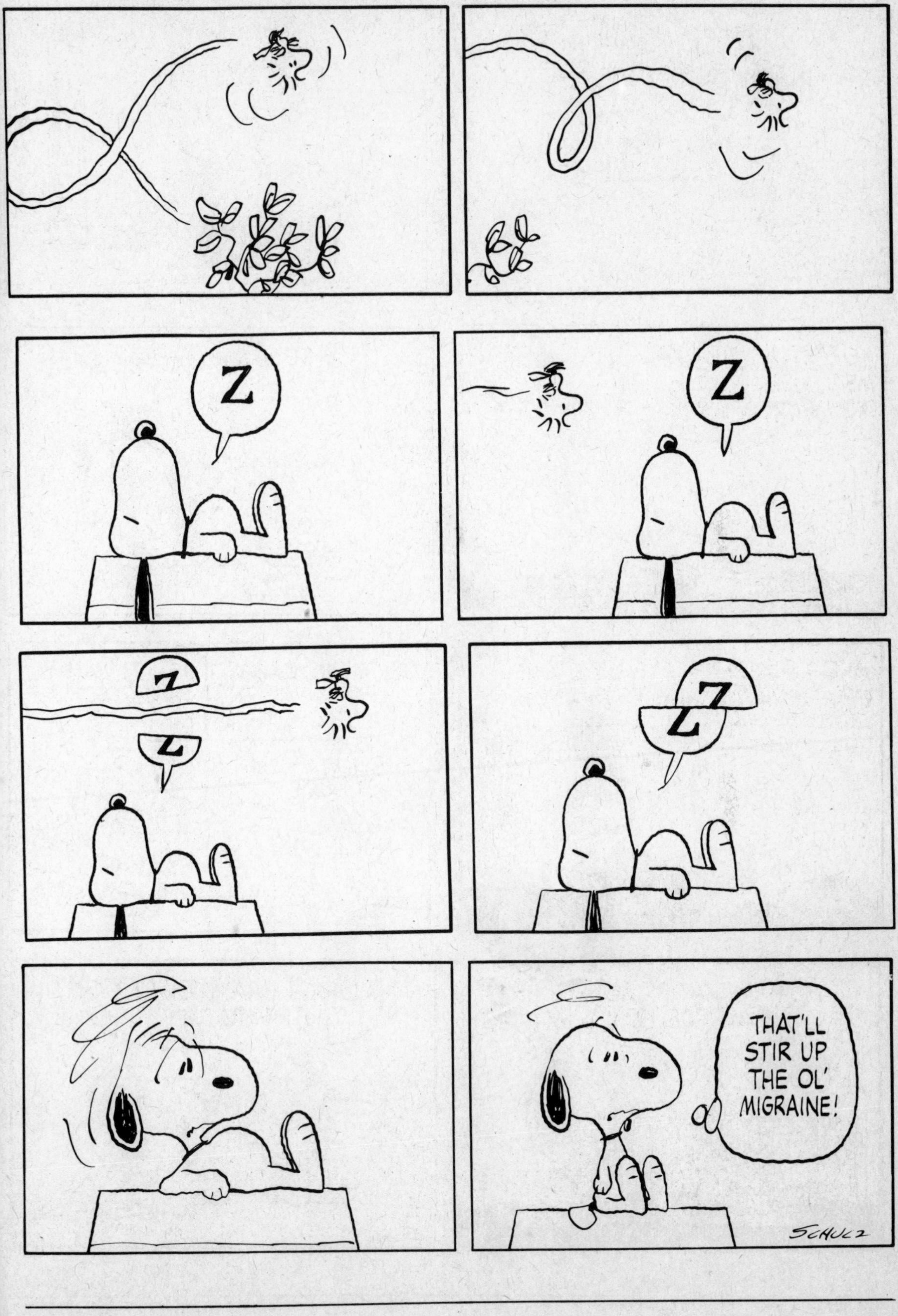
Z
Z
Z
Z
Z
Z
THAT'LL STIR UP THE OL' MIGRAINE!
SCHULZ

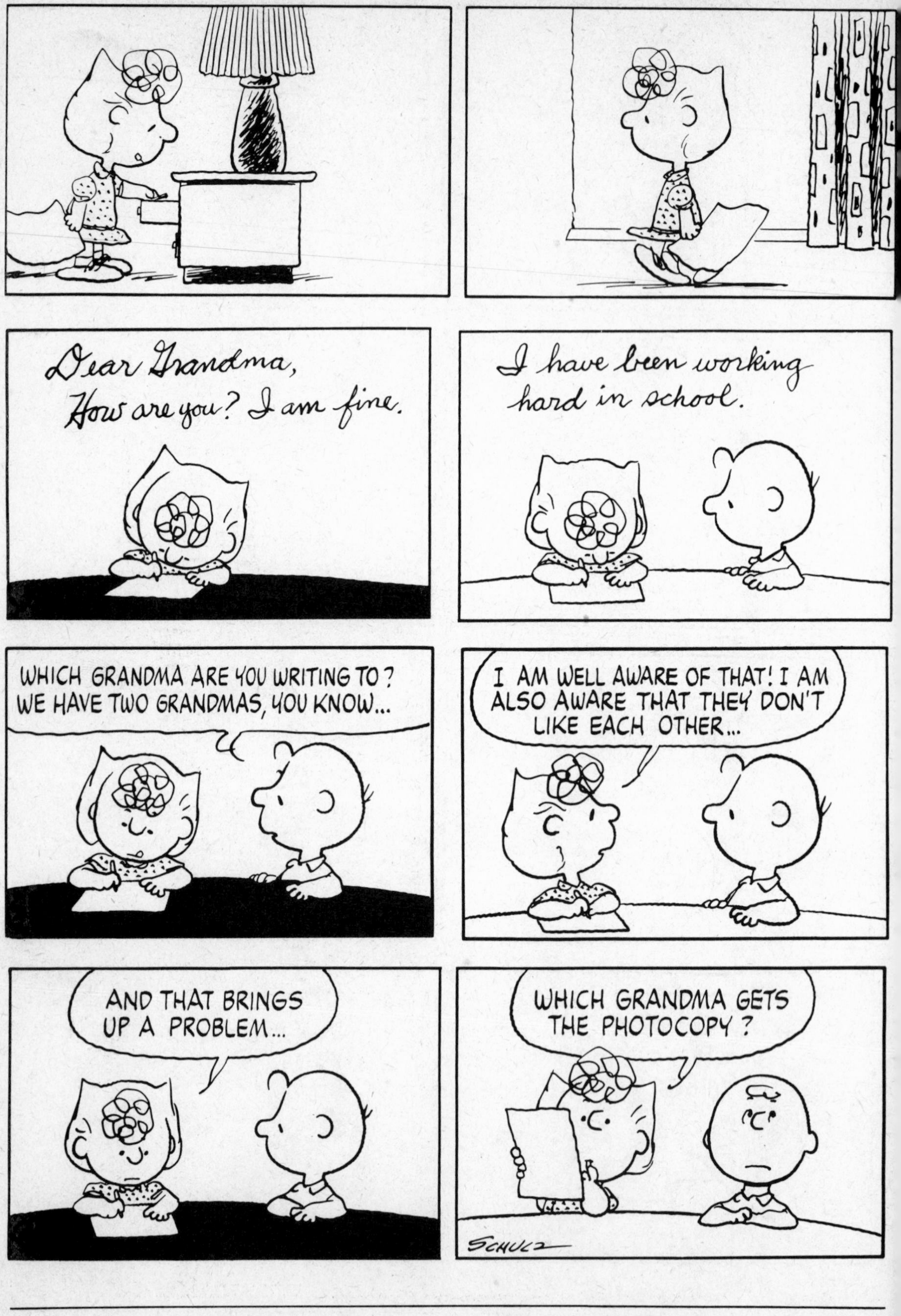
Dear Grandma,
How are you? I am fine.
I have been working hard in school.
WHICH GRANDMA ARE YOU WRITING TO? WE HAVE TWO GRANDMAS, YOU KNOW...
I AM WELL AWARE OF THAT! I AM ALSO AWARE THAT THEY DON'T LIKE EACH OTHER...
AND THAT BRINGS UP A PROBLEM...
WHICH GRANDMA GETS THE PHOTOCOPY?
SCHULZ

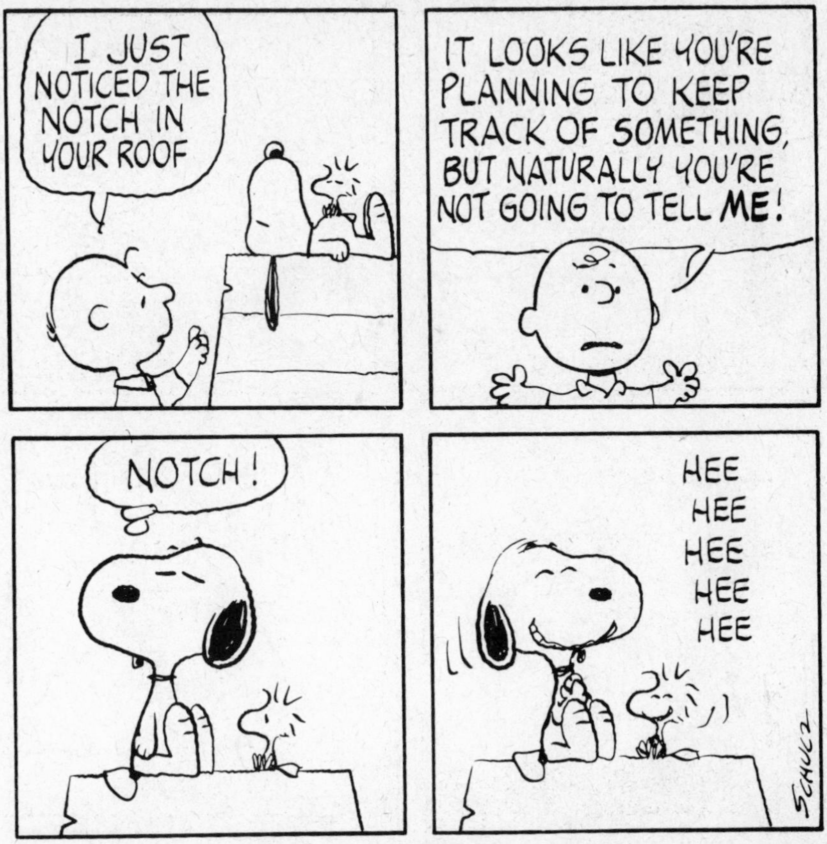
I JUST NOTICED THE NOTCH IN YOUR ROOF
IT LOOKS LIKE YOU'RE PLANNING TO KEEP TRACK OF SOMETHING, BUT NATURALLY YOU'RE NOT GOING TO TELL **ME**!
NOTCH!
HEE HEE HEE HEE HEE
SCHULZ

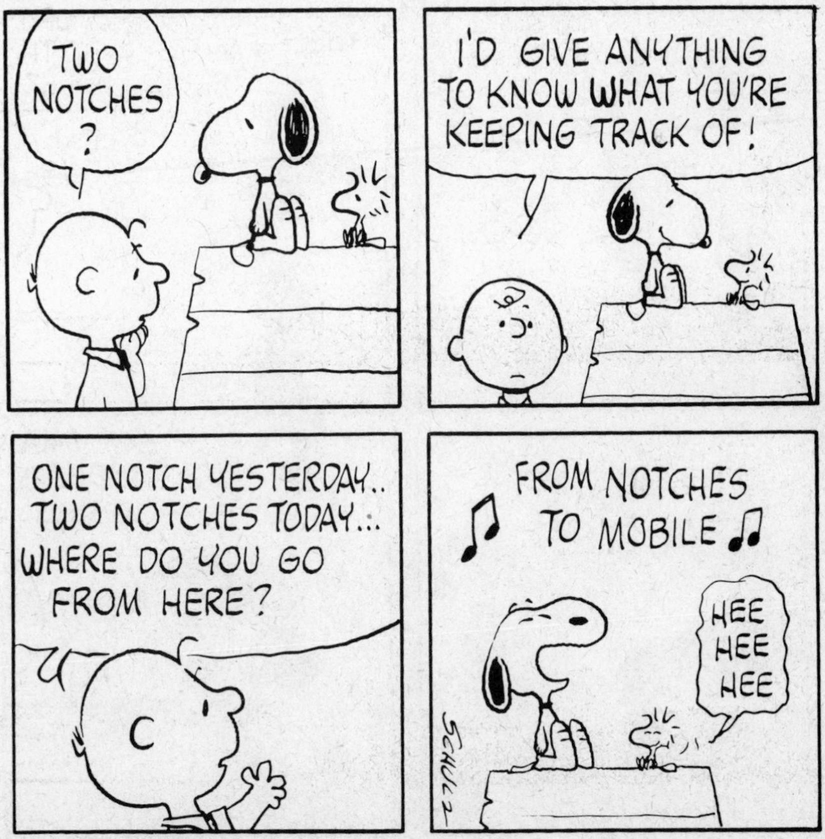
TWO NOTCHES ?
I'D GIVE ANYTHING TO KNOW **WHAT** YOU'RE KEEPING TRACK OF!
ONE NOTCH YESTERDAY.. TWO NOTCHES TODAY... WHERE DO YOU GO FROM HERE?
♪ FROM NOTCHES TO MOBILE ♫
HEE HEE HEE
SCHULZ

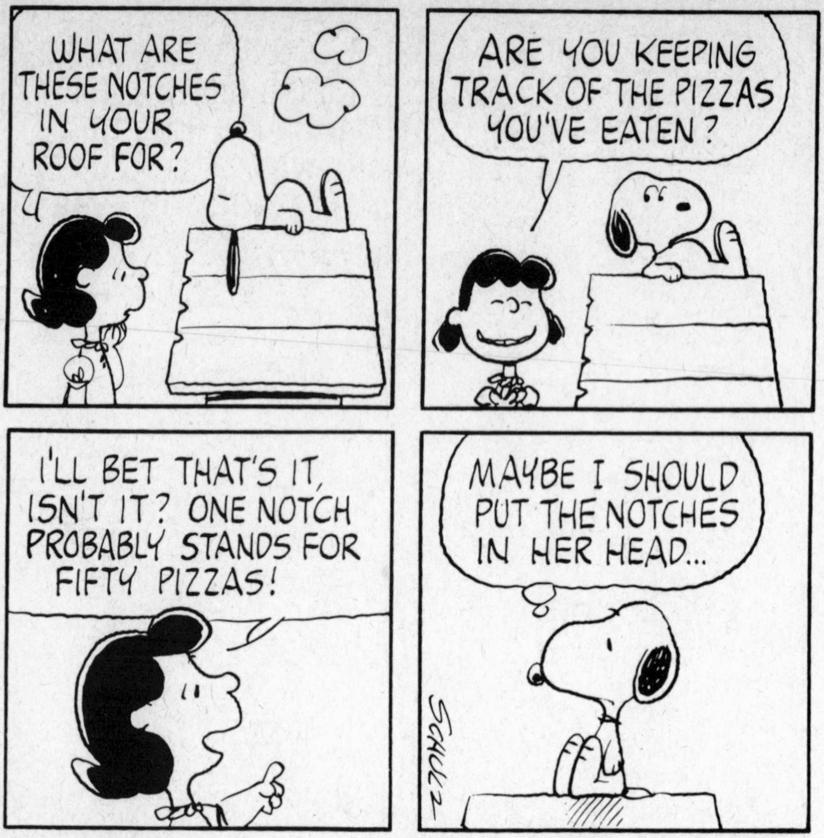
WHAT ARE THESE NOTCHES IN YOUR ROOF FOR?
ARE YOU KEEPING TRACK OF THE PIZZAS YOU'VE EATEN?
I'LL BET THAT'S IT, ISN'T IT? ONE NOTCH PROBABLY STANDS FOR FIFTY PIZZAS!
MAYBE I SHOULD PUT THE NOTCHES IN HER HEAD...
SCHULZ

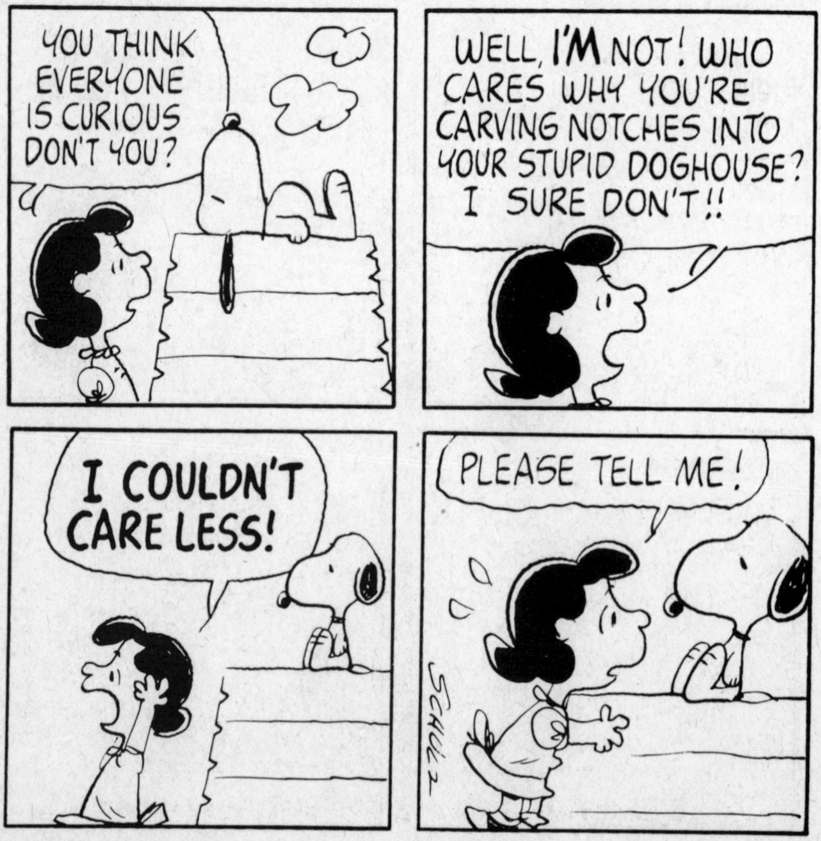
YOU THINK EVERYONE IS CURIOUS DON'T YOU?
WELL, I'M NOT! WHO CARES WHY YOU'RE CARVING NOTCHES INTO YOUR STUPID DOGHOUSE? I SURE DON'T!!
I COULDN'T CARE LESS!
PLEASE TELL ME!
SCHULZ

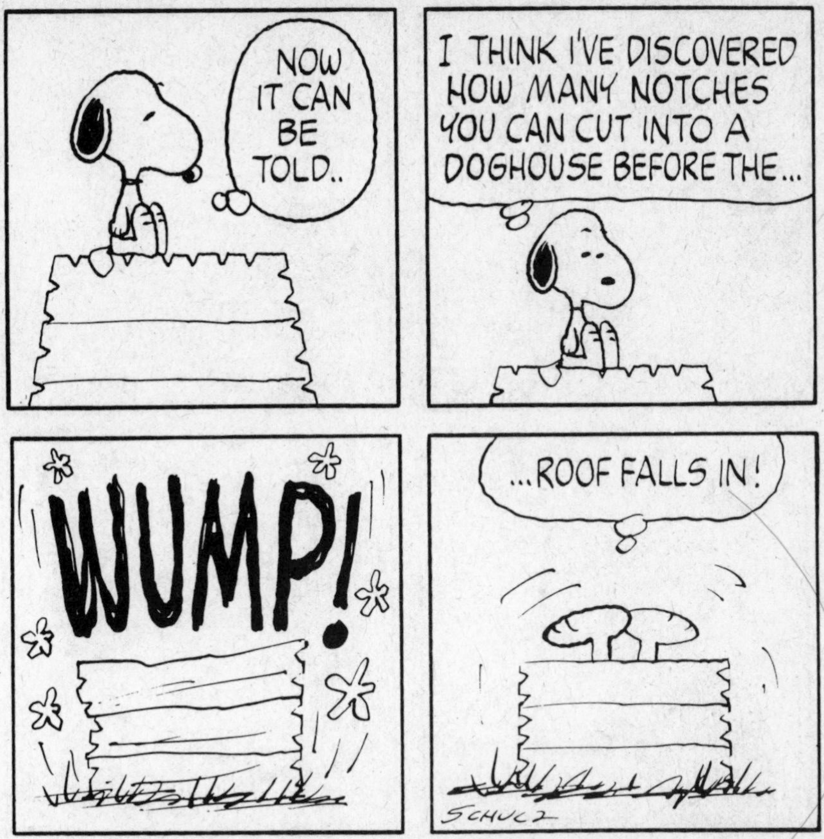
NOW IT CAN BE TOLD..
I THINK I'VE DISCOVERED HOW MANY NOTCHES YOU CAN CUT INTO A DOGHOUSE BEFORE THE...
WUMP!
...ROOF FALLS IN!

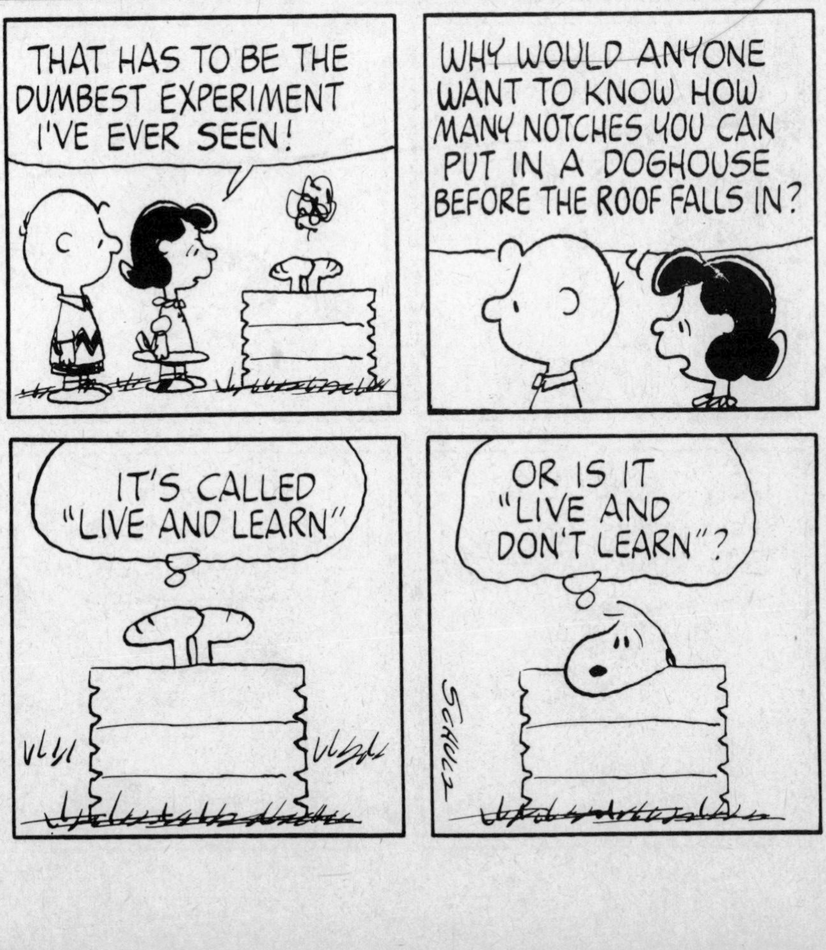
THAT HAS TO BE THE DUMBEST EXPERIMENT I'VE EVER SEEN!
WHY WOULD ANYONE WANT TO KNOW HOW MANY NOTCHES YOU CAN PUT IN A DOGHOUSE BEFORE THE ROOF FALLS IN?
IT'S CALLED "LIVE AND LEARN"
OR IS IT "LIVE AND DON'T LEARN"?

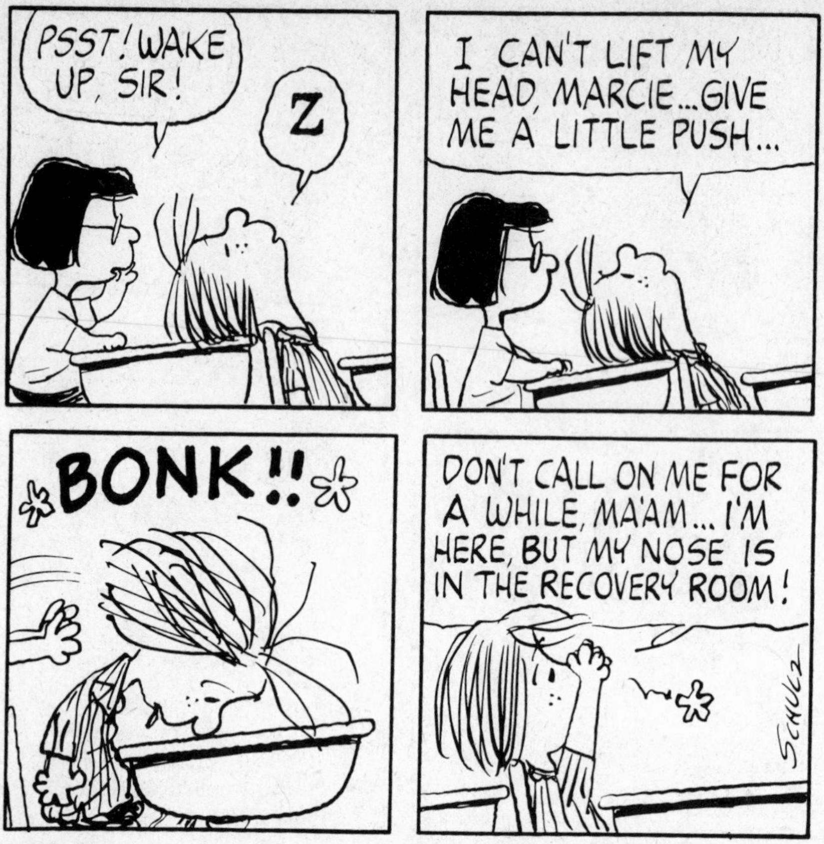
PSST! WAKE UP, SIR!
Z
I CAN'T LIFT MY HEAD, MARCIE...GIVE ME A LITTLE PUSH...
BONK!!
DON'T CALL ON ME FOR A WHILE, MA'AM... I'M HERE, BUT MY NOSE IS IN THE RECOVERY ROOM!
SCHULZ

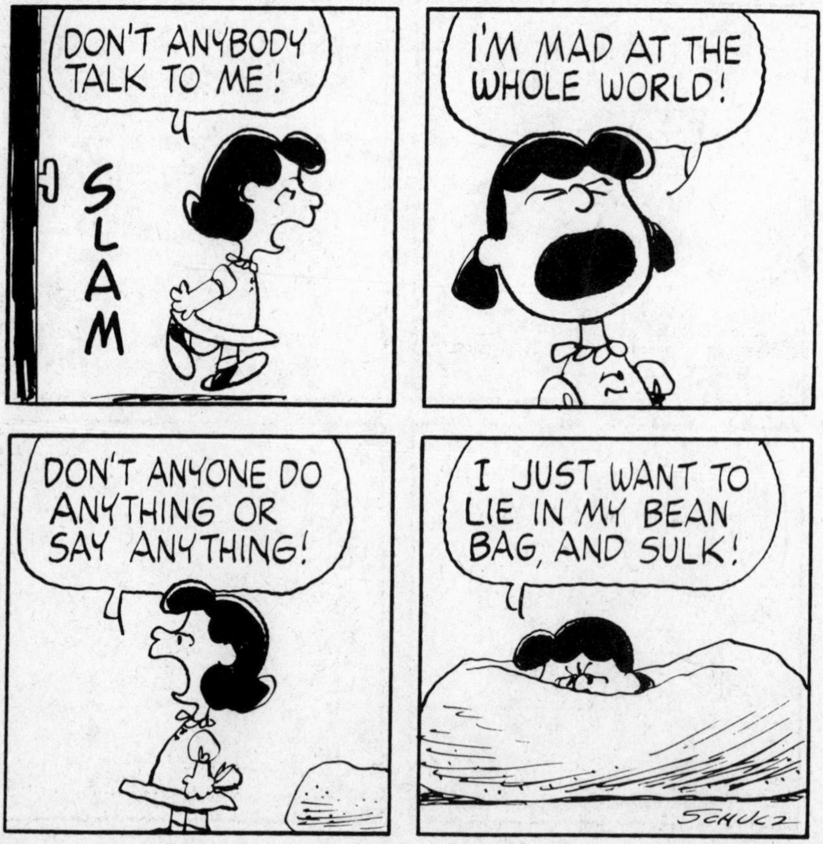
DON'T ANYBODY TALK TO ME!
SLAM
I'M MAD AT THE WHOLE WORLD!
DON'T ANYONE DO ANYTHING OR SAY ANYTHING!
I JUST WANT TO LIE IN MY BEAN BAG, AND SULK!
SCHULZ

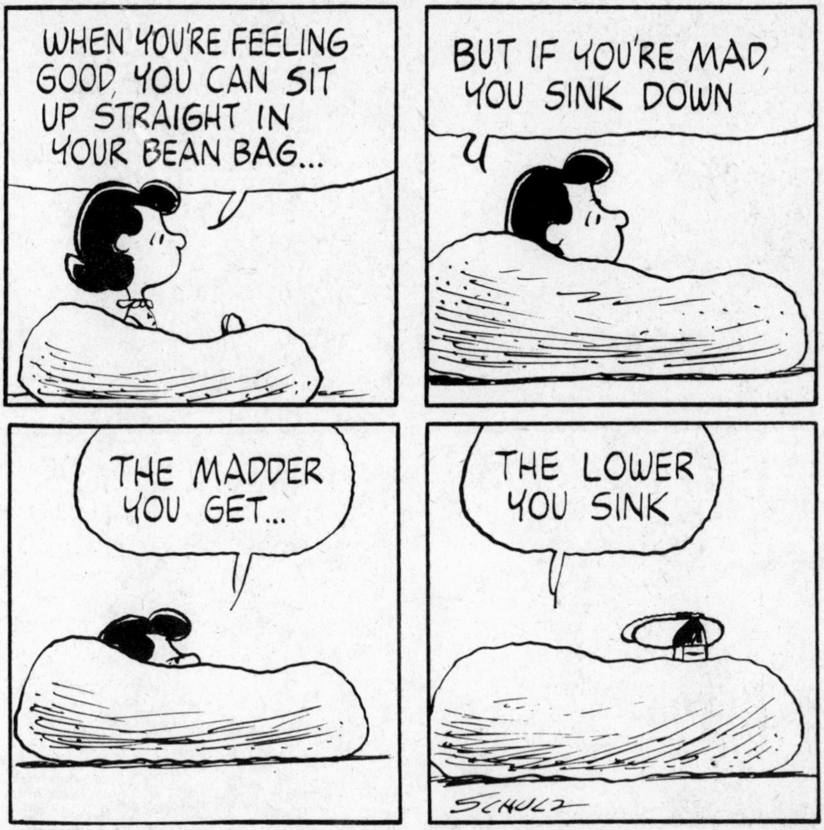
WHEN YOU'RE FEELING GOOD, YOU CAN SIT UP STRAIGHT IN YOUR BEAN BAG...
BUT IF YOU'RE MAD, YOU SINK DOWN
THE MADDER YOU GET...
THE LOWER YOU SINK

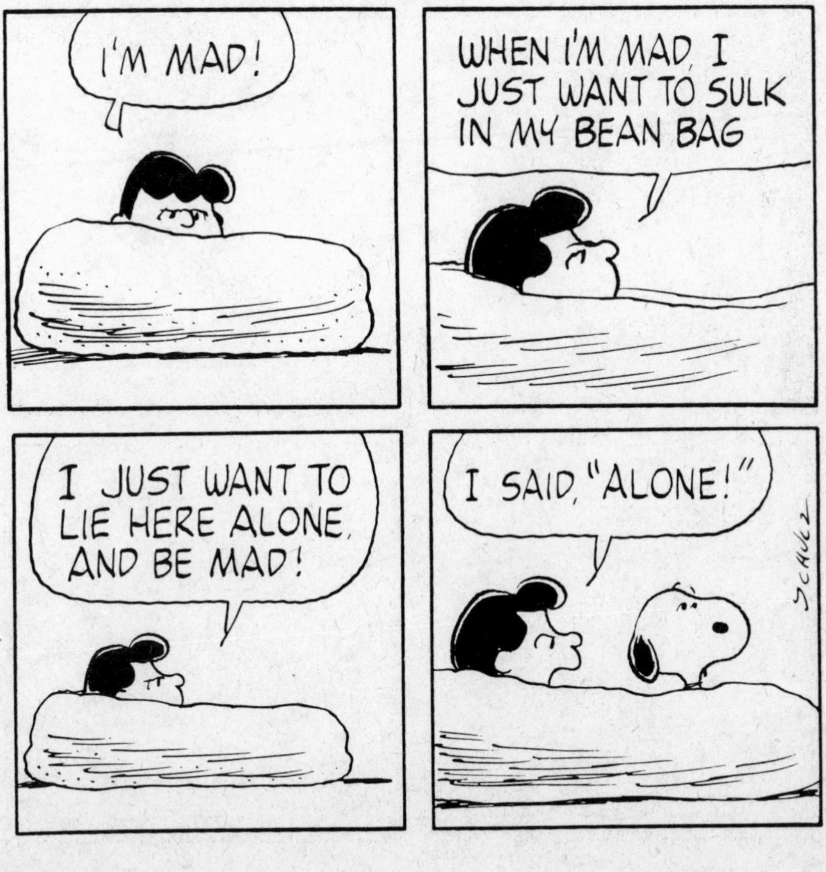
I'M MAD!
WHEN I'M MAD, I JUST WANT TO SULK IN MY BEAN BAG
I JUST WANT TO LIE HERE ALONE, AND BE MAD!
I SAID, "ALONE!"

PROBLEM NUMBER SIX...
"HOW MANY GALLONS OF CREAM CONTAINING 25% BUTTER FAT AND MILK CONTAINING 3½% BUTTER FAT MUST BE MIXED TO..
..OBTAIN 50 GALLONS OF CREAM CONTAINING 12½% BUTTER FAT?"
MA'AM, WOULD YOU SETTLE FOR TWENTY PUSH-UPS ?
SCHULZ

HERE COMES WOODSTOCK IN FOR A LANDING...
I CAN SEE ALREADY WHAT'S GOING TO HAPPEN..
TOO MUCH TOP SPIN!
SCHULZ

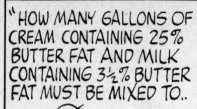

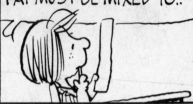

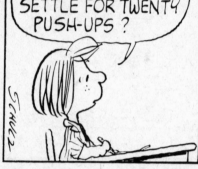

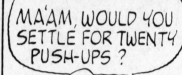

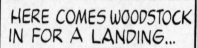

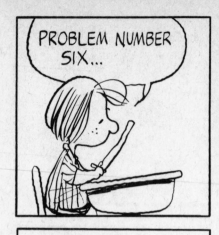

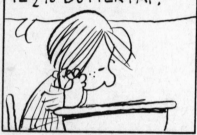

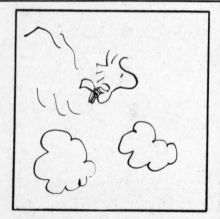

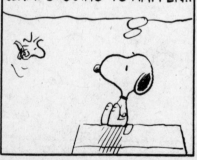

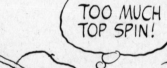

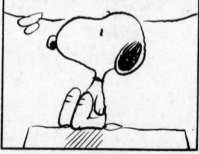

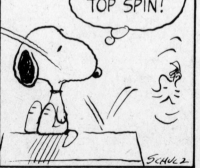

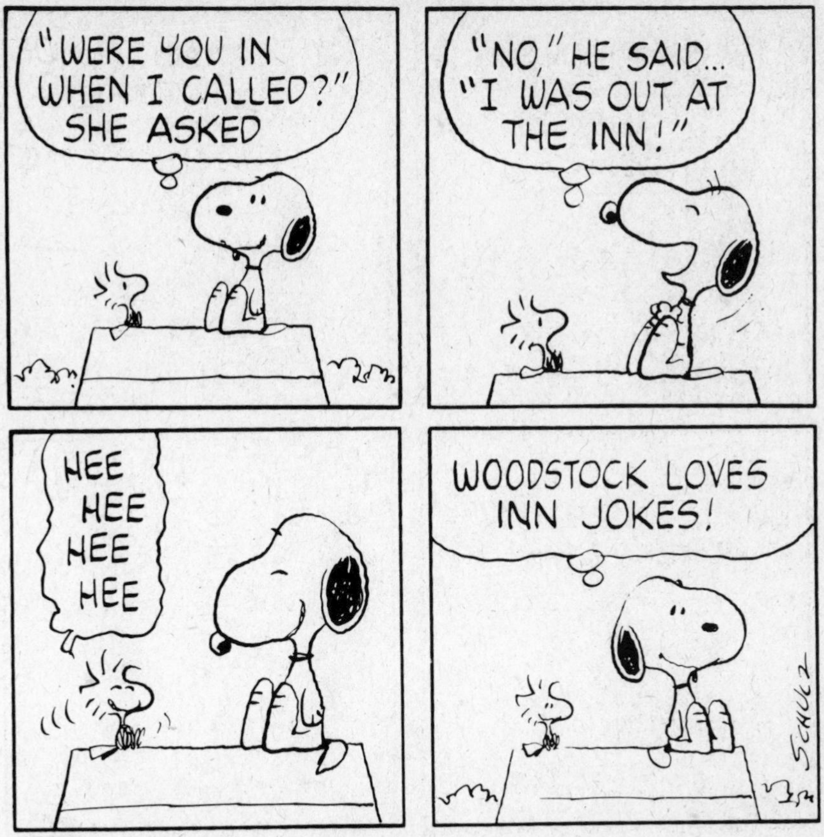
"WERE YOU IN WHEN I CALLED?" SHE ASKED
"NO," HE SAID... "I WAS OUT AT THE INN!"
HEE HEE HEE HEE
WOODSTOCK LOVES INN JOKES!
SCHULZ

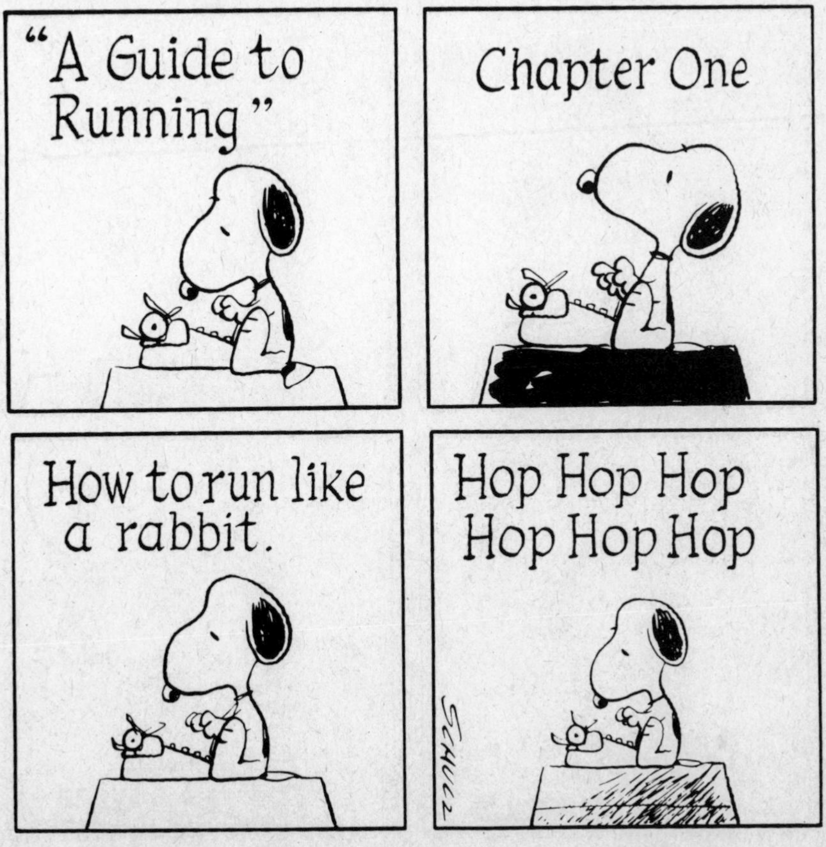
"A Guide to Running"
Chapter One
How to run like a rabbit.
Hop Hop Hop Hop Hop Hop
SCHULZ

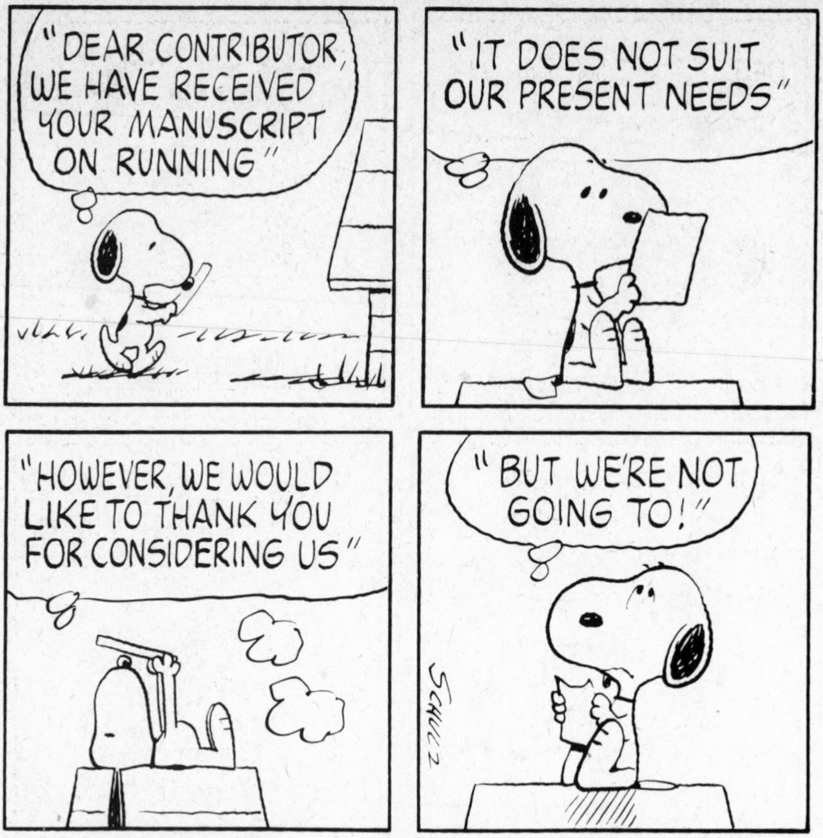
"DEAR CONTRIBUTOR, WE HAVE RECEIVED YOUR MANUSCRIPT ON RUNNING"
"IT DOES NOT SUIT OUR PRESENT NEEDS"
"HOWEVER, WE WOULD LIKE TO THANK YOU FOR CONSIDERING US"
"BUT WE'RE NOT GOING TO!"

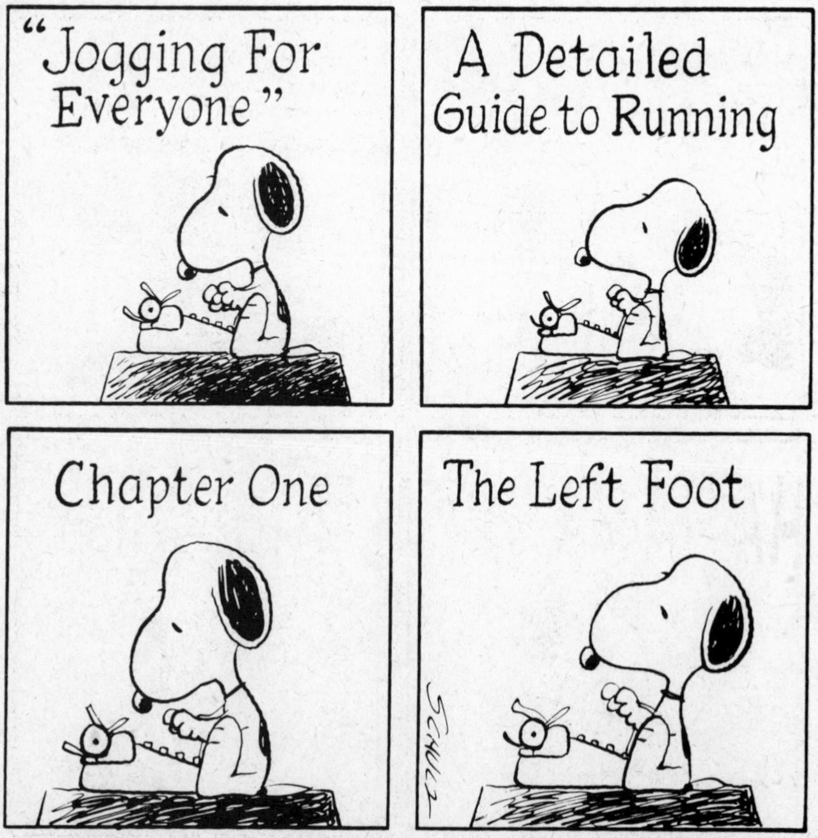
"Jogging For Everyone"
A Detailed Guide to Running
Chapter One
The Left Foot

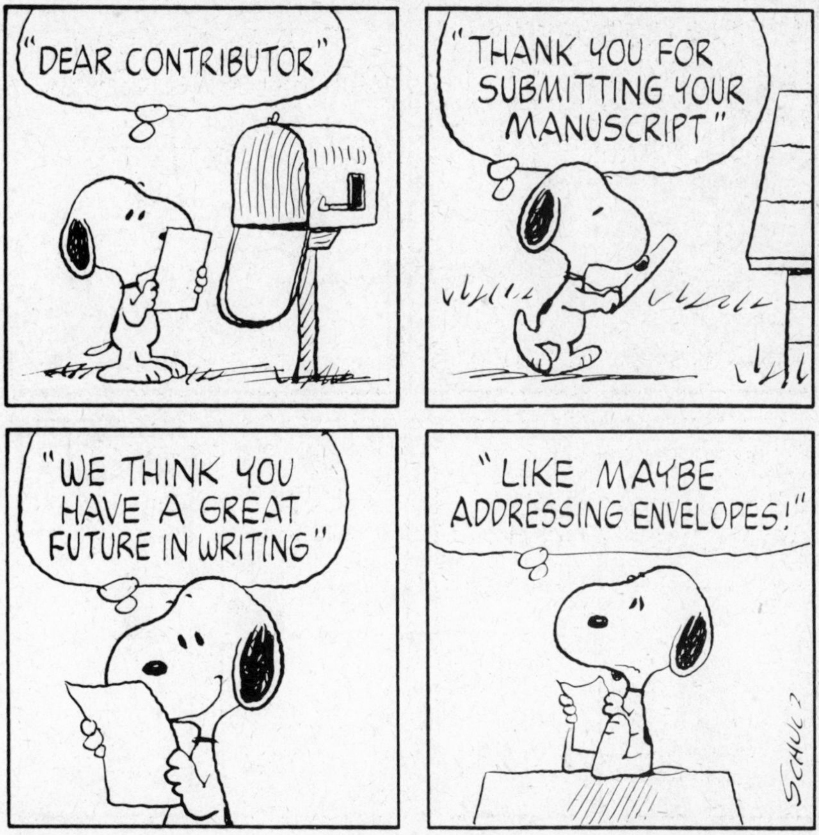
"DEAR CONTRIBUTOR"
"THANK YOU FOR SUBMITTING YOUR MANUSCRIPT"
"WE THINK YOU HAVE A GREAT FUTURE IN WRITING"
"LIKE MAYBE ADDRESSING ENVELOPES!"

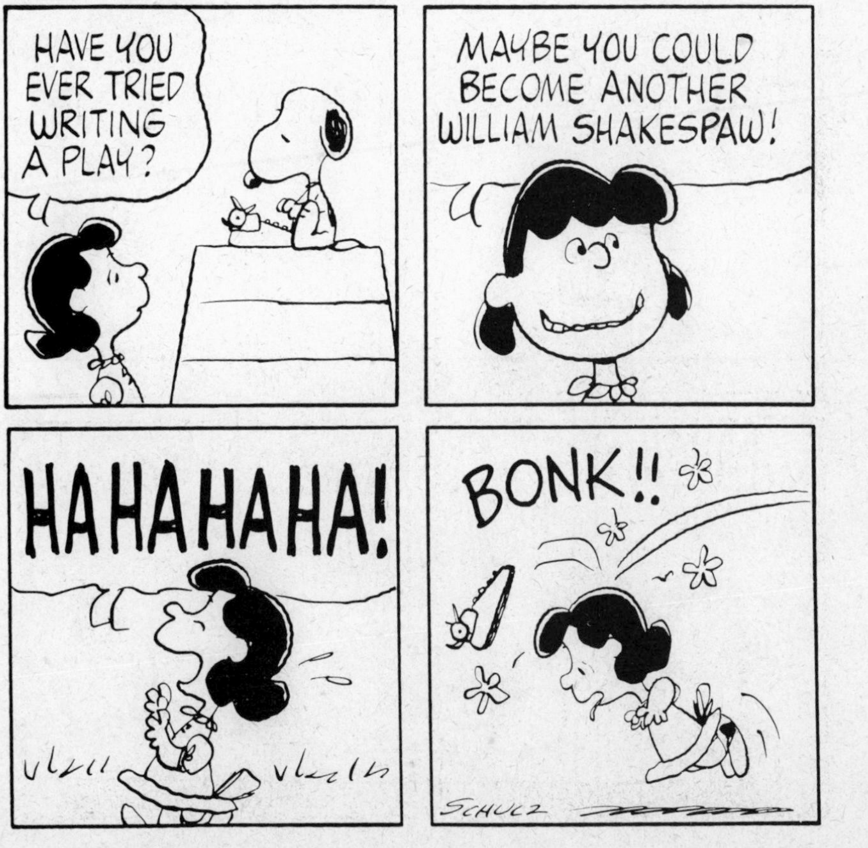
HAVE YOU EVER TRIED WRITING A PLAY?
MAYBE YOU COULD BECOME ANOTHER WILLIAM SHAKESPAW!
HAHAHAHA!
BONK!!

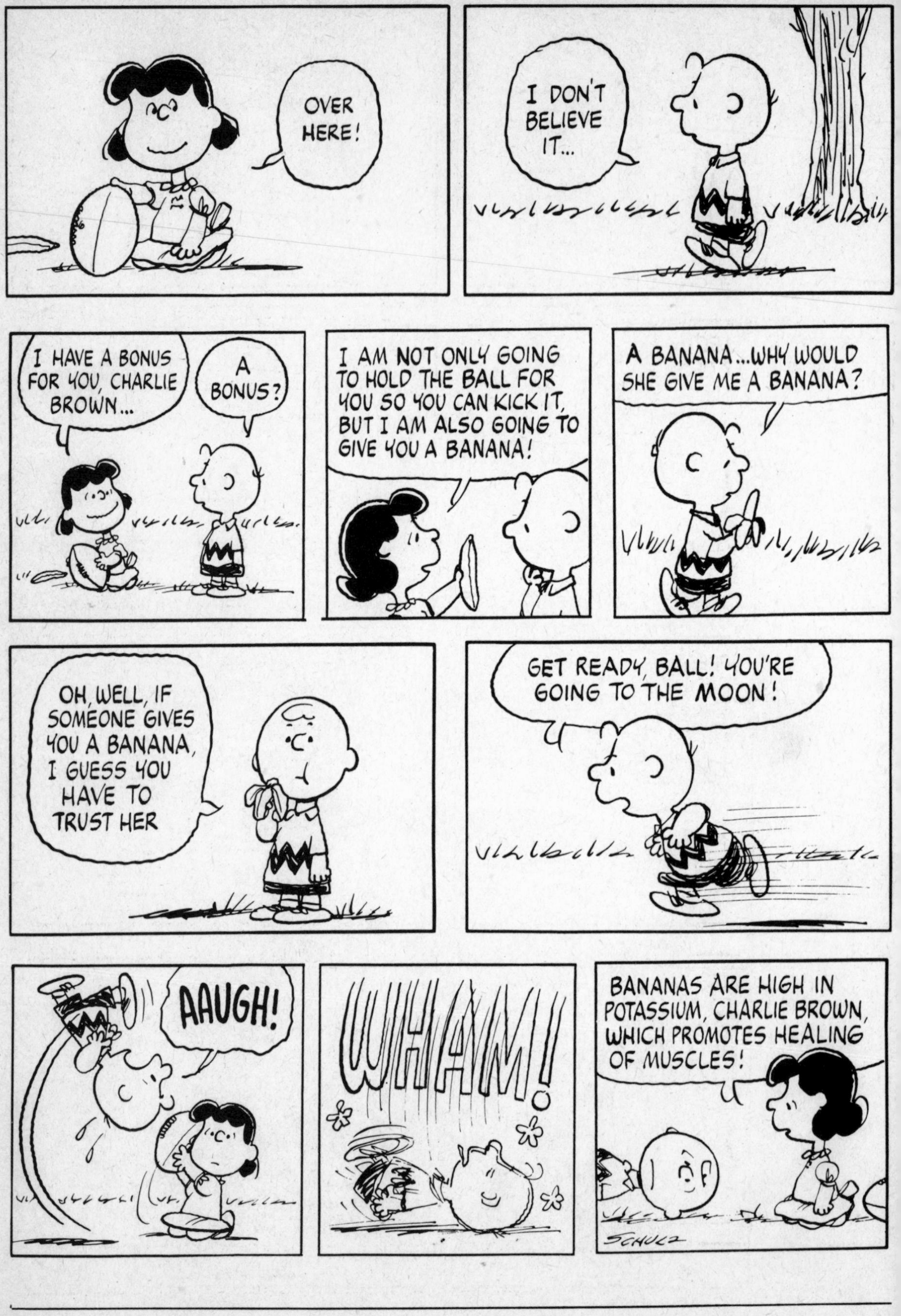
OVER HERE!
I DON'T BELIEVE IT...
I HAVE A BONUS FOR YOU, CHARLIE BROWN...
A BONUS?
I AM NOT ONLY GOING TO HOLD THE BALL FOR YOU SO YOU CAN KICK IT, BUT I AM ALSO GOING TO GIVE YOU A BANANA!
A BANANA...WHY WOULD SHE GIVE ME A BANANA?
OH, WELL, IF SOMEONE GIVES YOU A BANANA, I GUESS YOU HAVE TO TRUST HER
GET READY, BALL! YOU'RE GOING TO THE MOON!
AAUGH!
WHAM!
BANANAS ARE HIGH IN POTASSIUM, CHARLIE BROWN, WHICH PROMOTES HEALING OF MUSCLES!
SCHULZ

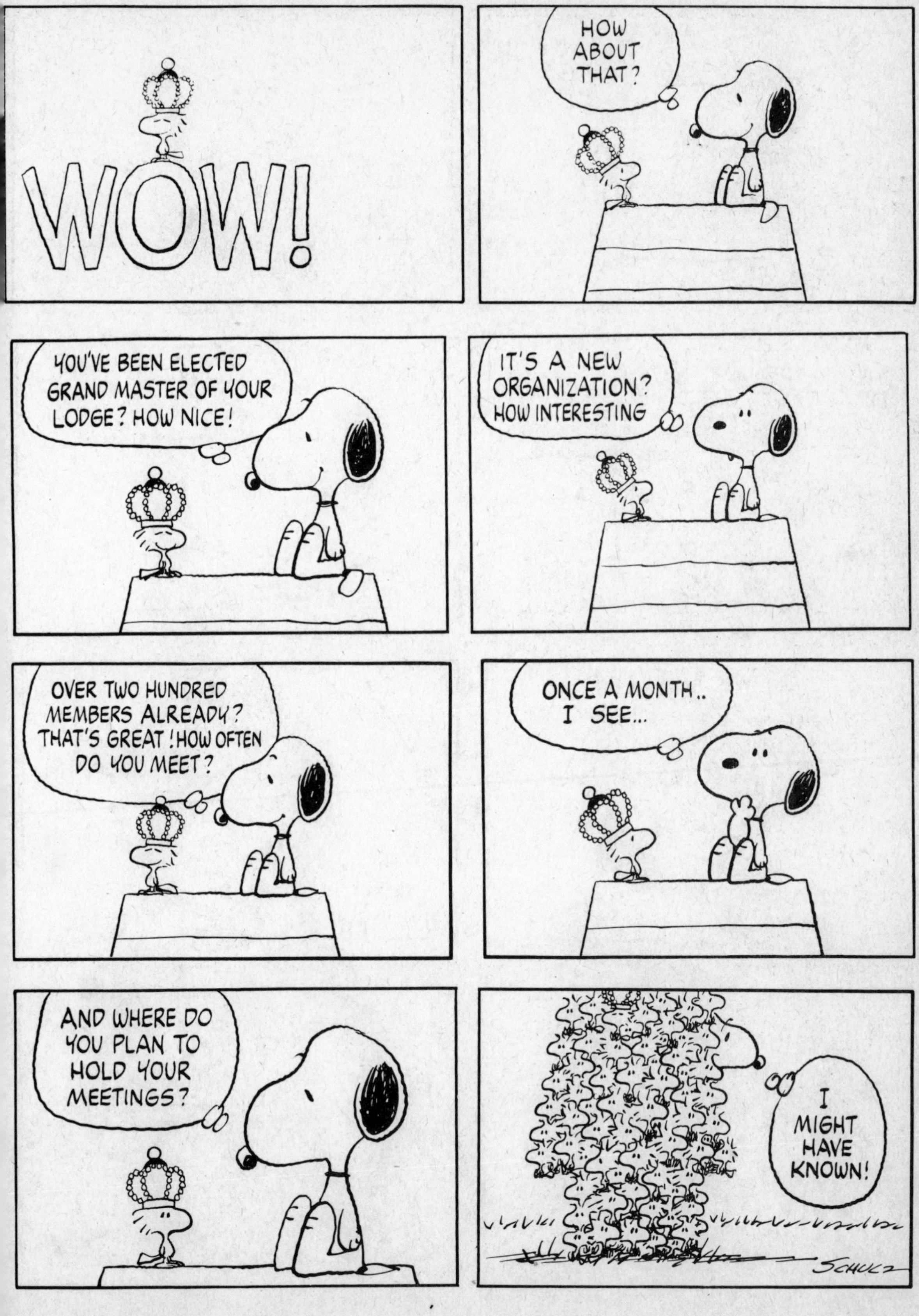
WOW!
HOW ABOUT THAT?
YOU'VE BEEN ELECTED GRAND MASTER OF YOUR LODGE? HOW NICE!
IT'S A NEW ORGANIZATION? HOW INTERESTING
OVER TWO HUNDRED MEMBERS ALREADY? THAT'S GREAT! HOW OFTEN DO YOU MEET?
ONCE A MONTH.. I SEE...
AND WHERE DO YOU PLAN TO HOLD YOUR MEETINGS?
I MIGHT HAVE KNOWN!
SCHULZ

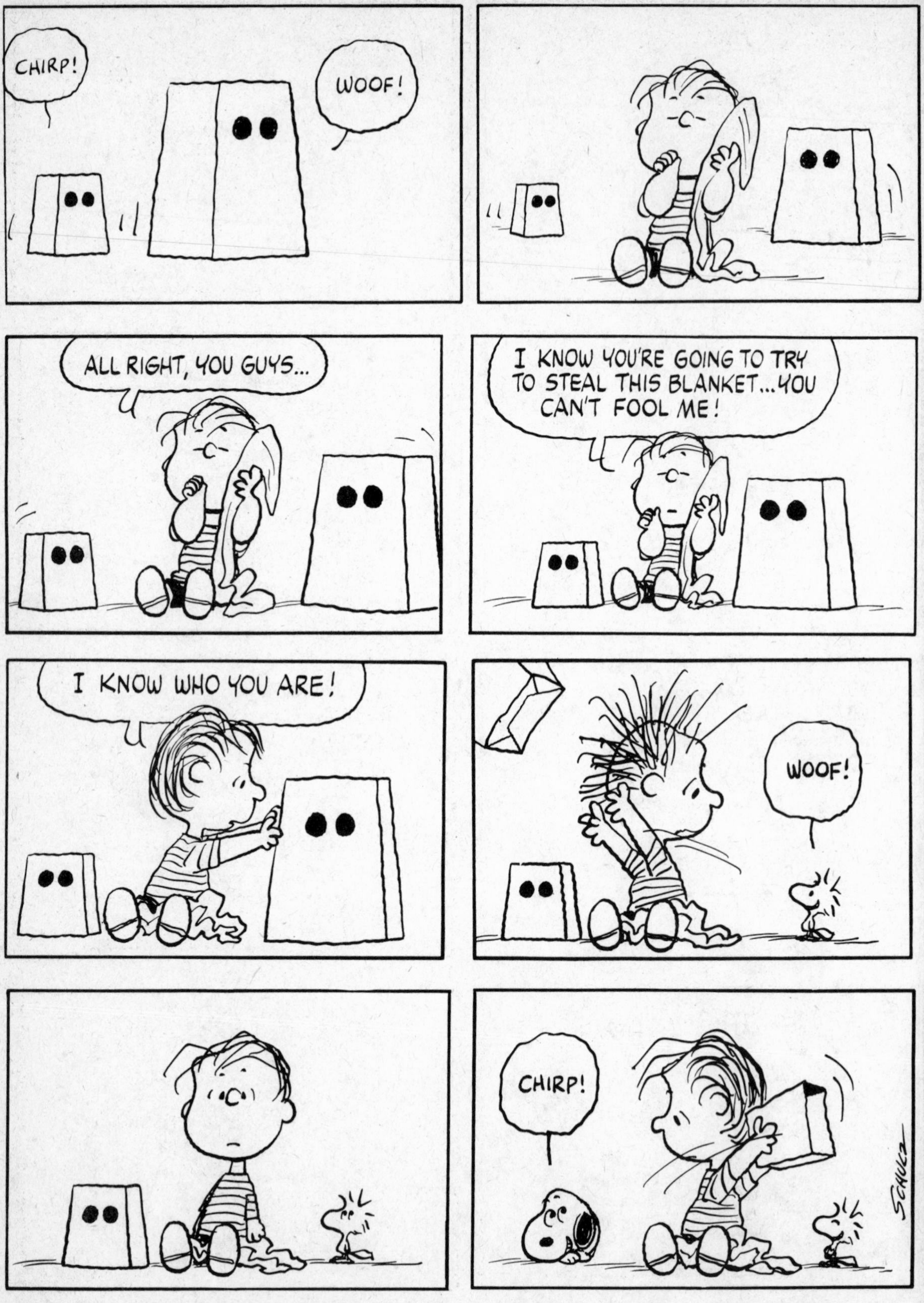
CHIRP!
WOOF!
ALL RIGHT, YOU GUYS...
I KNOW YOU'RE GOING TO TRY TO STEAL THIS BLANKET...YOU CAN'T FOOL ME!
I KNOW WHO YOU ARE!
WOOF!
CHIRP!
SCHULZ

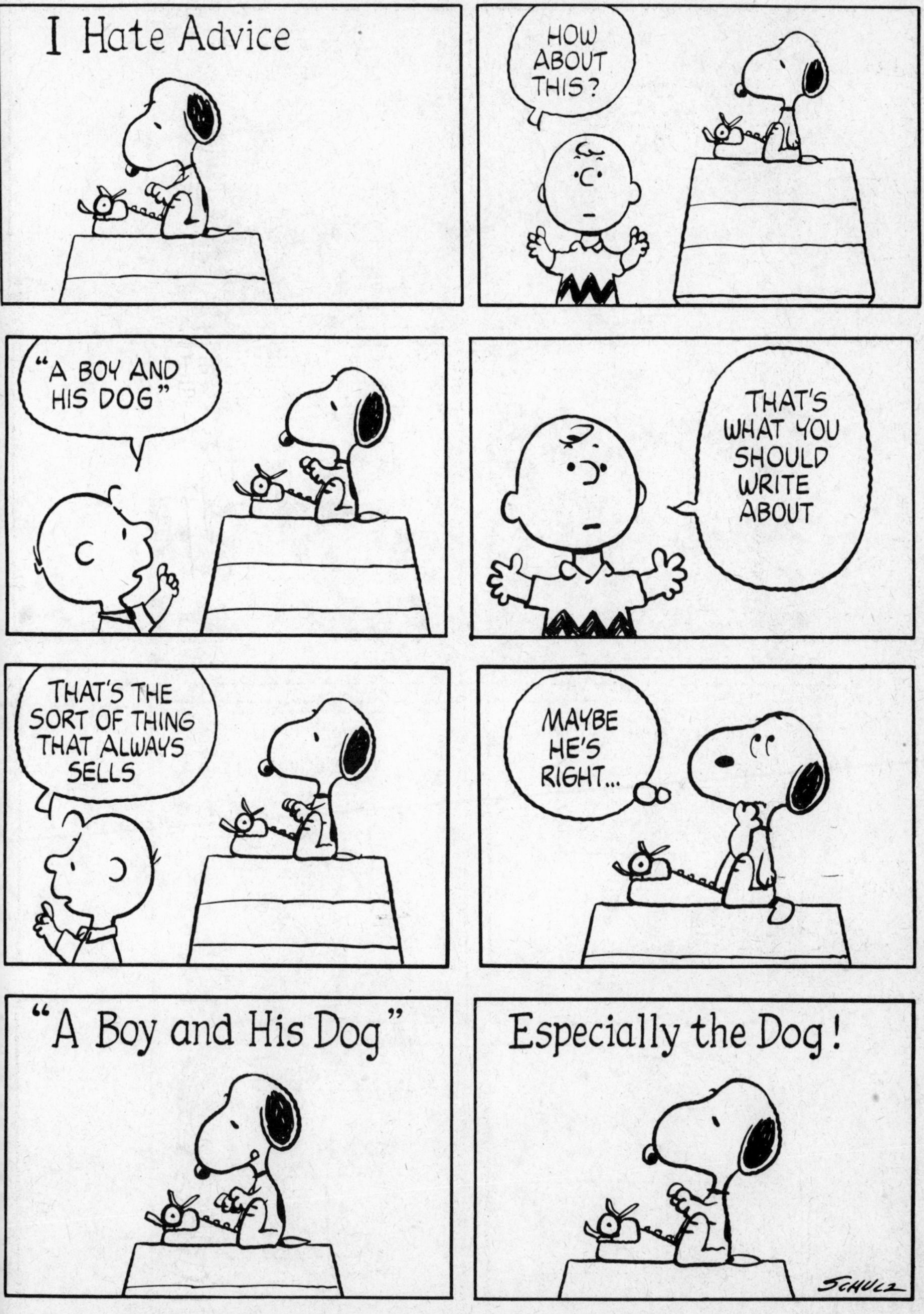
I Hate Advice
HOW ABOUT THIS?
"A BOY AND HIS DOG"
THAT'S WHAT YOU SHOULD WRITE ABOUT
THAT'S THE SORT OF THING THAT ALWAYS SELLS
MAYBE HE'S RIGHT...
"A Boy and His Dog"
Especially the Dog!
SCHULZ

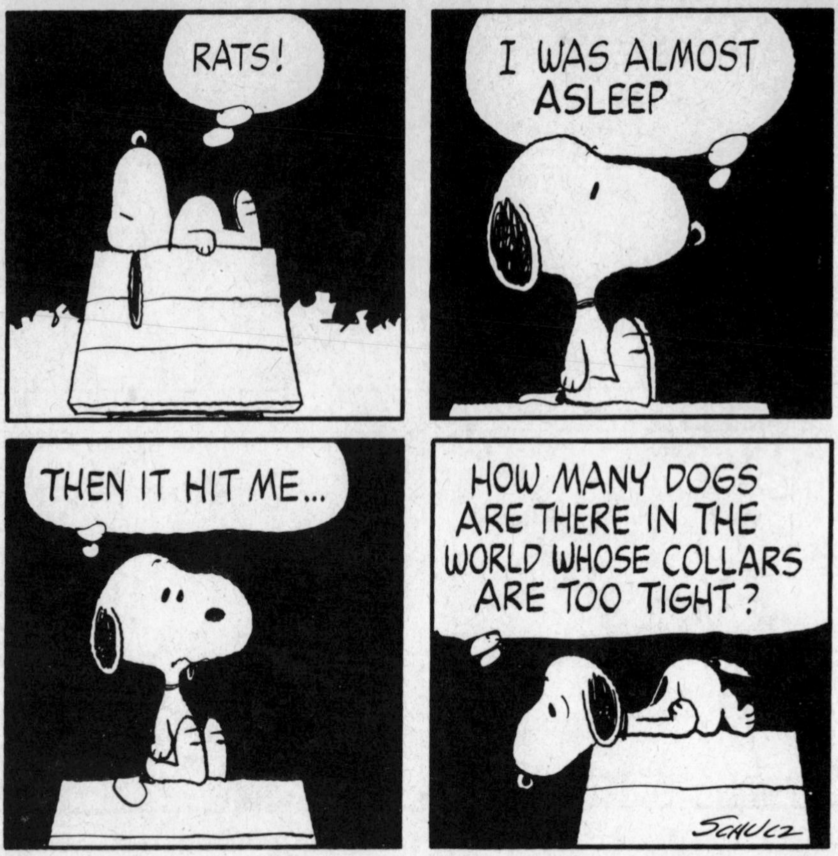
RATS!
I WAS ALMOST ASLEEP
THEN IT HIT ME...
HOW MANY DOGS ARE THERE IN THE WORLD WHOSE COLLARS ARE TOO TIGHT?
SCHULZ

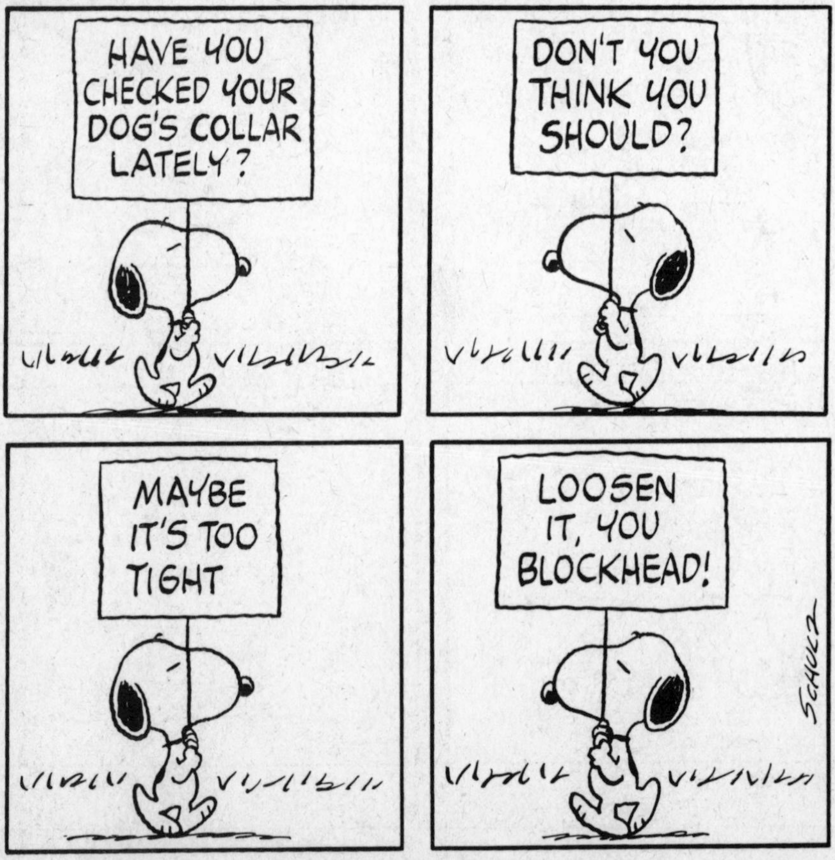
HAVE YOU CHECKED YOUR DOG'S COLLAR LATELY?
DON'T YOU THINK YOU SHOULD?
MAYBE IT'S TOO TIGHT
LOOSEN IT, YOU BLOCKHEAD!
SCHULZ

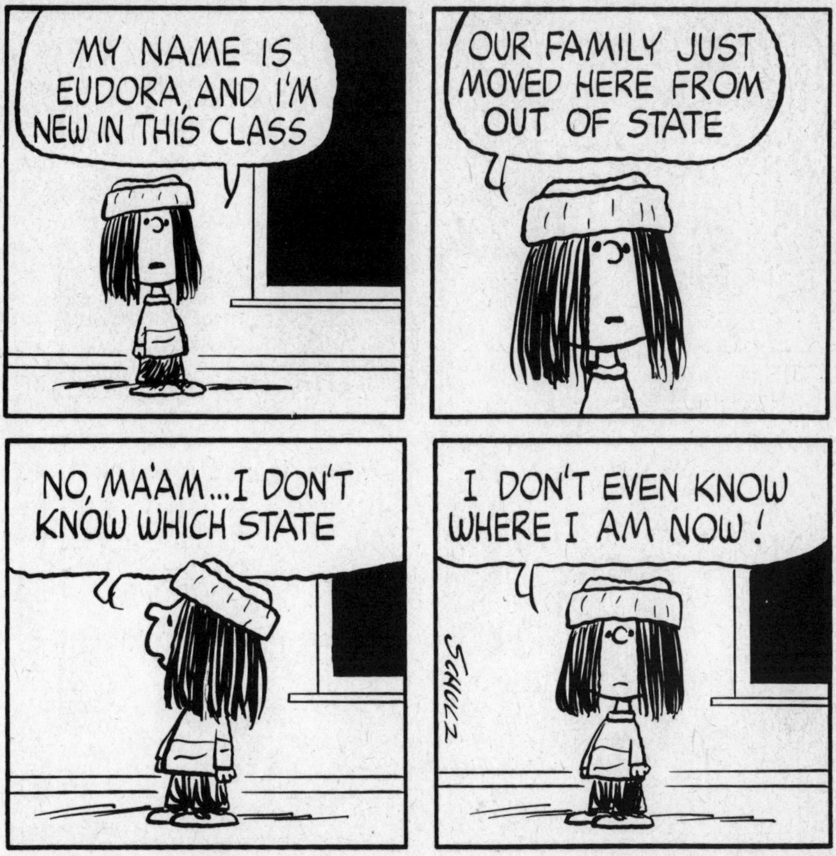
MY NAME IS EUDORA, AND I'M NEW IN THIS CLASS
OUR FAMILY JUST MOVED HERE FROM OUT OF STATE
NO, MA'AM...I DON'T KNOW WHICH STATE
I DON'T EVEN KNOW WHERE I AM NOW!
SCHULZ

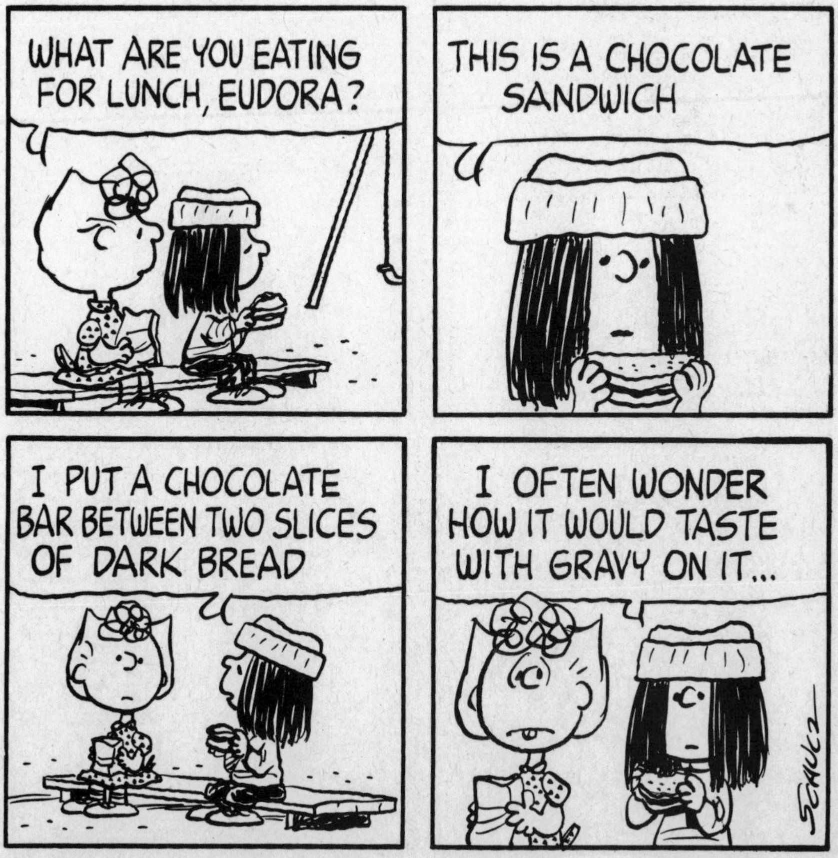
WHAT ARE YOU EATING FOR LUNCH, EUDORA?
THIS IS A CHOCOLATE SANDWICH
I PUT A CHOCOLATE BAR BETWEEN TWO SLICES OF DARK BREAD
I OFTEN WONDER HOW IT WOULD TASTE WITH GRAVY ON IT...
SCHULZ

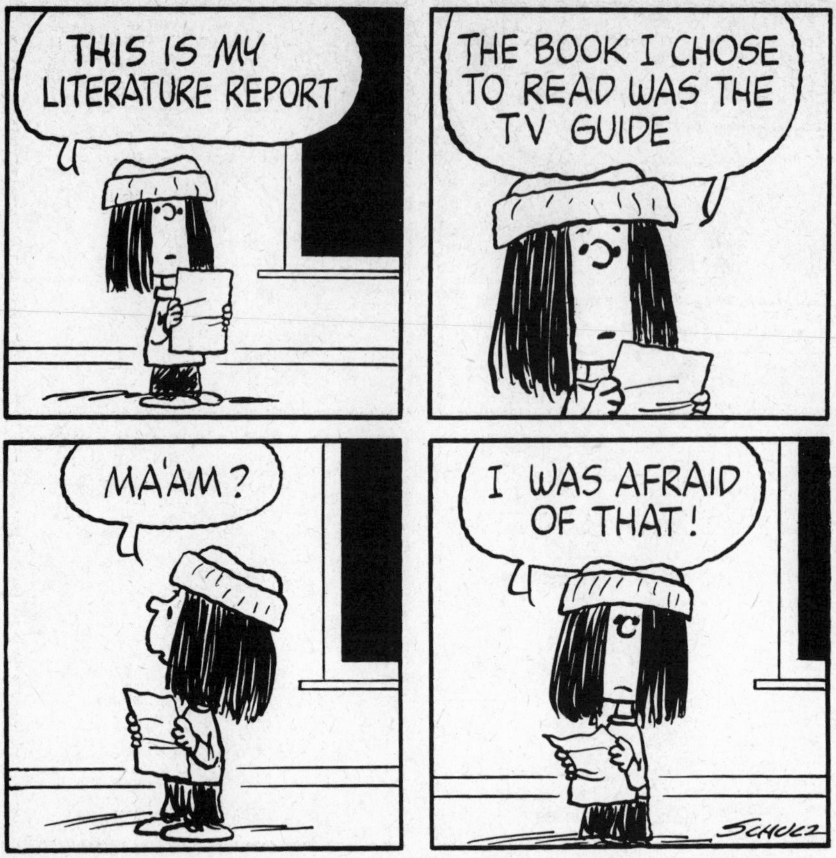
THIS IS MY LITERATURE REPORT
THE BOOK I CHOSE TO READ WAS THE TV GUIDE
MA'AM?
I WAS AFRAID OF THAT!
SCHULZ

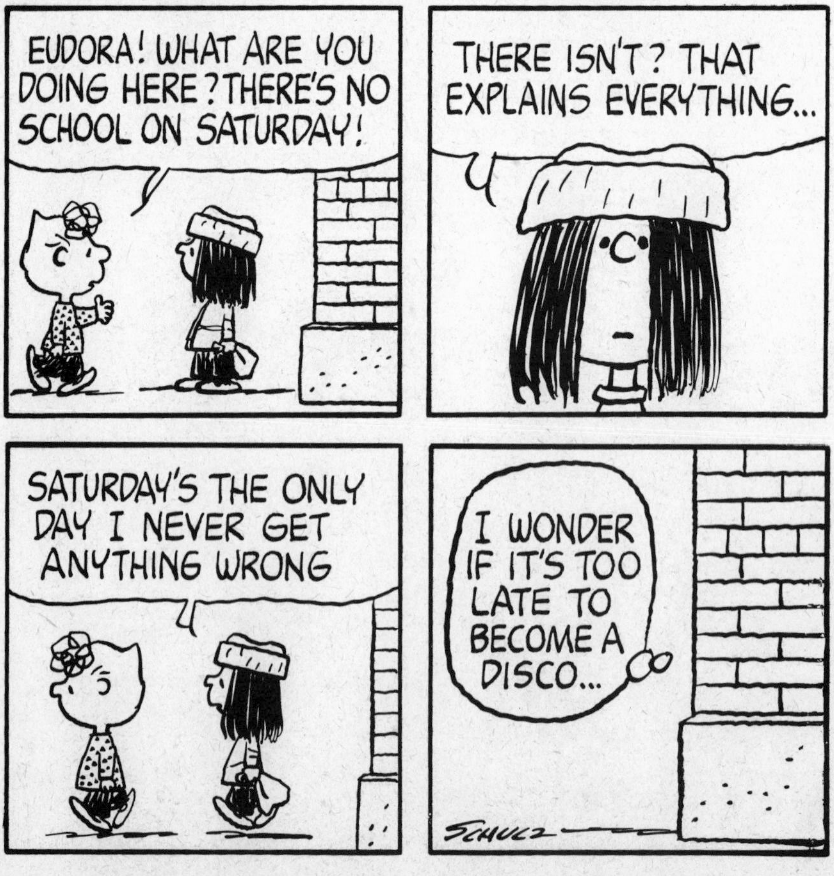
EUDORA! WHAT ARE YOU DOING HERE? THERE'S NO SCHOOL ON SATURDAY!
THERE ISN'T? THAT EXPLAINS EVERYTHING...
SATURDAY'S THE ONLY DAY I NEVER GET ANYTHING WRONG
I WONDER IF IT'S TOO LATE TO BECOME A DISCO...
SCHULZ

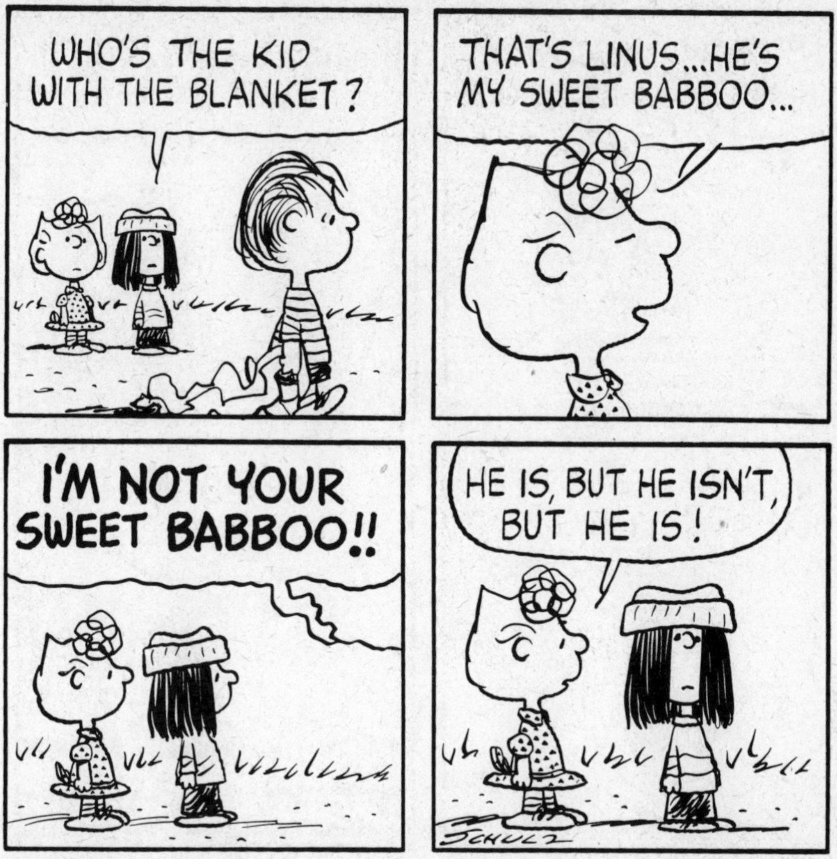
WHO'S THE KID WITH THE BLANKET?
THAT'S LINUS...HE'S MY SWEET BABBOO...
I'M NOT YOUR SWEET BABBOO!!
HE IS, BUT HE ISN'T, BUT HE IS!
SCHULZ

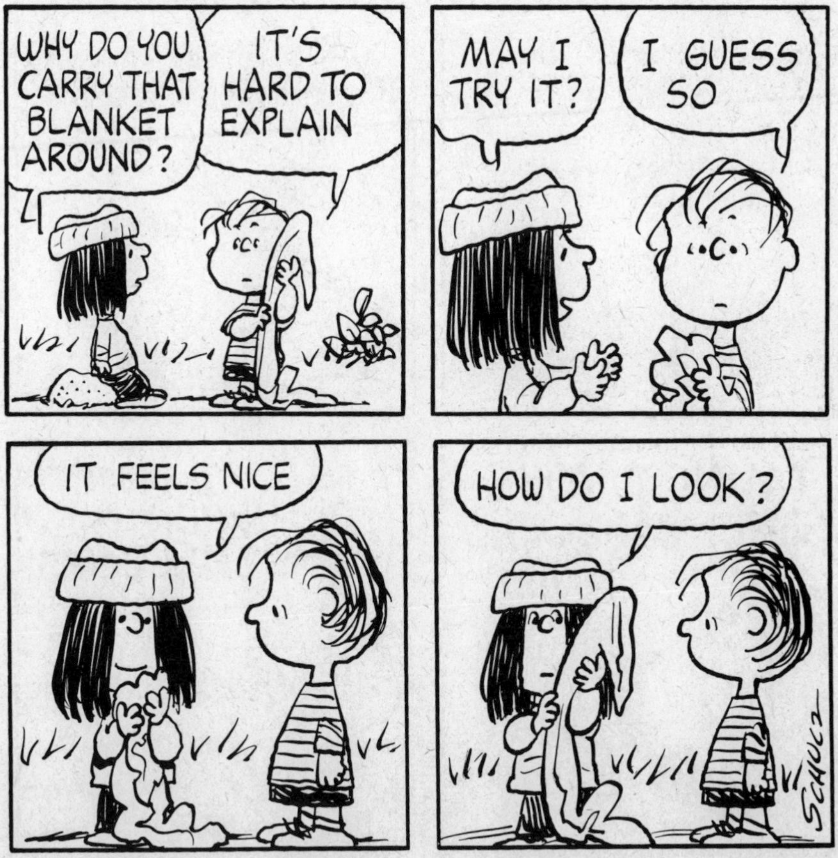
WHY DO YOU CARRY THAT BLANKET AROUND?
IT'S HARD TO EXPLAIN
MAY I TRY IT?
I GUESS SO
IT FEELS NICE
HOW DO I LOOK?
SCHULZ

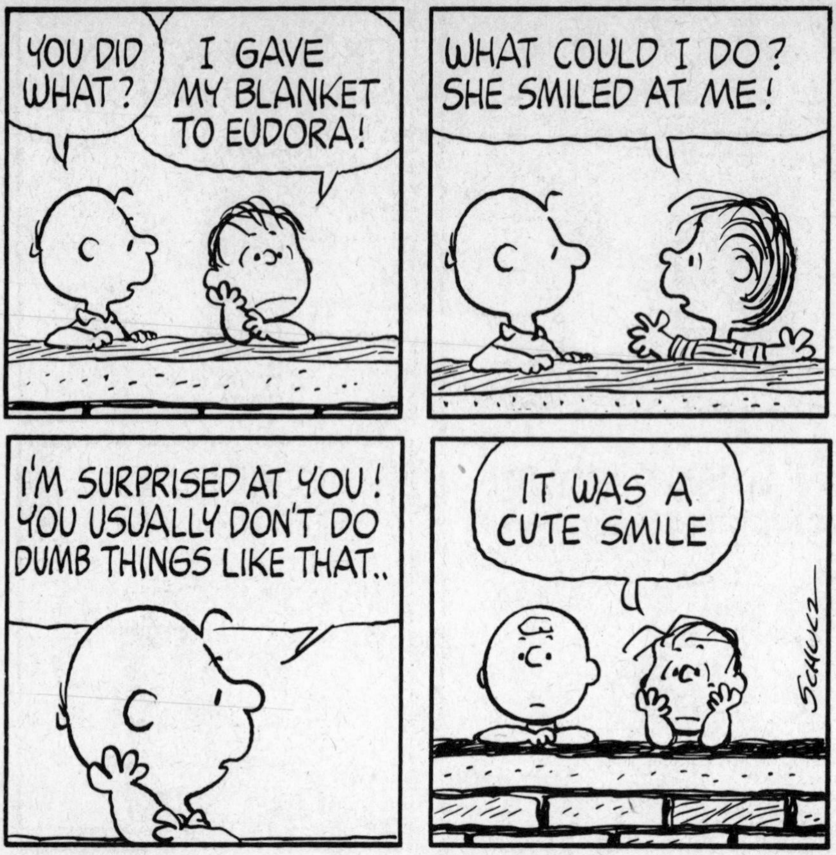
YOU DID WHAT?
I GAVE MY BLANKET TO EUDORA!
WHAT COULD I DO? SHE SMILED AT ME!
I'M SURPRISED AT YOU! YOU USUALLY DON'T DO DUMB THINGS LIKE THAT..
IT WAS A CUTE SMILE
SCHULZ

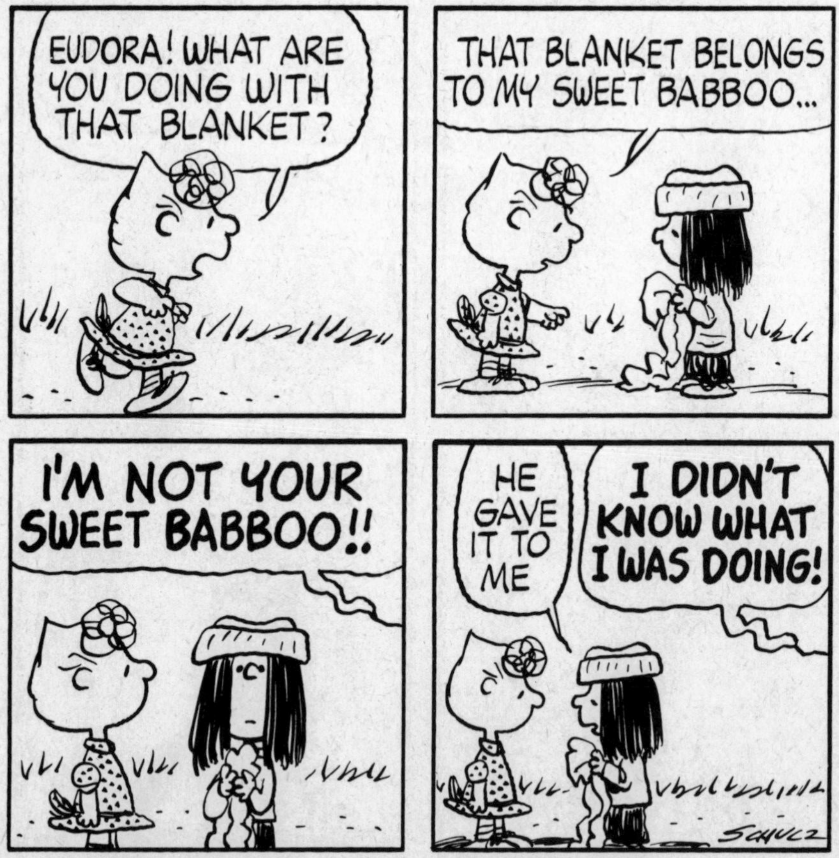
EUDORA! WHAT ARE YOU DOING WITH THAT BLANKET?
THAT BLANKET BELONGS TO MY SWEET BABBOO...
I'M NOT YOUR SWEET BABBOO!!
HE GAVE IT TO ME
I DIDN'T KNOW WHAT I WAS DOING!
SCHULZ

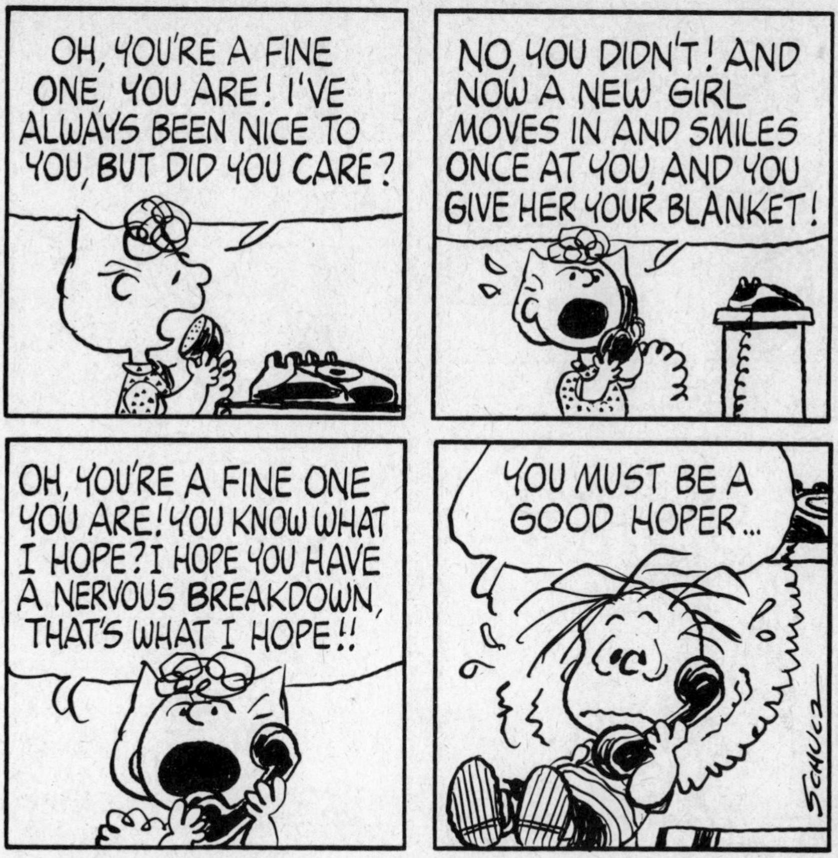
OH, YOU'RE A FINE ONE, YOU ARE! I'VE ALWAYS BEEN NICE TO YOU, BUT DID YOU CARE?
NO, YOU DIDN'T! AND NOW A NEW GIRL MOVES IN AND SMILES ONCE AT YOU, AND YOU GIVE HER YOUR BLANKET!
OH, YOU'RE A FINE ONE YOU ARE! YOU KNOW WHAT I HOPE? I HOPE YOU HAVE A NERVOUS BREAKDOWN, THAT'S WHAT I HOPE!!
YOU MUST BE A GOOD HOPER...
SCHULZ

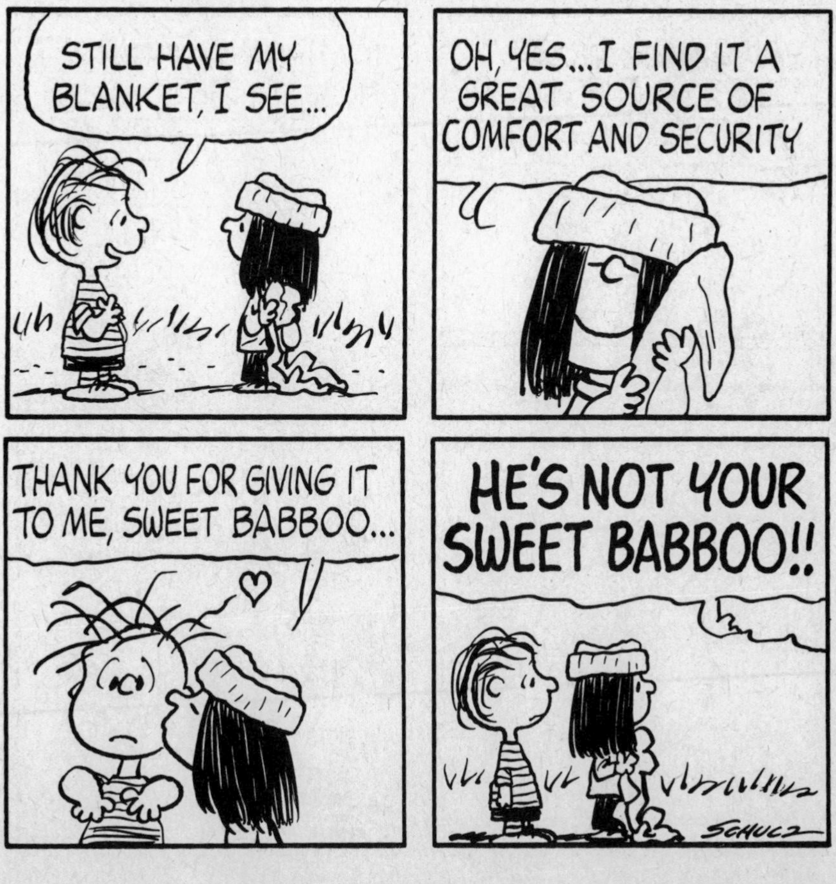
STILL HAVE MY BLANKET, I SEE...
OH, YES...I FIND IT A GREAT SOURCE OF COMFORT AND SECURITY
THANK YOU FOR GIVING IT TO ME, SWEET BABBOO...
HE'S NOT YOUR SWEET BABBOO!!
SCHULZ

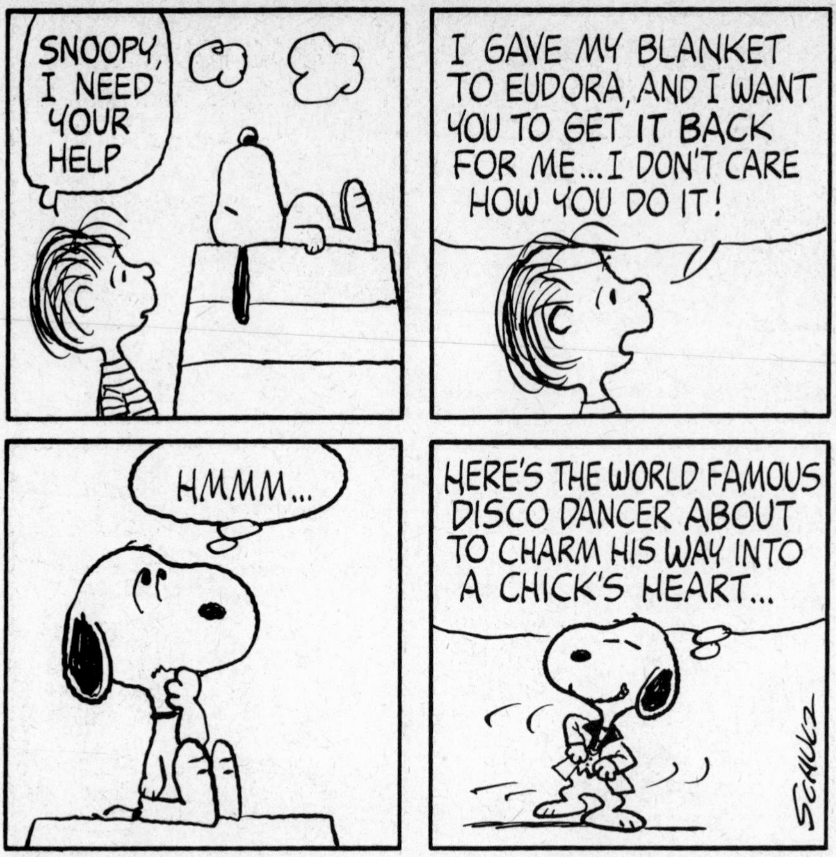
SNOOPY, I NEED YOUR HELP
I GAVE MY BLANKET TO EUDORA, AND I WANT YOU TO GET IT BACK FOR ME...I DON'T CARE HOW YOU DO IT!
HMMM...
HERE'S THE WORLD FAMOUS DISCO DANCER ABOUT TO CHARM HIS WAY INTO A CHICK'S HEART...
SCHULZ

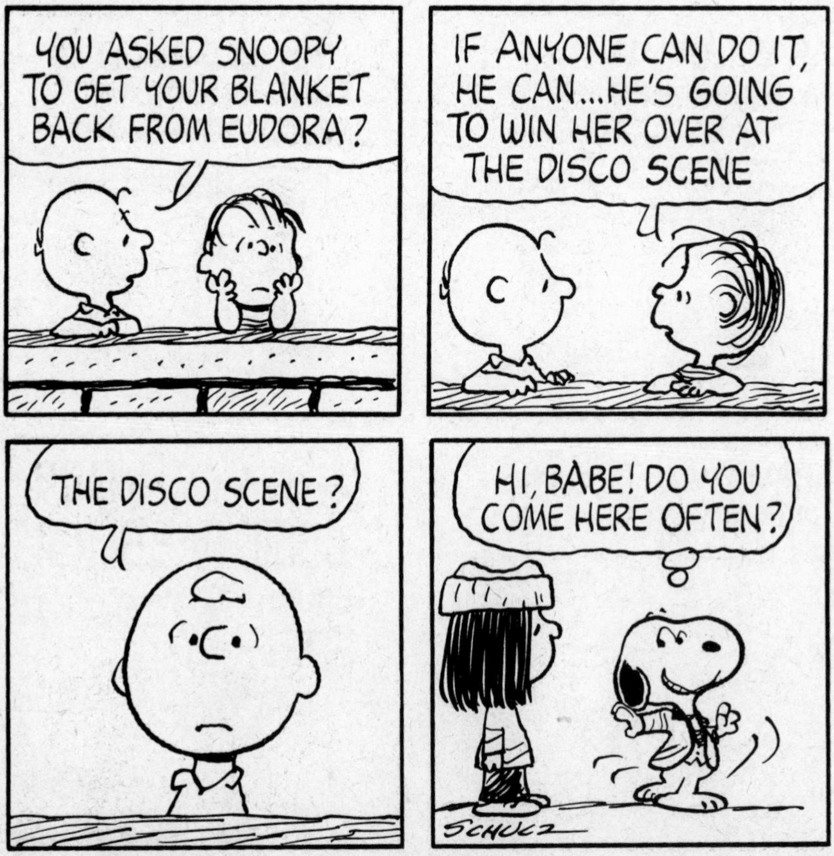
YOU ASKED SNOOPY TO GET YOUR BLANKET BACK FROM EUDORA?
IF ANYONE CAN DO IT, HE CAN...HE'S GOING TO WIN HER OVER AT THE DISCO SCENE
THE DISCO SCENE?
HI, BABE! DO YOU COME HERE OFTEN?
SCHULZ

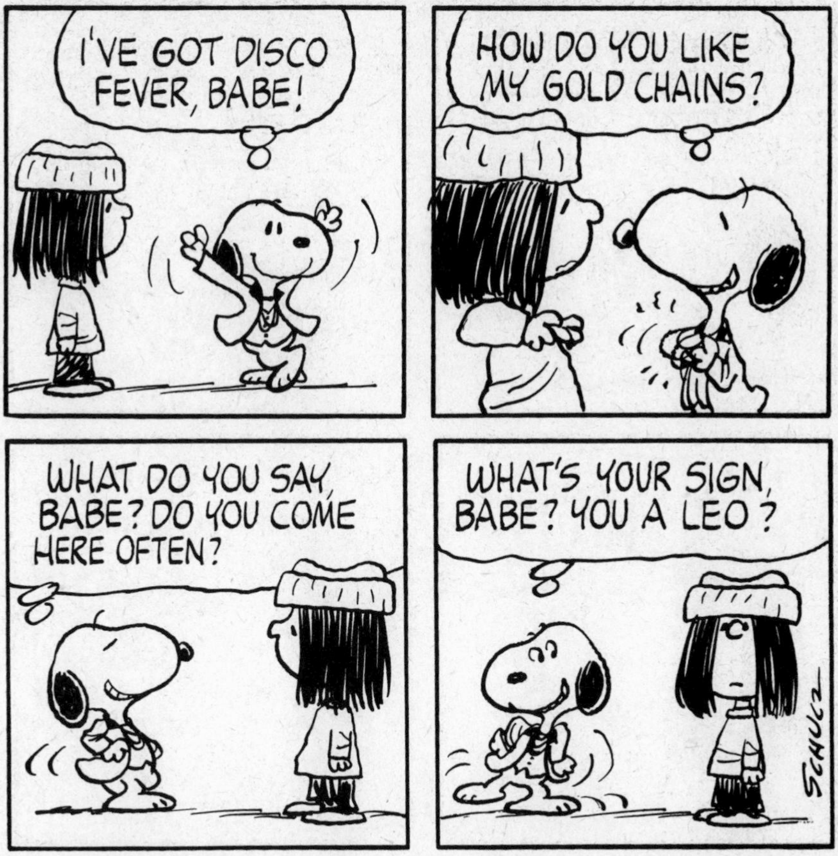
I'VE GOT DISCO FEVER, BABE!
HOW DO YOU LIKE MY GOLD CHAINS?
WHAT DO YOU SAY, BABE? DO YOU COME HERE OFTEN?
WHAT'S YOUR SIGN, BABE? YOU A LEO?
SCHULZ

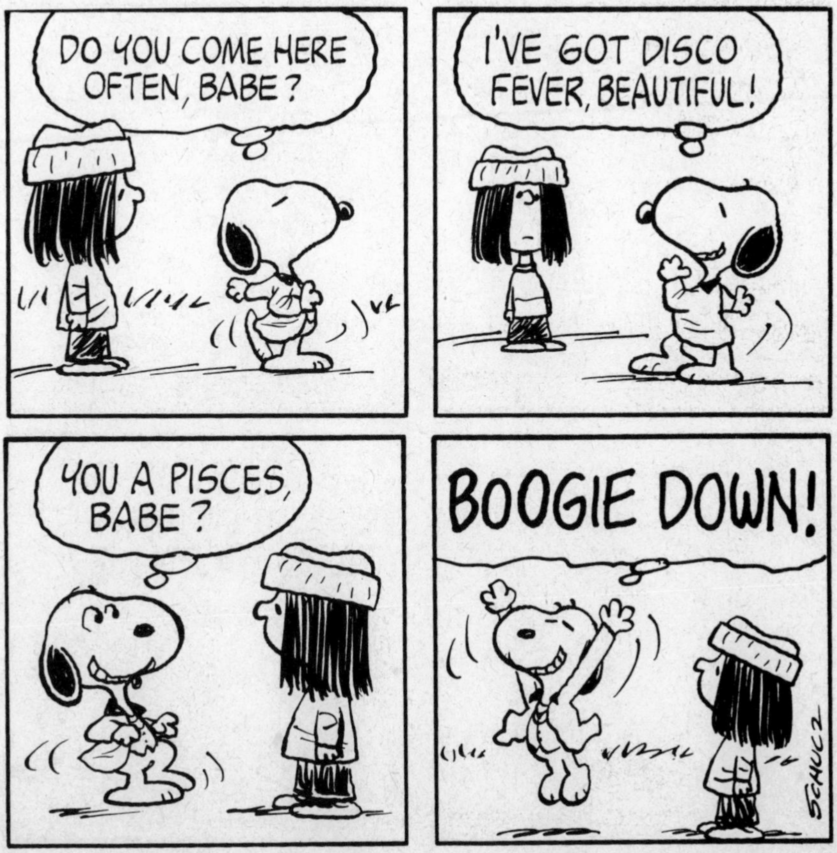
DO YOU COME HERE OFTEN, BABE?
I'VE GOT DISCO FEVER, BEAUTIFUL!
YOU A PISCES, BABE?
BOOGIE DOWN!
SCHULZ

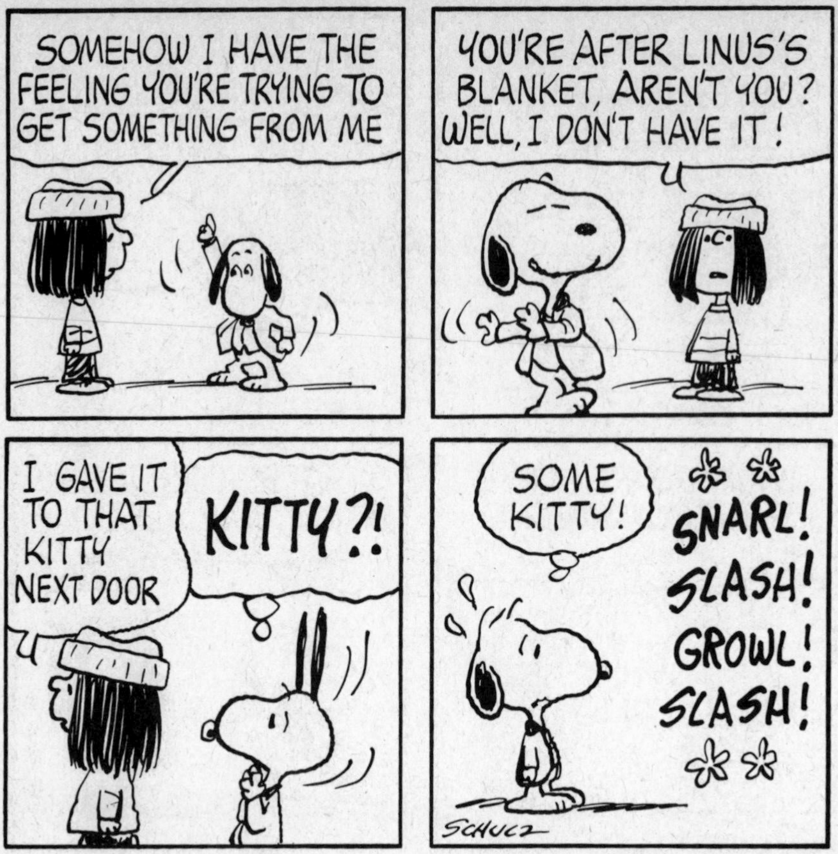
SOMEHOW I HAVE THE FEELING YOU'RE TRYING TO GET SOMETHING FROM ME
YOU'RE AFTER LINUS'S BLANKET, AREN'T YOU? WELL, I DON'T HAVE IT!
I GAVE IT TO THAT KITTY NEXT DOOR
KITTY?!
SOME KITTY!
SNARL!
SLASH!
GROWL!
SLASH!
SCHULZ

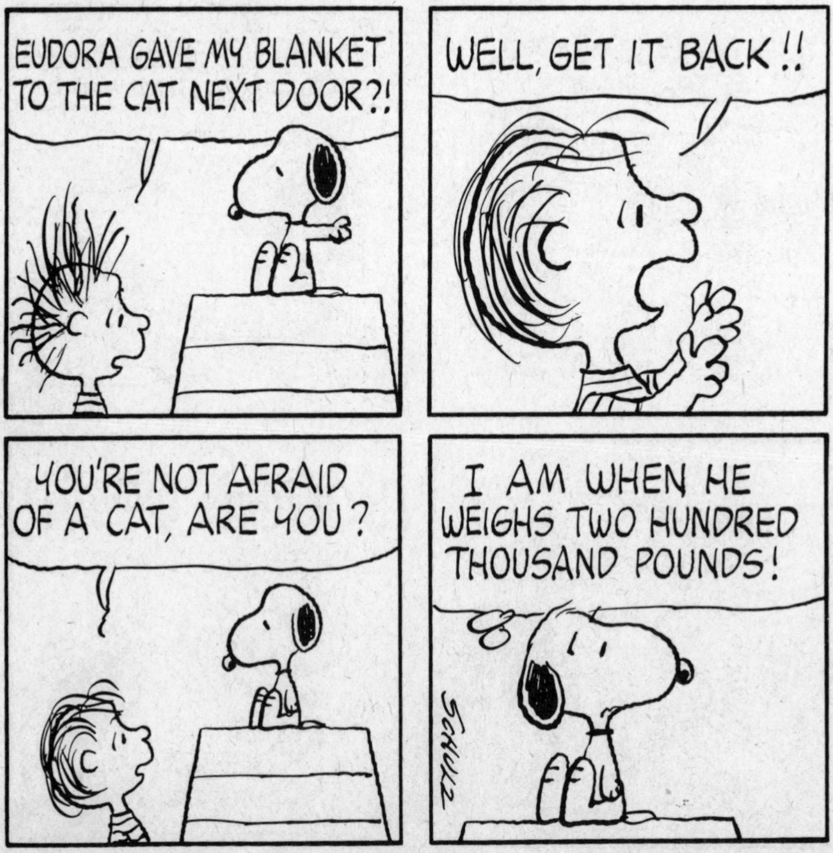
EUDORA GAVE MY BLANKET TO THE CAT NEXT DOOR?!
WELL, GET IT BACK!!
YOU'RE NOT AFRAID OF A CAT, ARE YOU?
I AM WHEN HE WEIGHS TWO HUNDRED THOUSAND POUNDS!
SCHULZ

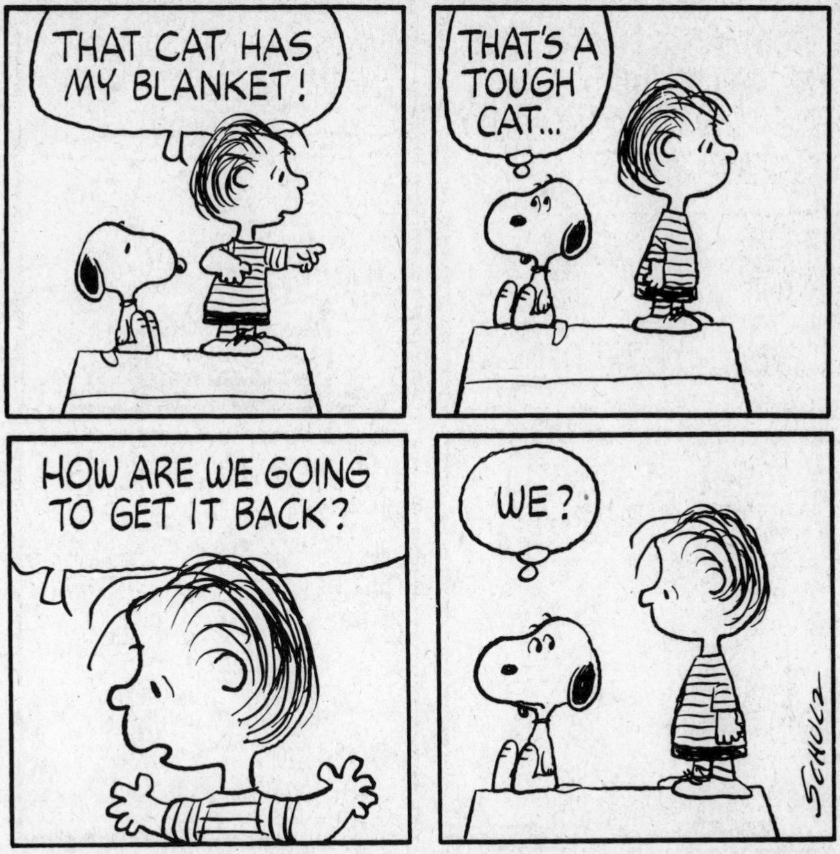
THAT CAT HAS MY BLANKET!
THAT'S A TOUGH CAT...
HOW ARE WE GOING TO GET IT BACK?
WE?
SCHULZ

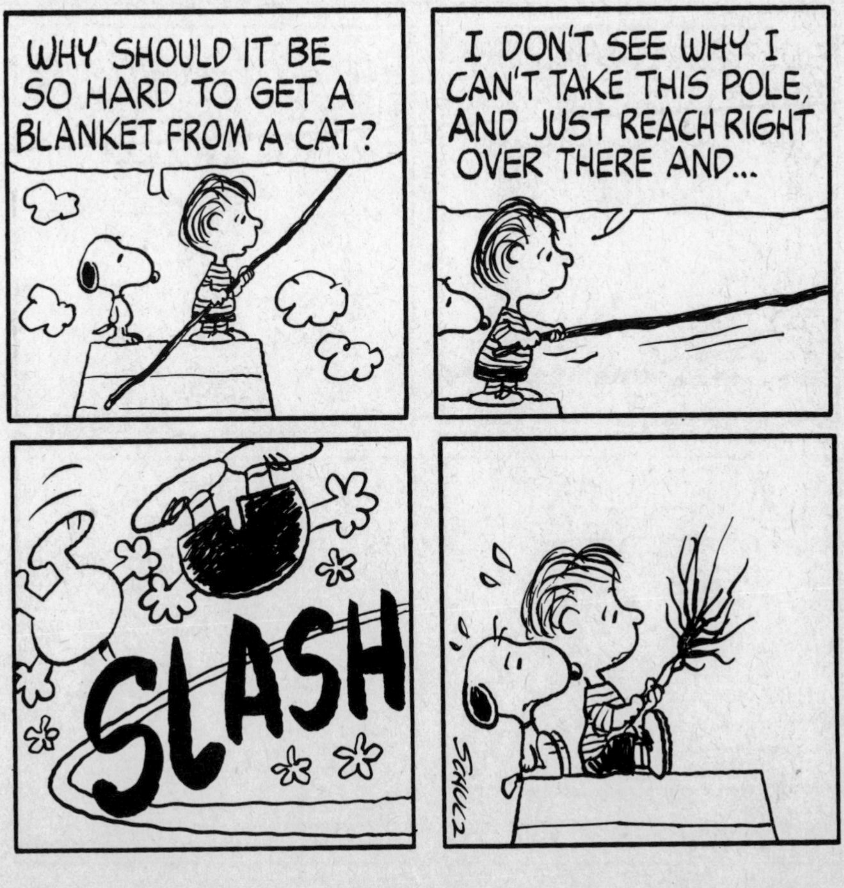
WHY SHOULD IT BE SO HARD TO GET A BLANKET FROM A CAT?
I DON'T SEE WHY I CAN'T TAKE THIS POLE, AND JUST REACH RIGHT OVER THERE AND...
SLASH
SCHULZ

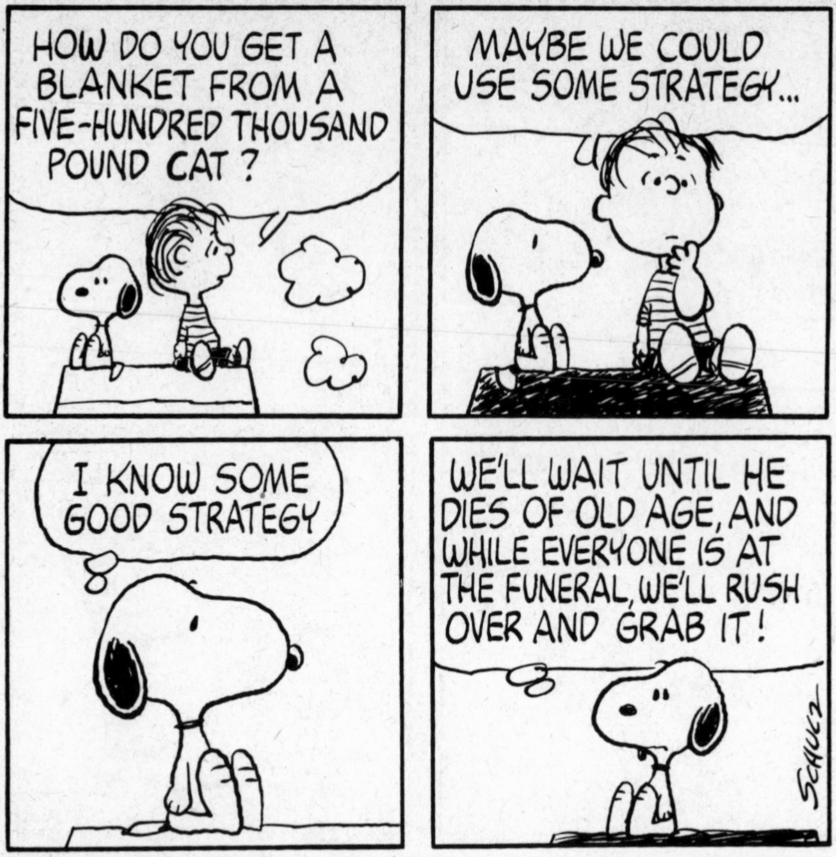
HOW DO YOU GET A BLANKET FROM A FIVE-HUNDRED THOUSAND POUND CAT?
MAYBE WE COULD USE SOME STRATEGY...
I KNOW SOME GOOD STRATEGY
WE'LL WAIT UNTIL HE DIES OF OLD AGE, AND WHILE EVERYONE IS AT THE FUNERAL, WE'LL RUSH OVER AND GRAB IT!
SCHULZ

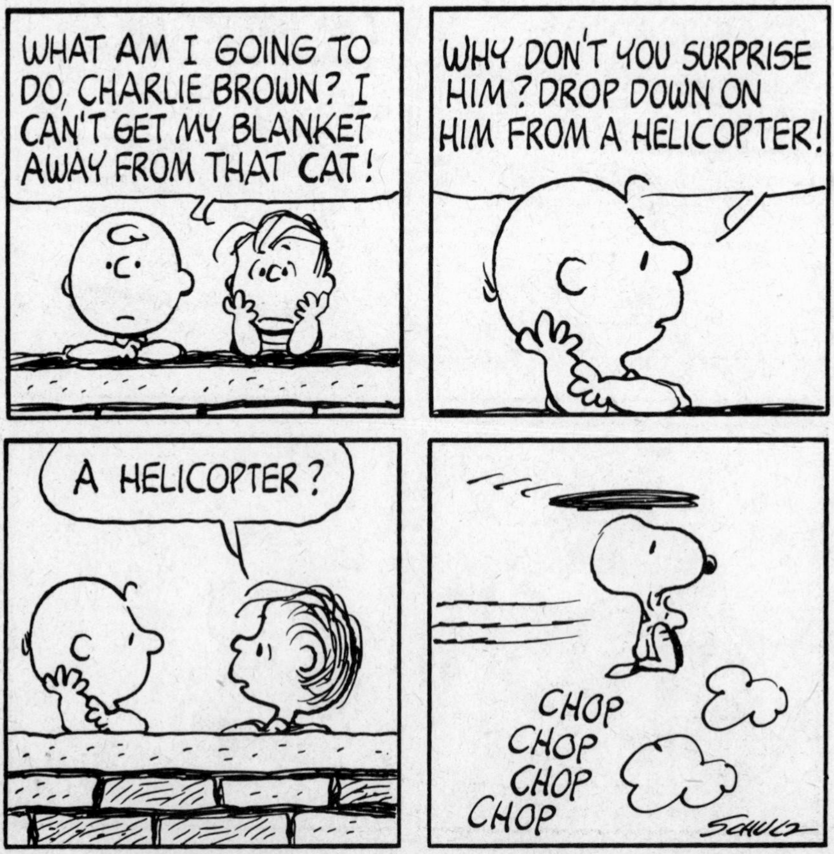
WHAT AM I GOING TO DO, CHARLIE BROWN? I CAN'T GET MY BLANKET AWAY FROM THAT CAT!
WHY DON'T YOU SURPRISE HIM? DROP DOWN ON HIM FROM A HELICOPTER!
A HELICOPTER?
CHOP
CHOP
CHOP
CHOP
SCHULZ

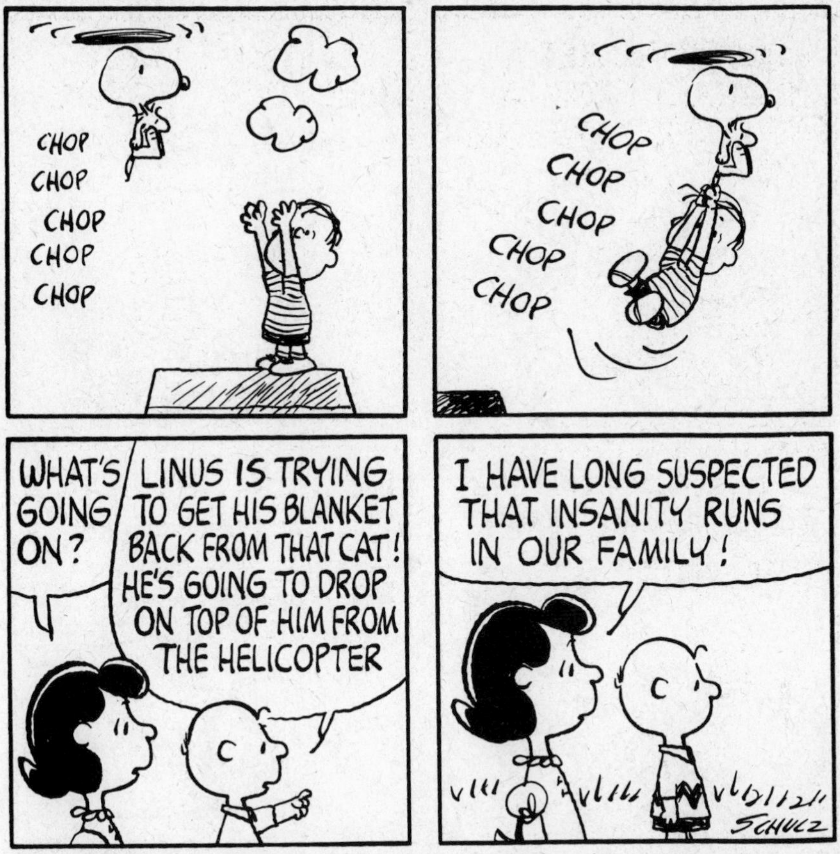
CHOP
CHOP
CHOP
CHOP
CHOP
CHOP
CHOP
CHOP
CHOP
CHOP
WHAT'S GOING ON?
LINUS IS TRYING TO GET HIS BLANKET BACK FROM THAT CAT! HE'S GOING TO DROP ON TOP OF HIM FROM THE HELICOPTER
I HAVE LONG SUSPECTED THAT INSANITY RUNS IN OUR FAMILY!
SCHULZ

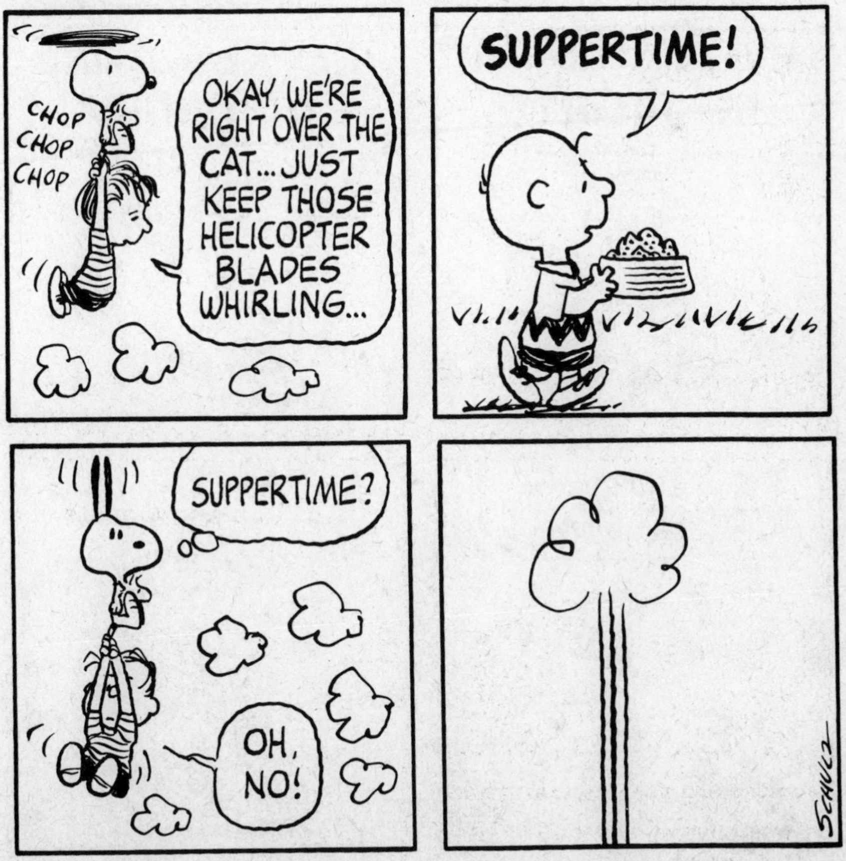
CHOP
CHOP
CHOP
OKAY, WE'RE RIGHT OVER THE CAT... JUST KEEP THOSE HELICOPTER BLADES WHIRLING...
SUPPERTIME!
SUPPERTIME?
OH, NO!
SCHULZ

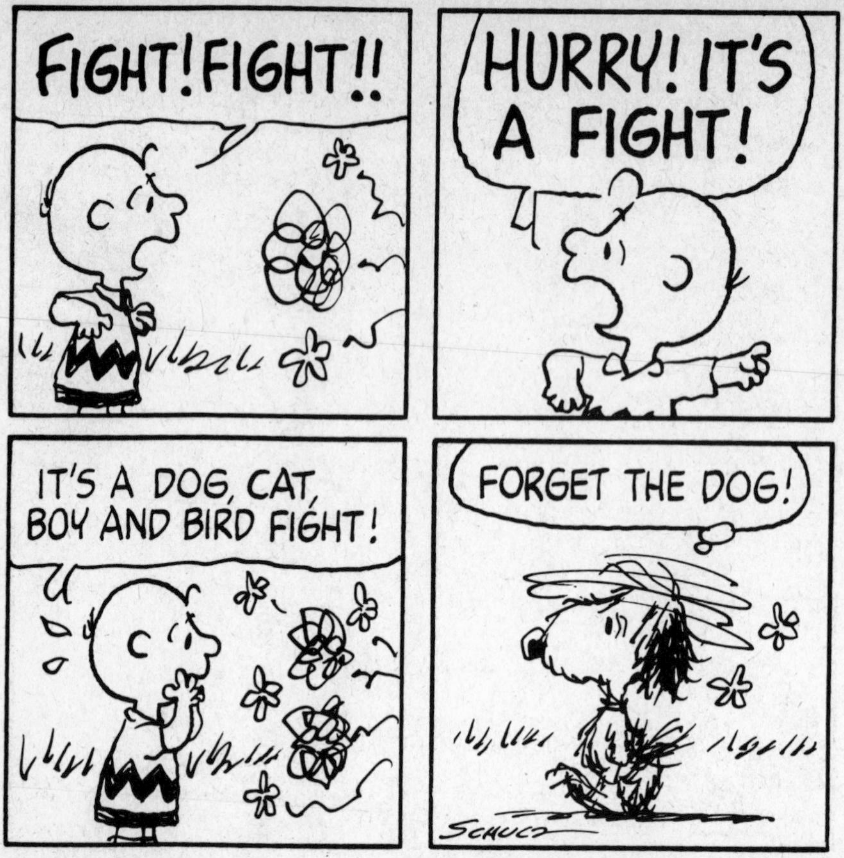
FIGHT! FIGHT!!
HURRY! IT'S A FIGHT!
IT'S A DOG, CAT, BOY AND BIRD FIGHT!
FORGET THE DOG!

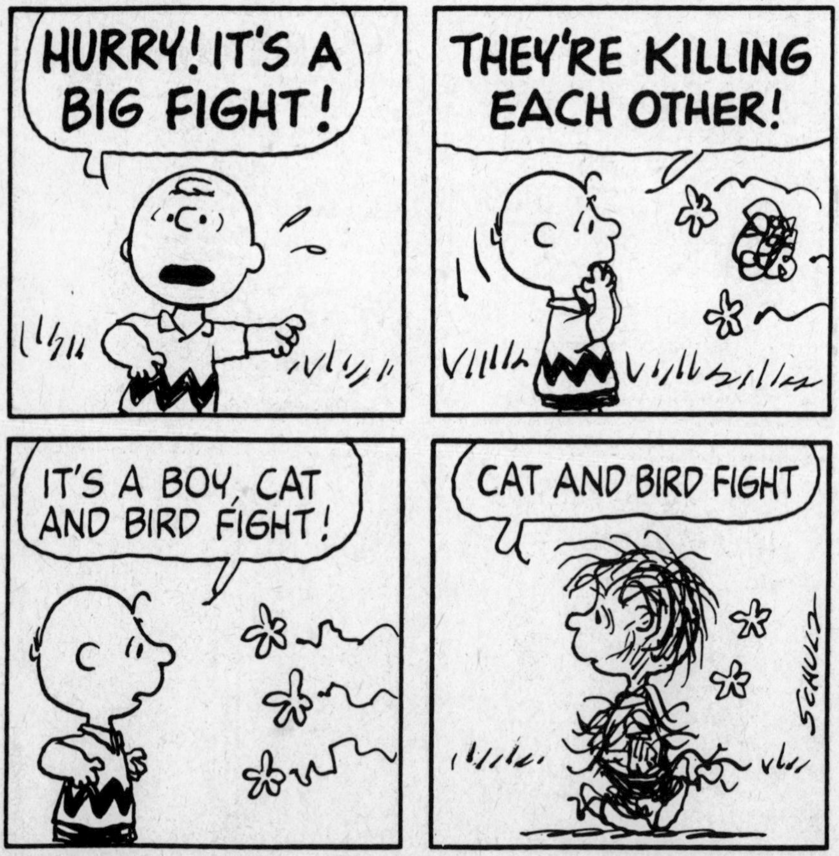
HURRY! IT'S A BIG FIGHT!
THEY'RE KILLING EACH OTHER!
IT'S A BOY, CAT AND BIRD FIGHT!
CAT AND BIRD FIGHT

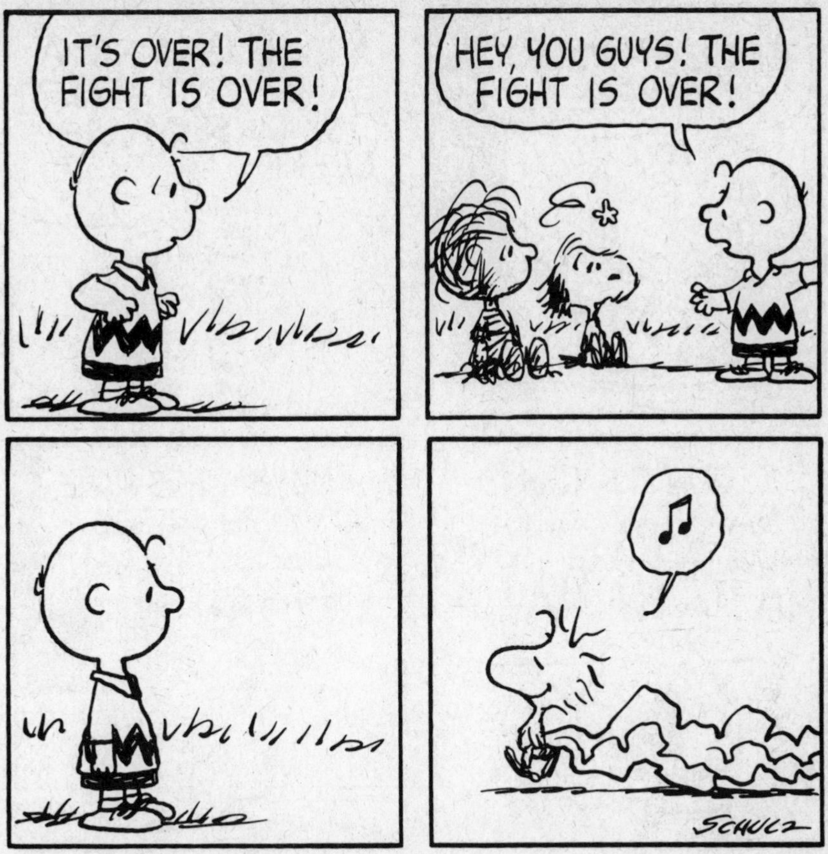
IT'S OVER! THE FIGHT IS OVER!
HEY, YOU GUYS! THE FIGHT IS OVER!

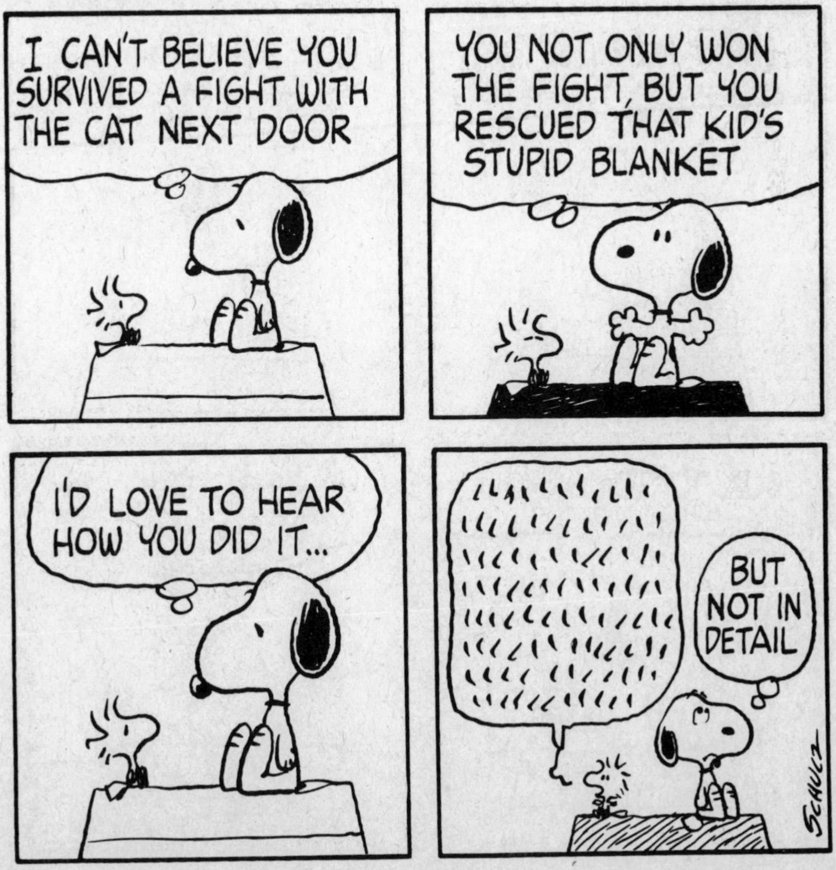
I CAN'T BELIEVE YOU SURVIVED A FIGHT WITH THE CAT NEXT DOOR
YOU NOT ONLY WON THE FIGHT, BUT YOU RESCUED THAT KID'S STUPID BLANKET
I'D LOVE TO HEAR HOW YOU DID IT...
BUT NOT IN DETAIL

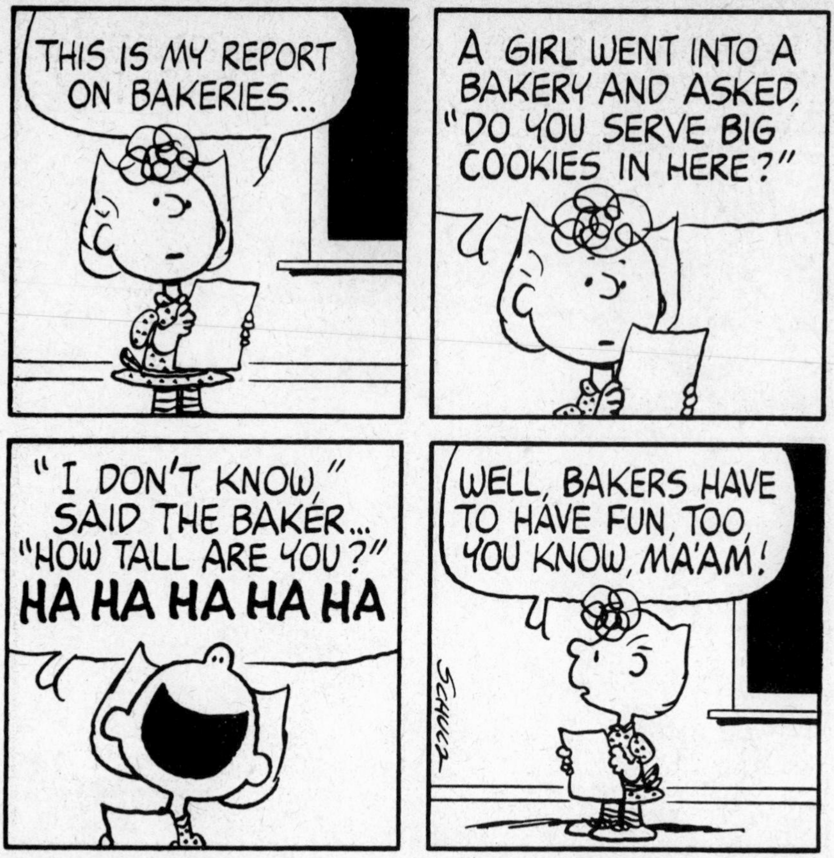
THIS IS MY REPORT ON BAKERIES...
A GIRL WENT INTO A BAKERY AND ASKED, "DO YOU SERVE BIG COOKIES IN HERE?"
"I DON'T KNOW," SAID THE BAKER... "HOW TALL ARE YOU?"
HA HA HA HA HA
WELL, BAKERS HAVE TO HAVE FUN, TOO, YOU KNOW, MA'AM!

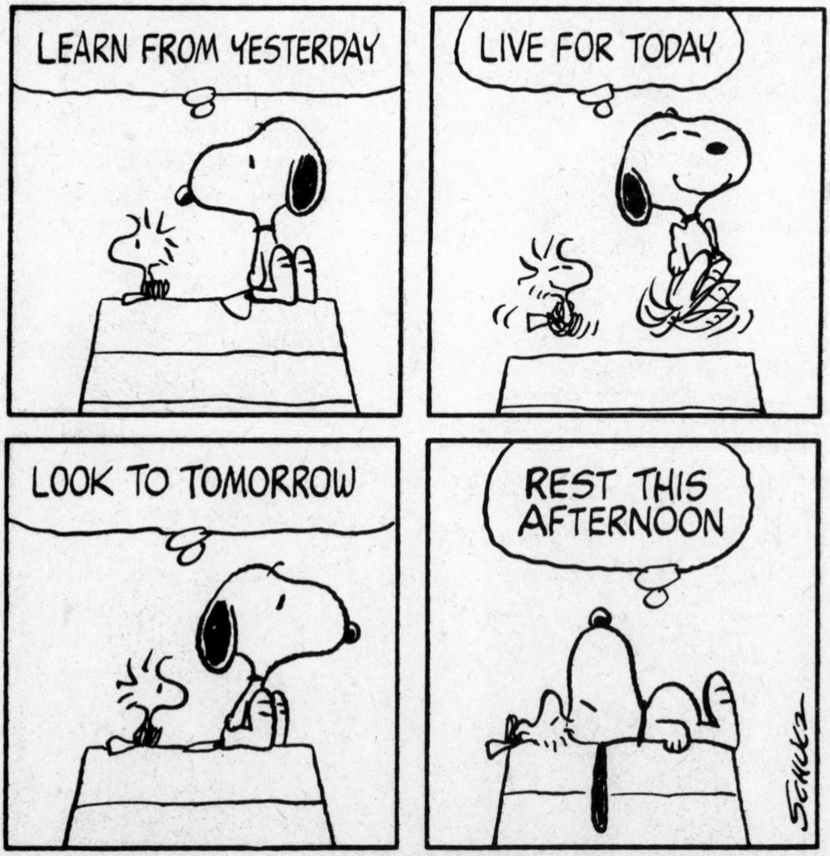
LEARN FROM YESTERDAY
LIVE FOR TODAY
LOOK TO TOMORROW
REST THIS AFTERNOON

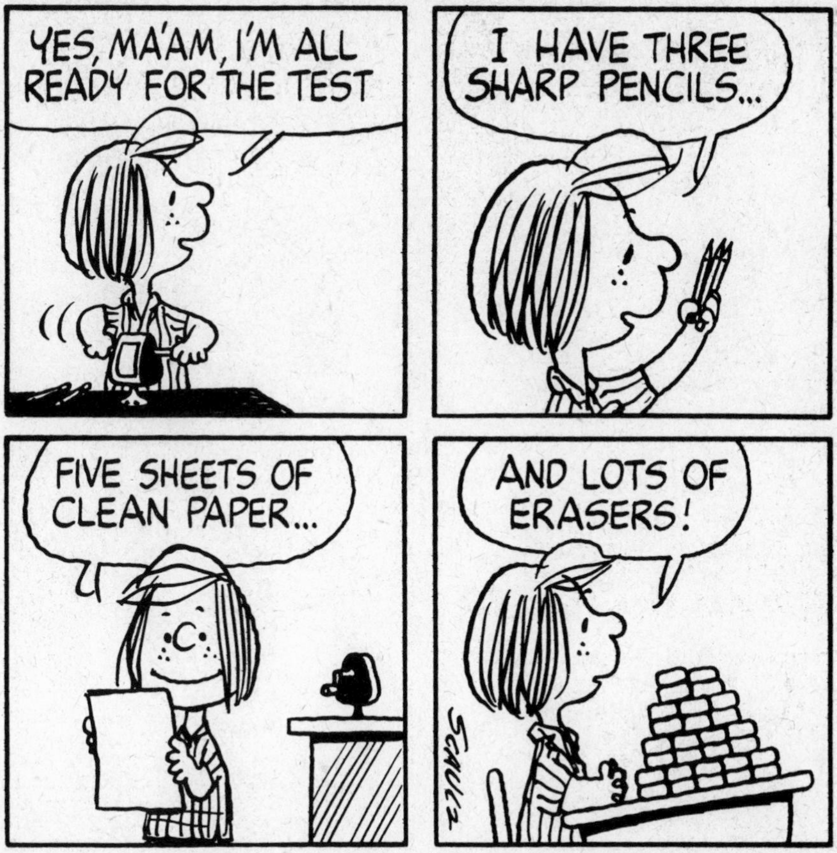
YES, MA'AM, I'M ALL READY FOR THE TEST
I HAVE THREE SHARP PENCILS...
FIVE SHEETS OF CLEAN PAPER...
AND LOTS OF ERASERS!

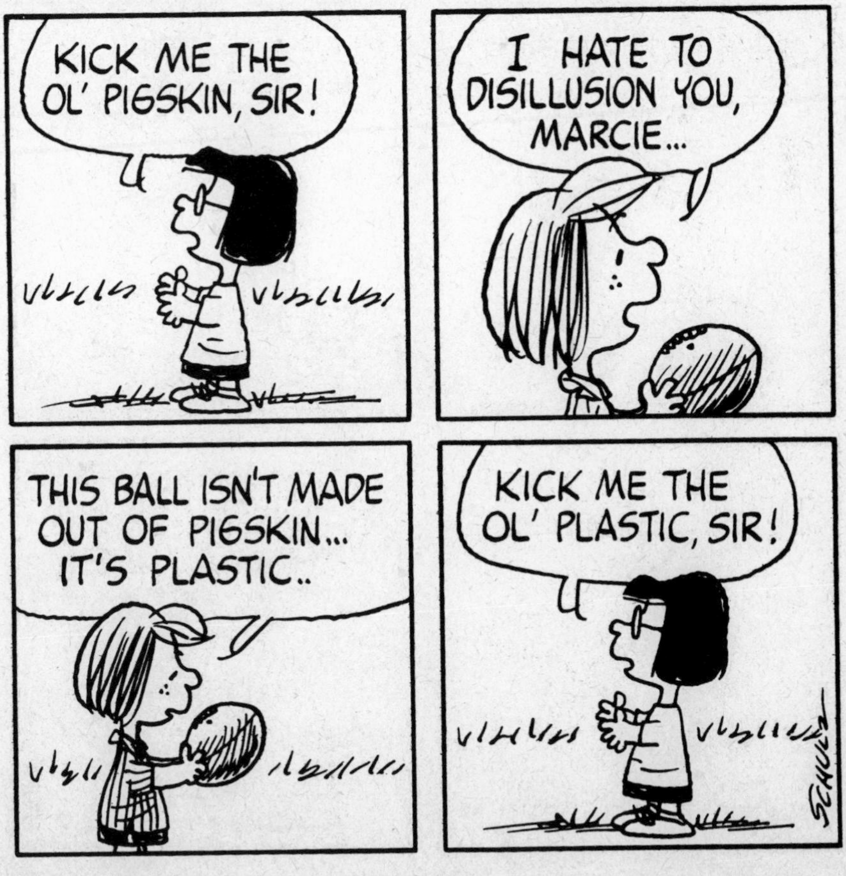
KICK ME THE OL' PIGSKIN, SIR!
I HATE TO DISILLUSION YOU, MARCIE...
THIS BALL ISN'T MADE OUT OF PIGSKIN... IT'S PLASTIC..
KICK ME THE OL' PLASTIC, SIR!

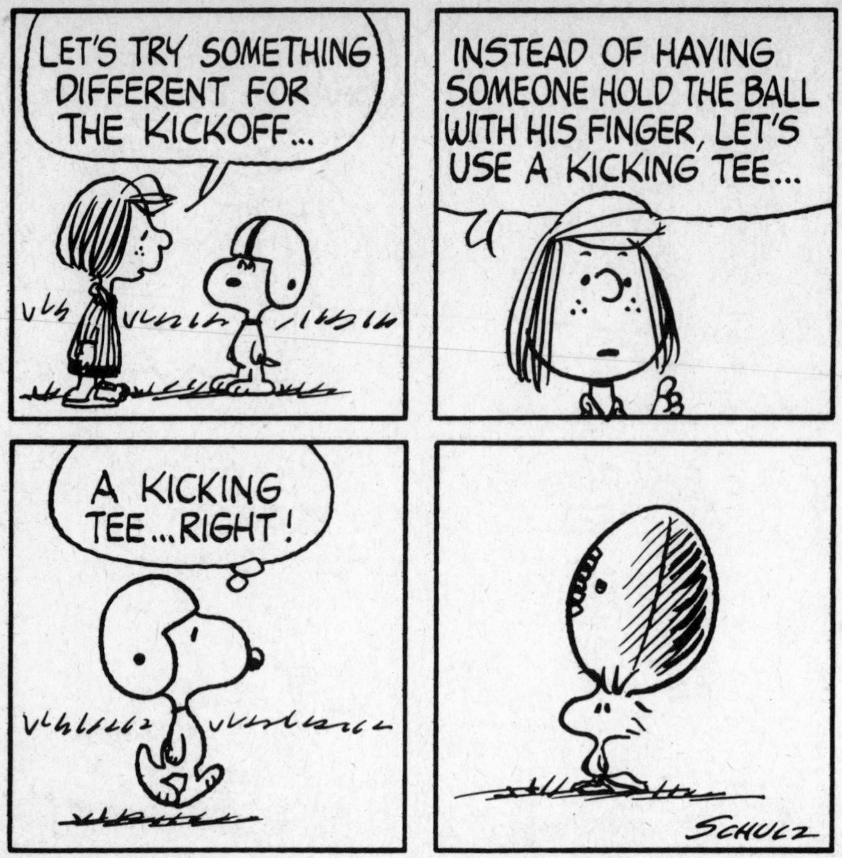
LET'S TRY SOMETHING DIFFERENT FOR THE KICKOFF...
INSTEAD OF HAVING SOMEONE HOLD THE BALL WITH HIS FINGER, LET'S USE A KICKING TEE...
A KICKING TEE...RIGHT!
SCHULZ

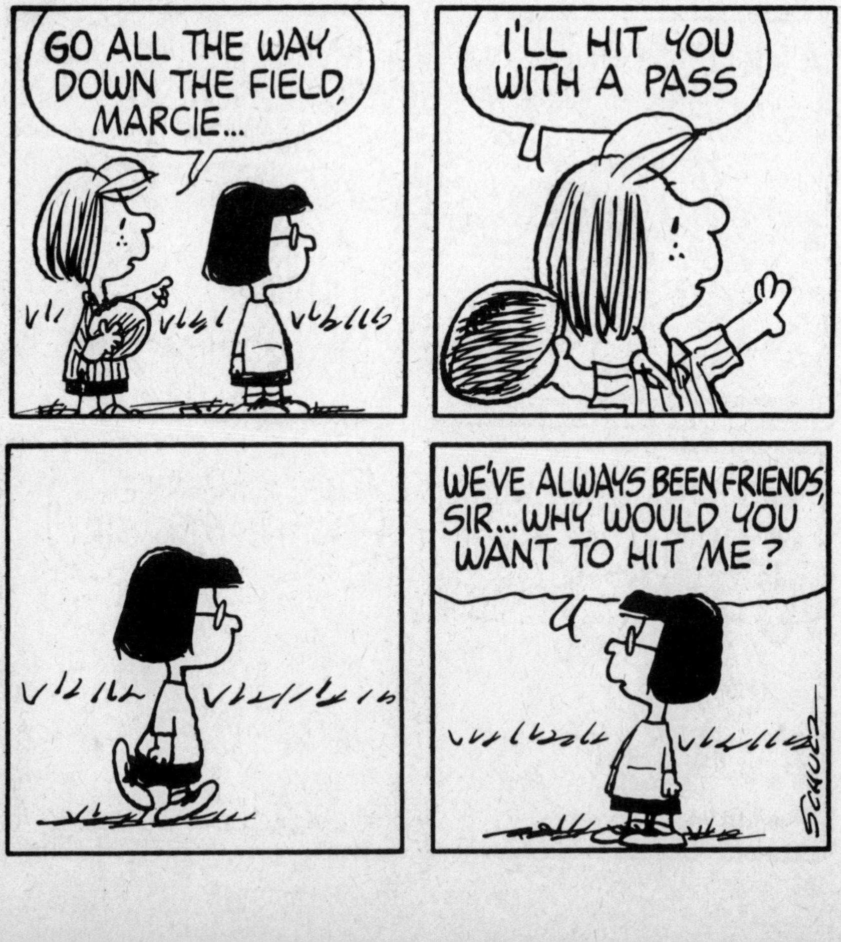
GO ALL THE WAY DOWN THE FIELD, MARCIE...
I'LL HIT YOU WITH A PASS
WE'VE ALWAYS BEEN FRIENDS, SIR...WHY WOULD YOU WANT TO HIT ME?
SCHULZ

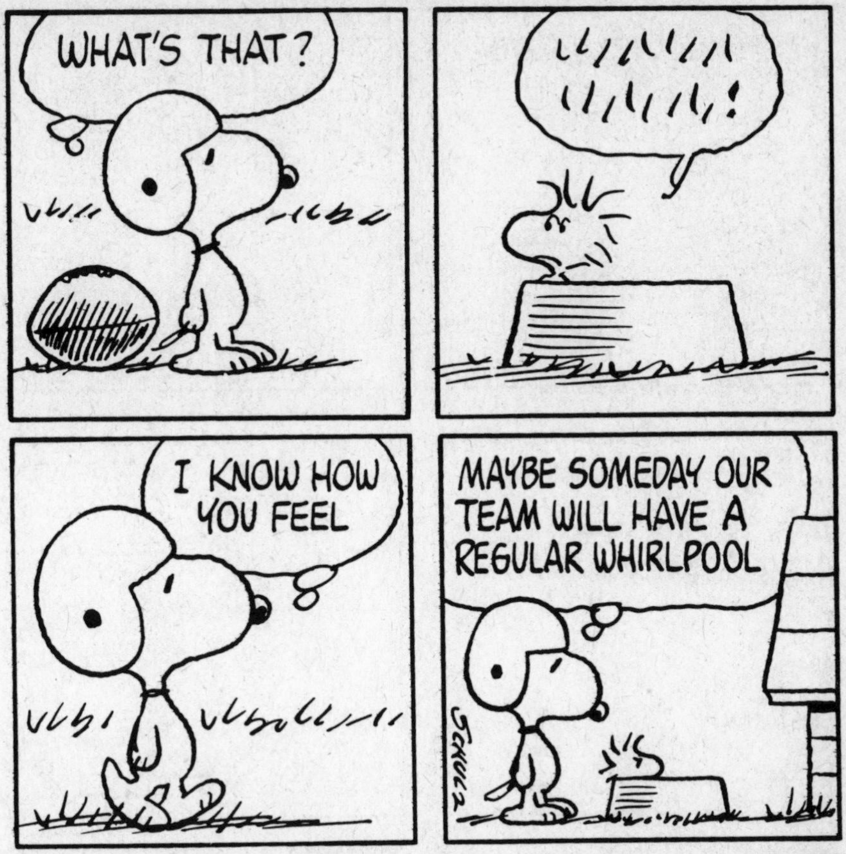
WHAT'S THAT?
I KNOW HOW YOU FEEL
MAYBE SOMEDAY OUR TEAM WILL HAVE A REGULAR WHIRLPOOL

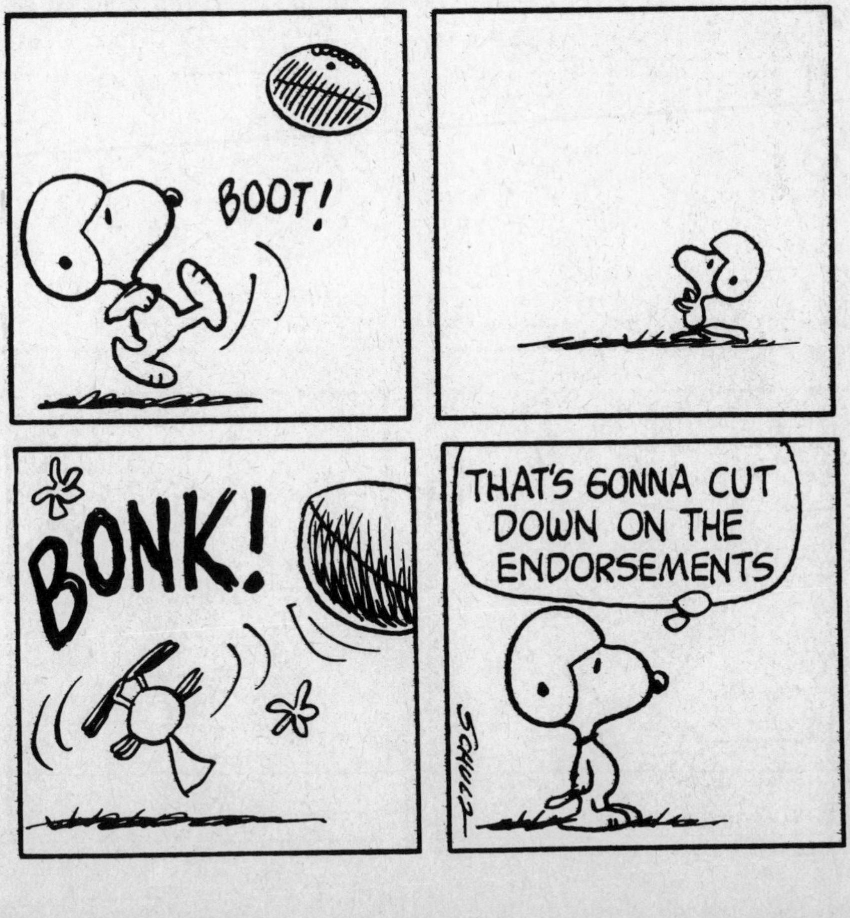
BOOT!
BONK!
THAT'S GONNA CUT DOWN ON THE ENDORSEMENTS

Favorite Quotations

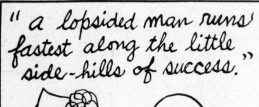

"*a lopsided man runs fastest along the little side-hills of success.*"

WHO SAID THAT, MOSES?

NO, A MAN NAMED FRANK MOORE COLBY...

IT SOUNDS LIKE SOMETHING MOSES WOULD HAVE SAID...

ACTUALLY, IT DOESN'T SOUND AT ALL LIKE SOMETHING MOSES WOULD HAVE SAID!

HOW DO YOU KNOW? YOU NEVER TALKED TO MOSES, DID YOU?

MOSES LIKED TO SAY THINGS LIKE THAT!

IF MOSES HAD THOUGHT OF IT, MOSES WOULD HAVE SAID IT!

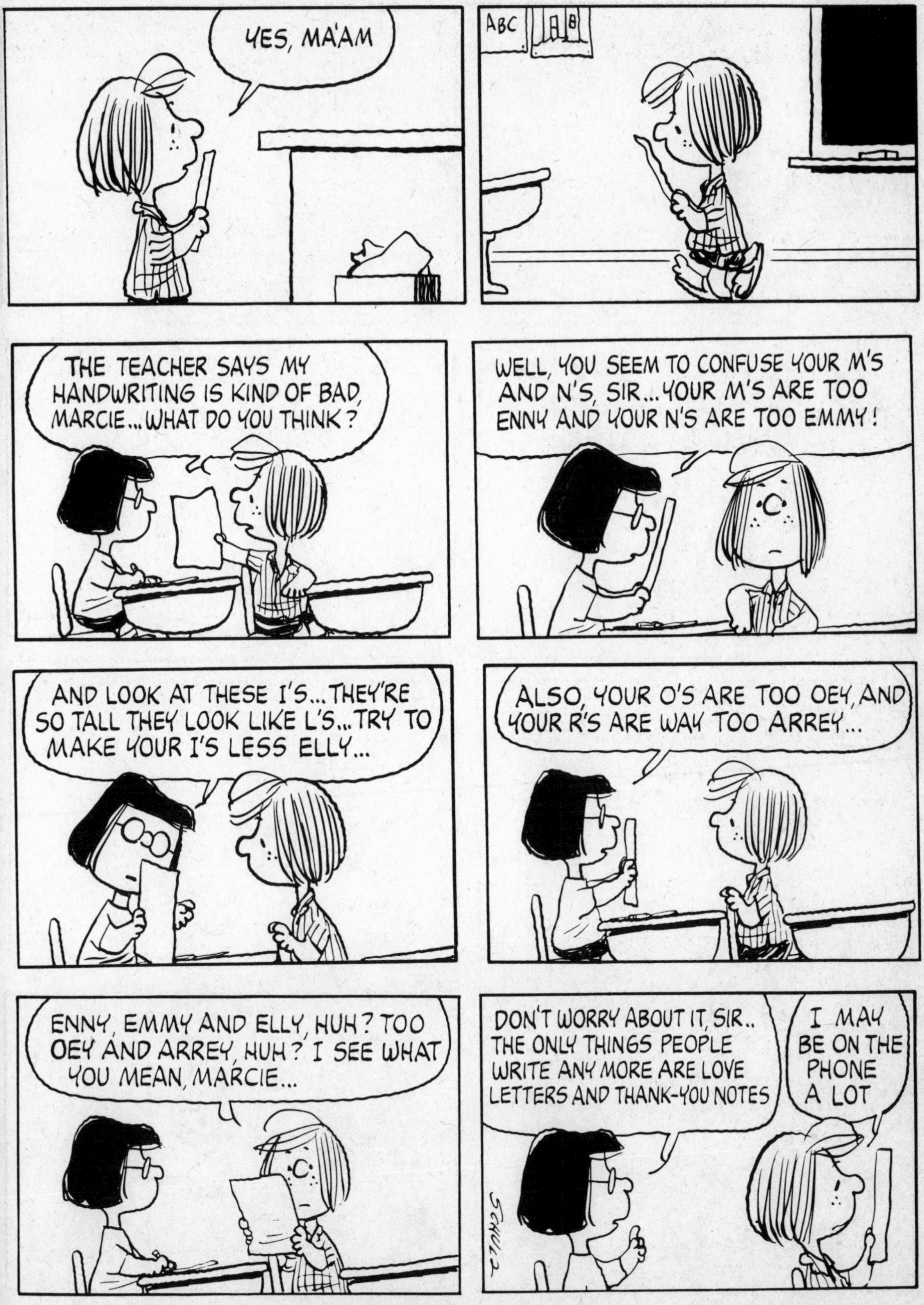
YES, MA'AM
ABC
THE TEACHER SAYS MY HANDWRITING IS KIND OF BAD, MARCIE...WHAT DO YOU THINK?
WELL, YOU SEEM TO CONFUSE YOUR M'S AND N'S, SIR...YOUR M'S ARE TOO ENNY AND YOUR N'S ARE TOO EMMY!
AND LOOK AT THESE I'S...THEY'RE SO TALL THEY LOOK LIKE L'S...TRY TO MAKE YOUR I'S LESS ELLY...
ALSO, YOUR O'S ARE TOO OEY, AND YOUR R'S ARE WAY TOO ARREY...
ENNY, EMMY AND ELLY, HUH? TOO OEY AND ARREY, HUH? I SEE WHAT YOU MEAN, MARCIE...
DON'T WORRY ABOUT IT, SIR.. THE ONLY THINGS PEOPLE WRITE ANY MORE ARE LOVE LETTERS AND THANK-YOU NOTES
I MAY BE ON THE PHONE A LOT
SCHULZ

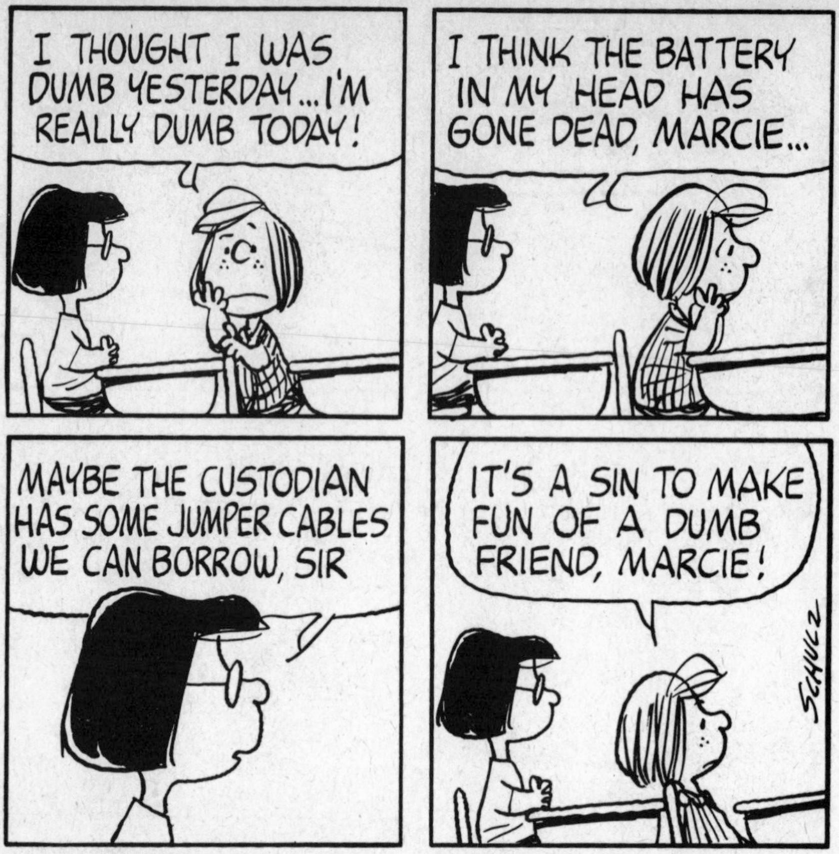
I THOUGHT I WAS DUMB YESTERDAY...I'M REALLY DUMB TODAY!
I THINK THE BATTERY IN MY HEAD HAS GONE DEAD, MARCIE...
MAYBE THE CUSTODIAN HAS SOME JUMPER CABLES WE CAN BORROW, SIR
IT'S A SIN TO MAKE FUN OF A DUMB FRIEND, MARCIE!
SCHULZ

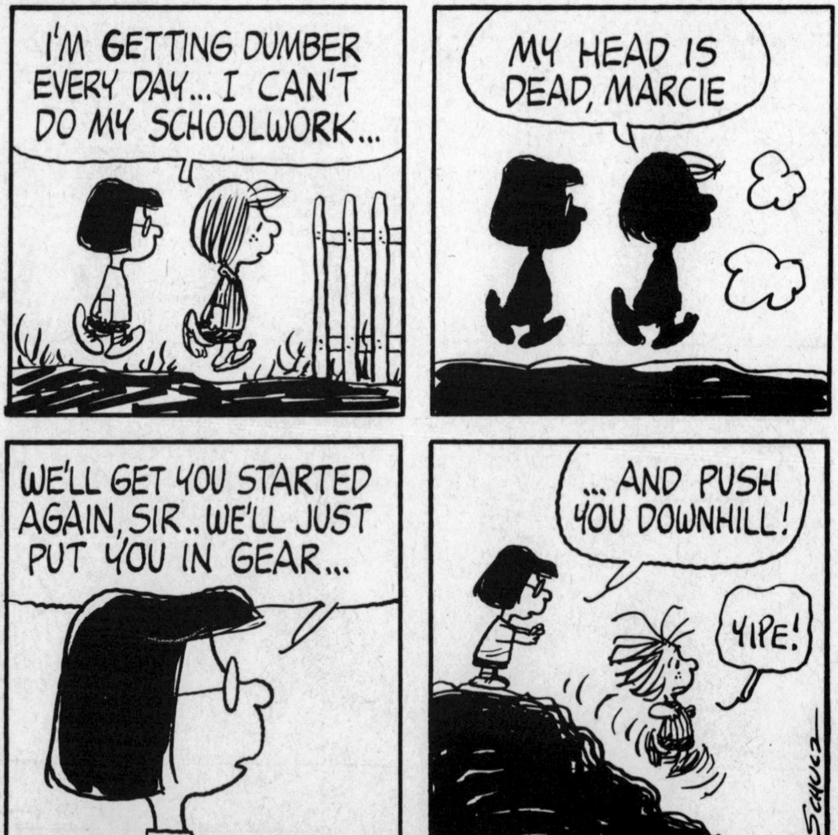
I'M GETTING DUMBER EVERY DAY... I CAN'T DO MY SCHOOLWORK...
MY HEAD IS DEAD, MARCIE
WE'LL GET YOU STARTED AGAIN, SIR.. WE'LL JUST PUT YOU IN GEAR...
... AND PUSH YOU DOWNHILL!
YIPE!
SCHULZ

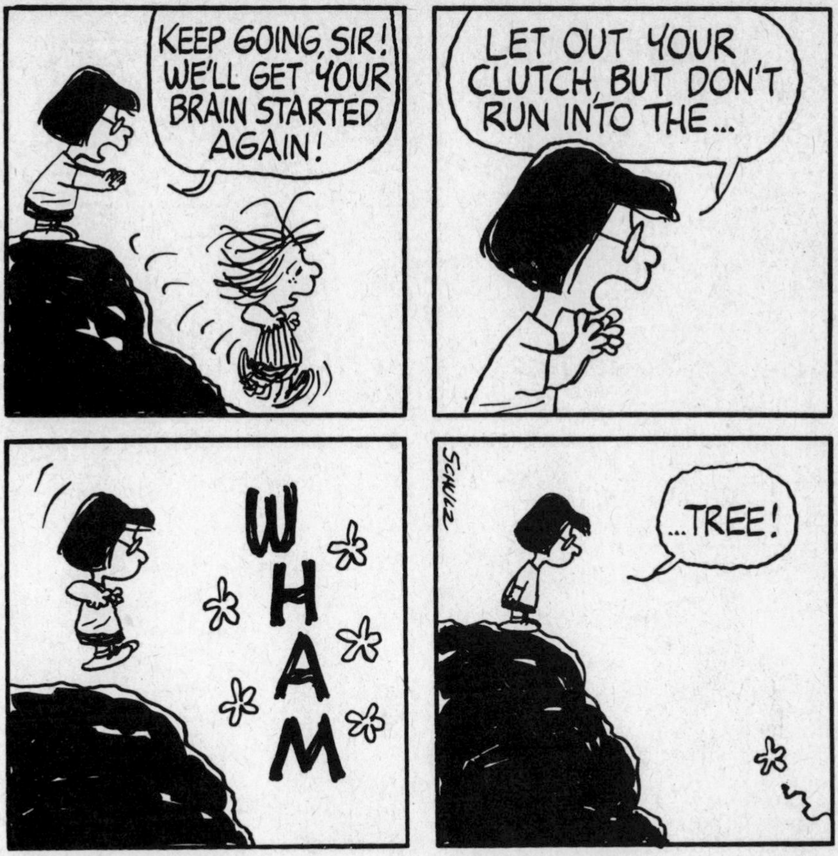

KEEP GOING, SIR! WE'LL GET YOUR BRAIN STARTED AGAIN!
LET OUT YOUR CLUTCH, BUT DON'T RUN INTO THE...
WHAM
...TREE!

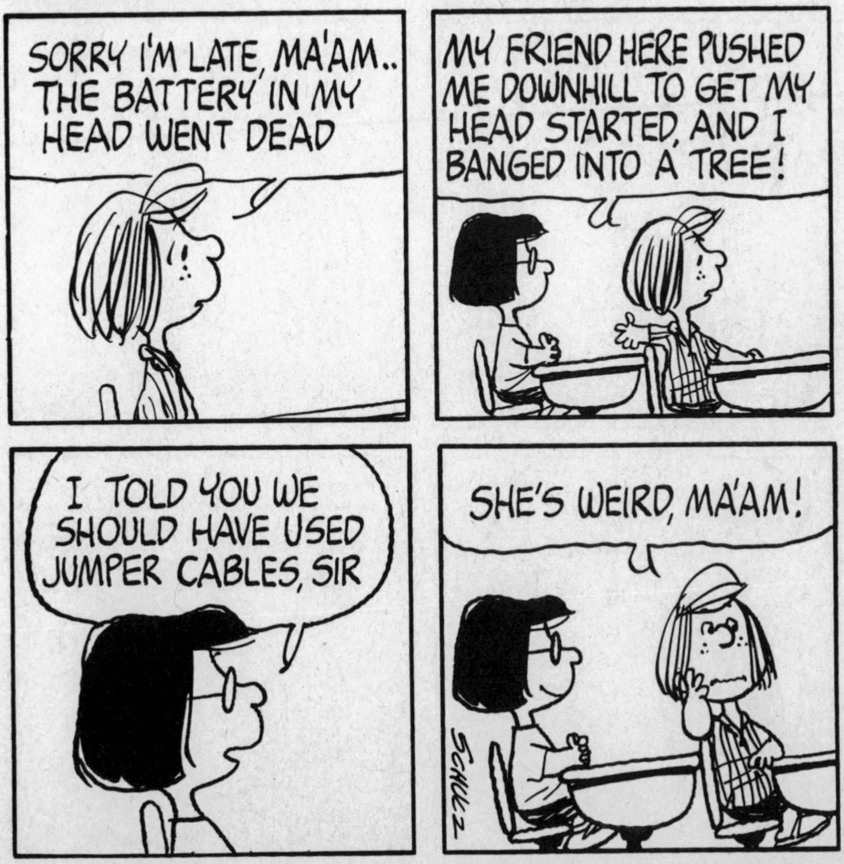

SORRY I'M LATE, MA'AM.. THE BATTERY IN MY HEAD WENT DEAD
MY FRIEND HERE PUSHED ME DOWNHILL TO GET MY HEAD STARTED, AND I BANGED INTO A TREE!
I TOLD YOU WE SHOULD HAVE USED JUMPER CABLES, SIR
SHE'S WEIRD, MA'AM!

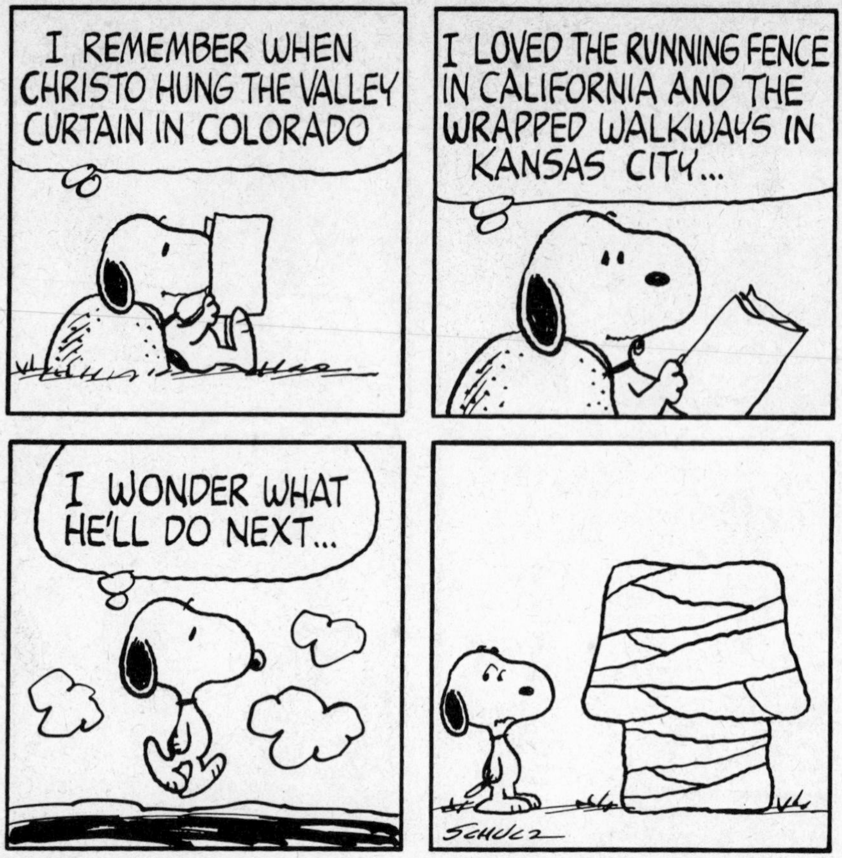
I REMEMBER WHEN CHRISTO HUNG THE VALLEY CURTAIN IN COLORADO
I LOVED THE RUNNING FENCE IN CALIFORNIA AND THE WRAPPED WALKWAYS IN KANSAS CITY...
I WONDER WHAT HE'LL DO NEXT...

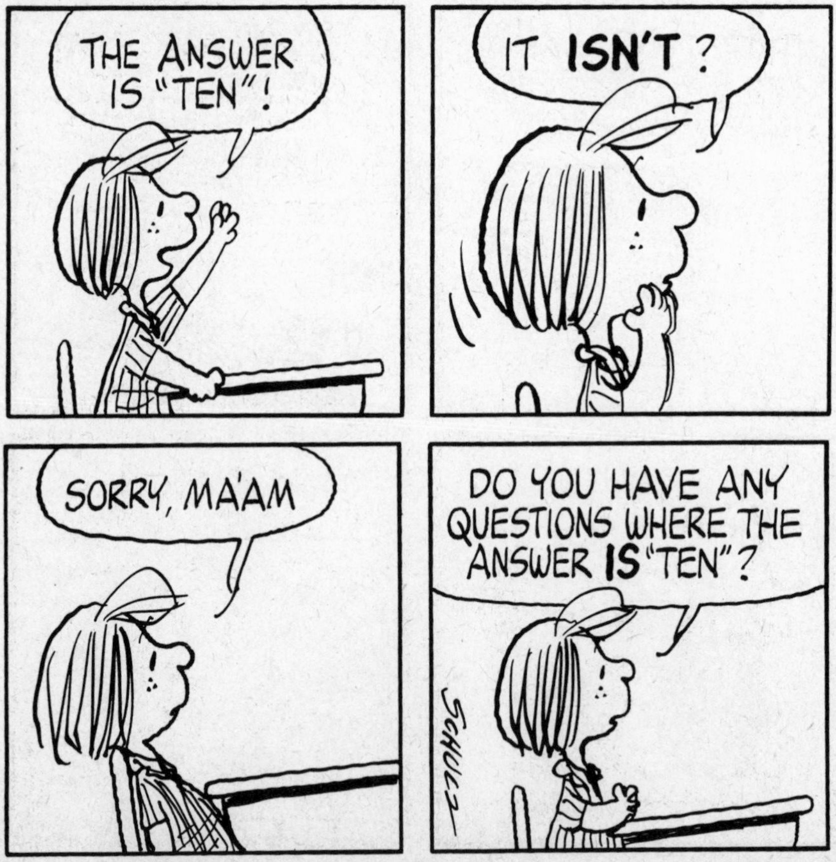
THE ANSWER IS "TEN"!
IT ISN'T ?
SORRY, MA'AM
DO YOU HAVE ANY QUESTIONS WHERE THE ANSWER IS "TEN"?

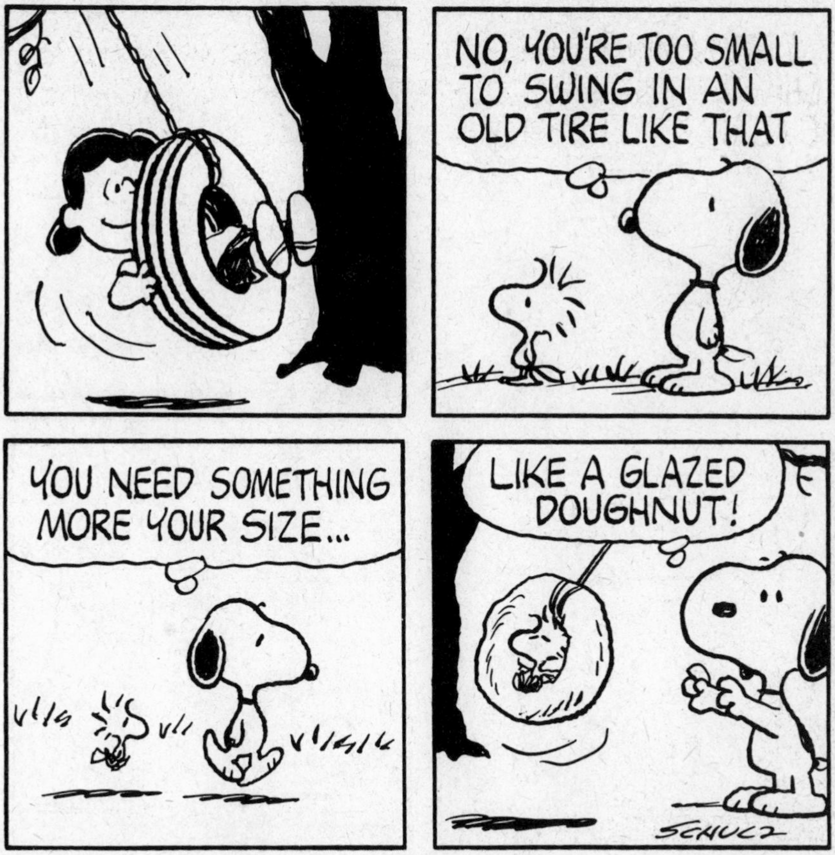
NO, YOU'RE TOO SMALL TO SWING IN AN OLD TIRE LIKE THAT
YOU NEED SOMETHING MORE YOUR SIZE...
LIKE A GLAZED DOUGHNUT!
SCHULZ

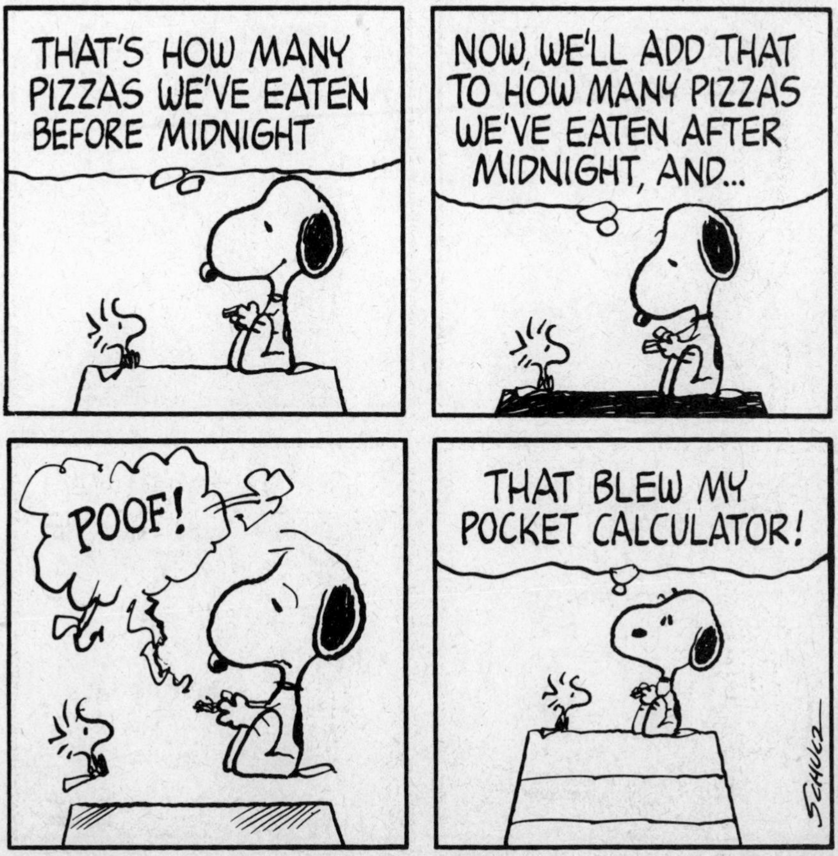
THAT'S HOW MANY PIZZAS WE'VE EATEN BEFORE MIDNIGHT
NOW, WE'LL ADD THAT TO HOW MANY PIZZAS WE'VE EATEN AFTER MIDNIGHT, AND...
POOF!
THAT BLEW MY POCKET CALCULATOR!
SCHULZ

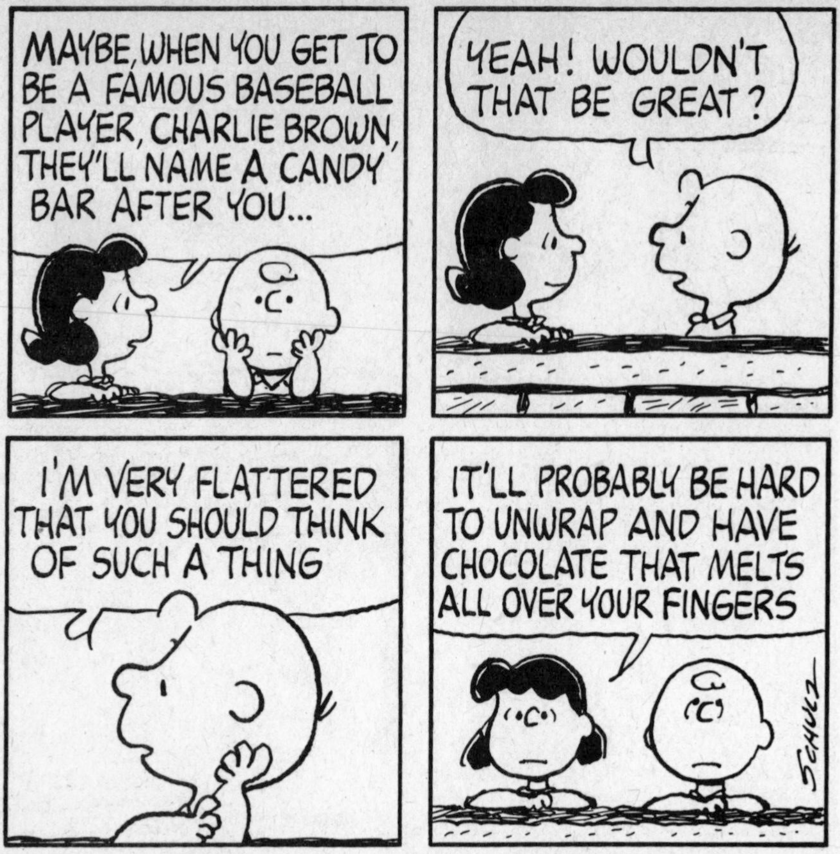
MAYBE, WHEN YOU GET TO BE A FAMOUS BASEBALL PLAYER, CHARLIE BROWN, THEY'LL NAME A CANDY BAR AFTER YOU...
YEAH! WOULDN'T THAT BE GREAT?
I'M VERY FLATTERED THAT YOU SHOULD THINK OF SUCH A THING
IT'LL PROBABLY BE HARD TO UNWRAP AND HAVE CHOCOLATE THAT MELTS ALL OVER YOUR FINGERS
SCHULZ

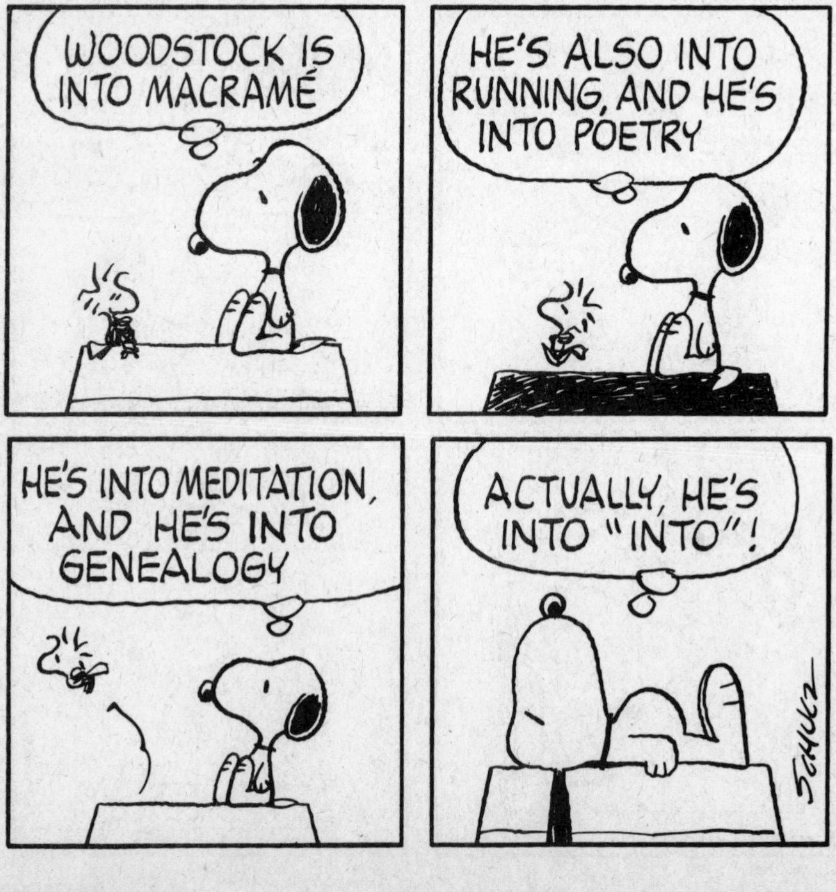
WOODSTOCK IS INTO MACRAMÉ
HE'S ALSO INTO RUNNING, AND HE'S INTO POETRY
HE'S INTO MEDITATION, AND HE'S INTO GENEALOGY
ACTUALLY, HE'S INTO "INTO"!
SCHULZ

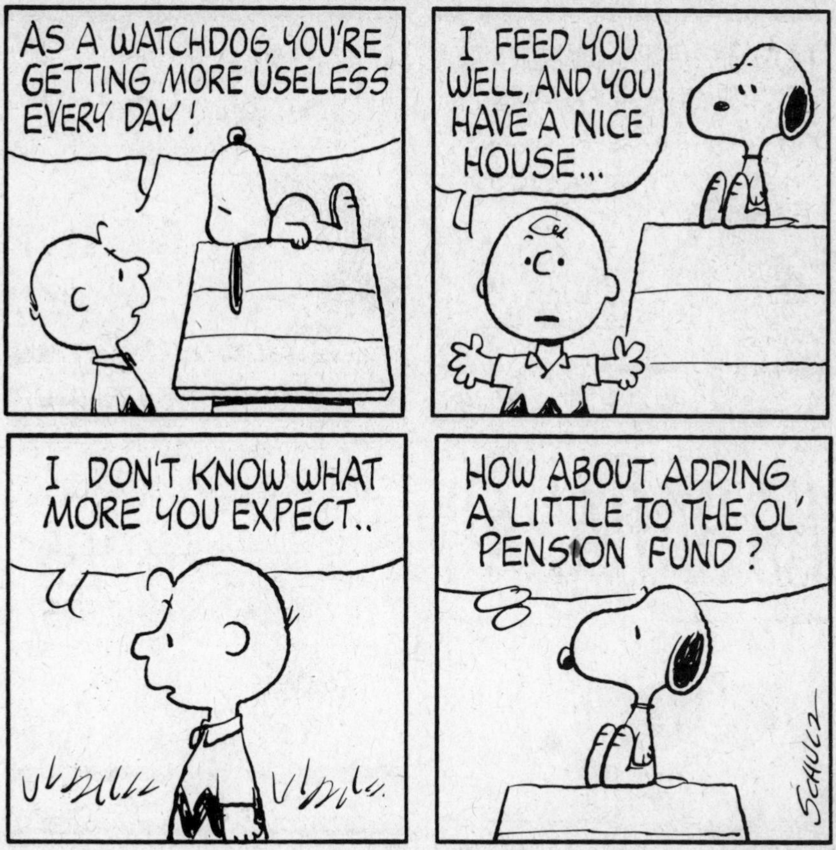
AS A WATCHDOG, YOU'RE GETTING MORE USELESS EVERY DAY!
I FEED YOU WELL, AND YOU HAVE A NICE HOUSE...
I DON'T KNOW WHAT MORE YOU EXPECT..
HOW ABOUT ADDING A LITTLE TO THE OL' PENSION FUND?
SCHULZ

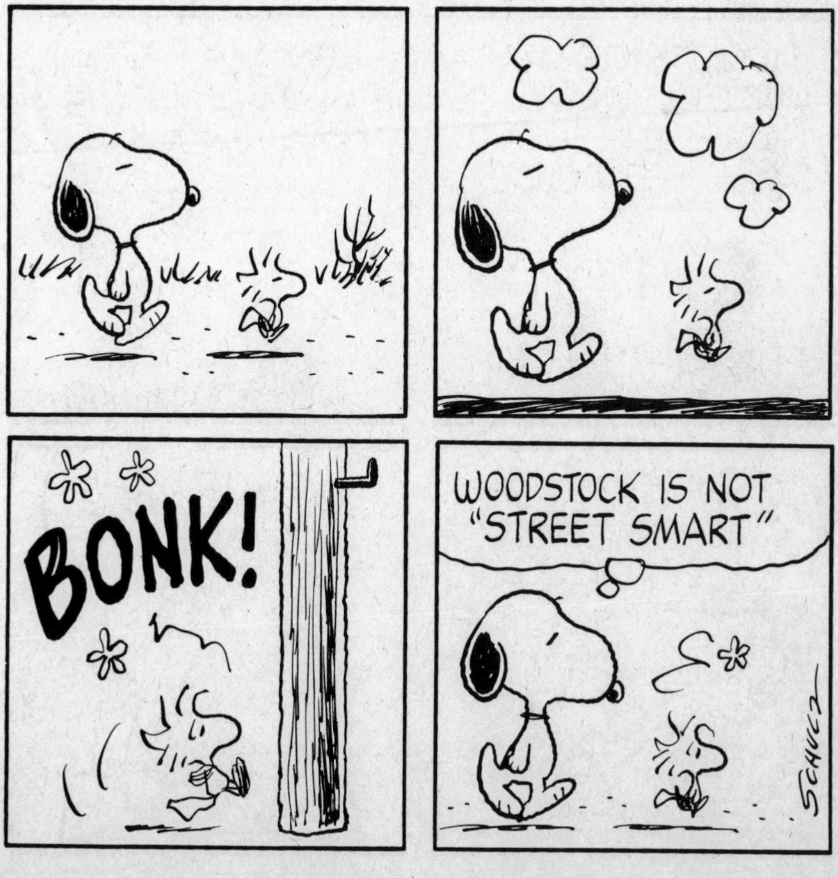
BONK!
WOODSTOCK IS NOT "STREET SMART"
SCHULZ

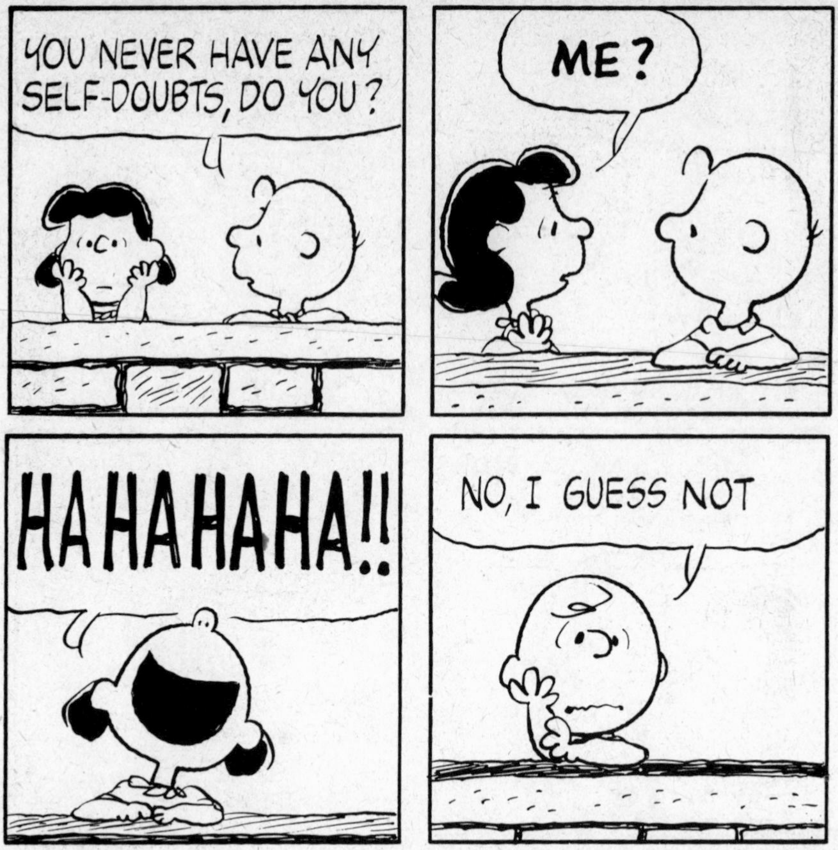
YOU NEVER HAVE ANY SELF-DOUBTS, DO YOU?
ME?
HAHAHAHA!!
NO, I GUESS NOT

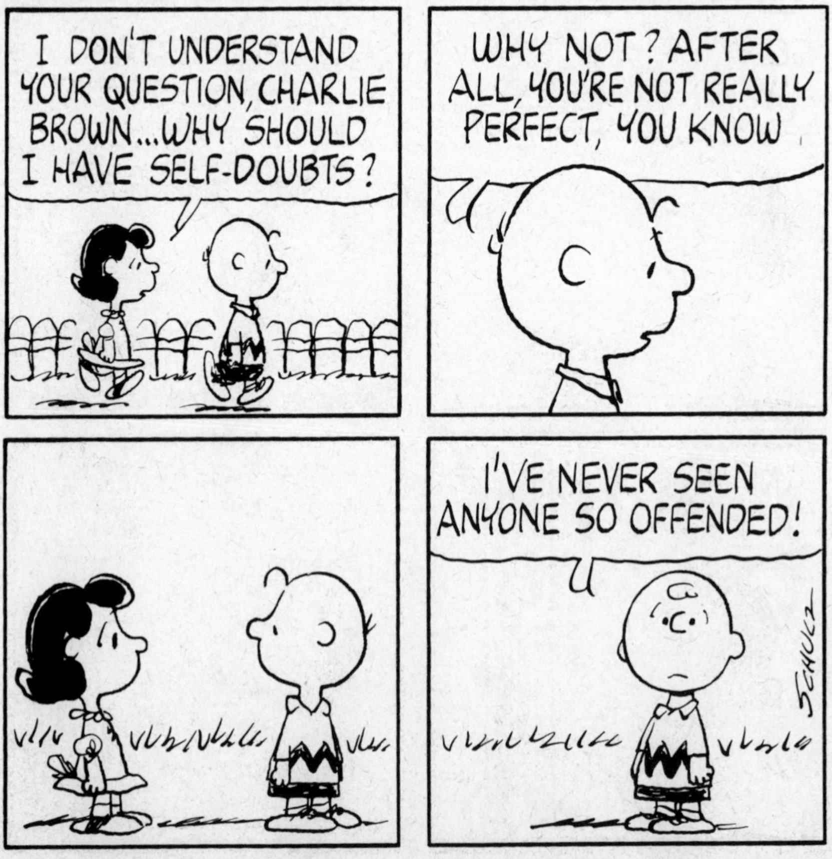
I DON'T UNDERSTAND YOUR QUESTION, CHARLIE BROWN...WHY SHOULD I HAVE SELF-DOUBTS?
WHY NOT? AFTER ALL, YOU'RE NOT REALLY PERFECT, YOU KNOW
I'VE NEVER SEEN ANYONE SO OFFENDED!
SCHULZ

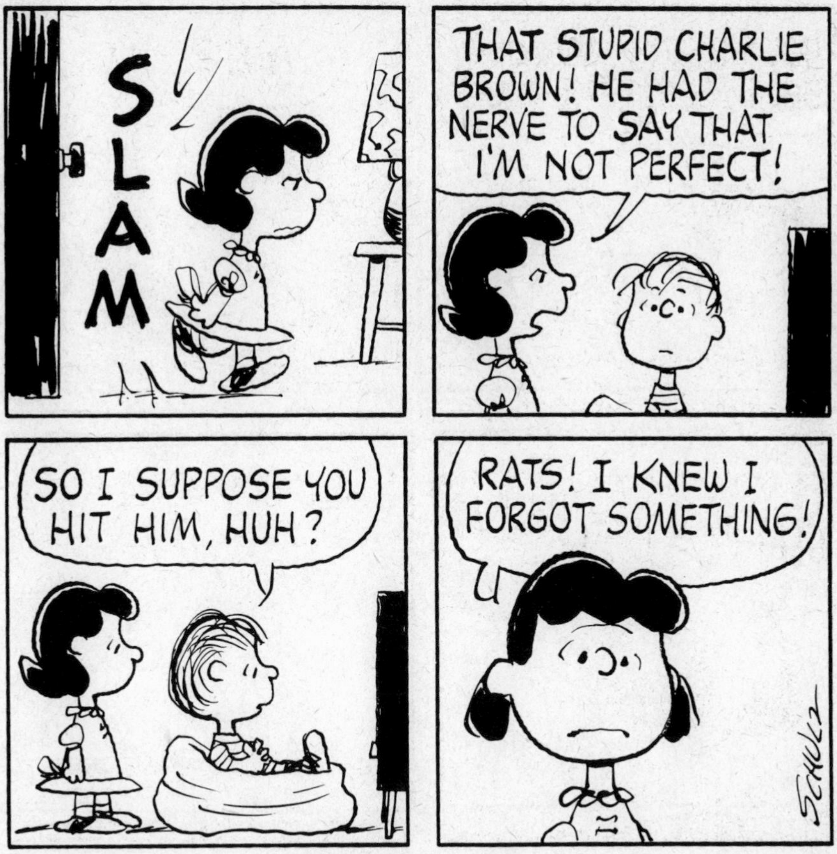
SLAM
THAT STUPID CHARLIE BROWN! HE HAD THE NERVE TO SAY THAT I'M NOT PERFECT!
SO I SUPPOSE YOU HIT HIM, HUH?
RATS! I KNEW I FORGOT SOMETHING!
SCHULZ

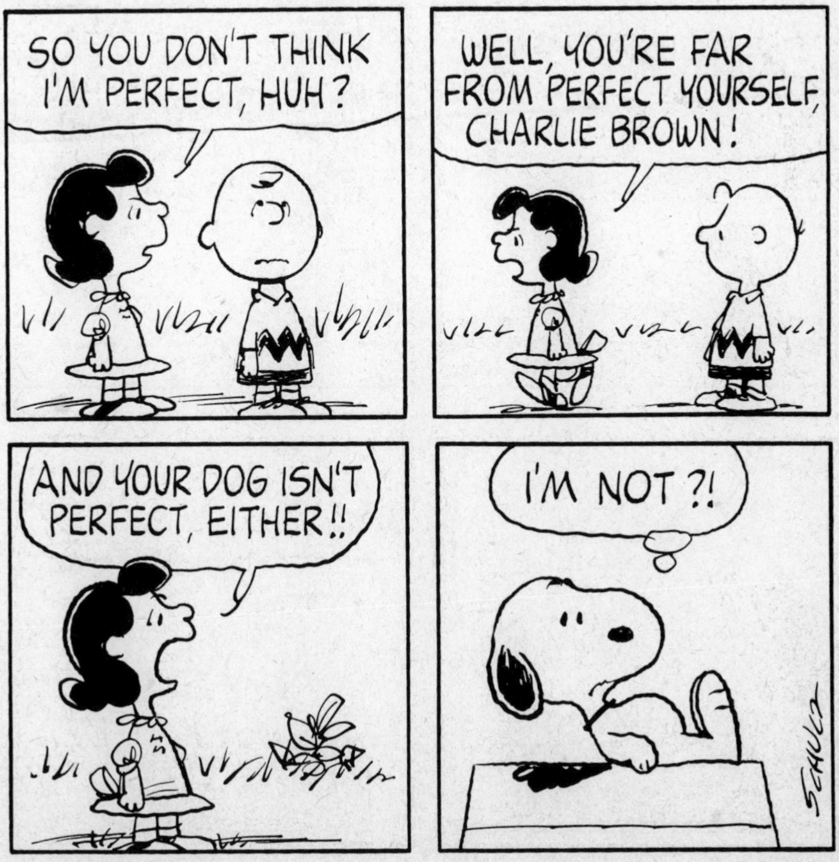
SO YOU DON'T THINK I'M PERFECT, HUH?
WELL, YOU'RE FAR FROM PERFECT YOURSELF, CHARLIE BROWN!
AND YOUR DOG ISN'T PERFECT, EITHER!!
I'M NOT ?!
SCHULZ

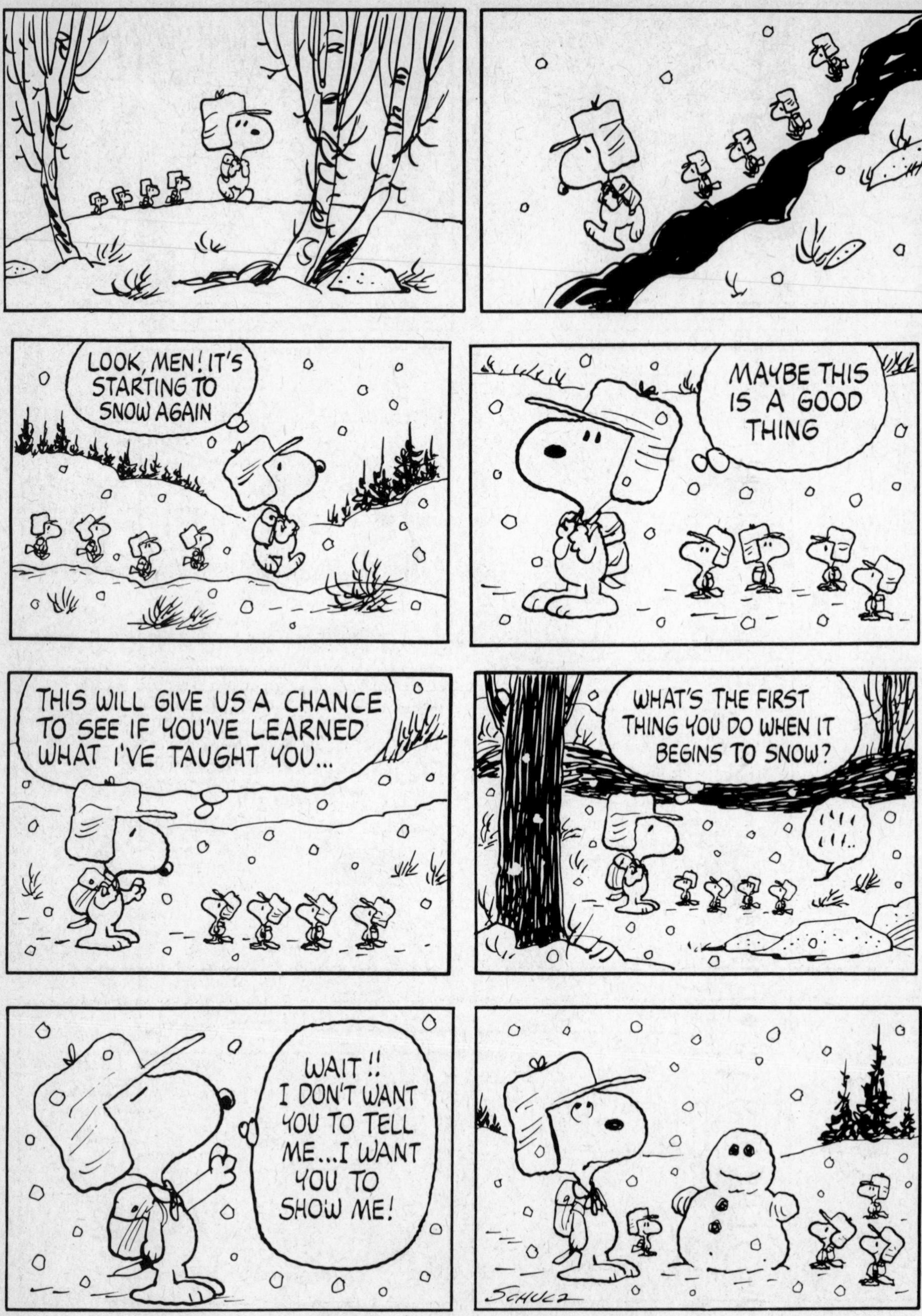
LOOK, MEN! IT'S STARTING TO SNOW AGAIN
MAYBE THIS IS A GOOD THING
THIS WILL GIVE US A CHANCE TO SEE IF YOU'VE LEARNED WHAT I'VE TAUGHT YOU...
WHAT'S THE FIRST THING YOU DO WHEN IT BEGINS TO SNOW?
WAIT!! I DON'T WANT YOU TO TELL ME...I WANT YOU TO SHOW ME!
SCHULZ

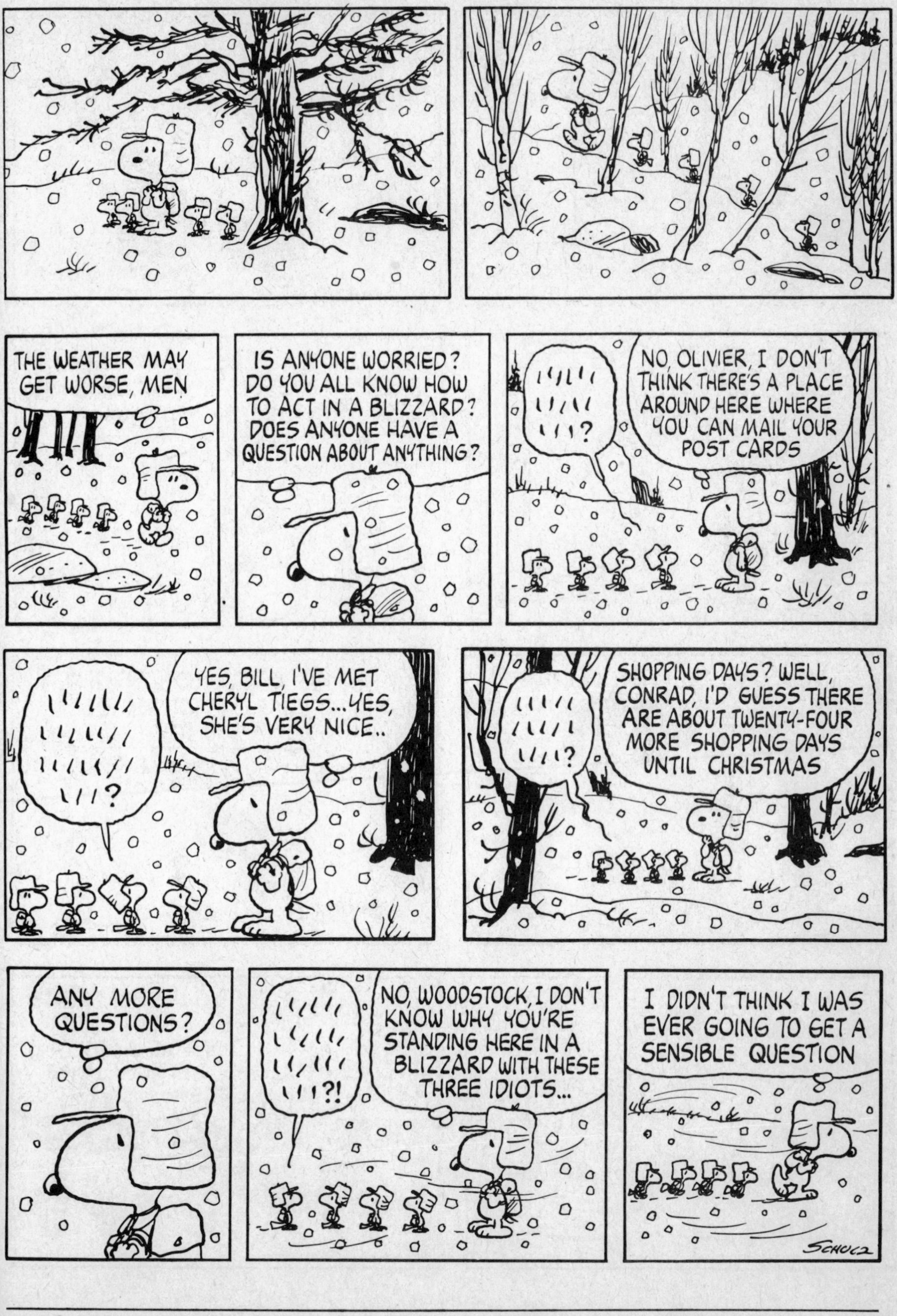
THE WEATHER MAY GET WORSE, MEN
IS ANYONE WORRIED? DO YOU ALL KNOW HOW TO ACT IN A BLIZZARD? DOES ANYONE HAVE A QUESTION ABOUT ANYTHING?
?
NO, OLIVIER, I DON'T THINK THERE'S A PLACE AROUND HERE WHERE YOU CAN MAIL YOUR POST CARDS
?
YES, BILL, I'VE MET CHERYL TIEGS...YES, SHE'S VERY NICE..
?
SHOPPING DAYS? WELL, CONRAD, I'D GUESS THERE ARE ABOUT TWENTY-FOUR MORE SHOPPING DAYS UNTIL CHRISTMAS
ANY MORE QUESTIONS?
?!
NO, WOODSTOCK, I DON'T KNOW WHY YOU'RE STANDING HERE IN A BLIZZARD WITH THESE THREE IDIOTS...
I DIDN'T THINK I WAS EVER GOING TO GET A SENSIBLE QUESTION
SCHULZ

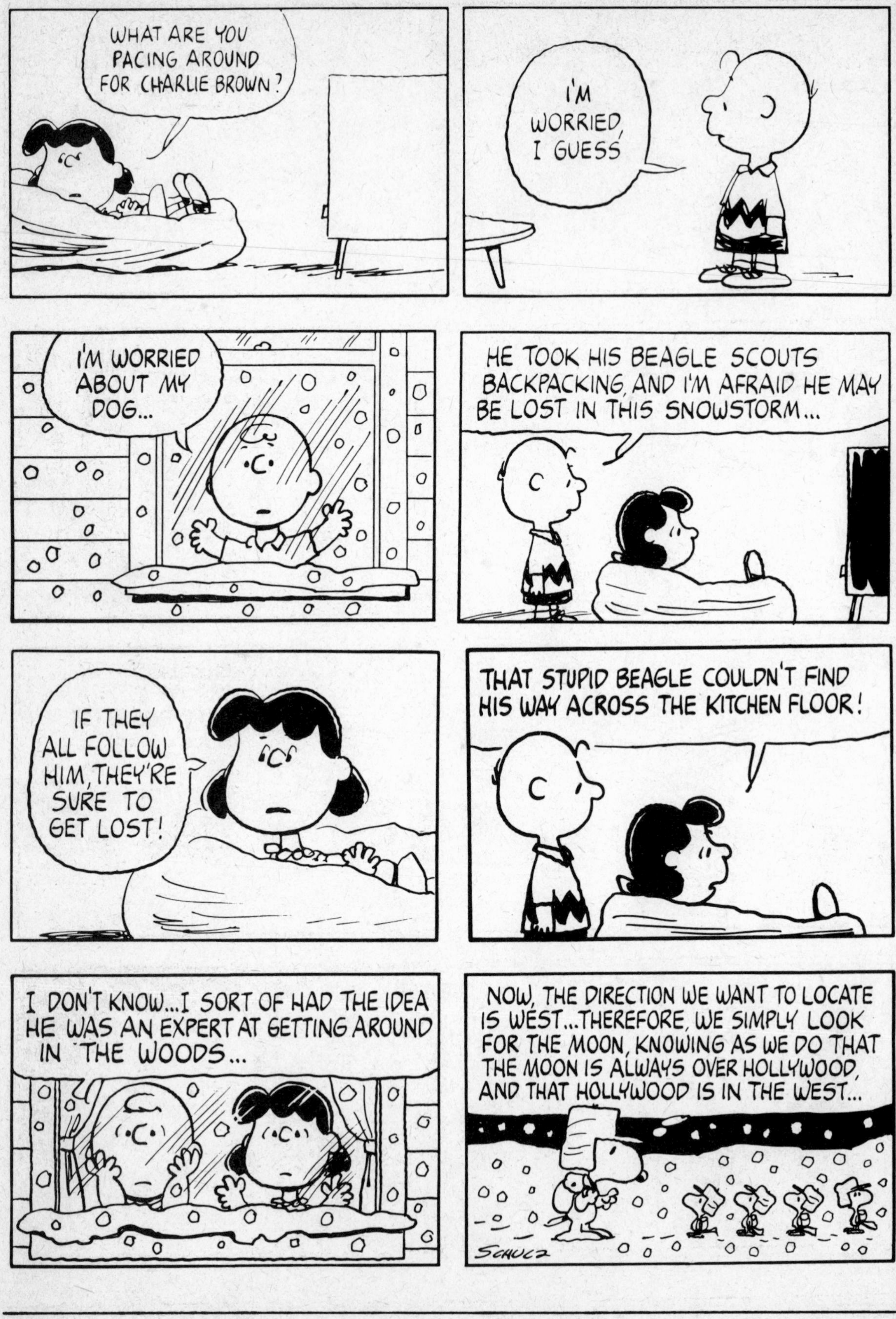

WHAT ARE YOU PACING AROUND FOR CHARLIE BROWN?
I'M WORRIED, I GUESS
I'M WORRIED ABOUT MY DOG...
HE TOOK HIS BEAGLE SCOUTS BACKPACKING, AND I'M AFRAID HE MAY BE LOST IN THIS SNOWSTORM...
IF THEY ALL FOLLOW HIM, THEY'RE SURE TO GET LOST!
THAT STUPID BEAGLE COULDN'T FIND HIS WAY ACROSS THE KITCHEN FLOOR!
I DON'T KNOW...I SORT OF HAD THE IDEA HE WAS AN EXPERT AT GETTING AROUND IN THE WOODS...
NOW, THE DIRECTION WE WANT TO LOCATE IS WEST...THEREFORE, WE SIMPLY LOOK FOR THE MOON, KNOWING AS WE DO THAT THE MOON IS ALWAYS OVER HOLLYWOOD, AND THAT HOLLYWOOD IS IN THE WEST...
SCHULZ

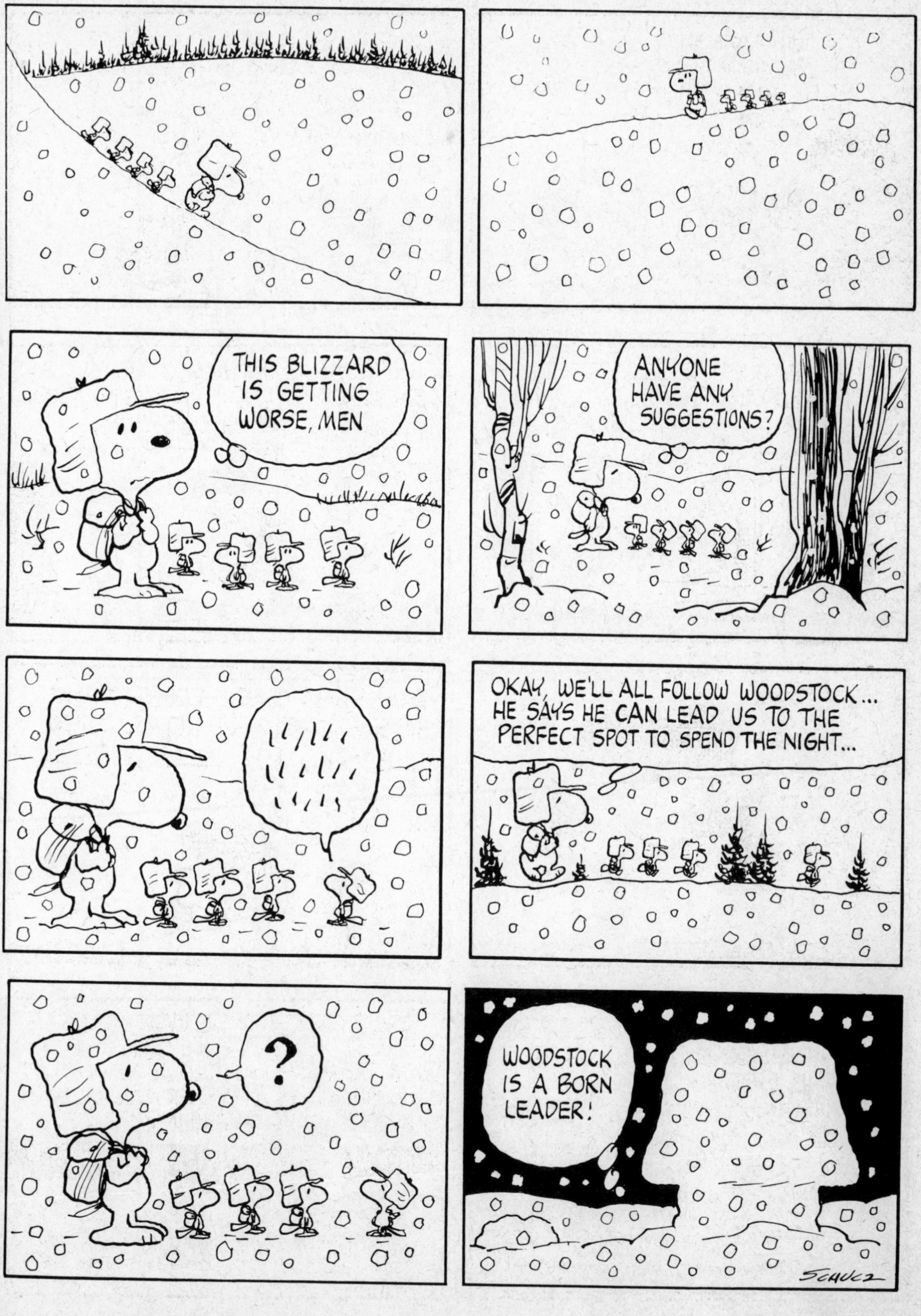
THIS BLIZZARD IS GETTING WORSE, MEN
ANYONE HAVE ANY SUGGESTIONS?
OKAY, WE'LL ALL FOLLOW WOODSTOCK... HE SAYS HE CAN LEAD US TO THE PERFECT SPOT TO SPEND THE NIGHT...
?
WOODSTOCK IS A BORN LEADER!
SCHULZ

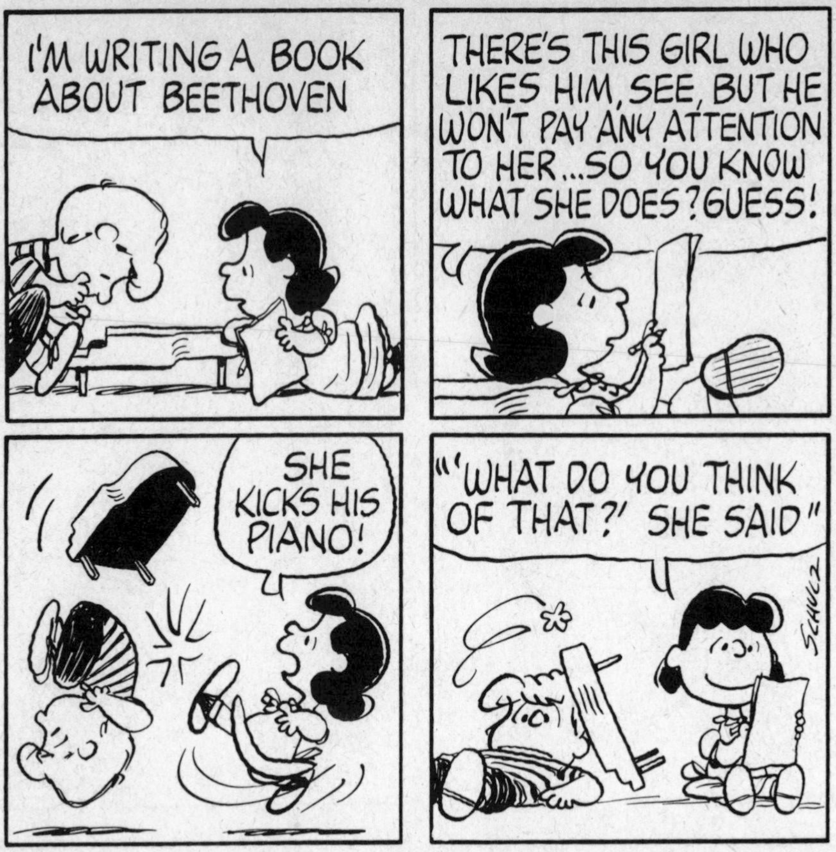
I'M WRITING A BOOK ABOUT BEETHOVEN
THERE'S THIS GIRL WHO LIKES HIM, SEE, BUT HE WON'T PAY ANY ATTENTION TO HER...SO YOU KNOW WHAT SHE DOES? GUESS!
SHE KICKS HIS PIANO!
"'WHAT DO YOU THINK OF THAT?' SHE SAID"
SCHULZ

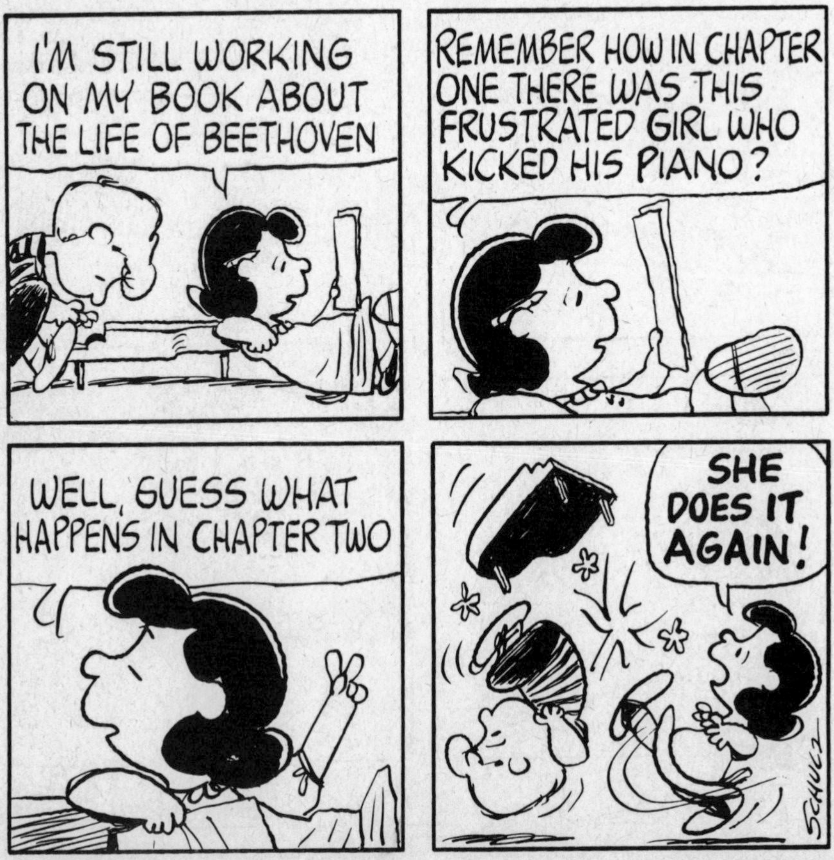
I'M STILL WORKING ON MY BOOK ABOUT THE LIFE OF BEETHOVEN
REMEMBER HOW IN CHAPTER ONE THERE WAS THIS FRUSTRATED GIRL WHO KICKED HIS PIANO?
WELL, GUESS WHAT HAPPENS IN CHAPTER TWO
SHE DOES IT AGAIN!
SCHULZ

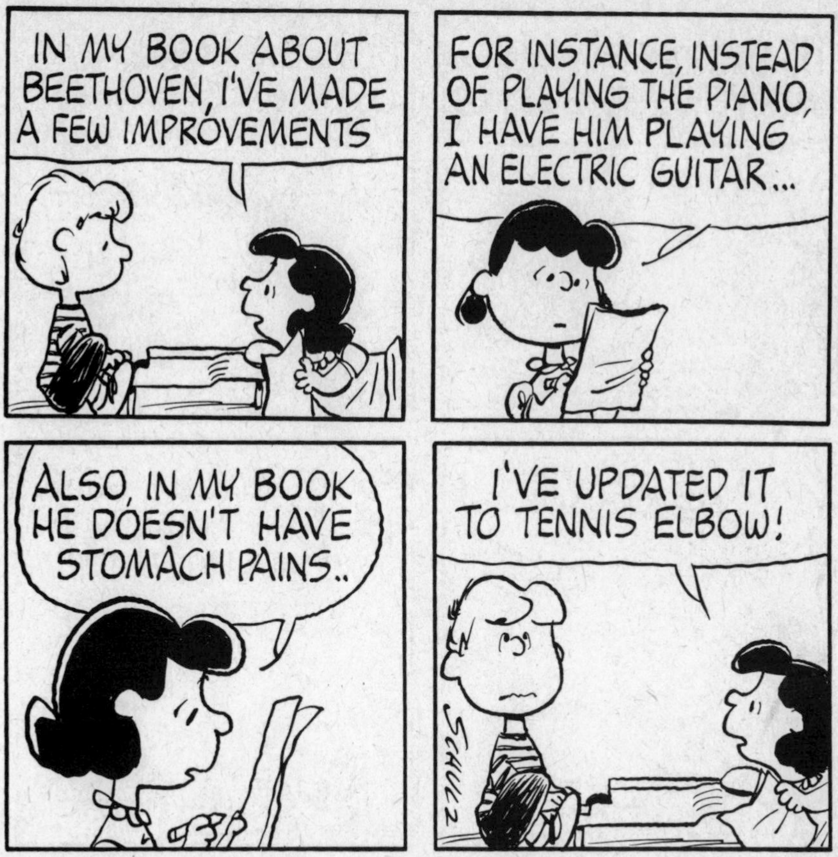
IN MY BOOK ABOUT BEETHOVEN, I'VE MADE A FEW IMPROVEMENTS
FOR INSTANCE, INSTEAD OF PLAYING THE PIANO, I HAVE HIM PLAYING AN ELECTRIC GUITAR...
ALSO, IN MY BOOK HE DOESN'T HAVE STOMACH PAINS..
I'VE UPDATED IT TO TENNIS ELBOW!

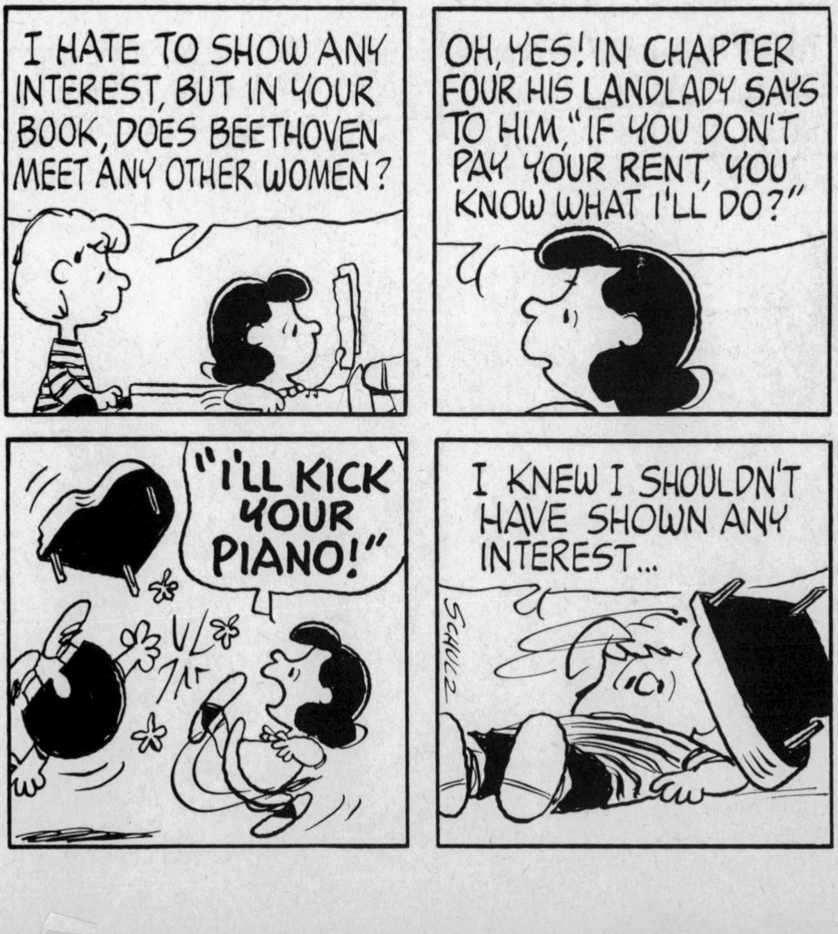
I HATE TO SHOW ANY INTEREST, BUT IN YOUR BOOK, DOES BEETHOVEN MEET ANY OTHER WOMEN?
OH, YES! IN CHAPTER FOUR HIS LANDLADY SAYS TO HIM, "IF YOU DON'T PAY YOUR RENT, YOU KNOW WHAT I'LL DO?"
"I'LL KICK YOUR PIANO!"
I KNEW I SHOULDN'T HAVE SHOWN ANY INTEREST...

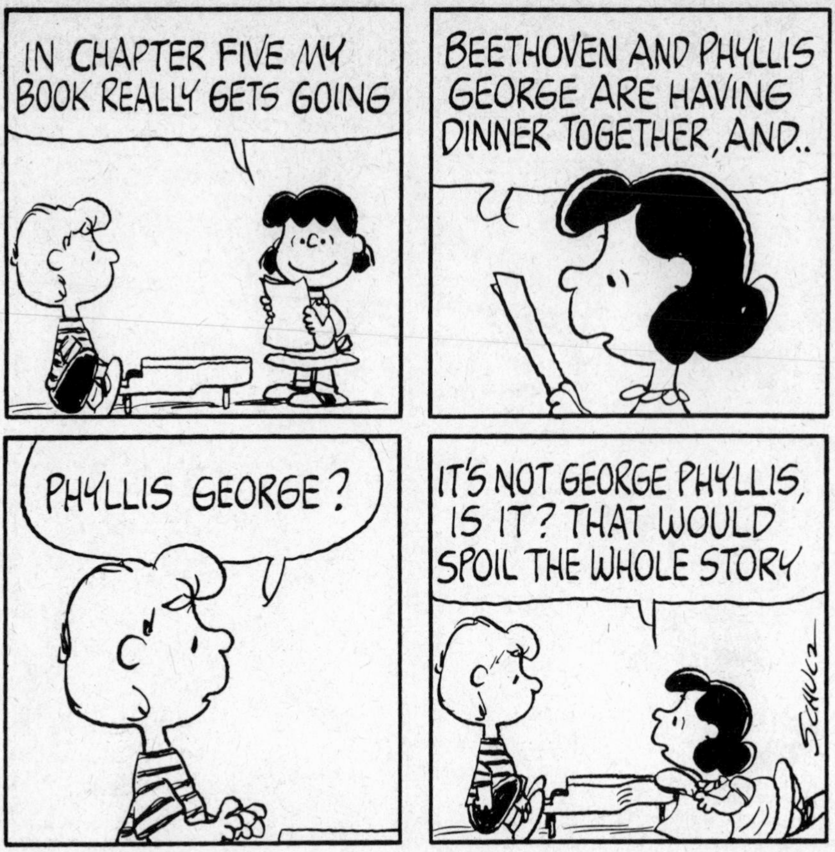
IN CHAPTER FIVE MY BOOK REALLY GETS GOING
BEETHOVEN AND PHYLLIS GEORGE ARE HAVING DINNER TOGETHER, AND..
PHYLLIS GEORGE?
IT'S NOT GEORGE PHYLLIS, IS IT? THAT WOULD SPOIL THE WHOLE STORY
SCHULZ

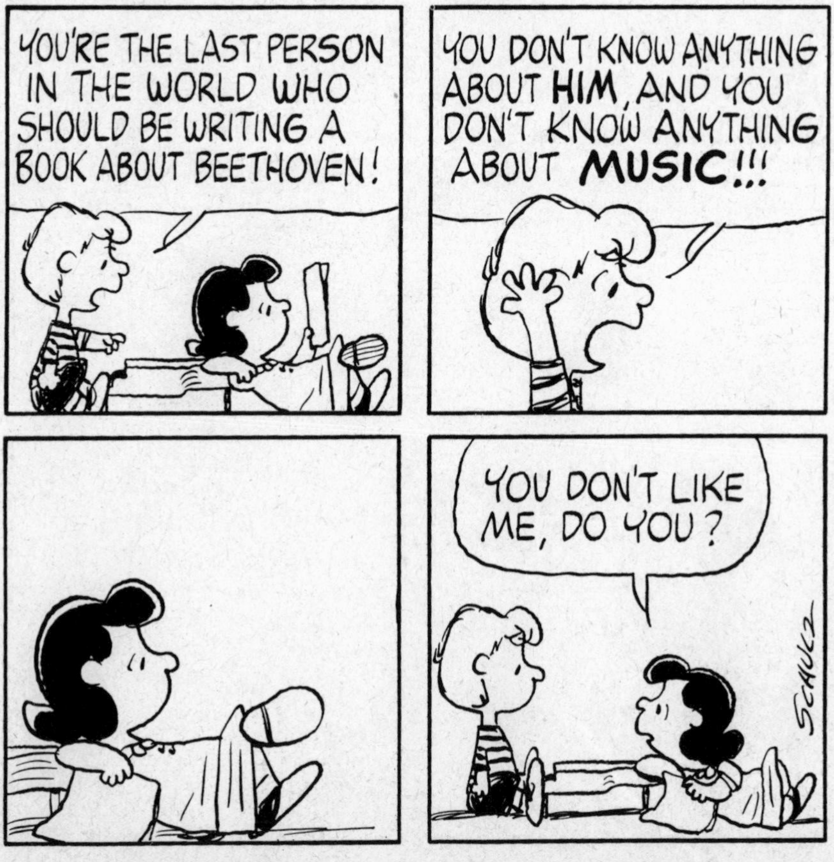
YOU'RE THE LAST PERSON IN THE WORLD WHO SHOULD BE WRITING A BOOK ABOUT BEETHOVEN!
YOU DON'T KNOW ANYTHING ABOUT **HIM**, AND YOU DON'T KNOW ANYTHING ABOUT **MUSIC**!!!
YOU DON'T LIKE ME, DO YOU?
SCHULZ

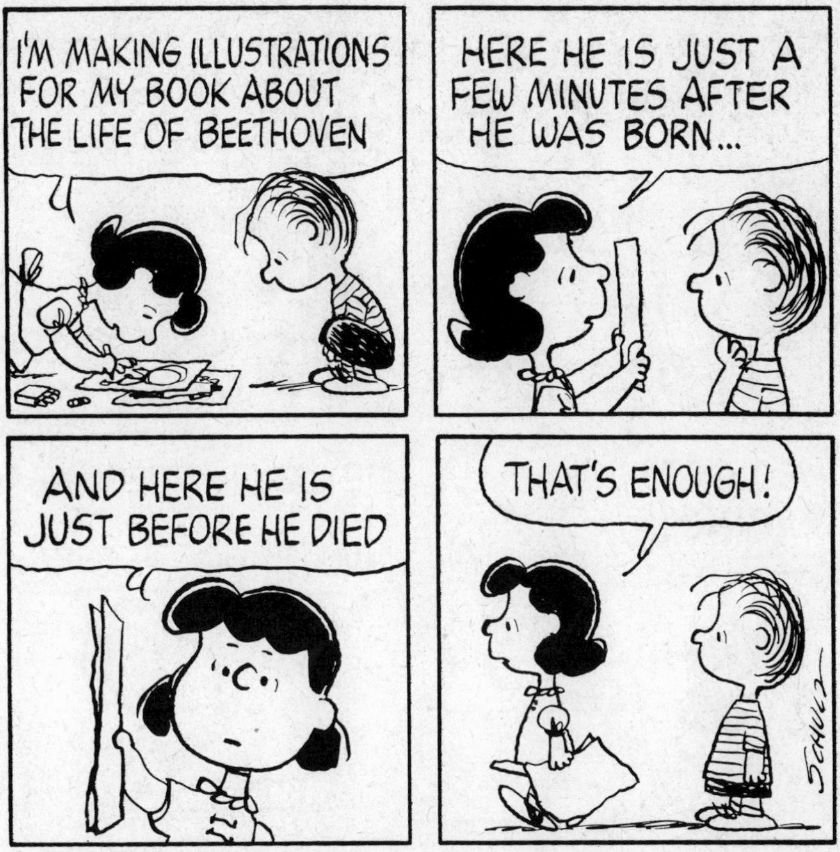
I'M MAKING ILLUSTRATIONS FOR MY BOOK ABOUT THE LIFE OF BEETHOVEN
HERE HE IS JUST A FEW MINUTES AFTER HE WAS BORN...
AND HERE HE IS JUST BEFORE HE DIED
THAT'S ENOUGH!
SCHULZ

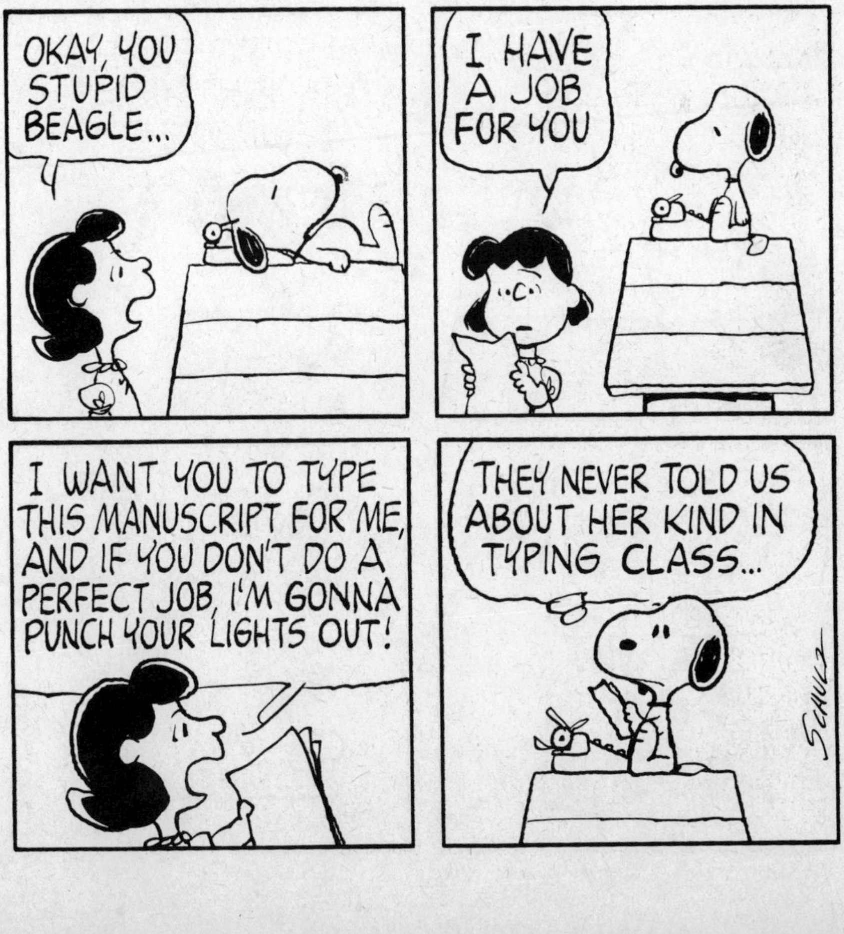
OKAY, YOU STUPID BEAGLE...
I HAVE A JOB FOR YOU
I WANT YOU TO TYPE THIS MANUSCRIPT FOR ME, AND IF YOU DON'T DO A PERFECT JOB, I'M GONNA PUNCH YOUR LIGHTS OUT!
THEY NEVER TOLD US ABOUT HER KIND IN TYPING CLASS...
SCHULZ

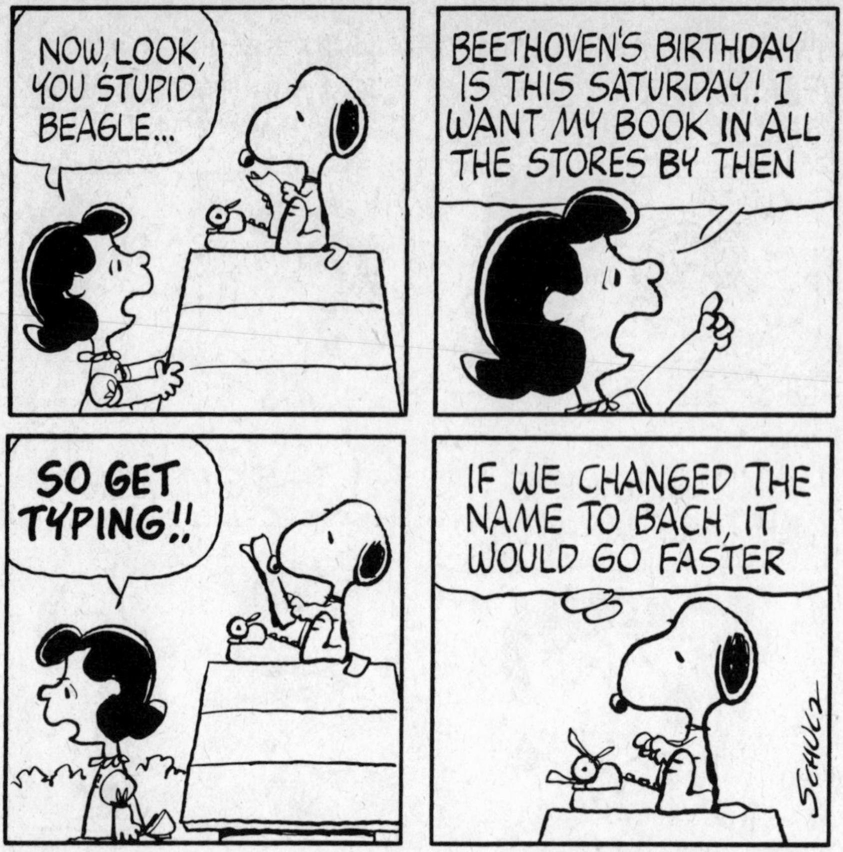
NOW, LOOK, YOU STUPID BEAGLE...
BEETHOVEN'S BIRTHDAY IS THIS SATURDAY! I WANT MY BOOK IN ALL THE STORES BY THEN
SO GET TYPING!!
IF WE CHANGED THE NAME TO BACH, IT WOULD GO FASTER
SCHULZ

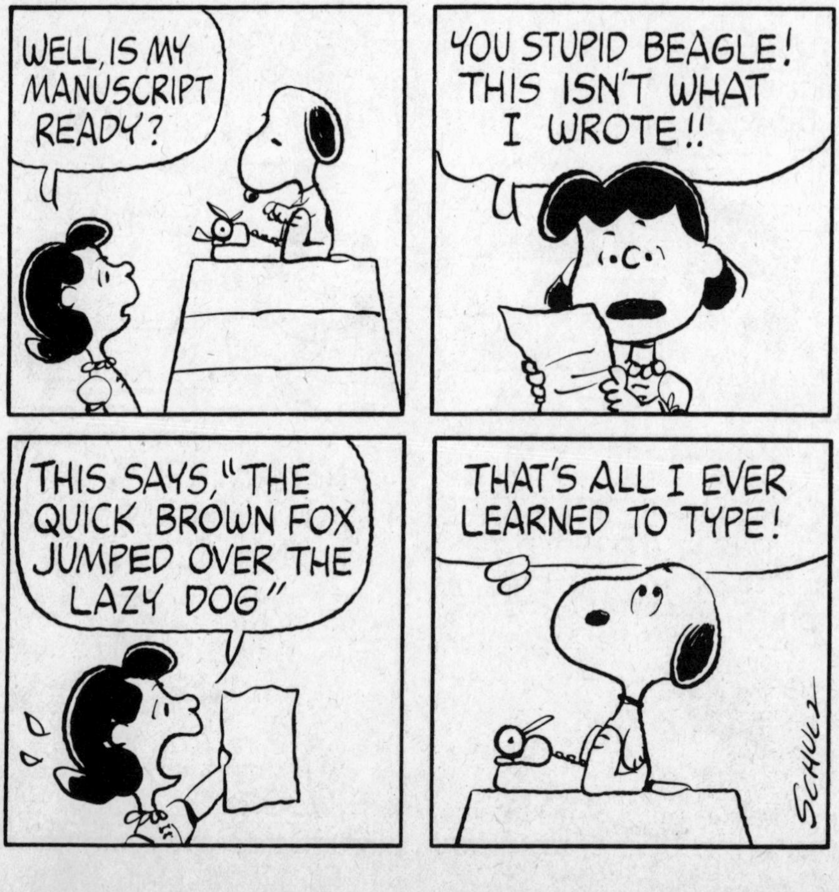
WELL, IS MY MANUSCRIPT READY?
YOU STUPID BEAGLE! THIS ISN'T WHAT I WROTE!!
THIS SAYS, "THE QUICK BROWN FOX JUMPED OVER THE LAZY DOG"
THAT'S ALL I EVER LEARNED TO TYPE!
SCHULZ

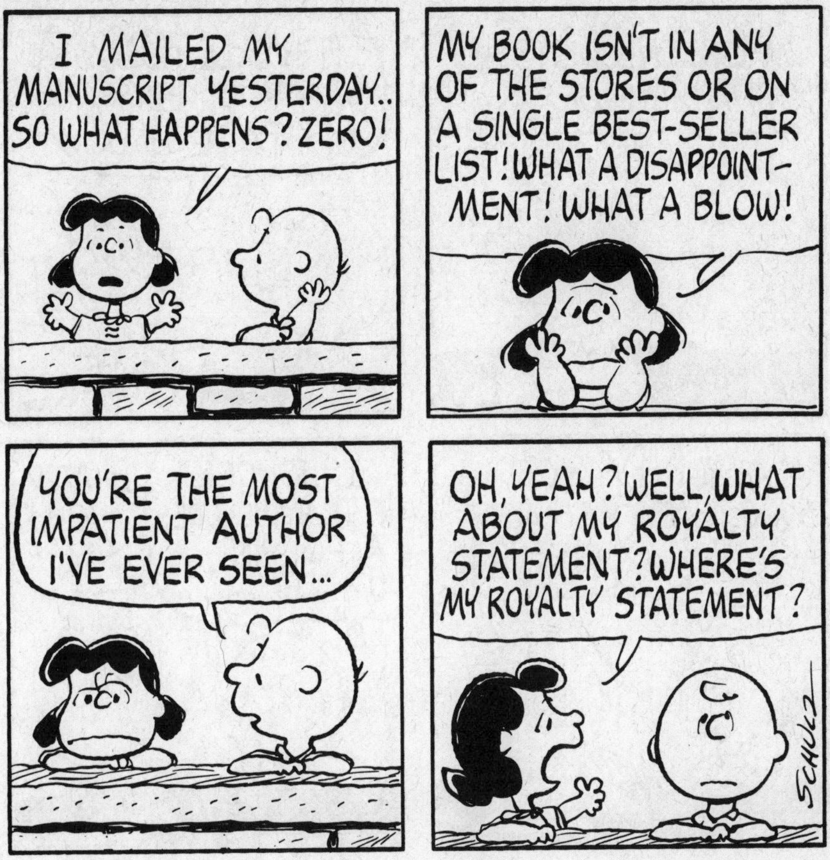
I MAILED MY MANUSCRIPT YESTERDAY.. SO WHAT HAPPENS? ZERO!
MY BOOK ISN'T IN ANY OF THE STORES OR ON A SINGLE BEST-SELLER LIST! WHAT A DISAPPOINTMENT! WHAT A BLOW!
YOU'RE THE MOST IMPATIENT AUTHOR I'VE EVER SEEN...
OH, YEAH? WELL, WHAT ABOUT MY ROYALTY STATEMENT? WHERE'S MY ROYALTY STATEMENT?
SCHULZ

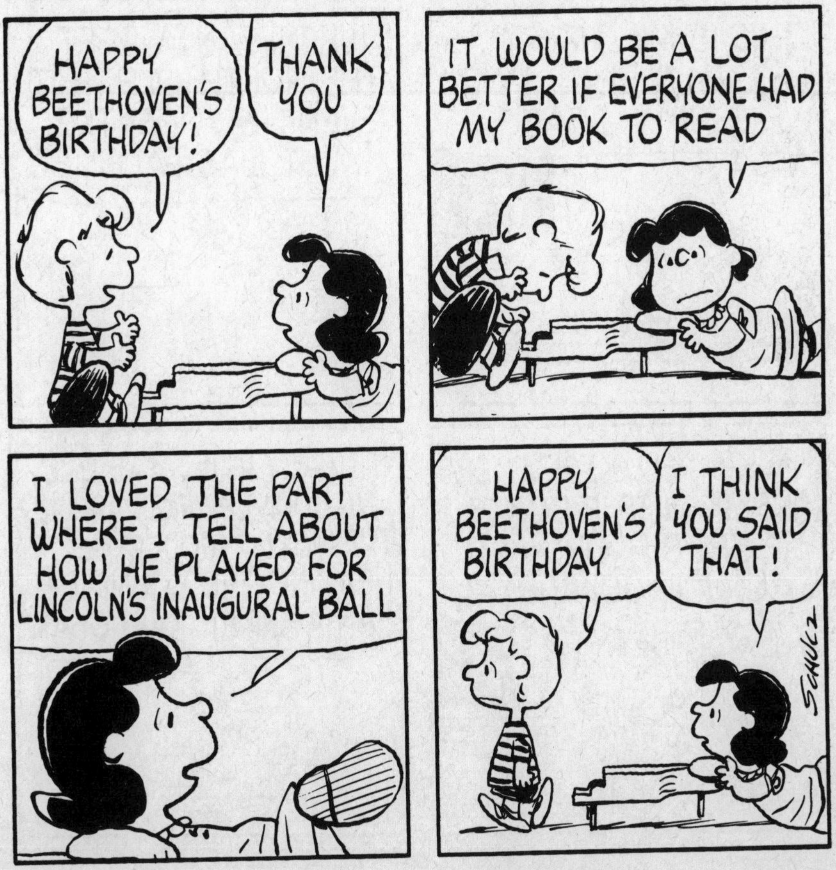
HAPPY BEETHOVEN'S BIRTHDAY!
THANK YOU
IT WOULD BE A LOT BETTER IF EVERYONE HAD MY BOOK TO READ
I LOVED THE PART WHERE I TELL ABOUT HOW HE PLAYED FOR LINCOLN'S INAUGURAL BALL
HAPPY BEETHOVEN'S BIRTHDAY
I THINK YOU SAID THAT!
SCHULZ

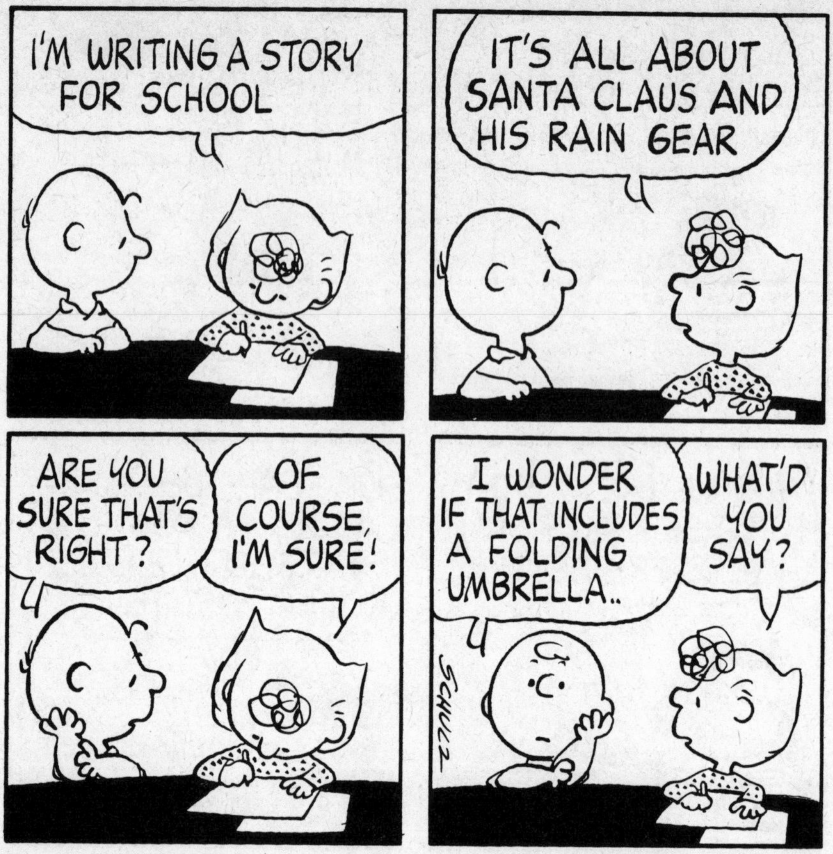
I'M WRITING A STORY FOR SCHOOL
IT'S ALL ABOUT SANTA CLAUS AND HIS RAIN GEAR
ARE YOU SURE THAT'S RIGHT?
OF COURSE, I'M SURE!
I WONDER IF THAT INCLUDES A FOLDING UMBRELLA..
WHAT'D YOU SAY?
SCHULZ

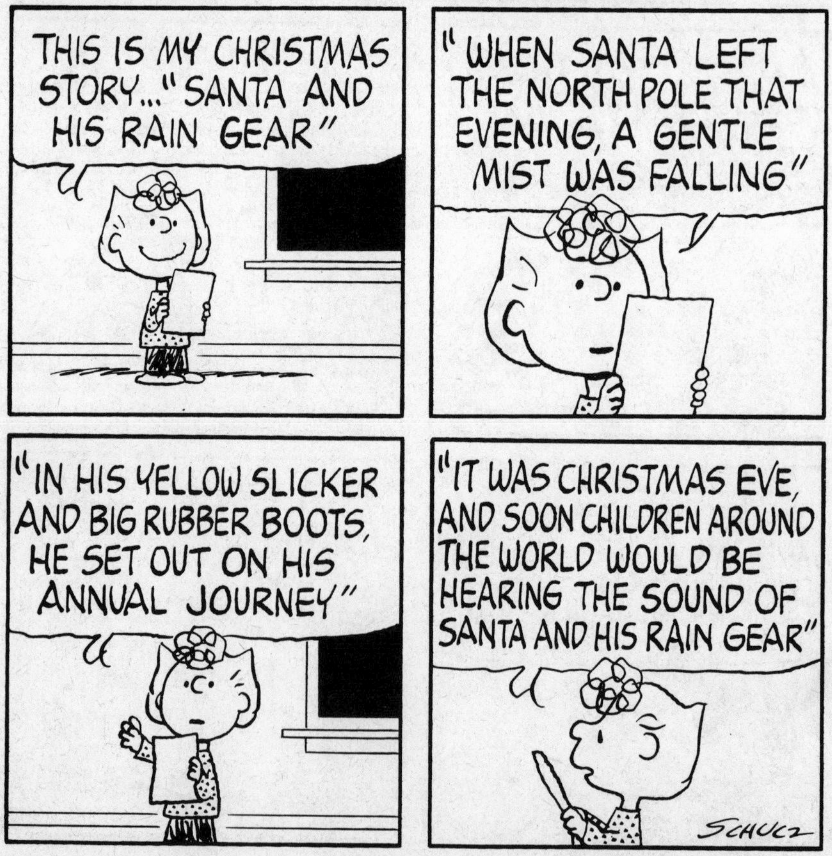
THIS IS MY CHRISTMAS STORY..."SANTA AND HIS RAIN GEAR"
"WHEN SANTA LEFT THE NORTH POLE THAT EVENING, A GENTLE MIST WAS FALLING"
"IN HIS YELLOW SLICKER AND BIG RUBBER BOOTS, HE SET OUT ON HIS ANNUAL JOURNEY"
"IT WAS CHRISTMAS EVE, AND SOON CHILDREN AROUND THE WORLD WOULD BE HEARING THE SOUND OF SANTA AND HIS RAIN GEAR"
SCHULZ

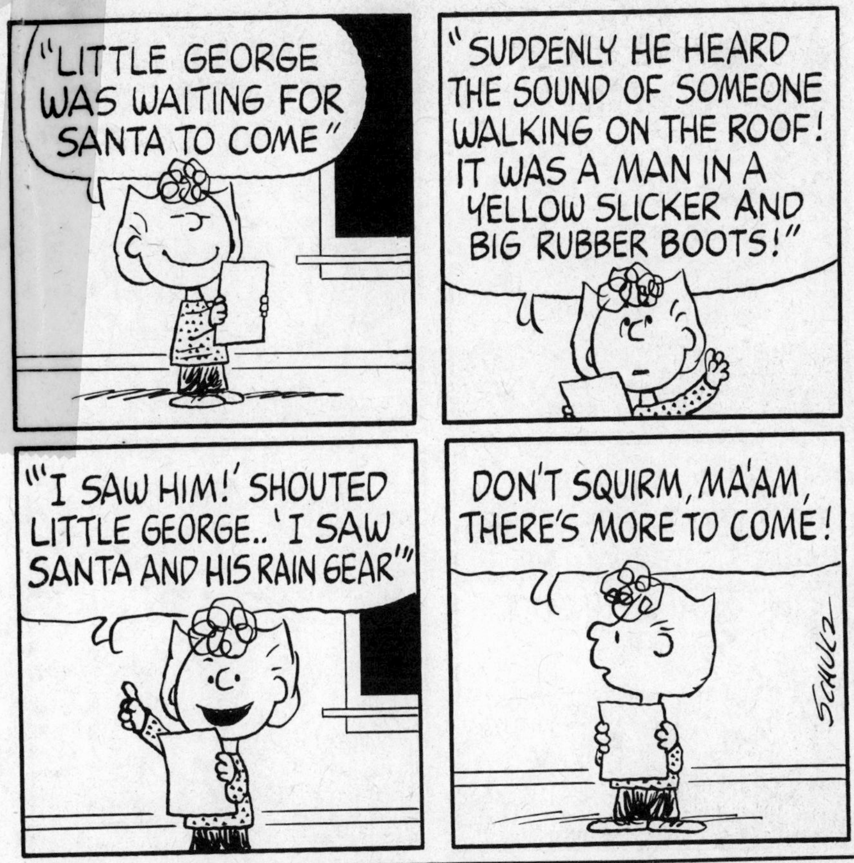
"LITTLE GEORGE WAS WAITING FOR SANTA TO COME"
"SUDDENLY HE HEARD THE SOUND OF SOMEONE WALKING ON THE ROOF! IT WAS A MAN IN A YELLOW SLICKER AND BIG RUBBER BOOTS!"
"'I SAW HIM!' SHOUTED LITTLE GEORGE..'I SAW SANTA AND HIS RAIN GEAR'"
DON'T SQUIRM, MA'AM, THERE'S MORE TO COME!
SCHULZ

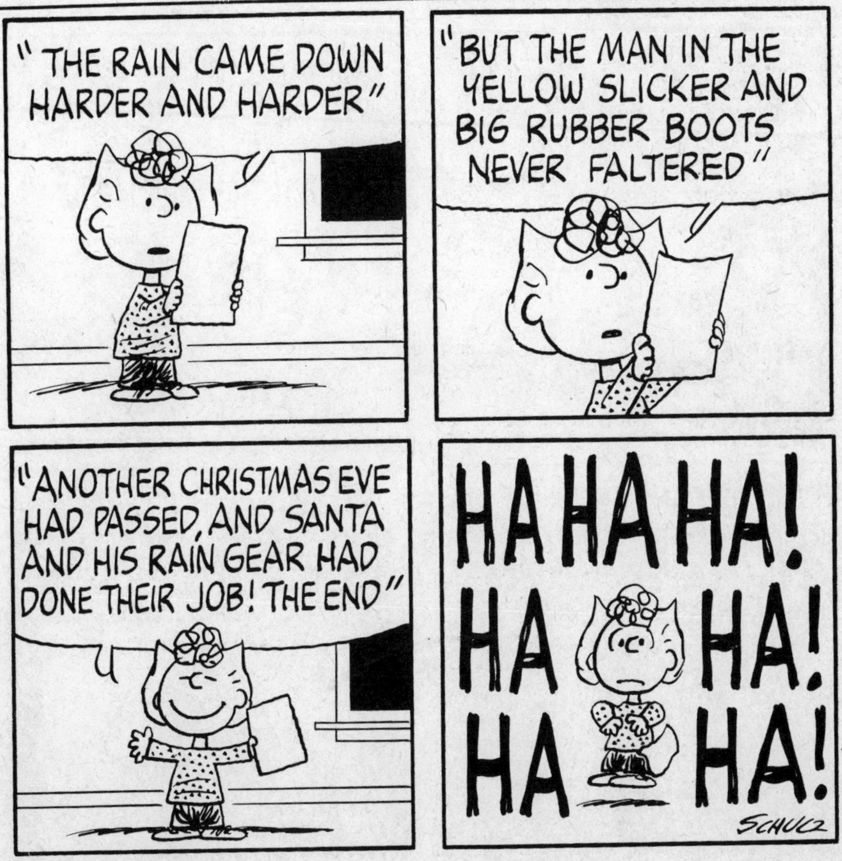
"THE RAIN CAME DOWN HARDER AND HARDER"
"BUT THE MAN IN THE YELLOW SLICKER AND BIG RUBBER BOOTS NEVER FALTERED"
"ANOTHER CHRISTMAS EVE HAD PASSED, AND SANTA AND HIS RAIN GEAR HAD DONE THEIR JOB! THE END"
HA HA HA HA! HA HA! HA HA!
SCHULZ

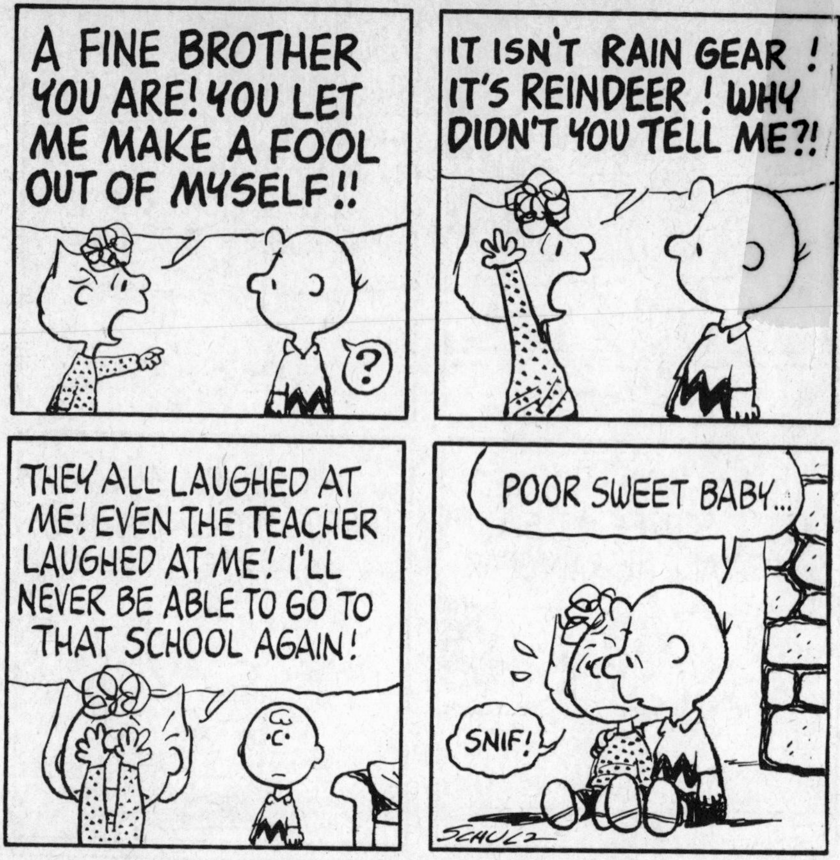
A FINE BROTHER YOU ARE! YOU LET ME MAKE A FOOL OUT OF MYSELF!!
?
IT ISN'T RAIN GEAR! IT'S REINDEER! WHY DIDN'T YOU TELL ME?!
THEY ALL LAUGHED AT ME! EVEN THE TEACHER LAUGHED AT ME! I'LL NEVER BE ABLE TO GO TO THAT SCHOOL AGAIN!
POOR SWEET BABY...
SNIF!
SCHULZ

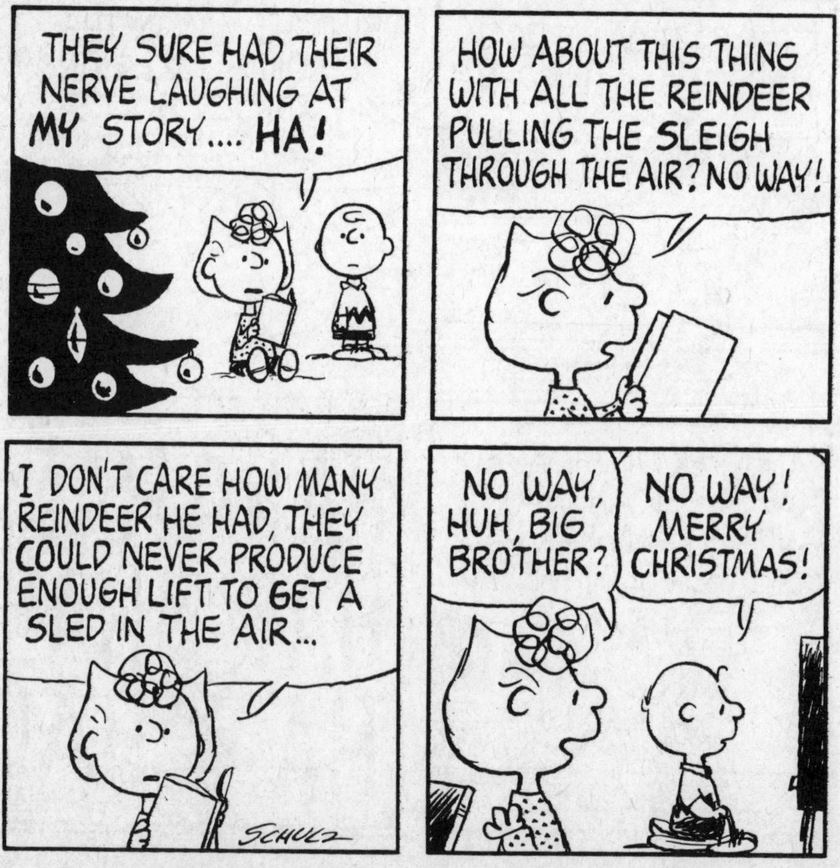
THEY SURE HAD THEIR NERVE LAUGHING AT MY STORY.... HA!
HOW ABOUT THIS THING WITH ALL THE REINDEER PULLING THE SLEIGH THROUGH THE AIR? NO WAY!
I DON'T CARE HOW MANY REINDEER HE HAD, THEY COULD NEVER PRODUCE ENOUGH LIFT TO GET A SLED IN THE AIR...
SCHULZ
NO WAY, HUH, BIG BROTHER?
NO WAY! MERRY CHRISTMAS!

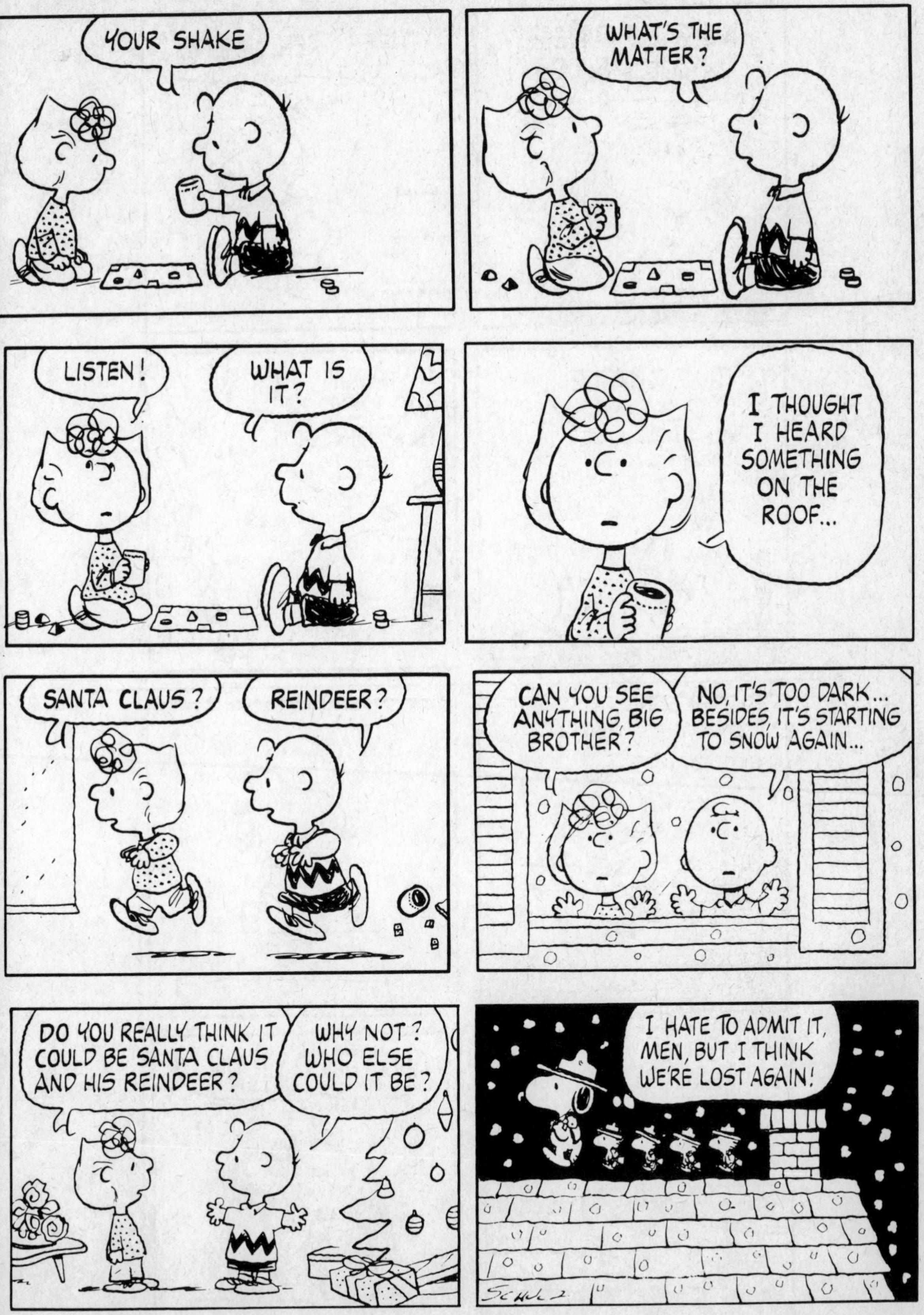
YOUR SHAKE
WHAT'S THE MATTER?
LISTEN!
WHAT IS IT?
I THOUGHT I HEARD SOMETHING ON THE ROOF...
SANTA CLAUS?
REINDEER?
CAN YOU SEE ANYTHING, BIG BROTHER?
NO, IT'S TOO DARK... BESIDES, IT'S STARTING TO SNOW AGAIN...
DO YOU REALLY THINK IT COULD BE SANTA CLAUS AND HIS REINDEER?
WHY NOT? WHO ELSE COULD IT BE?
I HATE TO ADMIT IT, MEN, BUT I THINK WE'RE LOST AGAIN!
SCHULZ

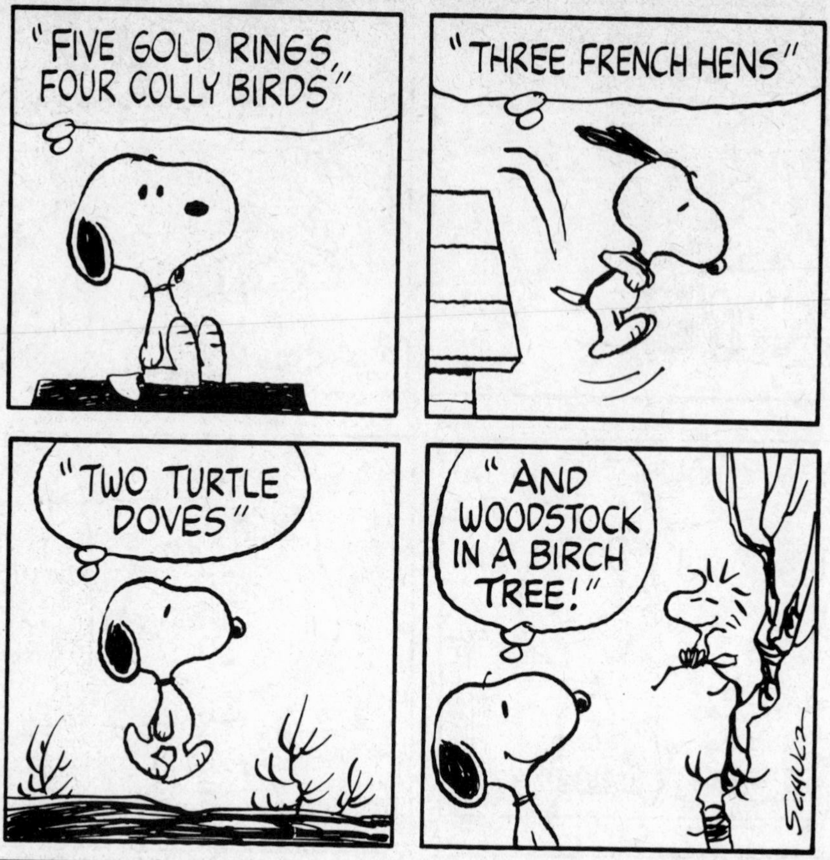
"FIVE GOLD RINGS, FOUR COLLY BIRDS"
"THREE FRENCH HENS"
"TWO TURTLE DOVES"
"AND WOODSTOCK IN A BIRCH TREE!"
SCHULZ

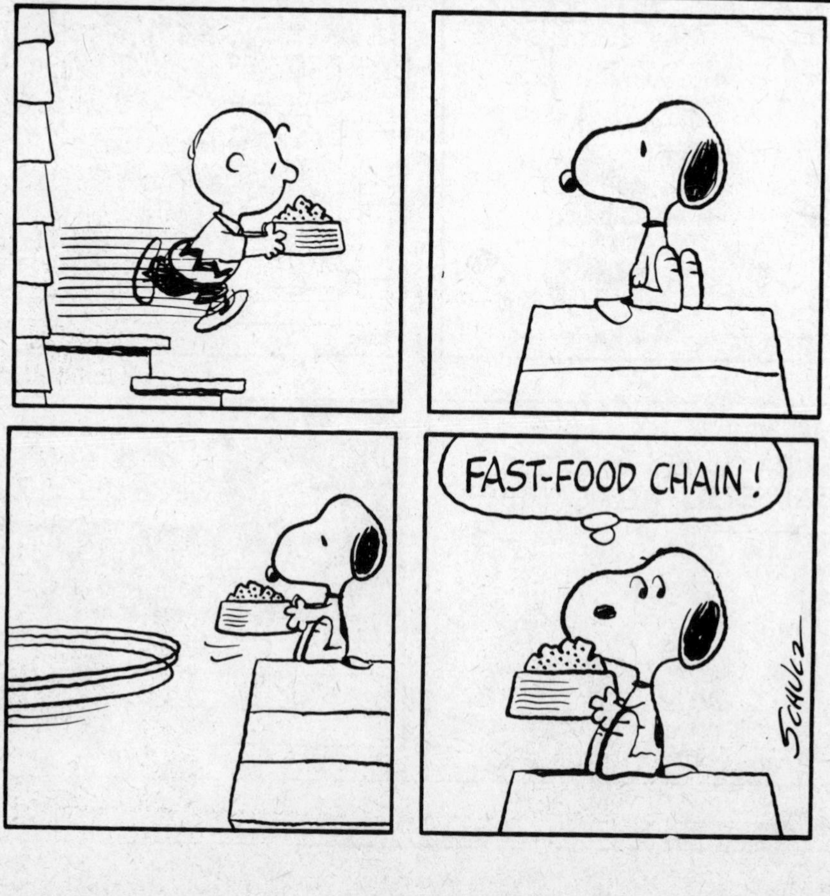
FAST-FOOD CHAIN!
SCHULZ

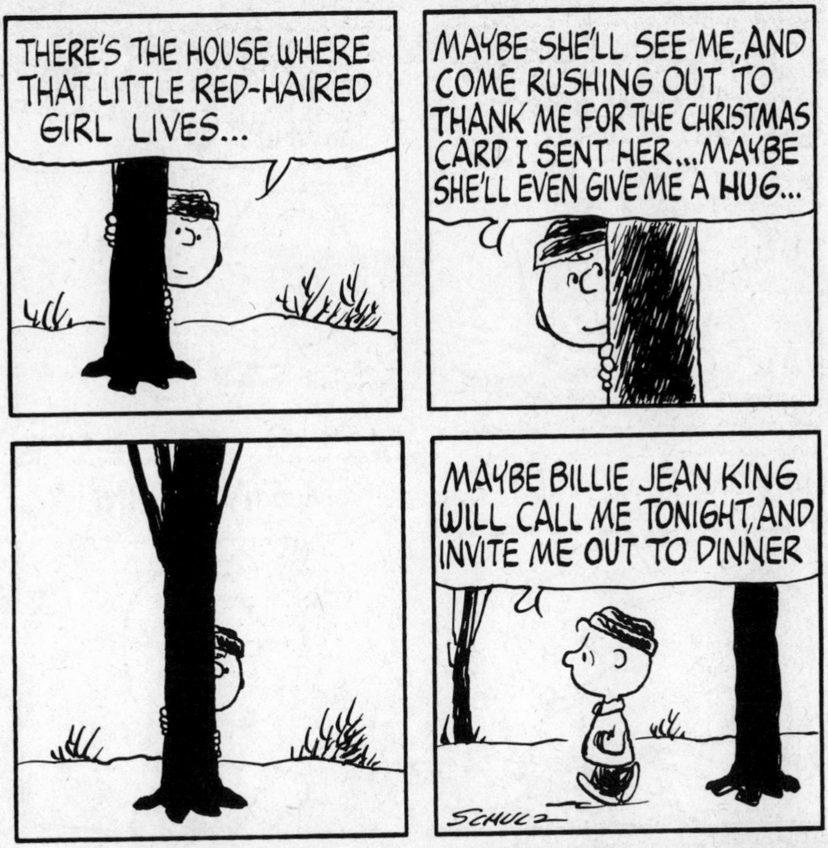
THERE'S THE HOUSE WHERE THAT LITTLE RED-HAIRED GIRL LIVES...
MAYBE SHE'LL SEE ME, AND COME RUSHING OUT TO THANK ME FOR THE CHRISTMAS CARD I SENT HER...MAYBE SHE'LL EVEN GIVE ME A **HUG**...
MAYBE BILLIE JEAN KING WILL CALL ME TONIGHT, AND INVITE ME OUT TO DINNER
SCHULZ

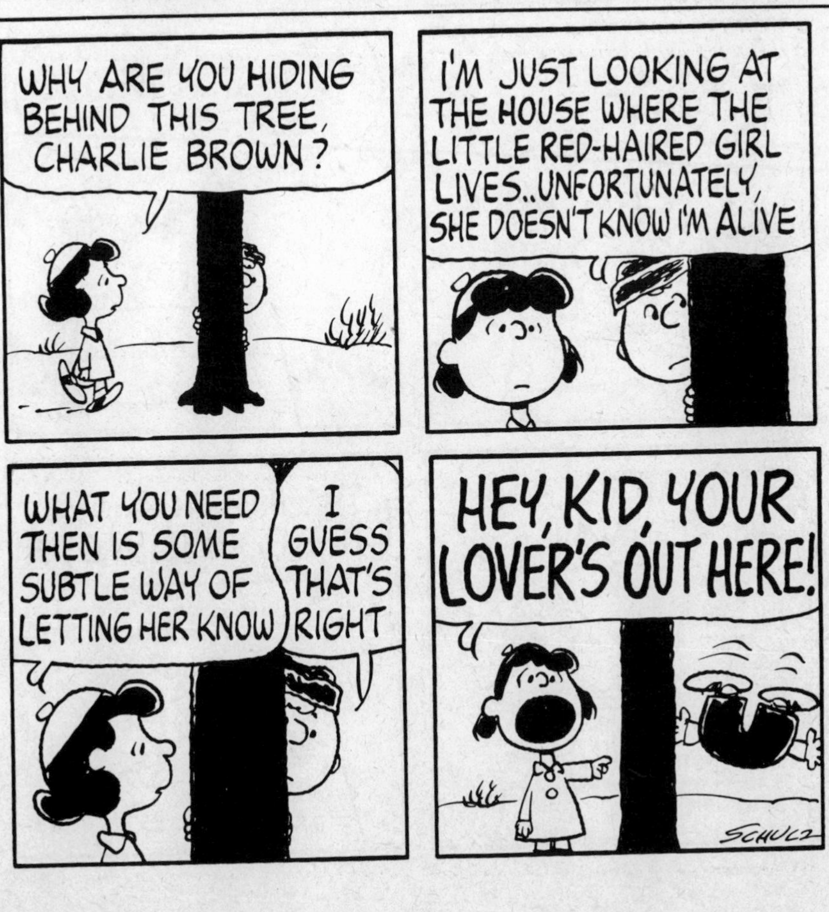
WHY ARE YOU HIDING BEHIND THIS TREE, CHARLIE BROWN?
I'M JUST LOOKING AT THE HOUSE WHERE THE LITTLE RED-HAIRED GIRL LIVES..UNFORTUNATELY, SHE DOESN'T KNOW I'M ALIVE
WHAT YOU NEED THEN IS SOME SUBTLE WAY OF LETTING HER KNOW
I GUESS THAT'S RIGHT
HEY, KID, YOUR LOVER'S OUT HERE!
SCHULZ

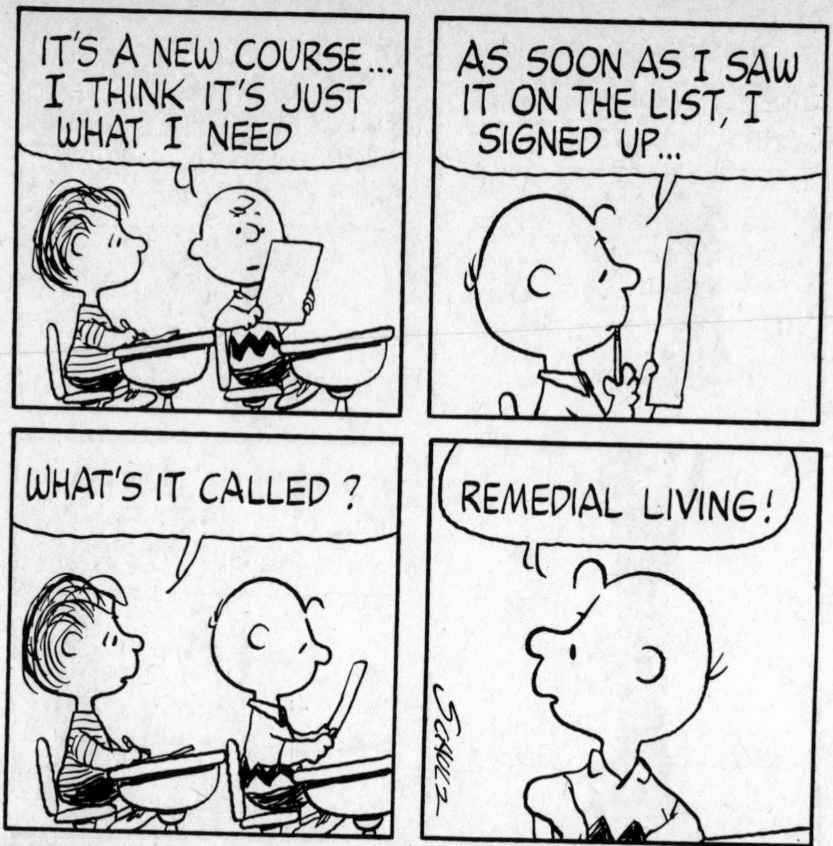
IT'S A NEW COURSE... I THINK IT'S JUST WHAT I NEED
AS SOON AS I SAW IT ON THE LIST, I SIGNED UP...
WHAT'S IT CALLED ?
REMEDIAL LIVING!
SCHULZ

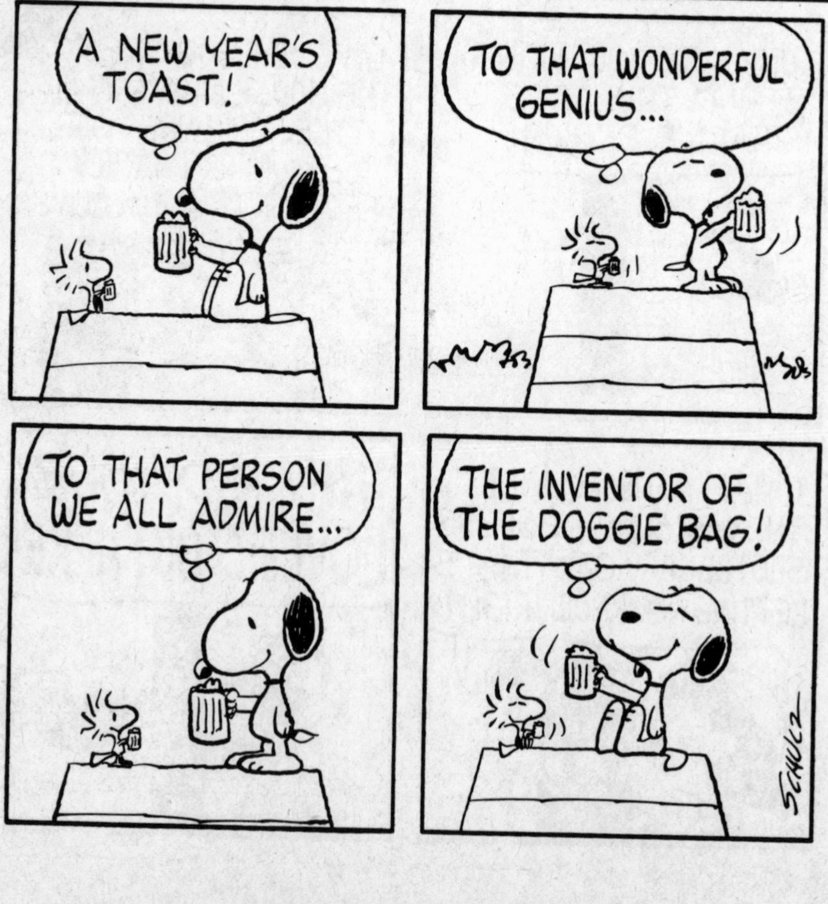
A NEW YEAR'S TOAST!
TO THAT WONDERFUL GENIUS...
TO THAT PERSON WE ALL ADMIRE...
THE INVENTOR OF THE DOGGIE BAG!
SCHULZ

Deer

THAT SHOULD BE "DEAR"

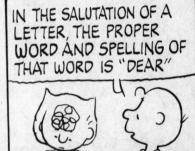

IN THE SALUTATION OF A LETTER, THE PROPER WORD AND SPELLING OF THAT WORD IS "DEAR"

Deer are beautiful animals found in most parts of the world.

I'M SORRY... I DIDN'T REALIZE YOU WERE WRITING ABOUT DEER... I APOLOGIZE...

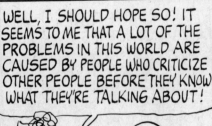

WELL, I SHOULD HOPE SO! IT SEEMS TO ME THAT A LOT OF THE PROBLEMS IN THIS WORLD ARE CAUSED BY PEOPLE WHO CRITICIZE OTHER PEOPLE BEFORE THEY KNOW WHAT THEY'RE TALKING ABOUT!

Dear Grandma,

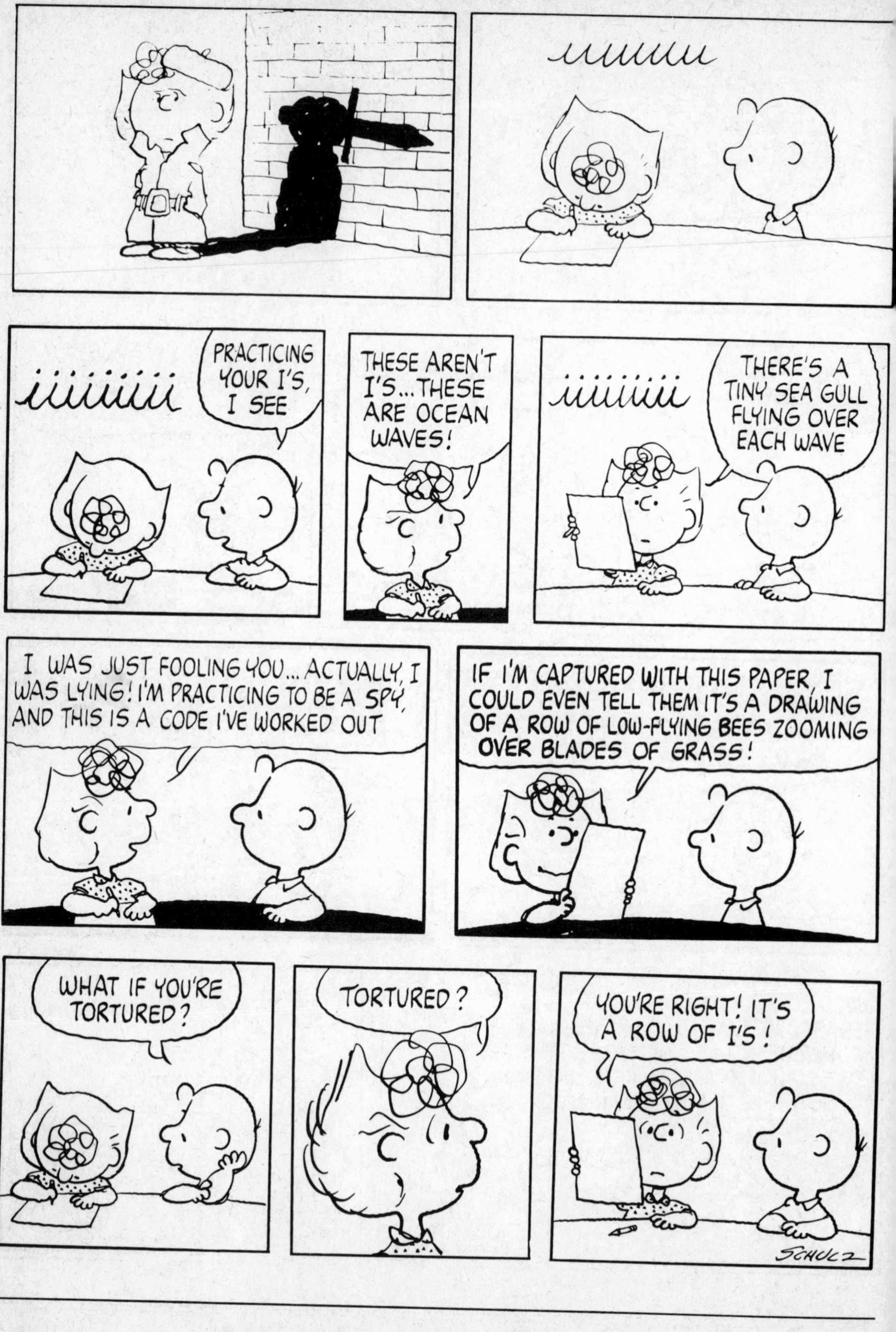

uuuuuu
iiiiiiii
PRACTICING YOUR I'S, I SEE
THESE AREN'T I'S...THESE ARE OCEAN WAVES!
iiiiiiii
THERE'S A TINY SEA GULL FLYING OVER EACH WAVE
I WAS JUST FOOLING YOU... ACTUALLY, I WAS LYING! I'M PRACTICING TO BE A SPY, AND THIS IS A CODE I'VE WORKED OUT
IF I'M CAPTURED WITH THIS PAPER, I COULD EVEN TELL THEM IT'S A DRAWING OF A ROW OF LOW-FLYING BEES ZOOMING OVER BLADES OF GRASS!
WHAT IF YOU'RE TORTURED?
TORTURED?
YOU'RE RIGHT! IT'S A ROW OF I'S!
SCHULZ

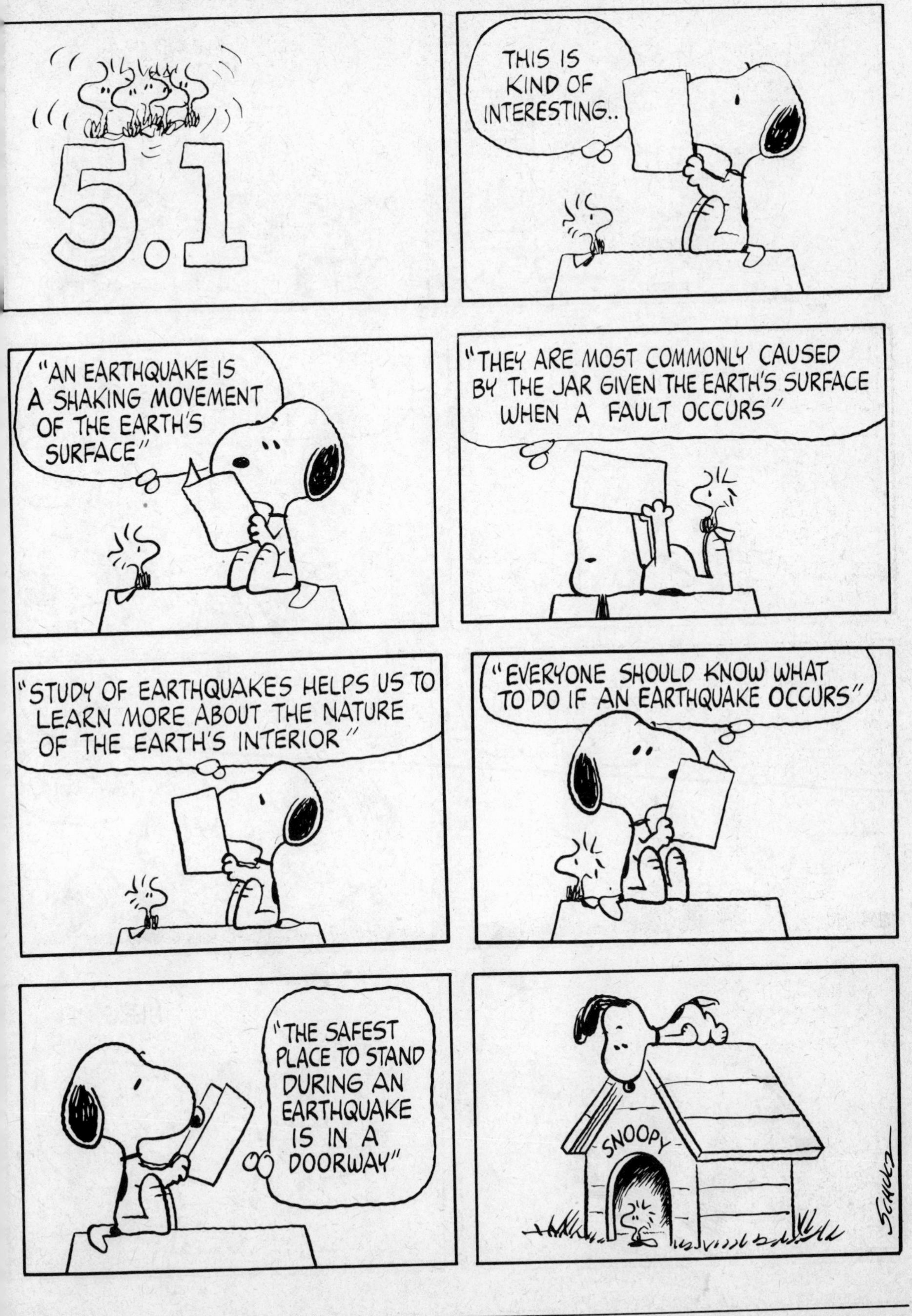
5.1
THIS IS KIND OF INTERESTING..
"AN EARTHQUAKE IS A SHAKING MOVEMENT OF THE EARTH'S SURFACE"
"THEY ARE MOST COMMONLY CAUSED BY THE JAR GIVEN THE EARTH'S SURFACE WHEN A FAULT OCCURS"
"STUDY OF EARTHQUAKES HELPS US TO LEARN MORE ABOUT THE NATURE OF THE EARTH'S INTERIOR"
"EVERYONE SHOULD KNOW WHAT TO DO IF AN EARTHQUAKE OCCURS"
"THE SAFEST PLACE TO STAND DURING AN EARTHQUAKE IS IN A DOORWAY"
SNOOPY
SCHULZ

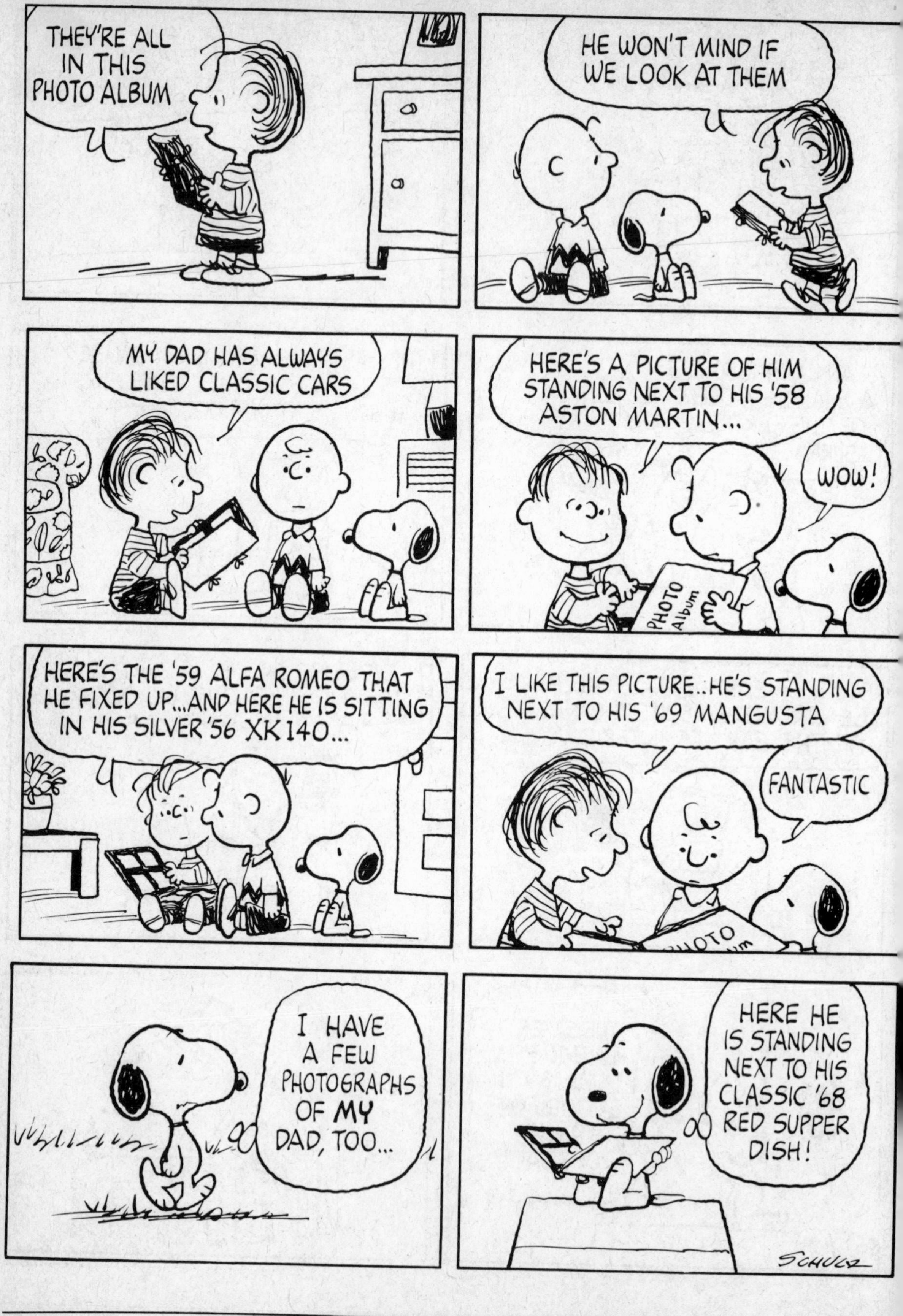
THEY'RE ALL IN THIS PHOTO ALBUM
HE WON'T MIND IF WE LOOK AT THEM
MY DAD HAS ALWAYS LIKED CLASSIC CARS
HERE'S A PICTURE OF HIM STANDING NEXT TO HIS '58 ASTON MARTIN...
WOW!
PHOTO Album
HERE'S THE '59 ALFA ROMEO THAT HE FIXED UP...AND HERE HE IS SITTING IN HIS SILVER '56 XK140...
I LIKE THIS PICTURE..HE'S STANDING NEXT TO HIS '69 MANGUSTA
FANTASTIC
I HAVE A FEW PHOTOGRAPHS OF MY DAD, TOO...
HERE HE IS STANDING NEXT TO HIS CLASSIC '68 RED SUPPER DISH!
SCHULZ

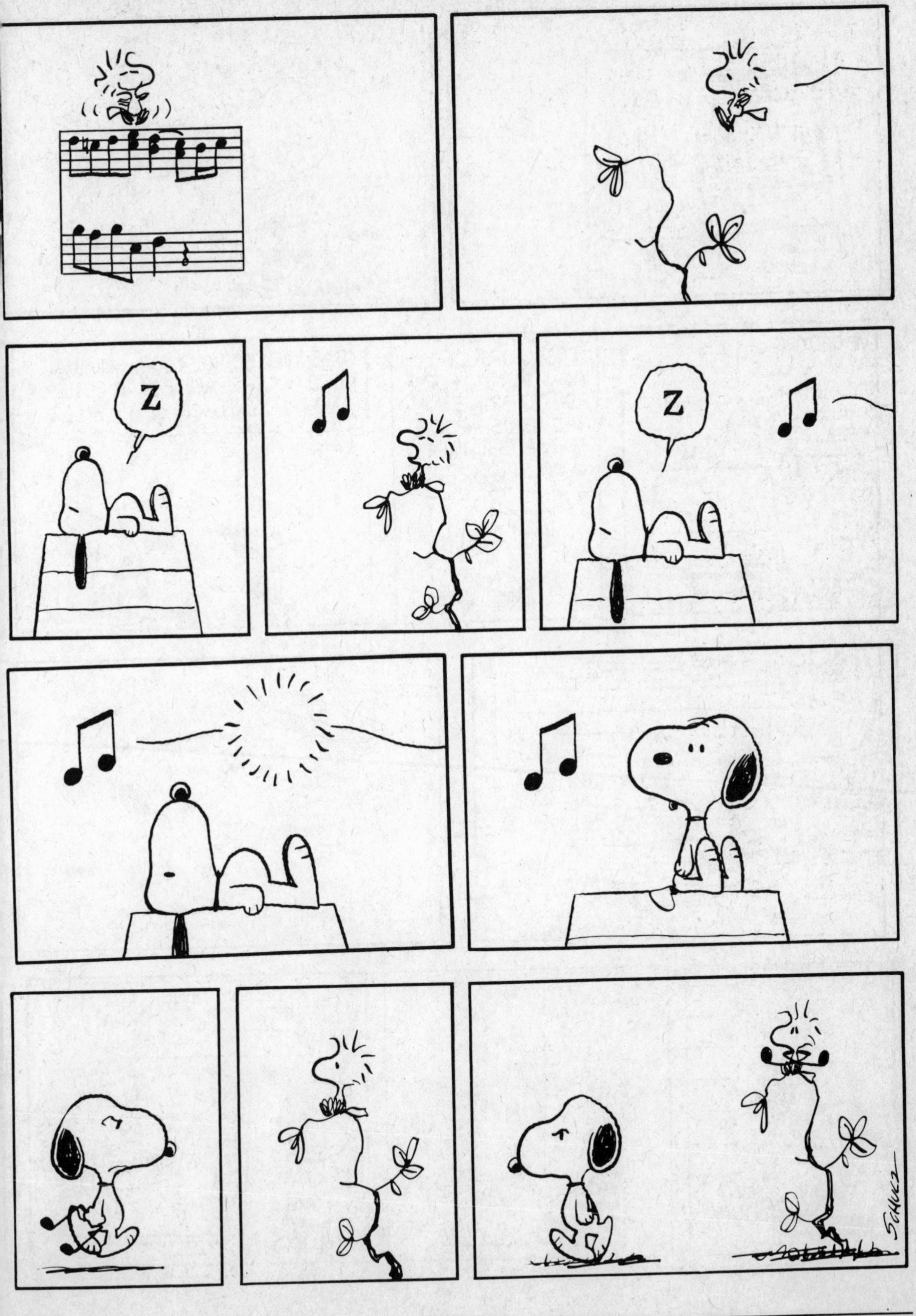
Z
Z
SCHULZ

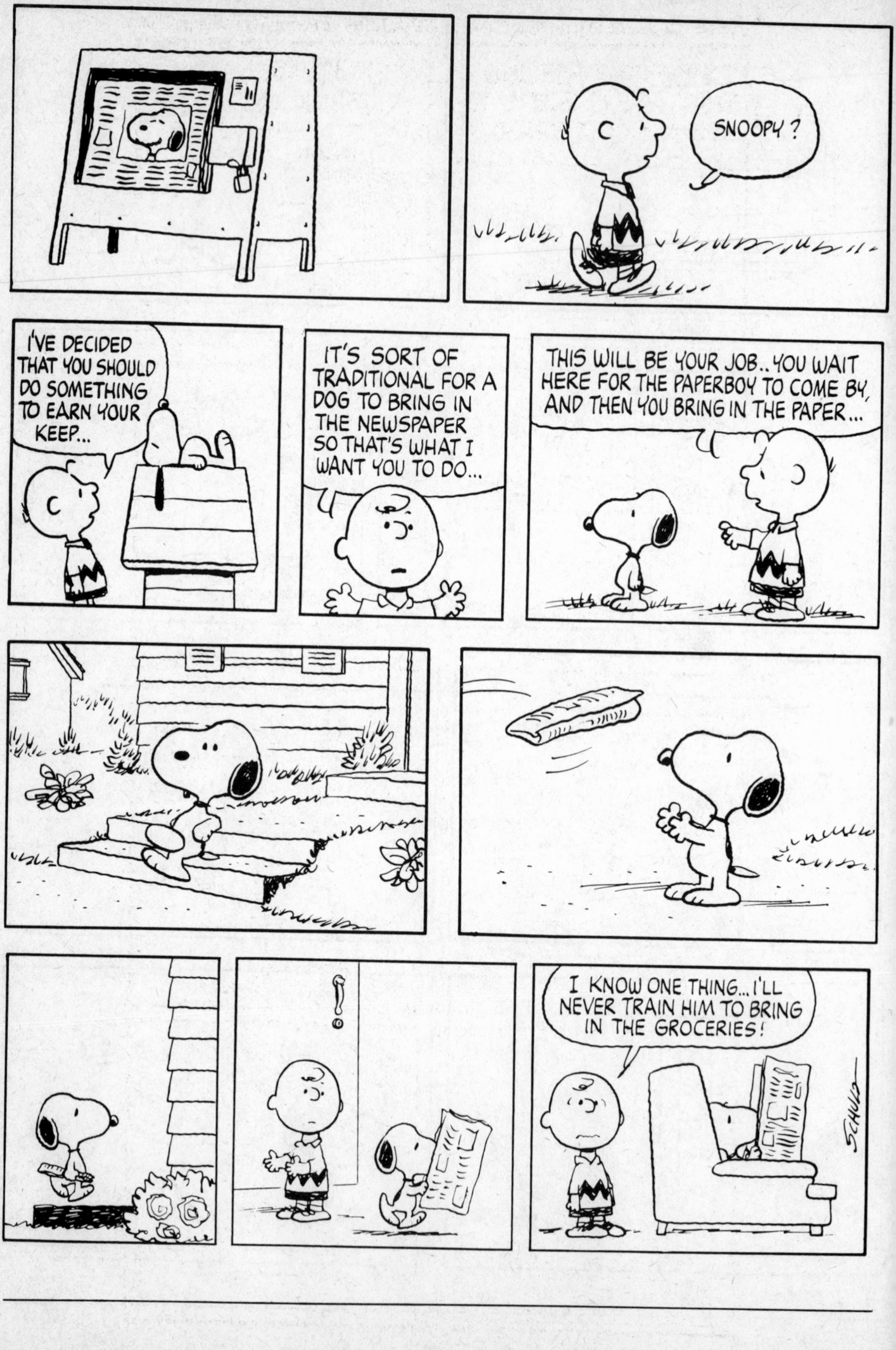
SNOOPY ?
I'VE DECIDED THAT YOU SHOULD DO SOMETHING TO EARN YOUR KEEP...
IT'S SORT OF TRADITIONAL FOR A DOG TO BRING IN THE NEWSPAPER SO THAT'S WHAT I WANT YOU TO DO...
THIS WILL BE YOUR JOB.. YOU WAIT HERE FOR THE PAPERBOY TO COME BY, AND THEN YOU BRING IN THE PAPER...
!
I KNOW ONE THING... I'LL NEVER TRAIN HIM TO BRING IN THE GROCERIES!
SCHULZ

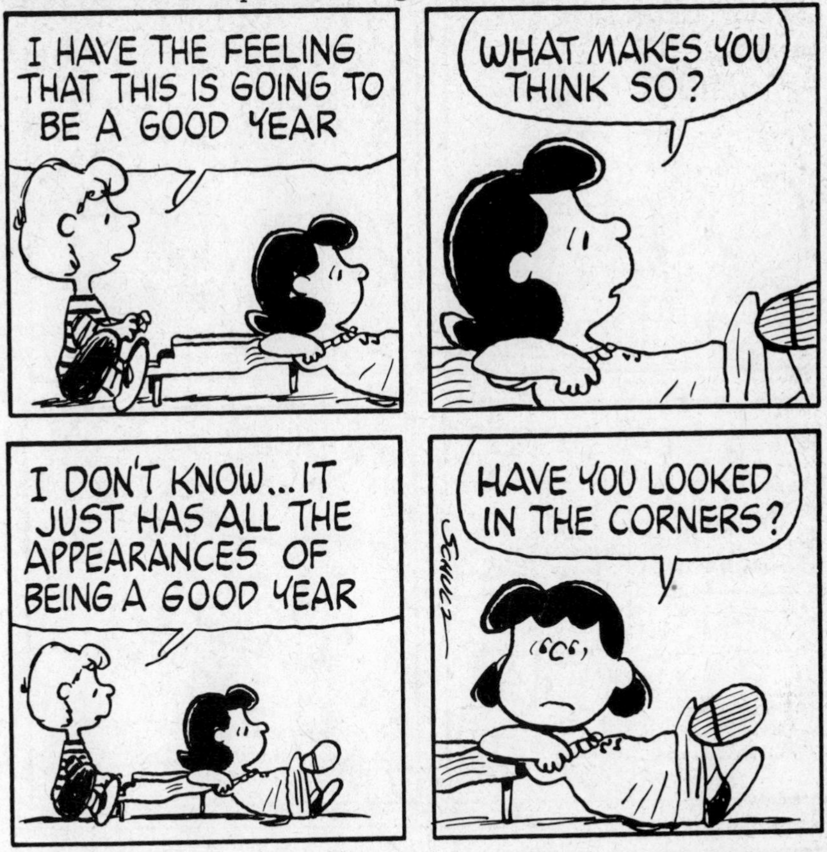
I HAVE THE FEELING THAT THIS IS GOING TO BE A GOOD YEAR
WHAT MAKES YOU THINK SO?
I DON'T KNOW... IT JUST HAS ALL THE APPEARANCES OF BEING A GOOD YEAR
HAVE YOU LOOKED IN THE CORNERS?
SCHULZ

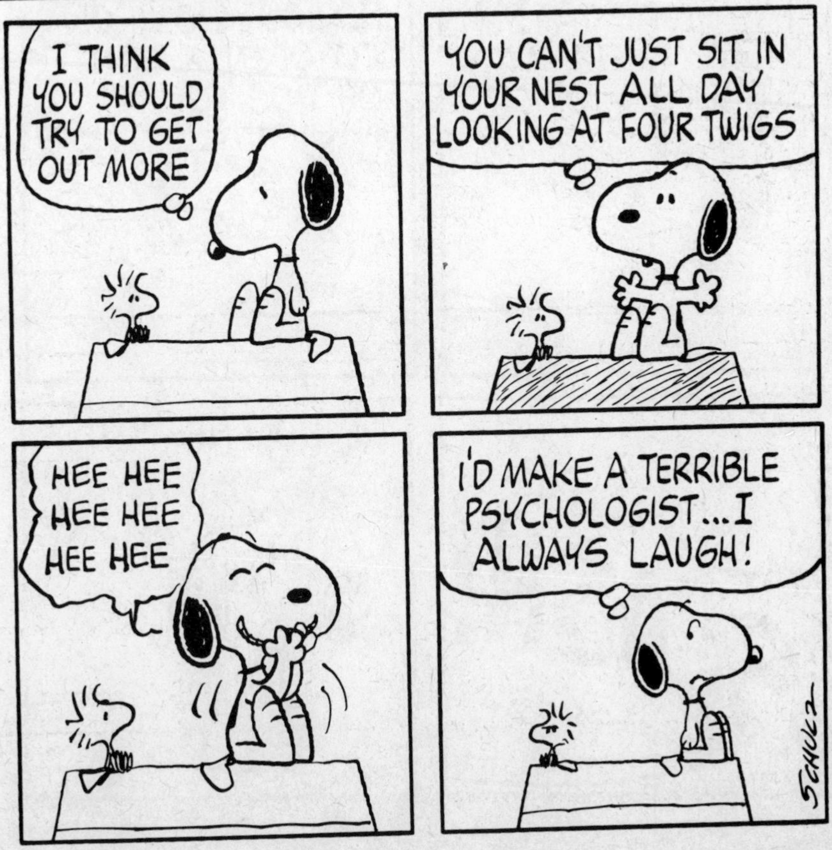
I THINK YOU SHOULD TRY TO GET OUT MORE
YOU CAN'T JUST SIT IN YOUR NEST ALL DAY LOOKING AT FOUR TWIGS
HEE HEE HEE HEE HEE HEE
I'D MAKE A TERRIBLE PSYCHOLOGIST... I ALWAYS LAUGH!
SCHULZ

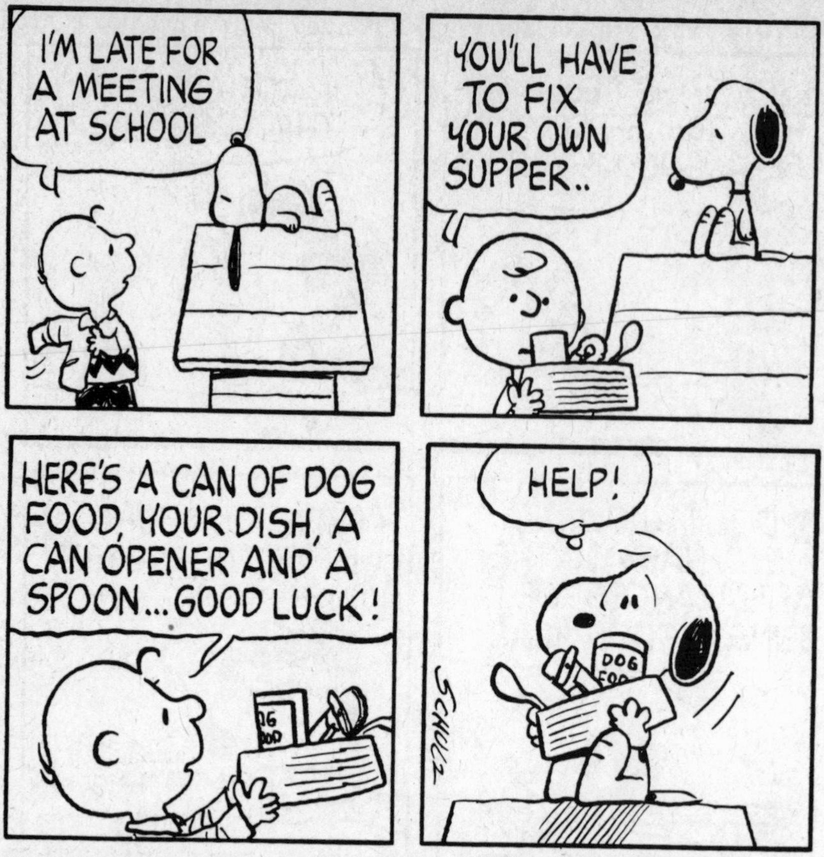
I'M LATE FOR A MEETING AT SCHOOL
YOU'LL HAVE TO FIX YOUR OWN SUPPER..
HERE'S A CAN OF DOG FOOD, YOUR DISH, A CAN OPENER AND A SPOON... GOOD LUCK!
HELP!
SCHULZ

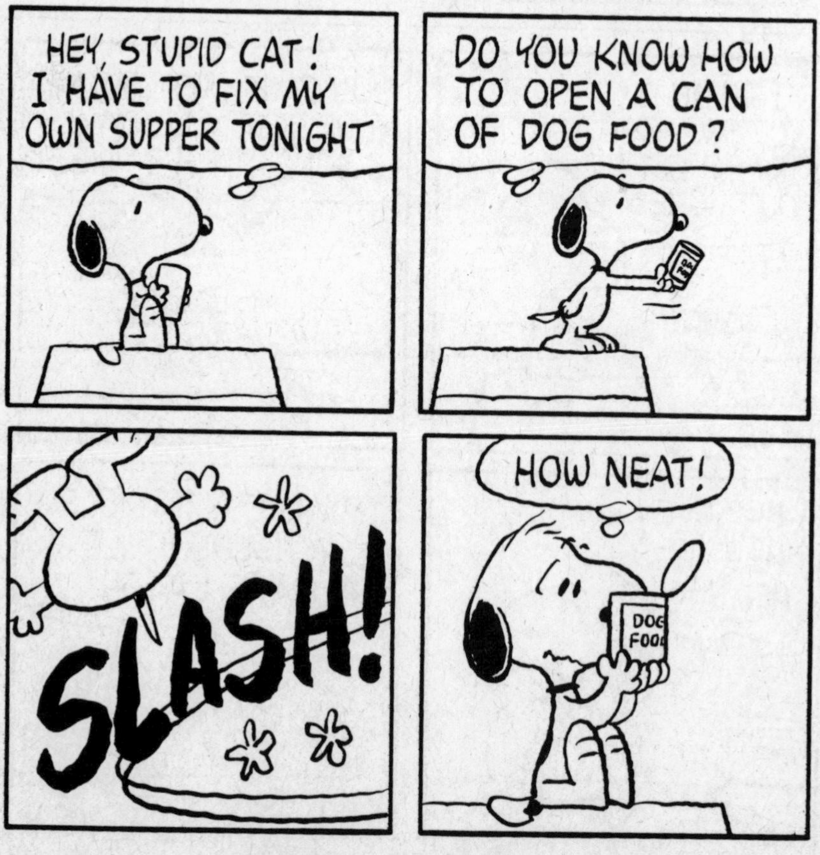
HEY, STUPID CAT! I HAVE TO FIX MY OWN SUPPER TONIGHT
DO YOU KNOW HOW TO OPEN A CAN OF DOG FOOD?
SLASH!
HOW NEAT!

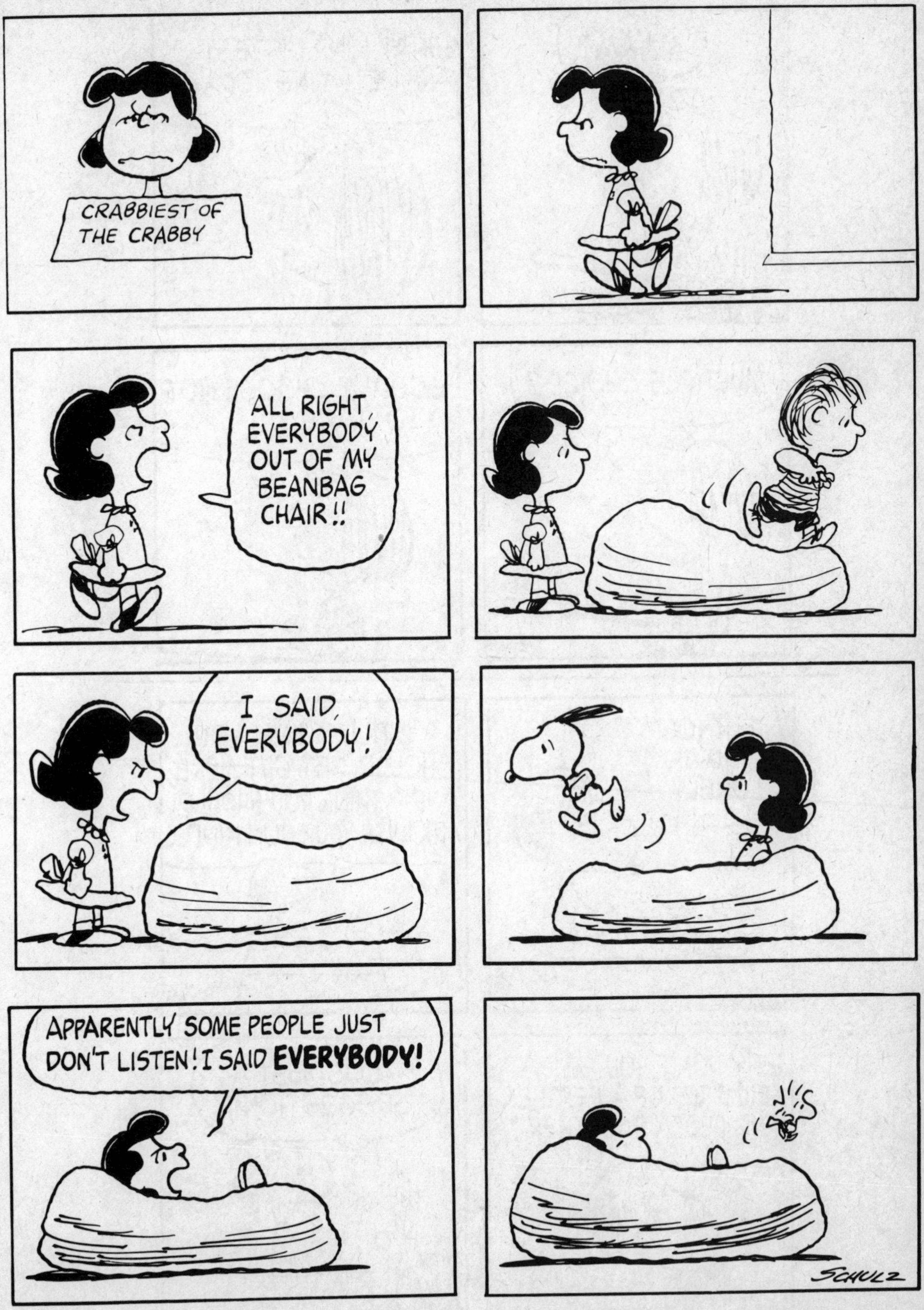
CRABBIEST OF THE CRABBY
ALL RIGHT, EVERYBODY OUT OF MY BEANBAG CHAIR!!
I SAID, EVERYBODY!
APPARENTLY SOME PEOPLE JUST DON'T LISTEN! I SAID **EVERYBODY!**
SCHULZ

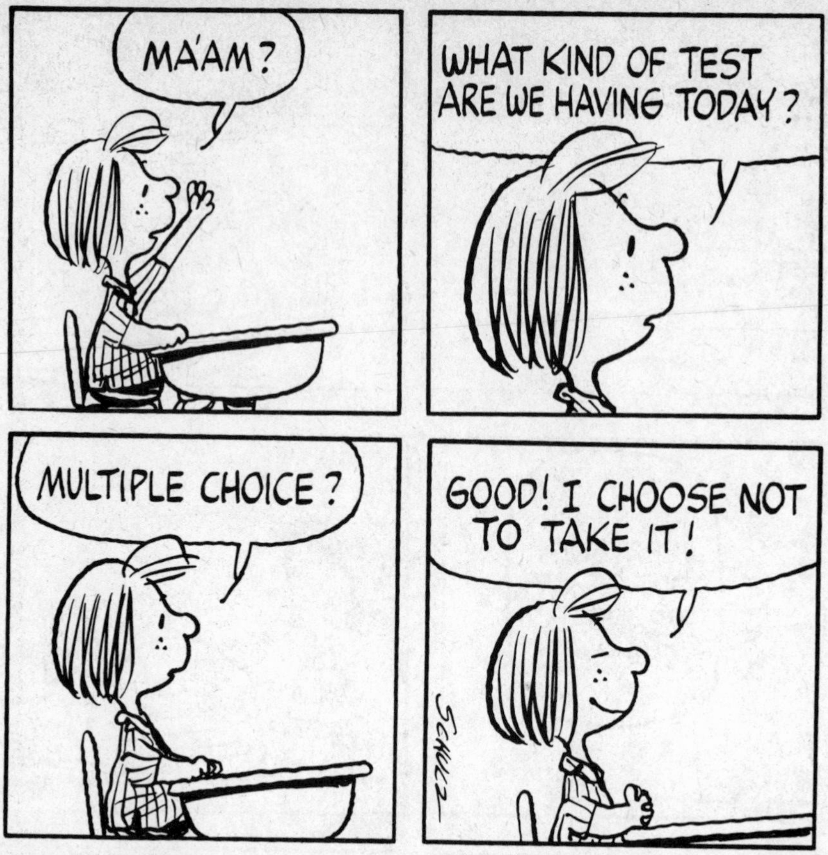
MA'AM?
WHAT KIND OF TEST ARE WE HAVING TODAY?
MULTIPLE CHOICE?
GOOD! I CHOOSE NOT TO TAKE IT!
SCHULZ

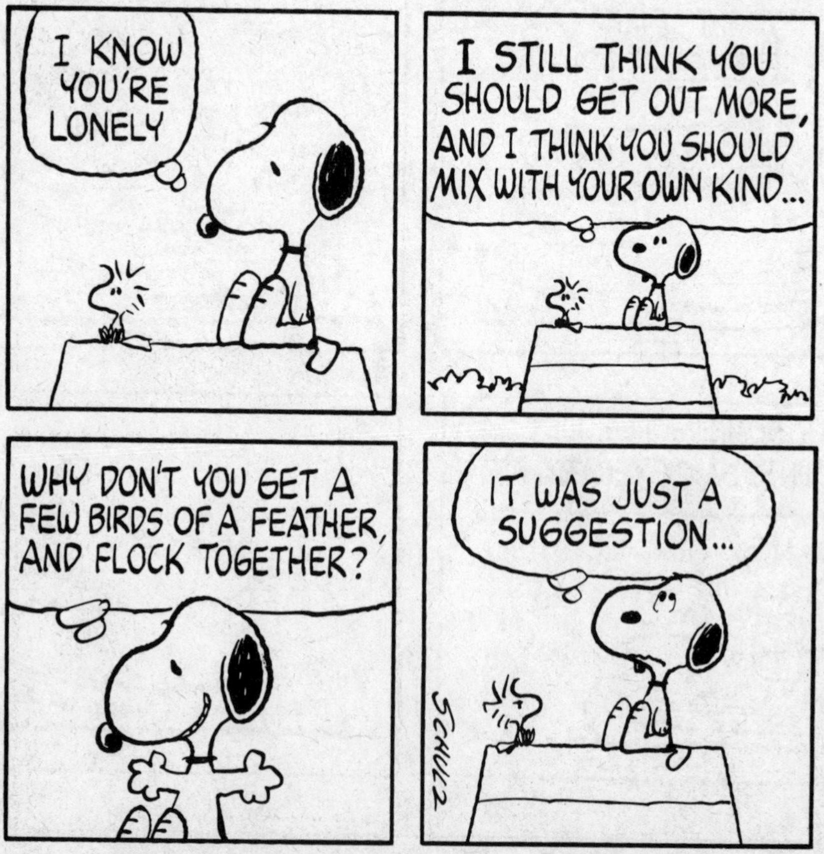
I KNOW YOU'RE LONELY
I STILL THINK YOU SHOULD GET OUT MORE, AND I THINK YOU SHOULD MIX WITH YOUR OWN KIND...
WHY DON'T YOU GET A FEW BIRDS OF A FEATHER, AND FLOCK TOGETHER?
IT WAS JUST A SUGGESTION...
SCHULZ

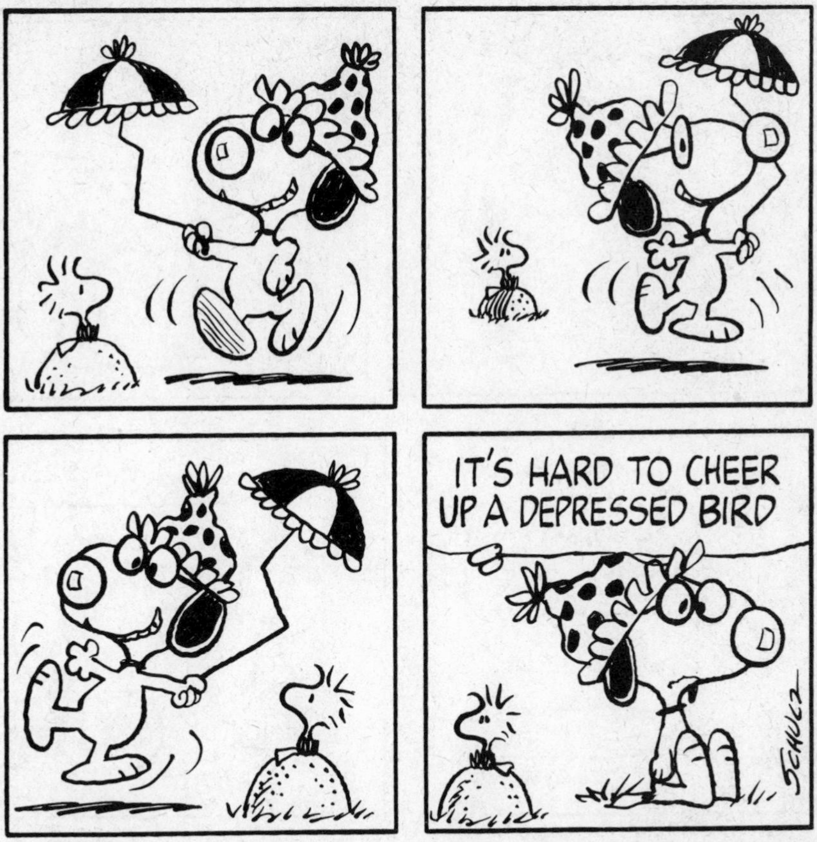
IT'S HARD TO CHEER UP A DEPRESSED BIRD

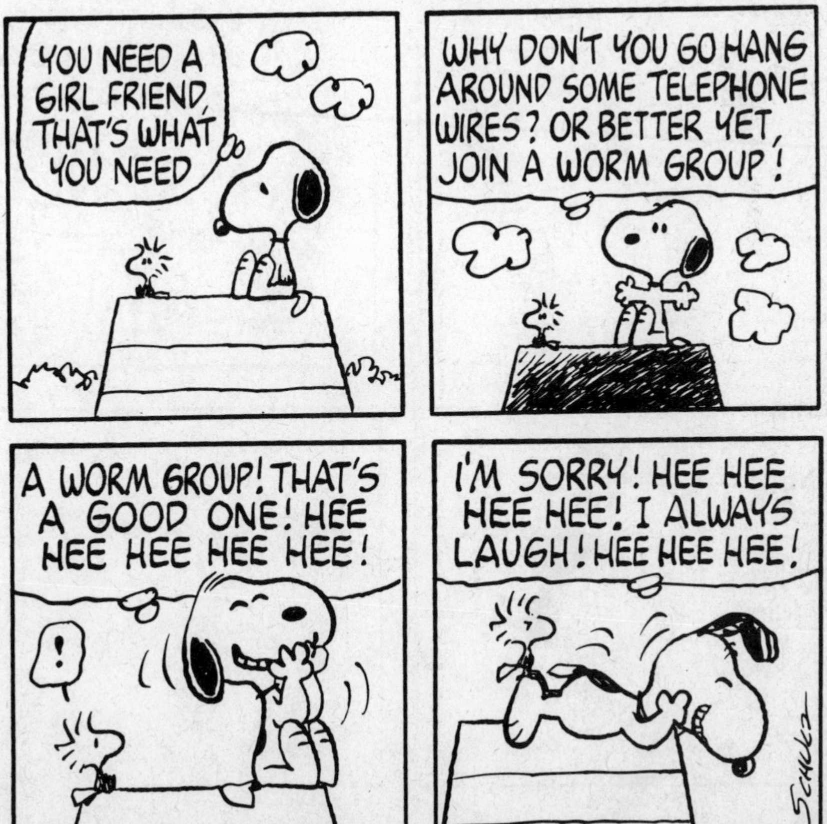
YOU NEED A GIRL FRIEND, THAT'S WHAT YOU NEED
WHY DON'T YOU GO HANG AROUND SOME TELEPHONE WIRES? OR BETTER YET, JOIN A WORM GROUP!
A WORM GROUP! THAT'S A GOOD ONE! HEE HEE HEE HEE HEE!
!
I'M SORRY! HEE HEE HEE HEE! I ALWAYS LAUGH! HEE HEE HEE!

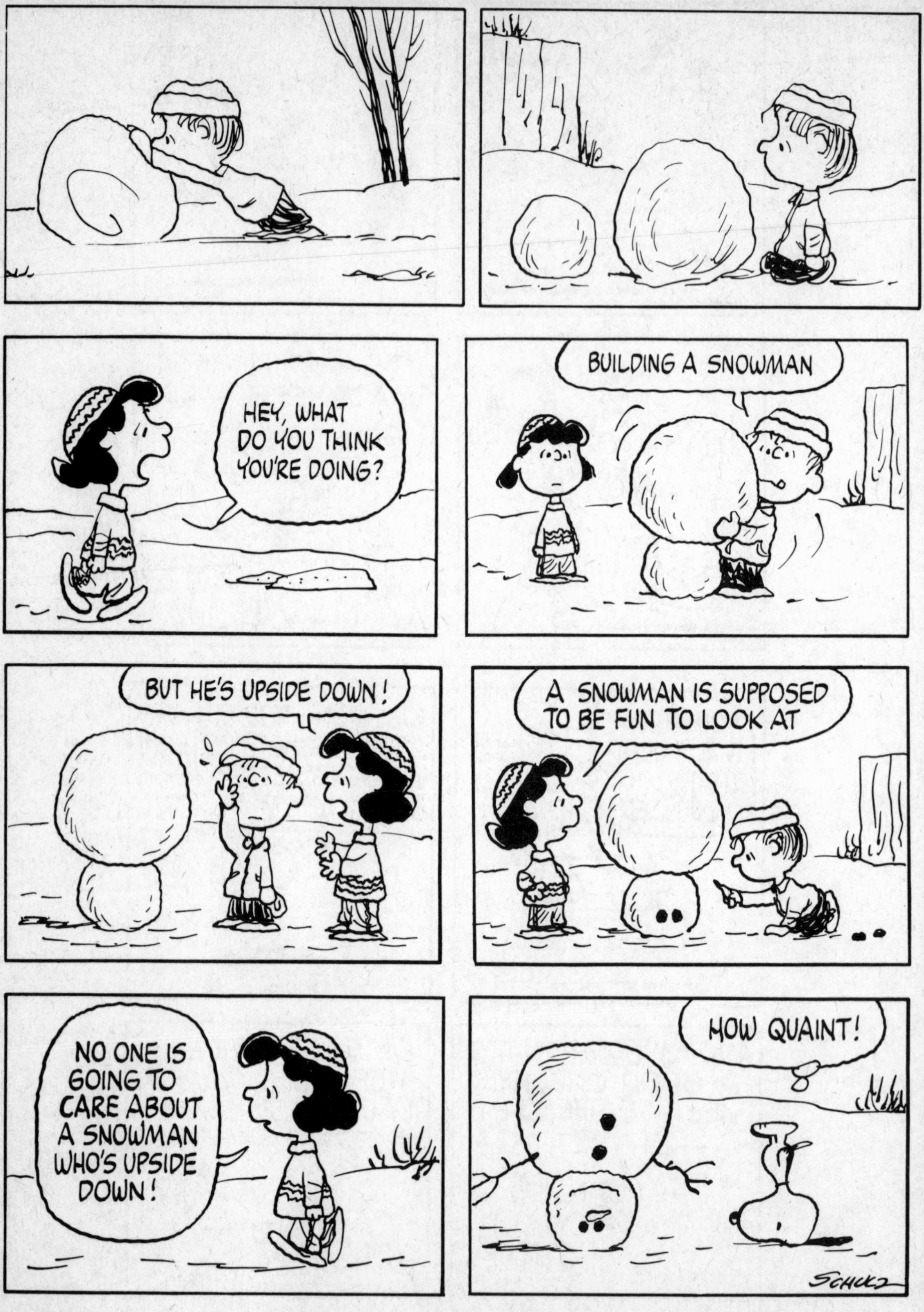
HEY, WHAT DO YOU THINK YOU'RE DOING?
BUILDING A SNOWMAN
BUT HE'S UPSIDE DOWN!
A SNOWMAN IS SUPPOSED TO BE FUN TO LOOK AT
NO ONE IS GOING TO CARE ABOUT A SNOWMAN WHO'S UPSIDE DOWN!
HOW QUAINT!
SCHULZ

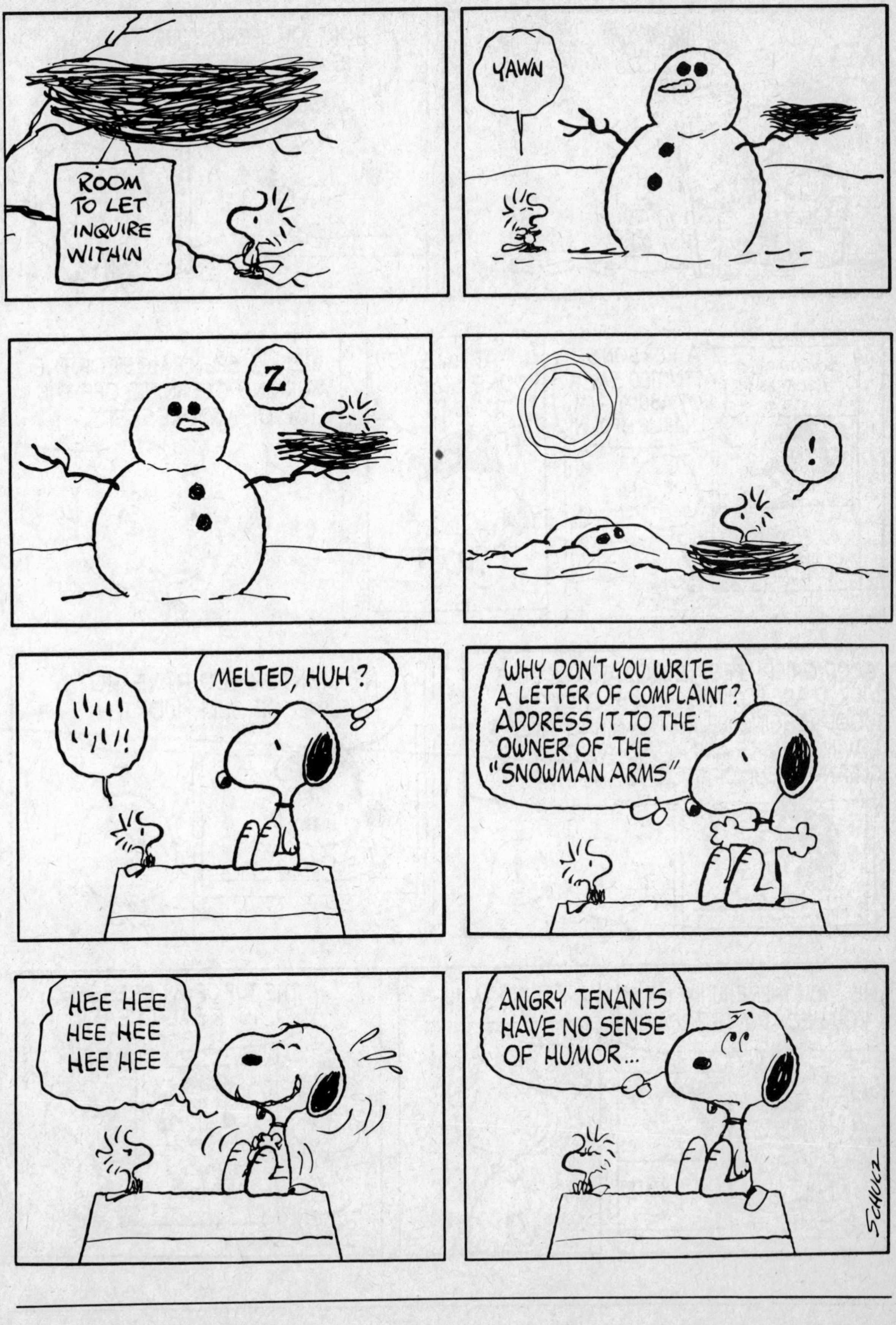
ROOM TO LET INQUIRE WITHIN
YAWN
Z
!
MELTED, HUH ?
WHY DON'T YOU WRITE A LETTER OF COMPLAINT? ADDRESS IT TO THE OWNER OF THE "SNOWMAN ARMS"
HEE HEE HEE HEE HEE HEE
ANGRY TENANTS HAVE NO SENSE OF HUMOR...
SCHULZ

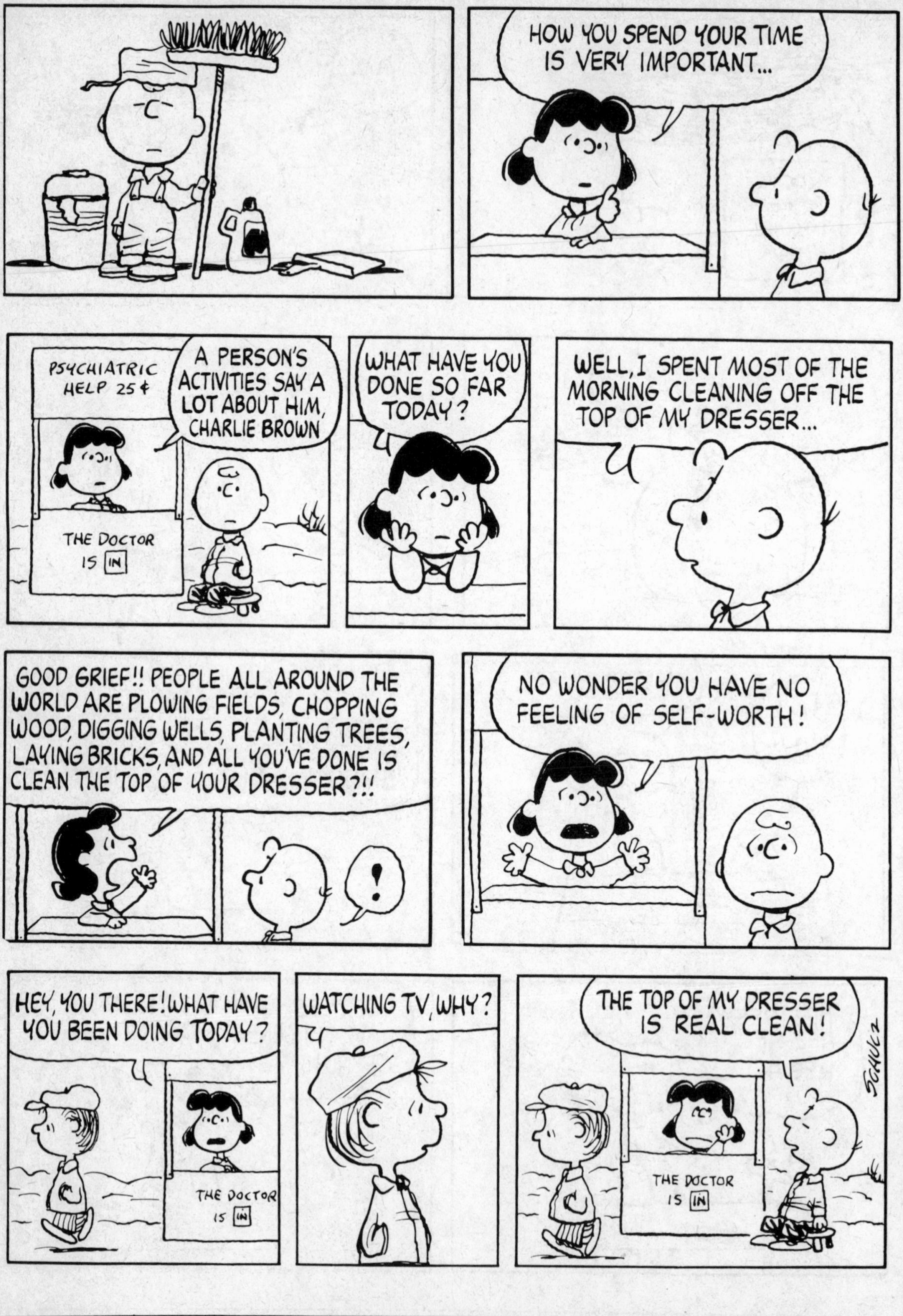
HOW YOU SPEND YOUR TIME IS VERY IMPORTANT...
PSYCHIATRIC HELP 25¢
A PERSON'S ACTIVITIES SAY A LOT ABOUT HIM, CHARLIE BROWN
THE DOCTOR IS IN
WHAT HAVE YOU DONE SO FAR TODAY?
WELL, I SPENT MOST OF THE MORNING CLEANING OFF THE TOP OF MY DRESSER...
GOOD GRIEF!! PEOPLE ALL AROUND THE WORLD ARE PLOWING FIELDS, CHOPPING WOOD, DIGGING WELLS, PLANTING TREES, LAYING BRICKS, AND ALL YOU'VE DONE IS CLEAN THE TOP OF YOUR DRESSER?!!
!
NO WONDER YOU HAVE NO FEELING OF SELF-WORTH!
HEY, YOU THERE! WHAT HAVE YOU BEEN DOING TODAY?
THE DOCTOR IS IN
WATCHING TV, WHY?
THE TOP OF MY DRESSER IS REAL CLEAN!
THE DOCTOR IS IN
SCHULZ

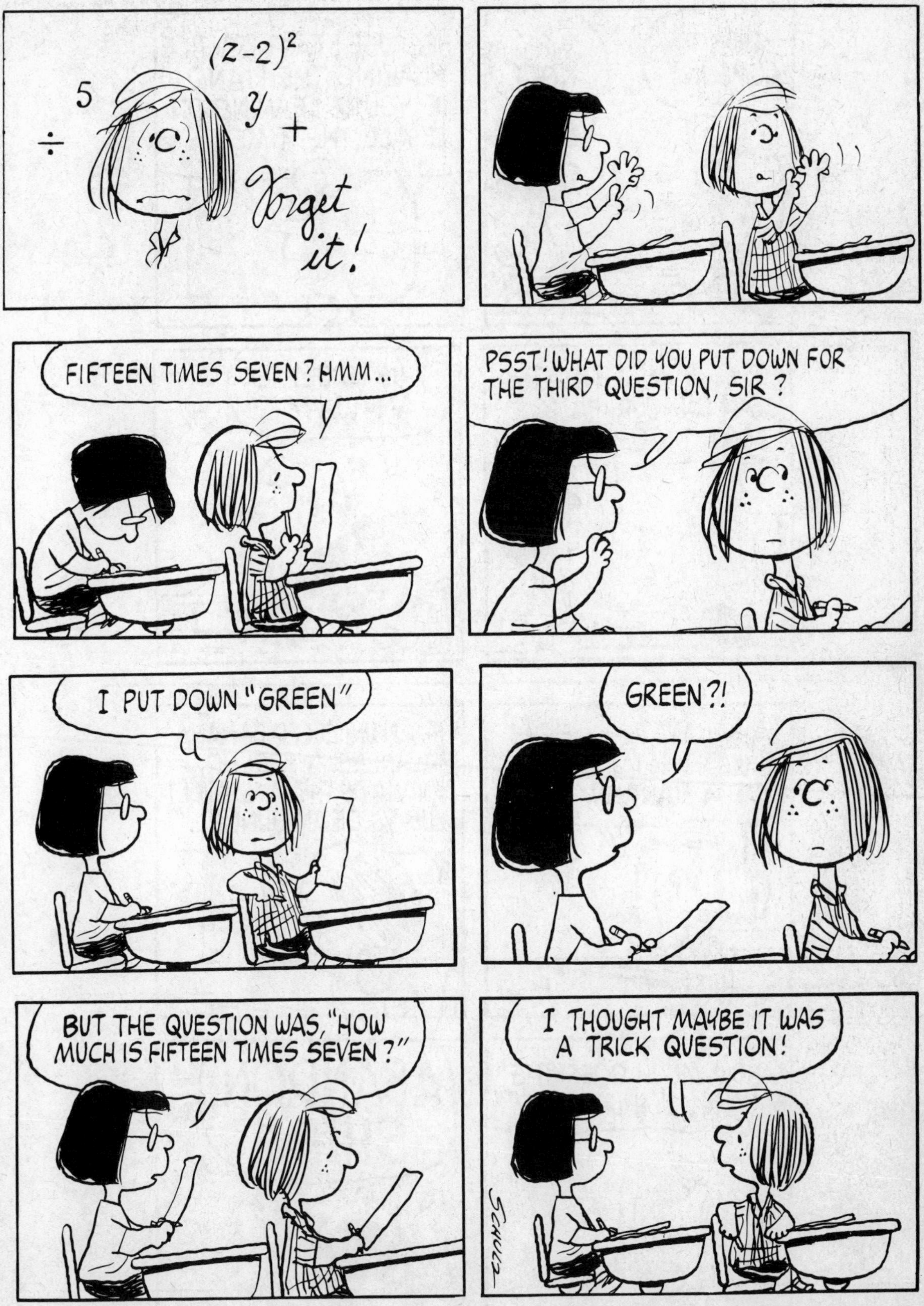

$(z-2)^2$
5
y
÷
+
Forget it!
FIFTEEN TIMES SEVEN? HMM...
PSST! WHAT DID YOU PUT DOWN FOR THE THIRD QUESTION, SIR?
I PUT DOWN "GREEN"
GREEN?!
BUT THE QUESTION WAS, "HOW MUCH IS FIFTEEN TIMES SEVEN?"
I THOUGHT MAYBE IT WAS A TRICK QUESTION!
SCHULZ

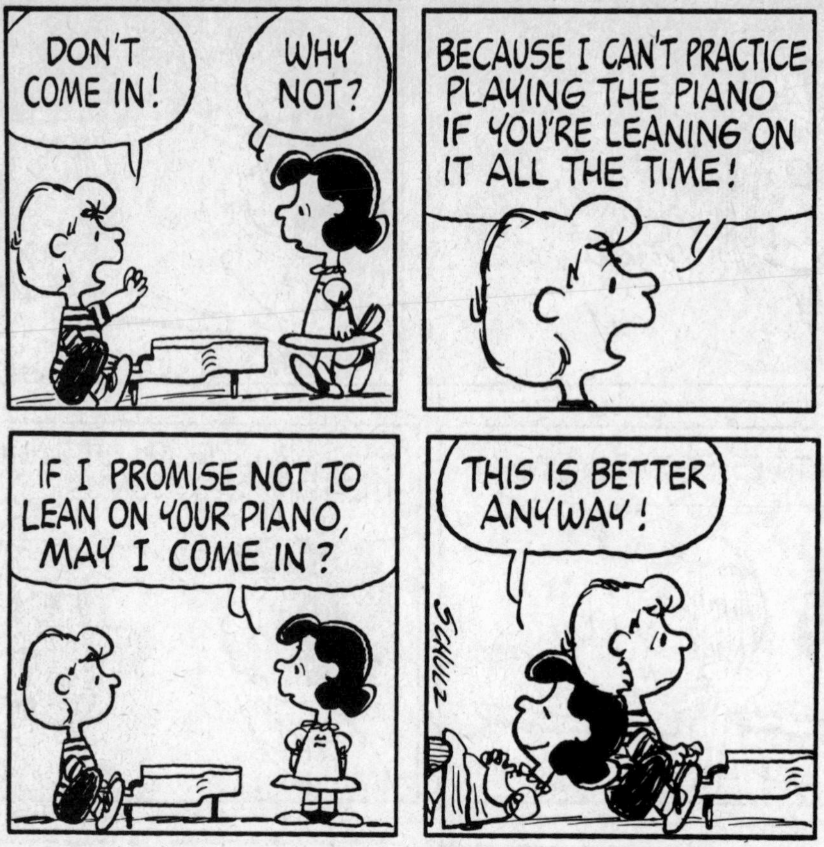
DON'T COME IN!
WHY NOT?
BECAUSE I CAN'T PRACTICE PLAYING THE PIANO IF YOU'RE LEANING ON IT ALL THE TIME!
IF I PROMISE NOT TO LEAN ON YOUR PIANO, MAY I COME IN?
THIS IS BETTER ANYWAY!
SCHULZ

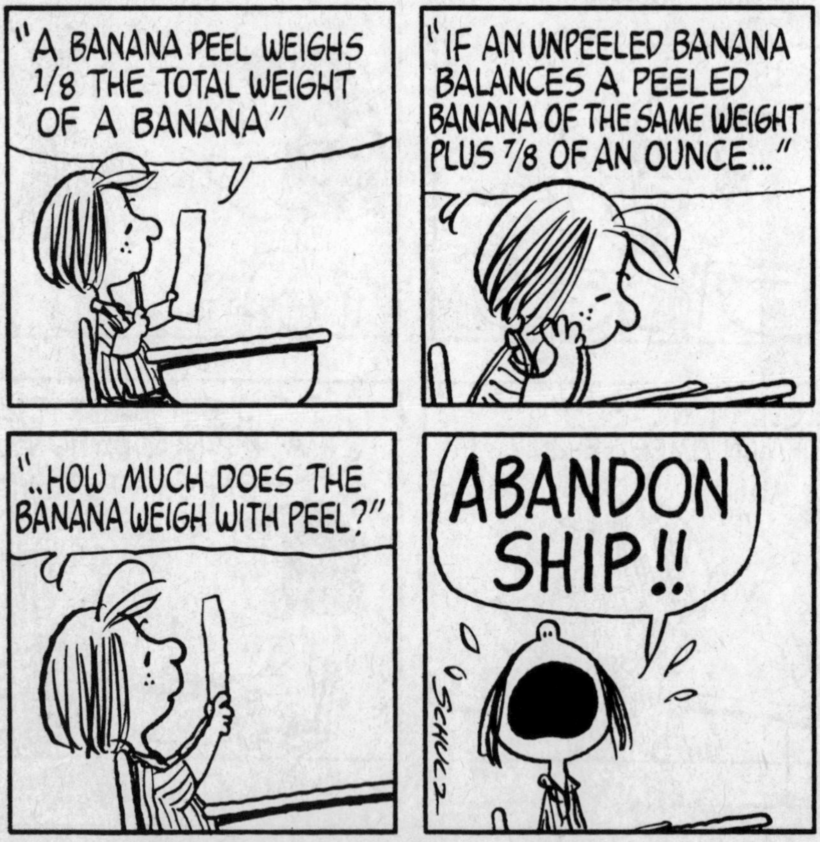
"A BANANA PEEL WEIGHS 1/8 THE TOTAL WEIGHT OF A BANANA"
"IF AN UNPEELED BANANA BALANCES A PEELED BANANA OF THE SAME WEIGHT PLUS 7/8 OF AN OUNCE..."
"..HOW MUCH DOES THE BANANA WEIGH WITH PEEL?"
ABANDON SHIP!!
SCHULZ

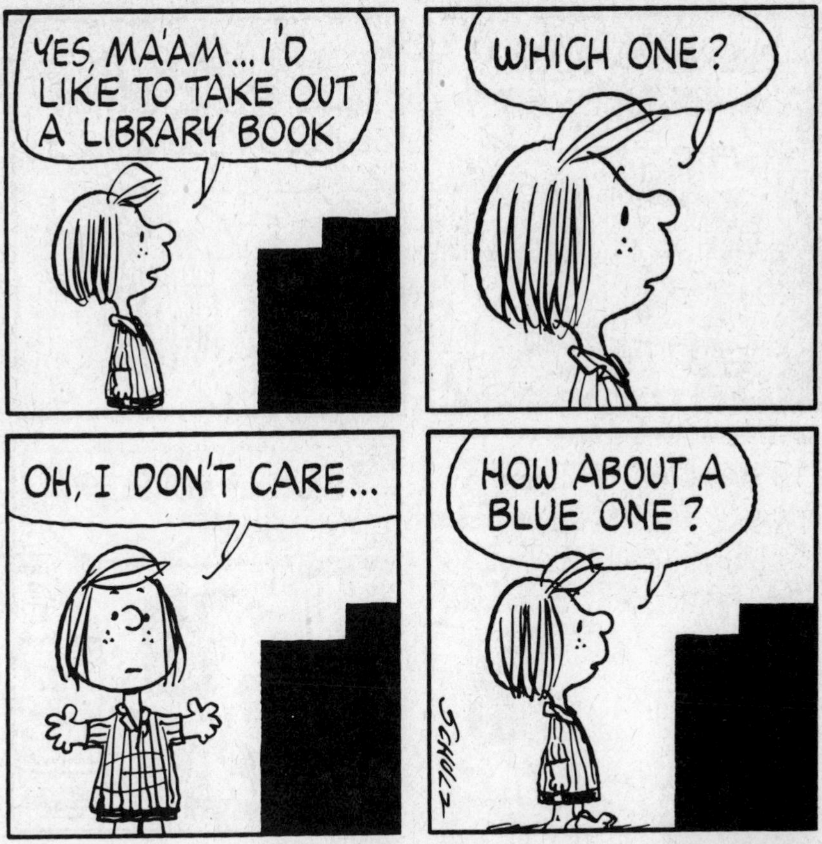
YES, MA'AM... I'D LIKE TO TAKE OUT A LIBRARY BOOK
WHICH ONE?
OH, I DON'T CARE...
HOW ABOUT A BLUE ONE?
SCHULZ

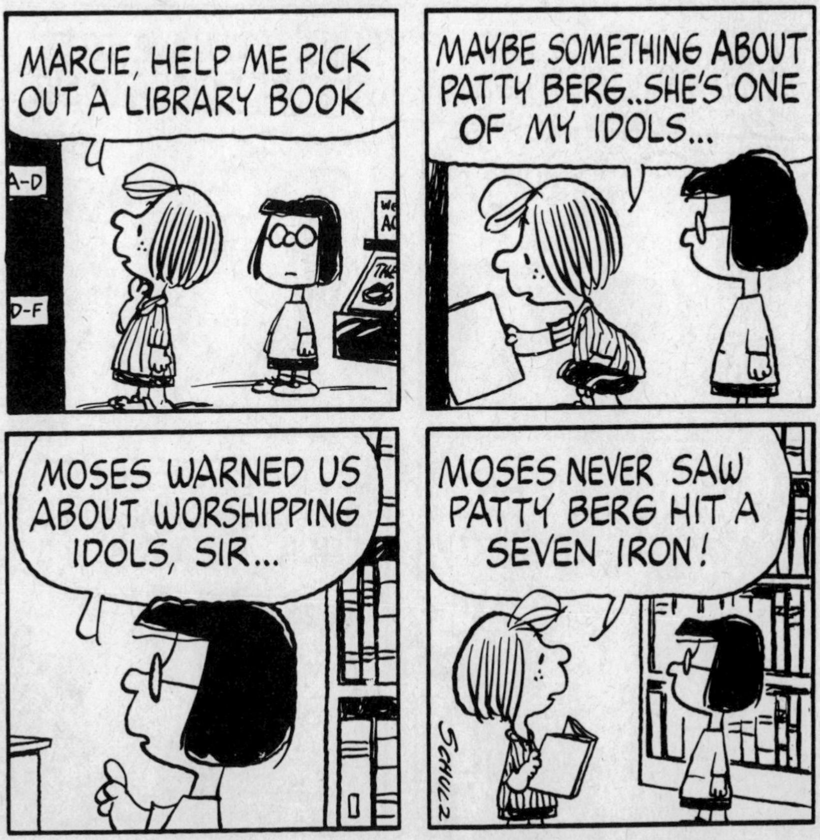
MARCIE, HELP ME PICK OUT A LIBRARY BOOK
A-D
D-F
MAYBE SOMETHING ABOUT PATTY BERG..SHE'S ONE OF MY IDOLS...
MOSES WARNED US ABOUT WORSHIPPING IDOLS, SIR...
MOSES NEVER SAW PATTY BERG HIT A SEVEN IRON!
SCHULZ

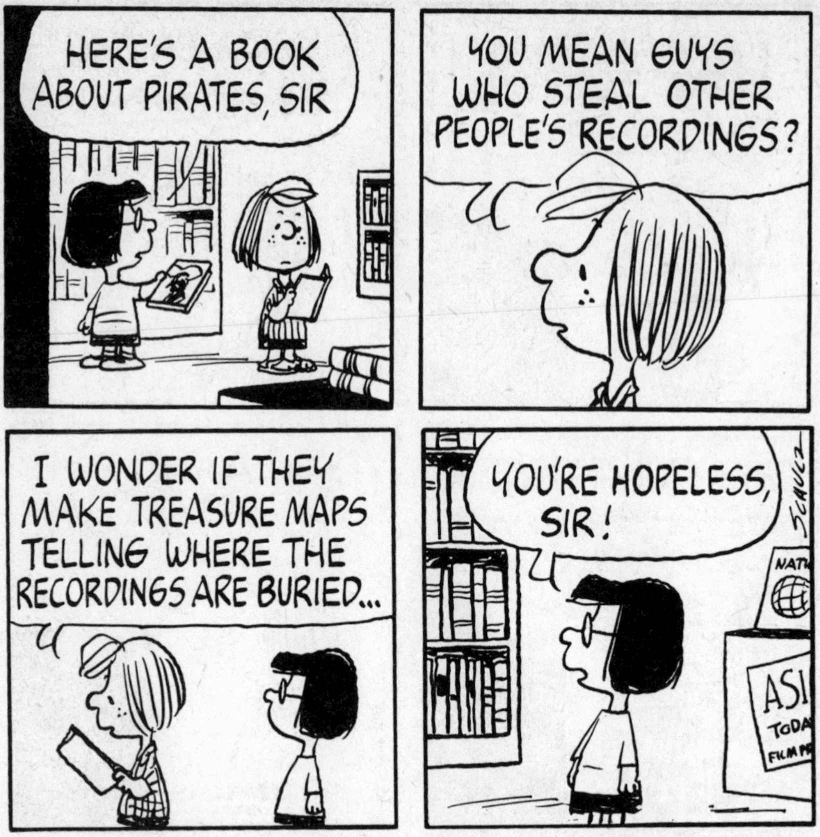
HERE'S A BOOK ABOUT PIRATES, SIR
YOU MEAN GUYS WHO STEAL OTHER PEOPLE'S RECORDINGS?
I WONDER IF THEY MAKE TREASURE MAPS TELLING WHERE THE RECORDINGS ARE BURIED...
YOU'RE HOPELESS, SIR!
SCHULZ

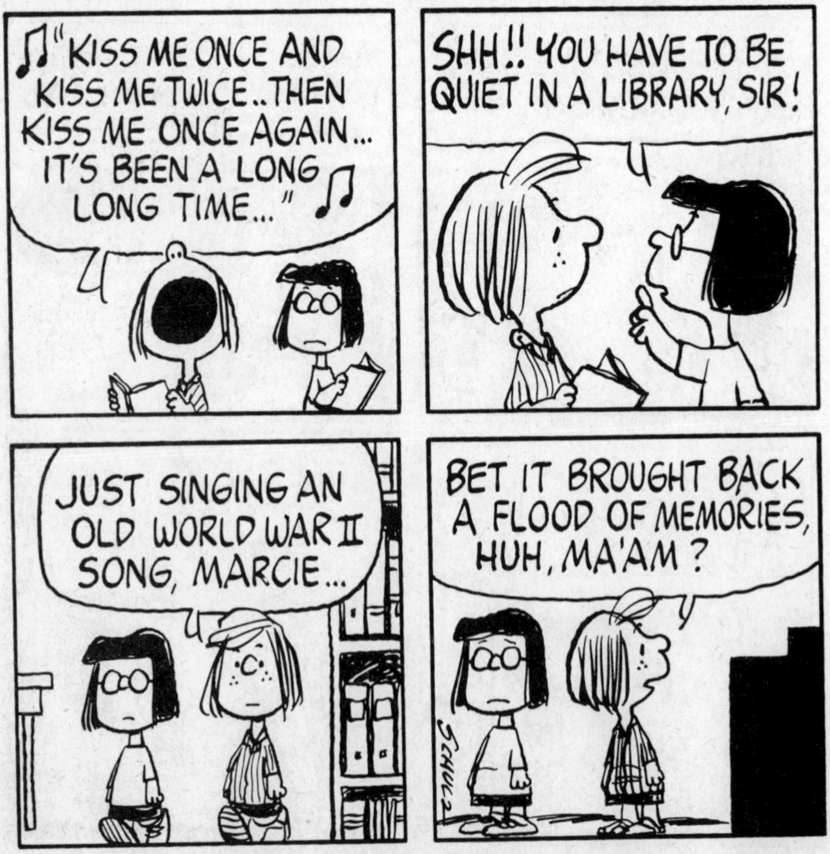
♫ "KISS ME ONCE AND KISS ME TWICE.. THEN KISS ME ONCE AGAIN... IT'S BEEN A LONG LONG TIME..." ♫
SHH!! YOU HAVE TO BE QUIET IN A LIBRARY, SIR!
JUST SINGING AN OLD WORLD WAR II SONG, MARCIE...
BET IT BROUGHT BACK A FLOOD OF MEMORIES, HUH, MA'AM?
SCHULZ

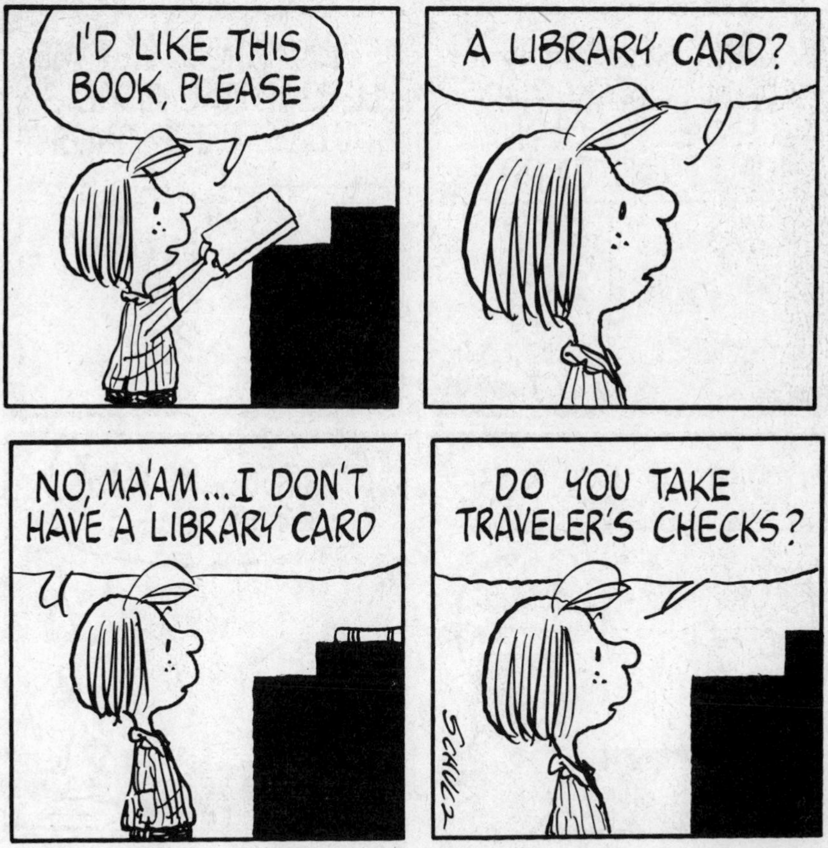
I'D LIKE THIS BOOK, PLEASE
A LIBRARY CARD?
NO, MA'AM... I DON'T HAVE A LIBRARY CARD
DO YOU TAKE TRAVELER'S CHECKS?
SCHULZ

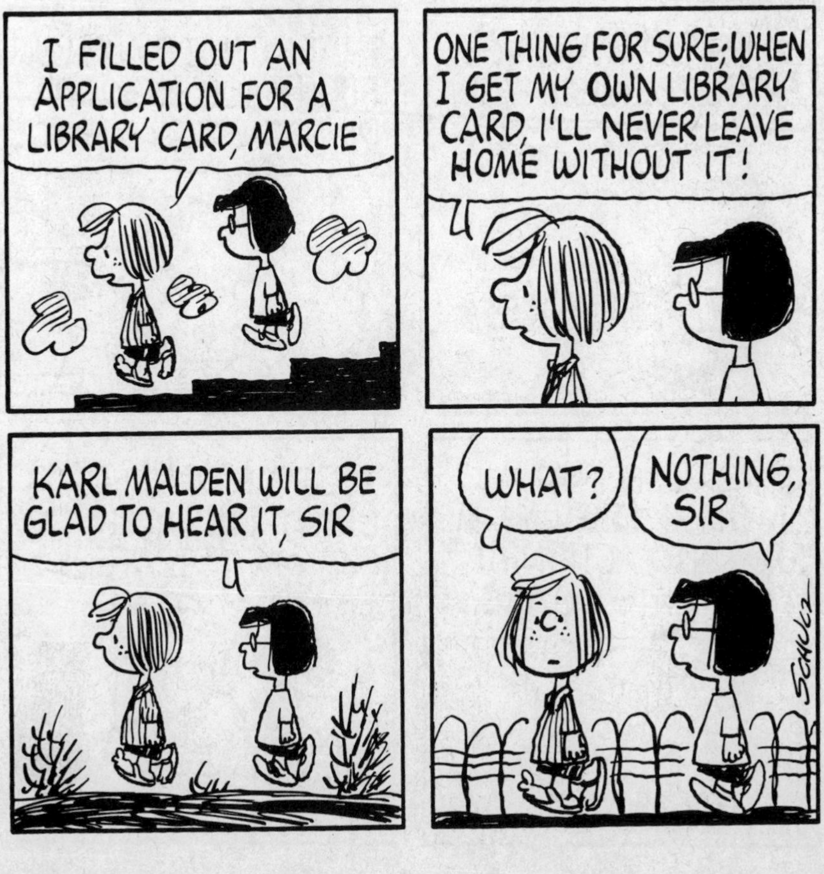
I FILLED OUT AN APPLICATION FOR A LIBRARY CARD, MARCIE
ONE THING FOR SURE; WHEN I GET MY OWN LIBRARY CARD, I'LL NEVER LEAVE HOME WITHOUT IT!
KARL MALDEN WILL BE GLAD TO HEAR IT, SIR
WHAT?
NOTHING, SIR
SCHULZ

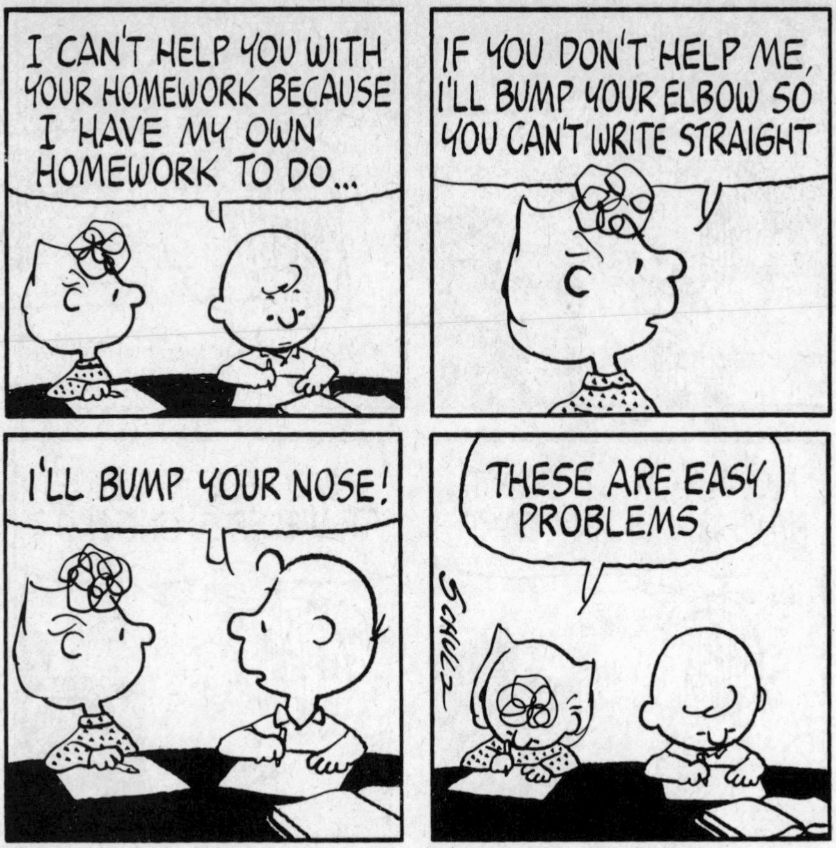
I CAN'T HELP YOU WITH YOUR HOMEWORK BECAUSE I HAVE MY OWN HOMEWORK TO DO...
IF YOU DON'T HELP ME, I'LL BUMP YOUR ELBOW SO YOU CAN'T WRITE STRAIGHT
I'LL BUMP YOUR NOSE!
THESE ARE EASY PROBLEMS
SCHULZ

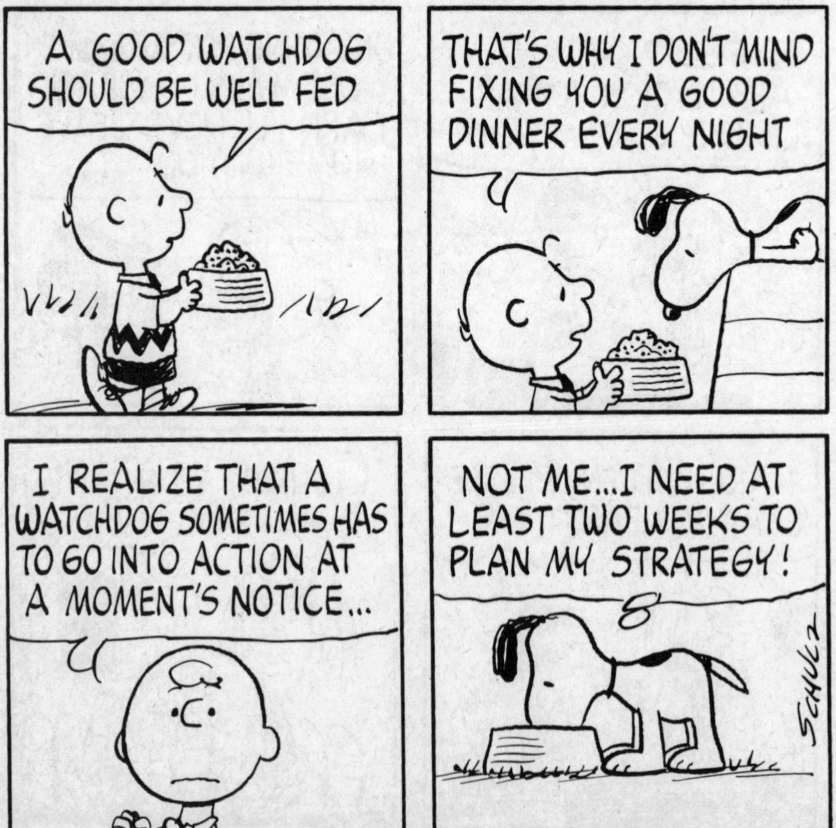
A GOOD WATCHDOG SHOULD BE WELL FED
THAT'S WHY I DON'T MIND FIXING YOU A GOOD DINNER EVERY NIGHT
I REALIZE THAT A WATCHDOG SOMETIMES HAS TO GO INTO ACTION AT A MOMENT'S NOTICE...
NOT ME...I NEED AT LEAST TWO WEEKS TO PLAN MY STRATEGY!
SCHULZ

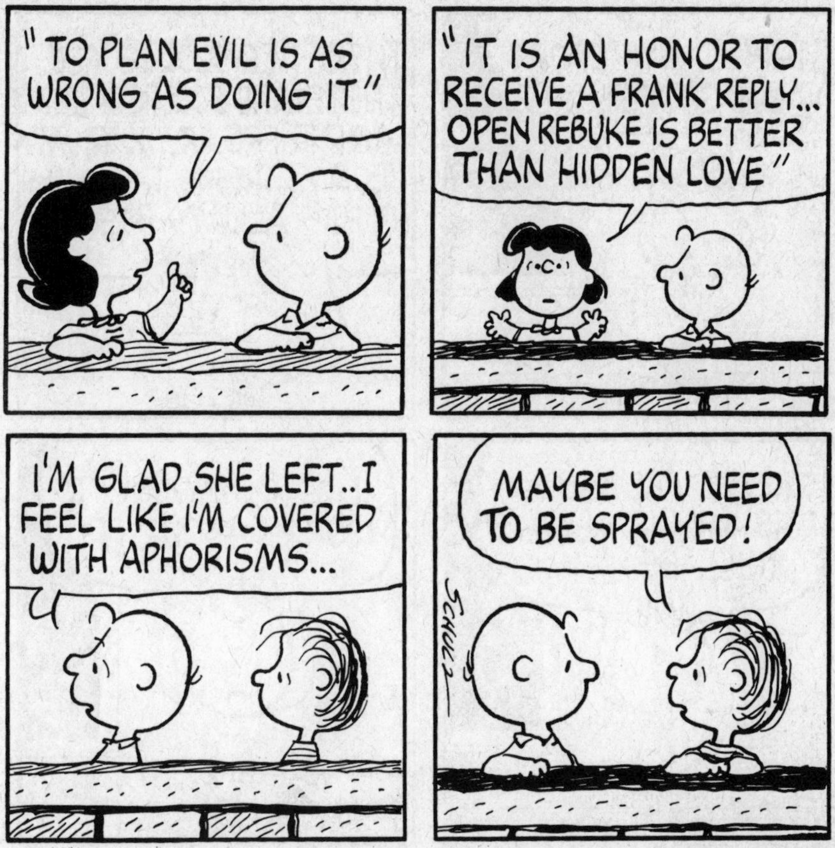
"TO PLAN EVIL IS AS WRONG AS DOING IT"
"IT IS AN HONOR TO RECEIVE A FRANK REPLY... OPEN REBUKE IS BETTER THAN HIDDEN LOVE"
I'M GLAD SHE LEFT..I FEEL LIKE I'M COVERED WITH APHORISMS...
MAYBE YOU NEED TO BE SPRAYED!
SCHULZ

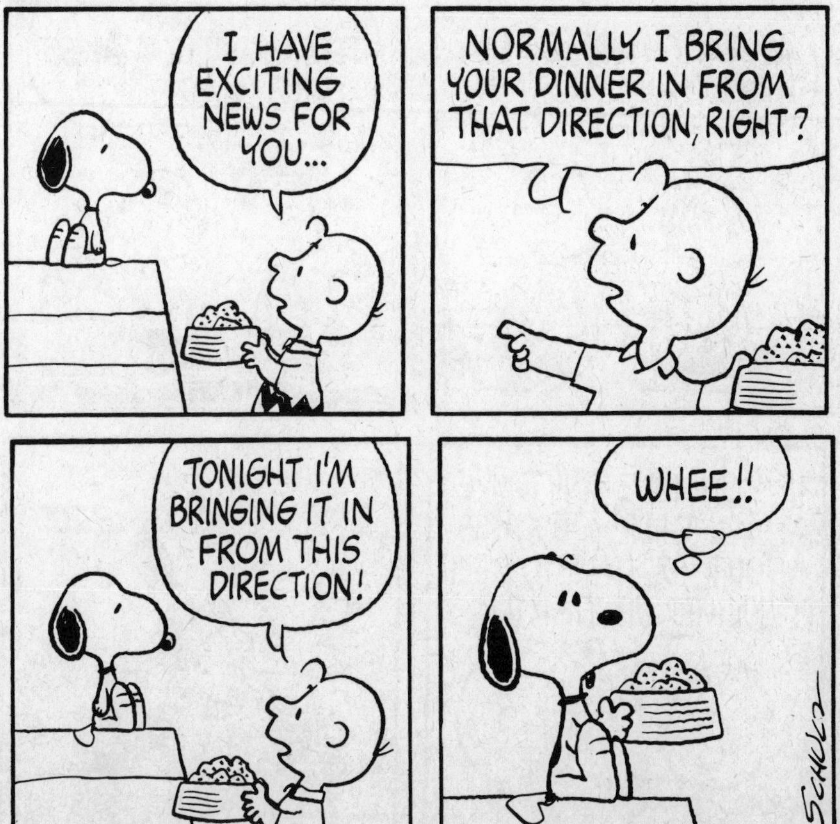
I HAVE EXCITING NEWS FOR YOU...
NORMALLY I BRING YOUR DINNER IN FROM THAT DIRECTION, RIGHT?
TONIGHT I'M BRINGING IT IN FROM THIS DIRECTION!
WHEE!!
SCHULZ

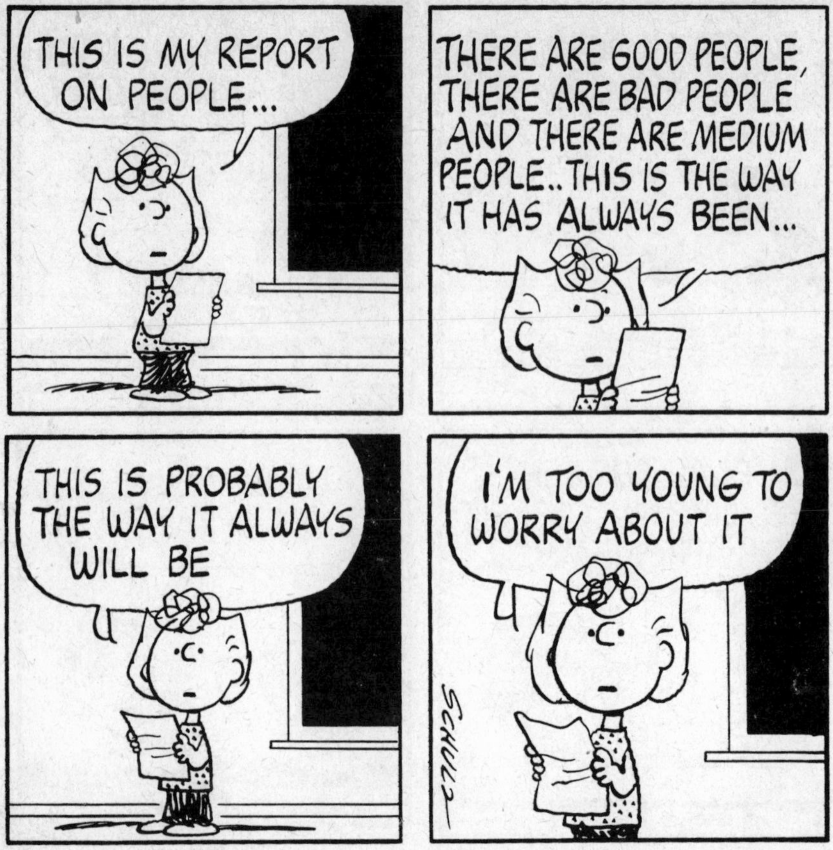
THIS IS MY REPORT ON PEOPLE...
THERE ARE GOOD PEOPLE, THERE ARE BAD PEOPLE AND THERE ARE MEDIUM PEOPLE..THIS IS THE WAY IT HAS ALWAYS BEEN...
THIS IS PROBABLY THE WAY IT ALWAYS WILL BE
I'M TOO YOUNG TO WORRY ABOUT IT
SCHULZ

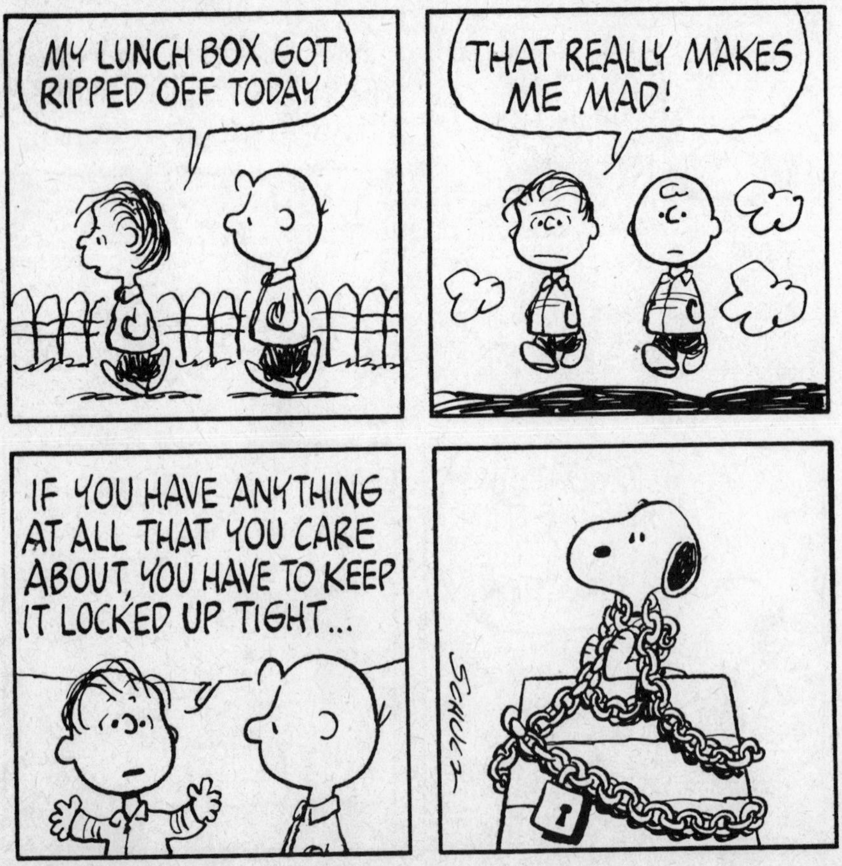
MY LUNCH BOX GOT RIPPED OFF TODAY
THAT REALLY MAKES ME MAD!
IF YOU HAVE ANYTHING AT ALL THAT YOU CARE ABOUT, YOU HAVE TO KEEP IT LOCKED UP TIGHT...
SCHULZ